WITHDRAWN FROM STOCK

THE DEFINITE ARTICLE

About the Author

Michael McDowell is a former Tánaiste, Minister for Justice and Attorney General of Ireland, and served three terms as a member of Dáil Éireann between 1987 and 2007.

He was founding chairman of the Progressive Democrats in 1985. From 1999 to 2007 he played a significant role in the implementation of the Good Friday Agreement and the St Andrews Agreement.

He was educated at Gonzaga College, Dublin, 1959–1968.

He graduated in Economics, Politics, Roman Law and Jurisprudence at University College Dublin. He qualified as a barrister in 1974 and was called to the Inner Bar in 1987. He practises as a Senior Counsel at The Bar of Ireland.

He has played a leading role in a succession of referendum debates in relation to amendments to the Irish Constitution. In 2016, at the request of the late Senator Feargal Quinn, he stood successfully for the NUI constituency in Seanad Éireann, and was re-elected in 2020 and in 2025, securing the largest ever NUI vote.

Michael McDowell is married to Professor Niamh Brennan, and they have three sons and two grandchildren.

THE DEFINITE ARTICLE

COLLECTED WRITINGS OF

MICHAEL McDOWELL

Published by
Red Stripe Press

email: info@redstripepress.com

www.redstripepress.com

© Michael McDowell, 2025

Hardback ISBN 978-1-78605-216-2
ePub ISBN 978-1-78605-217-9

A catalogue record for this book is available from the British Library. All rights reserved. No part of this publication may be reproduced, stored in a retrieval system or transmitted in any form or by any means, electronic, mechanical, photocopying, recording or otherwise, without the prior, written permission of the publisher.

This book is sold subject to the condition that it shall not, by way of trade or otherwise, be lent, resold, hired out, or otherwise circulated without the publisher's prior consent in any form of binding or cover other than that in which it is published and without a similar condition including this condition being imposed on the subsequent purchaser.

Typeset by www.typesetting.ie

Printed in Dublin by SPRINTBOOKS

For my parents, Tony and Eilis McDowell

Acknowledgements

At the outset, I must acknowledge the friendly encouragement of Michael Brennan of Red Stripe Press, at whose sole suggestion, and with his total support, this collection was made and published. Without that encouragement, it would simply never have crossed my mind to participate in such a project.

I also happily acknowledge that I still owe him the outstanding text of the other book mentioned in the preface. To that I must add my acknowledgement to the ever professional and unflappable editor, Eileen O'Brien of Red Stripe Press, who has been saintly in her care and oversight of the project.

Additionally, I owe a huge acknowledgement to the proprietors and editorial staff of the various newspapers in which the weekly articles first appeared. Never once was my topic chosen for me and never once was my article spiked or censored. That is what a free press is all about.

Closer to home, I must acknowledge the great support I have always received from Kate Edgar and Samantha Long – not least in ensuring that I met publication deadlines and for their valuable feedback.

Lastly, there are the thousands of readers who have written to me or crossed the street to talk to me so often and so unexpectedly, encouraging me to keep up my writing. Their kindness has always meant so much to me.

M. McDowell

Preface

This book, while replete with my ideas, was not my idea at all. I have to confess that it originates in my continuing failure to supply my publishers with the text of an entirely different book which remains 'stuck in the works' but will, when properly written and published, have as its subject matter the Anglo-Irish Treaty of 1921.

Over the last 15 years or so I have written a weekly column in a number of Irish newspapers. Michael Brennan of Red Stripe Press asked me for a cup of coffee one morning and suggested publication of a selection of those articles from a corpus of, I suppose, more than five hundred pieces. He thought it could be published while I toiled away at my magnum opus. I confess that I was as surprised as I was relieved at his suggestion.

The articles selected are mainly those which my publishers have chosen. They reflect much of the diversity of topics that I have dealt with over those 15 years but have been arranged into broad thematic categories which speak for themselves. Some have been proven wrong – such as my analysis of the Article 26 reference of the Judicial Appointments Commission Bill, which was saved by the scruff of its constitutional neck by a Supreme Court judgment which I still consider wrong, and my article about the chemical weapons use by Assad in Syria, which unduly exonerated his regime.

To the editors' selection I have added a few historical papers which I would like to bring to light again.

The Definite Article: Preface

While I have always been accorded free rein on the topic of my weekly pieces, I have always been equally subject to strict word count limits chosen by their publishers. This means that every word used must count and that conciseness skills taught to me at school using a great little book, *Elements of Style* by Strunk and White, have come in very handy decades later.

I hope the reader of this book derives as much enjoyment in perusing the pages as I have over the years in writing the pieces.

Michael McDowell
April 2025

Contents

1. History – Ireland Looking Back................... 1
2. Uniting the Irish........................... 67
3. Religion and Social Affairs................... 111
4. International Affairs......................... 157
5. Immigration and Asylum..................... 198
6. Irish Politics............................... 210
7. UK and Ireland Politics and Brexit............. 250
8. Defence, Policing and Security................ 289
9. Planning, Housing and Infrastructure.......... 304
10. Energy and Climate Policy.................... 345
11. Europe.................................... 354
12. Media..................................... 365
13. Trumpism – A Danger to America and World Democracy........................... 378
14. Referendums and Constitutional Issues......... 405

History – Ireland Looking Back

The greatness of Michael Collins

22 March 2009

RTE has commissioned a series of five programmes under the title *Ireland's Greatest*. The idea, loosely based on a BBC precedent, is that a poll was conducted among the general public with a view to identifying figures in Irish history who could be considered to be Ireland's greatest. A shortlist was compiled, consisting of Michael Collins, Bono, James Connolly, John Hume and Mary Robinson. This shortlist has attracted some criticism; many people rightly ask: what about Daniel O'Connell? W.B. Yeats? Charles Parnell? Michael Davitt? George Bernard Shaw? James Joyce? Éamon de Valera? and so on. Others have made the point that it's like comparing apples and oranges to compare people who are still alive (and whose ultimate status in Irish history is very hard to judge) with people who are long dead (and in respect of whom we know the sum total of their lives through history and biography).

Whatever about these criticisms, it does seem to me that it is a worthwhile use of broadcasting time to ask people, no matter how informally, to address their minds to what actually constitutes 'greatness' and judge what kind of figures really do amount to 'Ireland's greatest'.

Having agreed to advocate Michael Collins, I decided that I would not be drawn into a negative analysis of the other contenders. All of them, in different ways, seem to me to be estimable people who stand out from the ordinary and have, in one way or another, through their lives changed Ireland, both nationally and internationally.

Why then did I agree to champion Michael Collins? Having a keen interest in Irish history and a sense of pride in Ireland, Collins emerges, in my view, as being the towering figure in twentieth-century Irish history in terms of personality, achievement and charisma, and in terms of his transformative effect on his country.

So many books and films have been made about Michael Collins that he is now, in many senses, a figure of legend. Many biographies have been written, ranging from hagiographical to skeptical. One of the most recent, *Mick*, by the brilliant and sadly recently deceased Peter Hart, sets out to deconstruct the myth or legend of Collins and to analyse his significance in a detached and objective way. He follows the footsteps of major biographical works starting with Piaras Béaslaí, including Rex Taylor, Seán Ó Faoláin, Tim Pat Coogan, T. Ryle Dwyer, Léon Ó Broin, Margery Forester and many, many others. Peter Hart set out 'not to debunk the Story as such or to correct previous biographers. Instead, I would like to start from scratch and from a new, forensic perspective.' He said of his book *Mick*, 'What I hope readers find here is not the man of legend but a dynamic and fascinating man nonetheless: the most gifted, ruthless and powerful Irish politician of the twentieth century'. That description of him is, I think, true.

Some may question the term 'ruthless' when applied to Collins. Many feel it unfair to describe the man who delivered an independent Ireland from the hands of the Empire as 'ruthless'. The War of Independence was, like all war, violent but also, in many respects, cruel.

Yet no one would describe Michael Collins as a 'cruel man'. Though responsible for prosecuting a violent struggle for independence to its logical end, he did not revel in violence or in any sense glorify death or the letting of blood.

He was clear-minded and did not deceive himself on the moral issues involved in the War of Independence or the steps that were taken to win it.

People now use the term 'terrorism' rather loosely. Every struggle which does not consist of pitched battles between men in uniforms is not terrorism. The use of terror – i.e. bombing civilians to create fear and subjugation – is what terrorism is all about.

Moreover, Collins was dealing with a struggle for independence not merely from a much larger neighbouring island but from what was in the early twentieth century the most powerful empire on the globe. If there were to be a war of independence at all, it was never going to be one in which pitched battles (such as that brought about in 1916) would result in Ireland's freedom being won against the military power of the British Empire. It had to be based on the model of the Boer War, the most recent precedent for the struggle Collins hoped to lead.

No matter how revisionist we are asked to be by some commentators, the struggle of the Sinn Féin movement, coupled with the IRA, was essentially different from the political programme of the Irish Parliamentary Party, the 'Home Rulers'. John Redmond, leader of the Irish Parliamentary Party, spoke sincerely and eloquently of an Ireland with Home Rule, one in which young Irishmen would come to be willing to fight and die for what they regarded as 'their' Empire – a radically different vision from the separatist nationalists' agenda for Ireland.

How, then, do we differentiate between Collins in the early twentieth century and the Provos at the end of that century? Having seen, and been hugely depressed by, the futility of the 1916 Rising (and Collins admired James Connolly as the most adept of the leaders of that rising, in military terms), Collins was determined to seek Irish liberty and to put Ireland on the path to becoming a republic – 'the path to freedom' – and he committed himself to doing everything to bring about that freedom. The triumph of Sinn Féin in the 1918 election, and the subsequent electoral outcomes in which Sinn Féin again triumphed, justified him, in his and my mind, in viewing Dáil Éireann as the legitimate government of the Irish State. He was not serving a 'paper republic'. He was serving a truly democratic republic established by the votes of the people. He claimed morally the right to defend and to vindicate that state which Sinn Féin was mandated by the Irish people to create. He never lost or exceeded that mandate. His struggle was never rejected by the people at the ballot box. And he always accorded to the Irish people the right and the privilege to adjudicate through the ballot box on the way in which Irish freedom would be accomplished.

Without making a schoolboy hero of him, he was an immensely brave man. Very different from many later figures, he was really loved by those who were close to him. They saw him as a good person. He was never betrayed by those close to him. All of that speaks to his moral character.

As someone who considers himself a Republican, as someone who believes passionately in an independent Ireland, and as someone who believes that it was the entitlement of the Irish people through the ballot box to substitute their own government for an illegitimate British government, I cannot agree with those who now claim that Irish independence (as we now have it) would have come to us inevitably by constitutional means.

Where I may agree with some revisionist critics of the War of Independence is in the well-judged criticism that the Irish nationalists fundamentally misunderstood their Northern Unionist countrymen. The constant theme that Unionism was purely economic and was, in some sense, explicable only as a temporary result of British machination and selfish economic interest was wrong.

But Collins, along with de Valera, knew that there could be no coercion of the Northern Unionists. However inadequate their grasp of the reality of Unionism, they were not planning a genocidal civil war against the Unionists.

Finally, Collins is an intriguing complex character. He is no plaster saint. If you doubt me, can I recommend that you go to see Mary Kenny's play *Allegiance?*

I think Collins must be one of our greatest historical figures and that in 50 years' time or a 100 years' time they will still be writing books about him, writing plays about him, shooting films about him and, most of all, Irish people will still view his name with pride.

The centenary of the Ulster Covenant

An address to the Irish Association/IBIS conference at the Linen Hall, Belfast

22 September 2012

I am honoured to have been invited to participate in today's proceedings marking the 100th anniversary of the Ulster Covenant. My good friend Brian Kennaway asked me to speak about the Ulster Covenant from a republican and nationalist perspective and I am very glad to have been able to accept his kind invitation.

Decade of centenaries

It seems to me that one of the great potential benefits of the next ten years of significant centenaries in Irish political history is that it should encourage Irish men and women, and indeed our neighbours, to re-examine and re-assess many of the events that have shaped our present state, our problems and our challenges from a more objective historical perspective.

While centenaries are, as we well know, still capable of abuse for purely political ends and as opportunities for point-scoring, they also mark a point at which events are symbolically transported from the realm of what was recent controversy into the realm of what is viewed as largely 'historical'.

My theme

I will advance the view this morning that the Ulster Covenant, the central symbolic point in loyalist resistance to the 3rd Home Rule Bill, was also a point of departure – a central moment in the history of Ireland viewed from a nationalist and republican point of view. In so arguing, I acknowledge of course that the mobilisation of unionist opinion in what is now Northern Ireland was accompanied by a process of militarisation over a number of years and not simply on one day, 28 September 1912. It began in earnest in 1911 and culminated in the formal establishment of the Ulster Volunteer Force in January 1913.

Complacent nationalism?

By any standard, the campaign for Repeal of the Act of Union, chiefly supported by Irish Catholics, was protracted and complex. Their path of 'constitutionalism', as opposed to the use of force or the threat of force, in pursuit of Repeal was confronted at every turn by obstacles in the shape of the Ascendancy interest, the political interests of Empire, the party exigencies of British politics, and economic and social divergence among the people of Ireland, not least the old sectarian cleavage.

From a nationalist perspective, the alignment of political planets in 1910 to 1914 seemed to promise final delivery of Home Rule. The Orange Card appeared to have been, or to be about to be, 'trumped'. The Irish Party seemed to be about to deliver their most cherished ambition – Home Rule – a condition that was, in the eyes of Redmond and others, firmly fixed in the constellation of the Empire, as we shall see.

The extent and nature of loyalist resistance to Home Rule was something for which constitutional nationalists were simply not prepared. Of course, they understood that there would be political resistance to Home Rule. But the energy – approaching ferocity – of the organisation of armed resistance culminating in the establishment and arming of the Ulster Volunteer Force was a factor which they had not really addressed or prepared for adequately. And so, the political challenge that lay behind the promulgation of the Ulster Covenant was, in terms of scale and intensity, something for which the Irish Party, as a constitutional nationalist movement, was ill-prepared. Still less so, the Liberal Government.

The prospect of political violence as a consequence of Home Rule, not to mention the possibility of an armed, largely denominational struggle approaching civil war, was a spectre that constitutional nationalist politicians tended to simply wish away. They naively assumed that the will of Westminster would ultimately be imposed, and that the UVF threat to use force would ultimately crumble in the face of a clear imposition of the authority of the Imperial Parliament.

A Godsend to radical separatists

In that context, events that led from the Ulster Covenant and the emergence of the UVF created perfect laboratory conditions for the emergence in the Irish nationalist population of a counterforce.

To those who did not share John Redmond's view of Home Rule Ireland as an integral part of the Empire, the threat of armed loyalist resistance to Home Rule offered a God-sent opportunity to revive and tap into the physical force radicalism of the Fenian tradition as well as the possibility of radicalising cultural nationalism into a form of Irish separatism far removed from Redmond's worldview.

It was onto this stage that my grandfather Eoin Mac Néill, a Glensman from Antrim who was a leading figure in the cultural and legitimate national revival, stepped with his article 'The North Began'. Far from seeing the Covenant and the UVF as deadly threats to his political ambitions for Ireland, Mac Néill welcomed their emergence as an assertion of 'right' – akin to the concept of what we would now call the 'right of self-determination' – a useful precedent for any separatist countermovement. In modern parlance, they were 'game-changers'.

The Fenian tradition, through the IRB, also saw the Ulster Covenant and the UVF as creating the context for mobilising and militarising Irish nationalists in the cause of Irish independence. They grasped equally the usefulness of Mac Néill's intervention.

Redmond's initial disdain for the Irish Volunteers was based on his confidence that his goals would still be achieved by entirely constitutional means. But he soon changed course and attempted to subsume the Irish Volunteers into the broad nationalist movement as an ally of the Irish Party.

Viewed objectively, the Covenant's legal implication in the context of the UVF and the establishment of a Provisional Government was close to treasonable. Mobilisation and arming of a large section of the population to resist by force the implementation of laws enacted at Westminster was clearly seditious and bordering on actual treason. A.V. Dicey, the great 'father' of English constitutional law and theory, while signing the English variant of the Ulster Covenant, privately warned Carson and Craig that once the Bill became law it might be treasonable to take up arms against its implementation. The establishment of a Provisional Government for Ulster backed by the UVF would likewise have been an objectively treasonable step. Support from Bonar Law, F.E. Smith and others for the Covenant and for the UVF, in terms of British law, flirted with treason.

Tolerance of, or ambivalence about, the threat to use force to overthrow the will of parliament was, by any standards, an open invitation to those Irish separatists who could countenance the use of physical force to demand the same tolerance for any mobilisation and militarisation that they could bring about.

Indeed, it seems that the political and moral 'logic' of the Ulster Covenant and the Ulster Volunteer Force was that the people of Southern Ireland had an equivalent political and moral 'right' to prepare to use force to assure their preferred constitutional status – even if that meant political independence from Westminster and, in the ultimate, leaving the Empire. Those in the Establishment who were prepared to 'legitimate' armed loyalist resistance to Home Rule were logically 'legitimating' the use of force by the other side to decide the 'Irish Question'.

Small wonder then that the creation of the UVF, the Provisional Government for Ulster and the signing of the Ulster Covenant was looked to by radicals within Irish nationalism and republicanism as a potential precedent to drive their own agenda forward.

Did the Covenant succeed?

On one level, the Ulster Covenant was originally intended to de-rail the entire Home Rule project rather than to partition the island. Looked at in that way, it was in the ultimate a failure because, ironically, it became the victim of its own success.

The Covenant, the UVF and the threat of a Provisional Government brought about the exclusion of the majority of historical Ulster from Home Rule and, in the ultimate, from the Irish Free State. But it can be argued with some force that the separatist Irish

Free State, and ultimately the Irish Republic, owe a very great deal to the intransigent stance of the signatories to the Ulster Covenant.

The very existence of Northern Ireland as a Home Rule state can of course be claimed as a victory for the Covenant. But, I think, the question as to whether the Covenant generally delivered what its drafters intended is by no means so clear-cut.

Trading Redmond for Collins?

Speaking at a St Patrick's Day Dinner in London on 17 March 1913, John Redmond had this to say about his vision for Ireland under Home Rule:

We will, under Home Rule, devote our attention to education, reform of the Poor Law, and questions of that kind which are purely domestic, which are, if you like, hum-drum Irish questions, and the only way in which we will attempt to interfere in any Imperial question will be by our representatives on the floor of the Imperial Parliament at Westminster doing everything in our power to increase the strength and glory of what will be our empire at long last; and by sending in support of the empire the strong arms and brave hearts of Irish soldiers and Irish sailors to maintain the traditions of Irish valour in any part of the world. That is our ambition.

To the extent that the Ulster Covenant, the UVF and the Provisional Government, with the help of the English Tories and the Curragh Mutiny, created the conditions in which nationalist Ireland was diverted from this imperialist vision of Redmond to the republican vision of Michael Collins, the question that must be asked is whether the result was not in another sense a profound failure. Could Unionists not have lived in Redmond's Ireland?

Of course, some will argue that Home Rule in any event would have led to Irish independence over time. That is something about which we may debate but about which we can never know.

On a personal note, I incline to the belief that Irish independence, in which I am a strong believer, owes its existence to the armed resistance to Home Rule, and thus by supreme irony, it seems to me, the Ulster Covenant therefore numbers among the founding documents of Irish freedom. It was that perception that caused Mac Néill at the founding meeting of the Irish Volunteers in the Rotunda in Dublin in November 1913 and Casement at a subsequent Volunteer meeting in Cork to rather naively cause some confusion by calling for 'Three cheers for Carson's Volunteers'.

Because the English Establishment was so ambivalent about the threat of force articulated in the Covenant, it handed a perfect precedent to Irish separatists. It also may have poisoned the minds and hearts of those nationalists who found themselves on the wrong side of the Border in 1922 and right up to the Belfast Agreement in 1998.

We must also leave to the debaters of insoluble issues the other question as to whether the partition of Ireland avoided civil war between Nationalism and Unionism or whether, in a sense, it confined that civil war to a 'phony civil war' which here in Northern Ireland intermittently simmered and occasionally boiled over until the Belfast Agreement.

The Republican perspective

Speaking as an Irish Republican in the philosophical tradition of Tone, Davis and indeed Bulmer Hobson, I cannot identify completely with the separatist ideology of the Ulster Covenant. But it seems to me that Irish history – North and South – is moving on.

The establishment in the Belfast Agreement, as a matter of international law, of the right of the people of Northern Ireland alone to decide their own constitutional future is something I celebrate as an Irishman and which I profoundly respect.

I spoke a couple of years ago in the Magill Summer School about the logic of genuine republicanism and about what should be the true significance for Irish republicans of the Orange panel on the tricolour – it is not in my mind a flag of 'green, white and gold'.

The vocation of promoting reconciliation among Irish people in my view takes precedence over the promotion of more immediate constitutional projects. Those of us whose unconditional priority is for reconciliation between the identities on this island, and for the creation of genuine respectful partnership between those identities, take hope from the Belfast Agreement that we are about to enter upon an era of partnership, equality, reconciliation and mutual empathy between those traditions.

We all know that a straight line is said to be the shortest distance between two points. It has also been said that 'straight line extrapolation is the shortest distance between two mistakes.' I say that because I read an article by Gerry Moriarty in the *Irish Times* last January about some straws in the wind of Northern Ireland's demography. He was previewing the expected release of census data here later this year. He pointed out that figures from the educational sector show the emergence of a new balance between the two religious identities: 57% of school children are described as Catholics and 42% Protestant. In Queen's University there are 8,700 Catholic students and 6,700 Protestants. In Ulster University the numbers are 11,000 and 7,000 respectively.

A more recent article by Gerry Moriarty shows that Northern Ireland's population is now 1.8 million and the Republic's population is 4.6 million, giving the entire island a larger population (6.4 million) than at any time since the post-Famine census of 1851, and a higher population than ten European states, including Finland and Denmark.

My reaction to reading this news was that the newly established era of legal equality between the major identities in Northern Ireland seems to be happening in the context of a coming numerical equality between the two main traditions.

Rather than vainly attempting to extrapolate future political trends or outcome from present sectarian head counts, it seems to me that the real challenge on this island, in all its parts, is now to set about the demanding task – nay the imperative task – of recognition of the values, the dignity, the ideals, the histories and the aspirations of the mixed identities we have and share on this island.

In this spirit and with these reflections, in this week of the centenary of Ulster Day, 28 September 1912, genuine Irish republicans, myself included, extend a warm hand of friendship to the descendants of those who signed the Covenant.

Family connections to the decade of centenaries

23 May 2013

In the decade 2012 to 2022, frequently referred to nowadays in Ireland as 'a decade of centenaries', I have been asked in a number of different ways to reflect on some of those events from the perspective of a descendant of one of the leading figures in Ireland's national struggle for independence. I do not claim any special authority for family members of historical figures; it is, however, almost inevitable that family connections colour one's views of historical events.

Examining my own present family, I find that the events of the 'decade of centenaries' have left indelible marks. Put it this way – my sons' eight great-grandparents' lives were each dramatically affected by those events.

On my side of my family, Eoin Mac Néill, my maternal grandfather, played a well-known central role in the tumultuous events in the ten years leading up to the foundation of the independent Irish state. But my paternal grandfather, John M. McDowell, was in his own way closely involved as well. He was a prominent member of John Redmond's United Irish League, closely associated with Nationalist MPs John Redmond, John Dillon, John Nugent and Joseph Devlin, as their legal adviser in their struggle for Home Rule. In the immediate aftermath of 1916, he saw the way the wind was blowing, and, as a constitutional nationalist, urged his party to pursue Dominion Home Rule to ward off the Sinn Féin threat. He died suddenly in 1925 in London on a social trip in the company of his wife, John Nugent and Joseph Devlin.

My wife's grandparents' lives were equally affected by those events. Joseph Brennan, then a leading Sinn Féin member in Cahirciveen, had his home blown up as an official reprisal by British forces under martial law, and came to Dublin to pursue a career that would eventually see him elected to the Senate. Patrick McCarvill, her maternal grandfather, as a young doctor was heavily involved in the IRA in Monaghan, was elected as a Republican TD, was imprisoned by both the British and the Free State governments, and went on hunger strike. His fiancée and future wife, Eileen McGrane, was Michael Collins' secretary when he was on the run, was captured and imprisoned by the British and subsequently by the Free State government, joining McCarvill on hunger strike.

So, from the constitutional, nationalist Redmondite lawyer to the anti-Treaty Republican hunger strikers, my sons' eight great-grandparents span a broad spectrum of nationalist and separatist activity in those years. Three of them became parliamentarians; three served multiple prison terms. They each endured a great deal of personal tragedy and sacrifice.

John M. McDowell and his wife, Maud, lost their 19-year-old favourite orphan nephew, William, who had been reared in their home, in the slaughter of the Somme on 9 September 1916 in the Battle of Ginchy. His warm letters to them from the trenches make sad reading. Cut to pieces by machine-gun fire in the advance of the 7th Leinster Battalion at Guillemont, his body was never found. Such was the price of his family's loyalty to the constitutional politics of John Redmond.

Perhaps a better-known, and most obviously poignant, piece of my family's history concerns the shooting, in the course of the Irish Civil War, of Brian Mac Néill, the 22-year-old second eldest son of Eoin Mac Néill, on the slopes of Ben Bulben, in September 1922, by soldiers of the Free State Army serving his father's Government.

Brian, like his two brothers, Niall and Turlough, had enlisted in the South Dublin IRA's 6th Battalion. and were members of an active service unit that played a leading role in the War of Independence from 1919 to 1921. Their father's home was the battalion's hidden weapons dump, never discovered in the course of multiple British searches. All three boys were on the run and imprisoned during that period. During the Truce, Brian was sent by IRA HQ to help reorganise the IRA in Sligo, North Roscommon, and East Mayo. He was appointed divisional adjutant. When the IRA split over the Treaty, Brian's division went anti-Treaty. With a heavy heart, his loyalty to his division outweighed his loyalty to his father and to his brothers, both of whom became commissioned officers in the National Army.

Prior to the commencement of Civil War hostilities, Brian was a frequent visitor to the family home in Blackrock, sometimes giving his minister father, Eoin, a lift from there to Government Buildings in a commandeered Dodge motor car. Brian, a first-class honours second-year medical student, who had taken a year out to fulfil his IRA duties, was by all accounts his mother's favourite. Cheery and outgoing, he was also a very popular figure in the anti-Treaty movement in Sligo.

After the attack on the Four Courts, and the commencement of open civil war, Brian could no longer travel home but kept in regular touch with his parents and brothers in a warm and loving correspondence via safe houses in Sligo.

After the death of Michael Collins, General Richard Mulcahy put strong pressure on General Seán Mac Eoin, his Western commander, to bring a quick and decisive end to the Civil War in Sligo and the West.

By this time, Brian had informed the Republican leadership that the IRA in Sligo was going to adopt guerrilla tactics. From their stronghold at Rahelly near Sligo, they engaged in a hit-and-run campaign against the Free State forces, inflicting heavy casualties and losses in terms of men killed and matériel captured. Many brave Free State soldiers, including close comrades in the War of Independence of Seán Mac Eoin, died at their hands in roadside ambushes and full-scale incursions on towns held by the Free State. Free State intelligence officers were to be 'shot on sight'. Brigadier General Joe Ring and Paddy Callaghan (a previous member of Mac Eoin's Longford Flying Column) were killed in ambushes in Mayo and Sligo.

Dáil Éireann had passed a resolution giving the National Army powers to conduct field court martials and to execute 'Irregulars' found under arms. Mac Eoin was in no humour to show mercy to those who had shot his comrades. In the end, Free State forces cornered the leadership of the Republican forces between Rahelly and Ben Bulben.

The day after the decisive battle in which the Republicans were surrounded and routed, a number of them sought to escape the ring of steel surrounding them by crossing Ben Bulben in the hope of regrouping at a hidden cave above Glencar Lake. Brian Mac Néill and three others, Seamus Devins TD and Volunteers Carroll and Banks, were surprised and surrounded in a mountain gully by a party of Free Staters commanded by two officers, McGoohan and Sexton.

What happened next is not certain, but it appears most probable that they surrendered, were disarmed and shot by their captors. Apparently, Brian Mac Néill, realising what was about to happen, attempted to run and was shot a short distance from where the other three were gunned down. Certainly, the same party of Free State troops two hours later captured two more 'Irregulars', Volunteers Patrick Langan and Joseph Benson, and executed them, mangling their bodies with machine-gun fire after they were put standing in a deep bog hole on the top of the mountain. All the bodies were left where they lay.

The Free State forces published untrue and highly misleading accounts of the killings and privately gave the Mac Néill family a further untrue but consoling version of the shootings.

Sligo's Noble Six, as the victims became known, became symbols of Civil War cruelty. They remain embedded in the political and historical fabric of County Sligo to this day.

For Eoin Mac Néill, his wife, Taddie, and their children, this was a cause of unimaginable grief and misgivings, which they dealt with entirely privately, and a horrendous outcome to their participation in the struggle for Irish freedom. A letter written by Eoin Mac Néill at the height of the Civil War gives some insight into his grief, his pride in, and his love for his lost son.

In the end, Brian's coffin was borne by his brothers and by fellow IRA comrades now wearing Free State uniforms, to his family grave at Kilbarrack in Dublin. Such was, and is, the reality of Civil War.

All of this is part of my sons' family legacy.

Four myths about the Rising

13 March 2016

The centenary of the Easter Rising is surrounded by myth, moral ambiguity and historical revisionism, and by political re-interpretation and re-invention.

For those, like myself, who unambiguously value and cherish the establishment of an independent, sovereign Irish republic, 1916 is the starting point of its existence, albeit that it was not brought to fruition for years afterwards.

It is not that we glory in violence or in death; it is that we honour and celebrate those who set the achievement of our liberty in train.

The first myth

1916 was not the start of a century of political violence in Ireland, as is sometimes claimed; when the British Tory establishment from 1912 to 1914 backed the creation of the UVF, armed to the teeth with German weapons, and approbated the establishment of a provisional government in Ulster sworn to resist by violence both the will of the Irish people for Home Rule and the authority of the Westminster parliament, the use of force and threat of civil war was deliberately introduced into the politics of twentieth-century Ireland.

Those actions demonstrated beyond contradiction that the ambition of the great majority of Irish people to achieve some form of self-determination would be countered by force at the hands of those who controlled the largest empire on the face of the earth.

The second myth

Contrary to what is claimed, Irish independence was never available through the Home Rule Acts.

All one has to do is to look at the Government of Ireland Act 1920, the high point of Home Rule legislation, to realise that a divided Ireland was to be offered, within the United Kingdom, two assemblies posing as parliaments, each with very limited domestic autonomy, a council of ministers chosen by the Lord Lieutenant, no fiscal autonomy, no capacity to conduct international relations, no control over its armed forces, and subject to having any or all of its laws overridden at will by Westminster.

It is also utterly false to claim, as happened this week, that Home Rule under the 1920 Act was indistinguishable from independence under the 1922 Constitution. The two were radically different.

To quote John Redmond, speaking at a St Patrick's Day dinner in London in 1913, on his ambition for Home Rule:

We will under Home Rule, devote our attention to education, reform of the Poor Law, and questions of that kind which are purely domestic, which are, if you like, hum-drum Irish questions, and the only way we will attempt to interfere in any Imperial question will be by our representatives on the floor of the Imperial Parliament in Westminster doing everything in our power to increase the strength and glory of what will then be our empire at long last; and by sending in support of the Empire the strong arms and brave hearts of Irish soldiers and Irish sailors to maintain the traditions of Irish valour in every part of the world. That is our ambition.

That 'ambition' cannot be airbrushed from history; Redmond was entitled to hold it, but it ceased to be (if it ever was) the ambition of most Irish people within 24 months of the Rising. While we can honour Redmond as a patriot, we do not have to share or reinstate his particular ideas of patriotism or his ambition.

Furthermore, in relation to Redmond's ambition, anyone who believes that Home Rule would have avoided partition need only read Ronan Fanning's *Fatal Path* to be disabused of that delusion.

A third myth

A third popular delusion is that the Rising had any chance of short-term military success. Some have argued that the Rising might somehow have succeeded were it not for the loss of the *Aud* arms ship or the making of MacNeill's countermanding order.

Perhaps the most closely guarded myth is that Casement came ashore at Banna Strand to help the Rising. On the contrary, his diaries and papers show that his only aim was to make contact with MacNeill and others with a view to stopping the Rising, which he correctly viewed as doomed to failure – with or without the cargo of the *Aud*.

Casement understood, as did MacNeill, The O'Rahilly, Hobson and others, that the Volunteers outside Dublin were utterly under-equipped and unprepared, and that British military strength in Ireland would crush the Rising with ease.

That did not bother Pearse. He was intent on self-sacrifice to relight the flame of Irish freedom.

Most interestingly, Casement actually pleaded with intelligence officers on the Easter weekend in London after his arrest to be allowed communicate with MacNeill to prevent a Rising, but his interrogators intimated to him that they thought it better to allow a Rising happen so that its perpetrators could be excised from the body politic. There, if you want to find it, was perfidious Albion at its most cynical; and there, if you want to find it, was the greatest self-inflicted shot in the foot to the British interest in Ireland.

A fourth myth

It is sometimes claimed that the Rising somehow validates the Provo campaign from 1969 to 1998.

While there are some small elements in common between the two (chiefly the absence of any democratic mandate), there are also radical differences. The issue in Northern Ireland was and is, at its heart, an issue between Irish people.

Since 1949, the UK has legally acknowledged the principle of the right of a majority in Northern Ireland to decide whether to remain in or leave the UK for a united Ireland. The use of violence since 1969 to decide that constitutional issue is the use of violence to coerce the will of a majority in Northern Ireland.

It can be argued that Sunningdale would never have happened without the threat or use of violence; but it cannot be argued that a united Ireland could occur without the consent of a majority of Northern Ireland's people or without civil war.

Quite unlike MacNeill and Pearse, who were careful not to threaten the northern unionists with violence, the Provos used shocking violence, bombing of civilians, and terror to attempt to subvert the will of their fellow Irishmen, and to attempt to force them into a united socialist Ireland.

Independence is good

Without being unfair to anyone, I detect an attitudinal coincidence between hostility to the 1916 Rising and a hankering for Redmond's ambition which nowadays takes the form of an ambition for a strongly federal EU superstate instead of sovereign independent nation states.

Fair enough. You may have such ambitions if you like.

For my part, I believe that becoming and remaining a sovereign independent republic has been, and will be, good for Ireland and for the Irish – economically, socially and culturally. I do not believe that Ireland would have equally prospered if it had remained a province of the United Kingdom – as Wales, Scotland, Northern Ireland and northern England demonstrate.

Nor do I believe that we should, after one hundred years, fold up the proclamation and become to an EU superstate what North Dakota is to the US.

With due regard to all the moral ambiguity that necessarily attends every revolution in history, I celebrate 100 years of independence sparked into life by the Rising. We should honour our patriots, however they viewed the Rising, and we should celebrate their achievements this Easter Day.

Eoin MacNeill – a family perspective

Delivered at NUI MacNeill Seminar

28 June 2016

Any examination of Eoin MacNeill's part in the events of 1916 must start with a close understanding of his background. Born in Glenarm in County Antrim in 1867, his Catholic parents lived in the Glens, an enclave in Protestant East Ulster. His father, Archie, a tough local tradesman, was by times a shipwright, a baker, a builder and the proprietor of the local postal service in Glenarm, a mixed community. His mother, Rosetta, came from a more refined background. Archie was prosecuted and acquitted arising out of unrest during an Orange demonstration in Glenarm when Eoin was just five years old.

One of a family of eight, Eoin benefitted from a family determination to seek good education for the children. Unlike three of his brothers, who were sent to Belvedere in Dublin, Eoin was sent to St Malachy's in Belfast and obtained a scholarship to study in the Royal University, where he graduated in politics and economics in 1888. The previous year he had obtained by examination a junior clerkship in the Accountant General's office in the Four Courts, becoming the first Catholic to have such an appointment, which previously had been made on the basis of Dublin Castle patronage.

As an undergraduate, he had begun in 1887 to study the Irish language, which was virtually extinct in the Glenarm in his childhood. From basic learning of the spoken language (on grinds for which he spent a quarter of his small starting salary), he quickly graduated to the study of Old and Middle Irish, and quickly became an expert in matters Gaelic. Along with Douglas Hyde, he co-founded the Gaelic League (Conradh na Gaeilge), and started to develop a theory of Irish identity which was a blend of his political, linguistic and religious outlooks.

In his role as editor of the *Gaelic Journal*, co-editor of *Fáinne an Lae* and first editor of *An Claidheamh Soluis*, he became a leading figure in the Irish language movement. It was in this context that he met and befriended the young Pádraig Pearse, a relationship which became of central importance to later events in 1916.

At the turn of the nineteenth century, MacNeill became increasingly politically active and took a leading role in the debate on the University Question, which led to the foundation of the National University of Ireland (NUI) in 1908. He was appointed Professor of Early Irish History in University College Dublin (UCD) in 1909.

The Volunteers

Four years later, in 1913, he wrote a leading article in *An Claidheamh Soluis* entitled 'The North Began', calling for nationalists in Ireland to consider establishing a volunteer force to counterbalance the Ulster Volunteers of Edward Carson, and describing the Ulster Volunteers as a positive step towards national self-determination.

On foot of 'The North Began', MacNeill was approached by a number of figures in the Irish Republican Brotherhood (IRB) and some of their associates to ask him to lead the process of forming the Irish Volunteers. When John Redmond imposed himself on the Irish Volunteers, MacNeill at first cooperated but later, when Redmond pledged the Volunteers to the Great War effort, sided with Pearse, Tom Clarke, Thomas MacDonagh, Bulmer Hobson and others in the split between Redmond's 'National Volunteers' and the 'Irish Volunteers', of which MacNeill was president and commander-in-chief.

However, a further, largely unseen split was developing in the Irish Volunteers. A small IRB-based group, including Pearse, Clarke and later MacDonagh, formed a secret 'Military Council' within the IRB and spent 1915 secretly plotting to start an armed insurrection against British rule in Ireland while the Great War was in progress.

MacNeill's priority was to arm the Volunteers. With Roger Casement and others, he had planned the June 1914 Howth and Kilcoole gun-running operations, which were modest in scale compared with the massive UVF importation at Larne in March of that year.

MacNeill and Hobson (who although an IRB member was unaware of the Military Council's plans) had a different view from that of Pearse, Clarke and MacDonagh on the legitimate use of force. The IRB's own constitution prohibited any armed insurrection which had not the backing of the Irish people. MacNeill categorically rejected any notion of any violent coup unless it had a reasonable prospect of military success. In particular, MacNeill was wholly opposed to the notion of 'blood sacrifice' as a way of polarising or catalysing the Irish people into a political struggle with Britain.

MacNeill, aware of Pearse's romantic and idealistic notion that an insurrection would be justified as a blood sacrifice, struggled to persuade the Irish Volunteers' executive that the use of force would only be justified (i) if the British attempted to disarm or suppress the Volunteers or (ii) if the Volunteers were in a position, in terms of arms and organisation, to use force successfully to end British rule in Ireland.

The February 1916 Memorandum

His memorandum on this issue ('the 1916 Memorandum'), written in February 1916, was a forceful and convincing exposition of his views. He suspected but was not definitively aware, however, that Pearse and Clarke had already decided to stage an insurrection 'come what may', and did not suspect that they were willing to use any means, including deception, to bring about a 'rising'.

This memorandum lay unpublished until 1961, when Professor F.X. Martin revealed it in *Irish Historical Studies* in an article entitled 'Eoin MacNeill and the 1916 Rising'. Martin's article is easily available on the internet and makes compelling reading even today.

In 1961, F.X. Martin's article ran counter to the then prevalent 'national myth' of 1916, which had relegated MacNeill to the status of an indecisive, incompetent academic 'bit player' who had somehow brought about by his indecision the military failure of the Rising.

Hobson, though an IRB man, had attempted to alert MacNeill to the secret plotting for a rising. He and MacNeill believed that the Volunteers should not stage a rising during the Great War but should wait for its end, a scenario in which, regardless of the outcome of the war, there would be an influx of returning Irish soldiers to strengthen the Volunteers. In the meantime, MacNeill and Hobson argued that the greatest priority was to secure arms for the Volunteers. If the Volunteers were to be outlawed, they believed that a guerrilla-type campaign would be more successful (a view which Michael Collins was later to adopt and implement).

Compounding this dispute within the Volunteers was the determination of James Connolly to stage a violent socialist revolution through the involvement of the Irish Citizen Army, a group which had emerged in the context of the 1913 Lockout.

Because Connolly's Citizen Army revolution had no prospect of success, the Volunteers were naturally convinced that it would almost certainly be used by Dublin Castle as a pretext to disarm and suppress the Irish Volunteers. MacNeill, at the request of Pearse, met with Connolly to dissuade him from starting any armed conflict. Pearse was present at this meeting and later informed MacNeill that Connolly had been persuaded by MacNeill's argument to abandon any thought of unilateral action by the Citizen Army. But, in reality, Pearse had secretly assured Connolly that an early rising was being planned in which he and the Citizen Army could take part.

It was in that context that MacNeill wrote and circulated the 1916 Memorandum. It was discussed at a day-long meeting at MacNeill's residence in Woodtown Park in Rathfarnham, during which Pearse expressly disavowed any plan for armed insurrection.

In the opening words of the 1916 Memorandum, MacNeill stated:

The only reason that could justify general action – military measures as distinct from military preparations – on the part of Irish nationalists would be a reasonably calculated or estimate prospect of success.

Without that prospect, military action (not military preparation) would in the first place be morally wrong – and that consideration to my mind is final and conclusive.

To enter deliberately on a course of action which is morally wrong is to incur the guilt not only of that action itself but of all its direct consequences.

For example to kill any person in carrying out such a course of action is murder. The guilt of murder in that case falls on those who have planned and ordered the general course of action on the party which makes such course of action inevitable.

The success which is calculated or estimated must be success in the operation itself, not merely some further moral or political advantage which may be hoped for as the result of non-success.

The memorandum goes on to dismiss any policy based on 'feelings' or 'instincts' and pleas for reason to prevail. He argued strongly against any premature use of force with no prospect of military success and against any rising simply based on 'striking' while the Great War was in progress on the claim that 'Ireland has always struck too late'.

He said: 'We must listen to nothing except proper preparation and proper calculation.'

On Pearse's notion of a blood sacrifice, MacNeill's memorandum had this to say, clearly directed personally at Pearse:

There is a feeling in some minds that action is necessary, that lives must be sacrificed, in order to produce an ultimate effect on the national mind. As a principle of action, I have heard that feeling disclaimed, but I did not fully accept the disclaimer. In fact, it is a sounder principle than any of the others I have dealt with.

If the destruction of our nationality was in sight, and we came to the conclusion that at best the vital principle of nationality was to be saved by laying down our lives, then we should make that sacrifice without hesitation. It would not be a military act in any sense, and it does not come within the scope of our military counsels.

This passage clearly demonstrates that MacNeill understood and was partly sympathetic with Pearse's fervour, but also underlines his conviction that it was morally wrong to drag other innocent people into a futile self-sacrifice or to kill others in pursuit of self-sacrifice. He was simply not willing to sacrifice the Irish Volunteers as a movement and all the inevitable victims of an early insurrection to 'produce an ultimate effect on the national mind'. This, then, was the line of intellectual and moral cleavage between the patriots who met that day in March 1916 at Woodtown Park in Rathfarnham.

MacNeill's memorandum had spelt out at length the inevitability of a military defeat for any rising and pointed out to the conspirators that the Volunteers' state of preparation outside Dublin was negligible.

But he wrote:

> ... [W]hereas in my conscientious judgment an armed revolt at present would be wrong and unpatriotic and criminal, it is quite a different case with regard to the possession and retention of our arms. I have not the slightest doubt on the point that we are morally and in every way justified in keeping by all necessary force such arms as we have got or can get. I hold myself entitled to resist to the death any attempt to deprive me of my arms or ammunition or other military articles that I have or can protect for myself or the Irish Volunteers. If in such resistance, any man meets his death through my act or counsel or command, I shall have no guilt on my conscience.

The Castle Document

The Pearse, Clarke and MacDonagh faction affected to accept MacNeill's argument at the Woodtown Park meeting, but secretly they decided to subvert it by composing a forged document purporting to be a Dublin Castle decision to disarm, arrest and suppress the Irish Volunteers. Knowing that MacNeill would authorise the use of violence in such a scenario, all they had to do was to produce false but convincing evidence – and that is why they concocted the famous 'Castle document'.

As F.X. Martin put it:

> In the light of MacNeill's attitude it is obvious that the 'Castle document' was 'a most opportune document' for the members of the IRB who were trying to manoeuvre MacNeill to support for an armed

rebellion. It was the news on Holy Friday morning of the expected arrival of the Aud *with arms for the Volunteers which decided him to support the plan for gun-running at Fenit, and thereby risk an almost inevitable collision with the British forces.*

The great historical value of MacNeill's memorandum of March 1916 is that it was written before the Rising and is therefore completely devoid of post factum justification or reasoning.

The 1917 Memorandum

In a second memorandum ('the 1917 Memorandum'), written in the latter half of 1917 at the request of Hobson, MacNeill, who had been released from a life sentence imposed on him by a general court martial in 1916 for his part in the Rising, set out at length his account of what happened in the period November 1915 to April 1916.

The 1917 Memorandum makes compelling reading too. It is also available online. It shows how the Pearse, Clarke and MacDonagh plan was concealed from MacNeill and how they forged the 'Castle document' to win him over to armed action. It gives a very vivid account of MacNeill's journey from Woodtown Park in Rathfarnham to St Enda's in Rathfarnham on Holy Thursday 1916, where MacNeill confronted Pearse with his knowledge of their plan for a rising.

MacNeill's account shows him as having been resigned to a rising up until midday on Easter Saturday when The O'Rahilly and Seán Fitzgibbon came to Woodtown Park and revealed to MacNeill that orders for a rising had been issued on the false basis that they were authorised by MacNeill, and, crucially, that the 'Castle document' was a forgery designed to bring him over to the planned Rising.

It was in that context that MacNeill at last countermanded the Rising – an order that was largely effective except in Dublin where the Rising's planners were in control of the Volunteers.

MacNeill states:

It is also untrue that I changed my mind several times. For a few hours I was convinced that all was over with our movement and nothing left for us except to sell our lives as dearly as possible. When The O'Rahilly and Fitzgibbon came to me on Holy Saturday, we agreed that the situation was by no means so desperate and that the rising ought to be prevented. The O'Rahilly gave me more help than any other person to prevent it.

But Pearse, while assuring MacNeill in a written message as late as Easter Saturday that the countermanding order would be implemented, was in reality busily re-scheduling the Rising for Easter Monday.

F.X. Martin, commenting on the two memoranda which were published for the first time in 1961, said:

Perhaps the most noticeable characteristic of both memoranda is their dispassionate line. MacNeill condemns nobody, though he might have considered himself to have reasonable grounds for resentment.

Pearse, in his last dispatch from the GPO, on Friday 28 April, declared that 'Both Eoin MacNeill and we have acted in the best interests of Ireland', and MacNeill was no less courteous during his court martial to the revolutionary leaders.

MacNeill actually remained unaware that a 'Military Council of Four' within the IRB had pre-determined on a rising until he met with Mrs Tom Clarke in the aftermath of his release from prison in 1917 while assisting Éamon de Valera in his campaign for the Clare East by-election.

Mrs Clarke, Countess Markievicz and Helena Molony had previously bitterly attacked MacNeill at the Sinn Féin convention in 1917 for his action in countermanding the Rising. The great majority, however, vigorously defended MacNeill. In the result, MacNeill topped the poll in the election for the Sinn Féin Ard-Chomhairle, leaving his critics far behind him in terms of votes.

Also elected on that occasion, with the narrowest of margins, was a young 1916 veteran called Michael Collins. Collins never doubted MacNeill's sincerity or integrity. Indeed, in 1922, when asked by American journalist Hayden Talbot to comment on MacNeill's decision to countermand the Rising, Collins told Talbot that he had never discussed the issue with MacNeill, and urged him to interview MacNeill on the matter. Talbot did so and Collins, on learning of the account given by MacNeill in the interview, accepted MacNeill's explanation.

MacNeill was quoted by Talbot as having described the executed 1916 leaders as 'patriots' motivated by 'pure martyrdom'. He ascribed the result of their execution as their 'fondest dreams' being 'exceeded'.

Furthermore, he is quoted by Talbot as saying that if it were argued that their pre-vision was good and his bad, he could make no comment except that even if he had known fully of their plan, he would still have countermanded the Rising. He believed it was the madness of British reactive violence in suppressing the Rising and executing its leaders that created the conditions for Irish independence.

It is also notable that MacNeill unreservedly backed the War of Independence. His three eldest sons became active members and officers in the 6th Battalion of the Irish Republican Army (IRA) in South Dublin.

During the War of Independence his home at Netley in Booterstown was raided and searched on a number of occasions. MacNeill and members of his family were arrested. But none of the searches ever revealed the secret compartment specially built into the ground floor of the house which was the arms dump for the 6th Battalion. By using his home in this way MacNeill was again putting his life on the line for Irish freedom.

An indication of MacNeill's personal commitment to the morality of the War of Independence can be gleaned from a letter he sent to the Archbishop of Tuam on 22 July 1920, in the context of the archbishop being reported as saying that the shooting of two Royal Irish Constabulary (RIC) men near Tuam, although a 'dastardly crime', could not justify the subsequent sacking of the town by Black and Tans in reprisal.

MacNeill, a devout Catholic, wrote to the archbishop:

Either we Irishmen are morally entitled to carry arms or we are not. If we are, we are entitled to defend our right and if the so-called 'police', who are well known to Your Grace to be no police but a mere branch of the British military forces, endanger our lives in the exercise of that right, Your Grace can define the extent of resistance that is morally justifiable.

It is surely not a case for vagueness, and till we know our rights supposing the present belief of the people in general and their present conscientious conviction to be mistaken – we are justified in protesting against your Lordship's use of the term 'murder' even without the qualifying adjective.

If on the other hand we have no right to bear arms, surely Your Grace ought to say so, for undoubtedly the bearing of arms, being the occasion of shooting on sight by those in command of the so-called police, will also be the occasion of the so-called police being shot at sight.

For my part I have not the slightest doubt that I am entitled to bear arms in defence of Ireland against the British forces, and that I am also entitled to resist being disarmed to the same degree as I may resist an attempt to destroy my house or my life or the lives of my family.

I am not bound to put up my hands when ordered to do so by any subordinate of the British Government. I have the clearest evidence therefore that my life and the rights I am entitled to defend unto death are always threatened by the so-called 'police'. Does Your Grace really believe that this state of mind implies that I am at heart and in conscience a murderer, not to say a dastard.

I am, my Lord Archbishop,

Your Grace's faithful servant

Eoin MacNeill

The echoes of his 1916 Memorandum are striking.

One can only assume that MacNeill had believed in 1920–22 (and rightly as it turned out) that the War of Independence had a good 'calculation of success', while in March to April 1916 he judged that a rising had none.

For a man who two years later, on 20 September 1922, lost his second son Brian to an on-the-spot execution by his own Irish Free State forces on the slopes of Ben Bulben, the moral complexities of Eoin MacNeill's views on the use of force are striking.

So, too, was his defence of the notorious summary Mountjoy executions on 8 December 1922, in reprisal for the shooting of two pro-Treaty TDs. On that occasion he informed the Dáil that it was a case of clear legal and moral justification and invited anyone to prosecute him for murder.

These events show that MacNeill's views on the morality of the use of force were based always on deep subjective conviction tempered by his strong sense of principle.

For all these and many other reasons, MacNeill deserves close and detached study; his influence on Irish history is significant. In more than one sense he was a foremost author of Irish history.

The Definite Article: HISTORY – IRELAND LOOKING BACK

The trial of Roger Casement

Lecture at the Bar of Ireland's series on famous Irish trials, Green Street Courthouse

29 September 2016

I

There are few figures in Irish history that excite and command as much debate and controversy as Roger Casement. He remains at the centre of public discourse largely because he embodied in one life so many different and seemingly contradictory personalities.

We have in this one man many and varied characters: Casement the international humanitarian; Casement the British Empire diplomat; Casement the avowed enemy of the British Empire: Casement the English king's grateful knight; Casement the Hohenzollern pawn; Casement born of landed gentry; Casement the Irish revolutionary; Casement the Edwardian liberals' moral hero; Casement the low-life homosexual; Casement the victim of dirty tricks; Casement the creator of his own myth; Casement the victim of Crown injustice; and Casement the Irish martyr.

His trial and the appeal on charges of high treason at the height of the Great War were clearly thought at the time to be a very major event in English legal history, meriting depiction in Lavery's great canvas, now in King's Inns, and the immediate publication in book form of a comprehensive account of both proceedings, which was obsequiously dedicated jointly to the presiding judges at the trial and appeal.

Casement's trial and execution did not bring its intended end to his standing as an historical figure. Far from bringing down the curtain of history on his life, the hangman's lever launched Roger Casement into more than one kind of immortality; he instantly became the unquenchable object of passionate inquiry, speculation and debate.

The trial of Roger Casement

Far from being an ignominious place of punishment for treachery, the gallows at Pentonville instead became a stage on which the character of Roger Casement still treads the boards with all the dramatic fascination of Hamlet, and, I think, he will always do so.

Like Hamlet, we also have Casement the tortured soul. His papers show him to have been, by turns, idealistic, vainglorious, sensitive, naïvely optimistic and frequently despondent. His friends and acquaintances admired him almost to the point of idolising him; few, if any, could see far into his secret, darker and more private world.

If Casement was ever on intimate terms with anyone other than himself, we have no record of it. His poetry, perhaps, is the one window into his inner nature and self-image.

In the end, each of us is left at liberty to imagine and even to judge his real character as we choose.

II

To understand the context and significance of the Casement trial, it is necessary to briefly describe his upbringing and career up to 1914.

Casement was born into the family of an impoverished Anglo-Irish ex-officer living in Sandycove, Dublin, and later in England. After his father's death, he was educated on the fringes of the families of wealthier relatives in County Antrim.

Leaving school at 16 to work as a clerk in a shipping company, he eventually was employed by the African International Association, which acted as the means whereby King Leopold II of the Belgians established and exploited a personal colony in the vast Congo basin as part of the European carve-up known as the Scramble for Africa.

Casement later joined the British Colonial Service and was commissioned to write a report on human rights abuses of the

Congolese natives under the cruel personal regime of King Leopold. His report, when published, gave rise to international outcry and led to the transfer of ownership of the Congo from Leopold personally to the Belgian state.

Later, he was posted to South America where he eventually wrote yet another report into appalling human rights abuses, this time by a British-registered enterprise of the Amazon's Putamayo Indians. The Liberal government in England, with a slight conscience over its own imperialism, fêted and decorated Casement for these reports, making him a knight in 1911.

Casement, however, had in the meantime fallen totally out of sympathy with the British Empire. He had joined the Gaelic League in 1904 and Arthur Griffith's Sinn Féin in 1905. His youthful, romantic view of Ireland was transformed into a strong commitment to the cause of self-government for Ireland.

In 1913, having just retired from the consular service, he became involved, with Eoin Mac Néill, in the establishment of the Irish Volunteers, although neither of them was in the Irish Republican Brotherhood. He played a major part in organising the Howth gun-running and went in July 1914 to the US to raise money for the Irish Volunteers.

Taking the view that the recently started Great War was an Allied injustice against the Germans, in October 1914 Casement travelled, at the request of veteran Fenian John Devoy, from America to Kristiania, the capital of the neutral, recently independent Kingdom of Norway, and from there to Germany to obtain the Kaiser's support for the cause of Irish independence.

By now Casement was under very close surveillance by the British secret services while in America. At one point, by irony, he was being trailed both by private detectives hired by the IRB to verify his bona fides and by British agents.

Prior to his departure from America, Casement had written a formal letter to the German Emperor seeking Germany's support for Irish freedom. In the course of that letter he said the following:

Hoping as we do that Germany will win this war so unrighteously forced upon her by a combination of assailants each lacking the courage to act alone, we earnestly commend to Your Majesty's attention this fundamental fact that to restore the equilibrium of sea power so grievously injured by Great Britain, to the detriment of the whole world since the Napoleonic Wars, Ireland must be freed from British control.

While the fortune of war may not bring German troops to Ireland, the hearts of thousands of Irishmen go out to the German shores today. Thousands of Irishmen are prepared to do their part to aid the German cause, for they recognise that it is their own. ...

On these grounds alone, did not natural sympathy and admiration for a people fighting against such heavy odds lead us to address Your Majesty, we should hope for a German triumph over an enemy who is also our enemy. We pray for that triumph for Germany; and we pray with it Your Majesty may have power, wisdom and strength of purpose to impose a lasting peace upon the seas by effecting the independence of Ireland and securing its recognition as a fixed condition of the terms of final settlement of the great maritime powers.

That letter was signed by the entire executive of Clann na Gael in America.

III

There is one particular incident in late 1914 that has an important bearing on the later trial of Roger Casement. En route to Germany in his pursuit of German assistance for the Volunteers, Casement travelled under a false name, accompanied by his man-servant and occasional sexual partner, Adler Christensen, aged 24 and from Norway. British intelligence was trailing Casement from America to Norway.

Christensen, a manipulative character, either contacted or was contacted by the British legation in Kristiania. His loyalties are unclear and were probably mixed and possibly for sale. He was, on Casement's account, promised £5,000 by the British to have Casement 'knocked on the head'.

During the negotiations with Adler Christensen, the British Minister in Norway, one Mansfeldt de Cardonnel Findlay, learned that Casement and Christensen were sexual partners. Findlay also obtained corroboration of Casement's homosexuality from other Norwegian sources. He passed this information onto the Foreign Office in London in late 1914.

The plot to kill him became an obsession with Casement, who called it 'the Findlay Affair'. Fearing that he would be eliminated by the British in Norway, Casement expedited his departure for Germany via Copenhagen under German escort.

Once in Germany, he set about dealing with their Foreign Office, proposing the establishment of an Irish Brigade and a declaration of German intentions in relation to Irish independence. He then sought evidence of the Findlay Affair, and arranged that Adler Christensen would obtain a written offer of £5,000 signed in Oslo by Findlay for his capture, and hoped to persuade the Germans to lay a trap for British intelligence to expose their dirty dealings. All of this was fed by a pre-occupation that his activities in America and Germany would be raised in the Houses of Parliament as proof of treachery.

He composed and circulated an open letter to Sir E. Grey, setting out his version of the Findlay Affair and ending with a renunciation of his knighthood. This letter was circulated to foreign embassies in Berlin. The letter is notable for two reasons. It would, if produced at his trial, (i) have totally deflated the Attorney General's opening speech to the jury which placed great emphasis on Casement's obsequious letter of grateful acceptance of his knighthood written in 1911, and (ii) would have severely discredited the Crown's tone of moral outrage by exposing the 'dirty dealings' of British intelligence. To try a man for treason in respect of actions taken after the Crown had conspired to murder him might appear a little unjust.

But the letter's production at trial would, as the letter's text makes clear, have also constituted a clear written admission in terms of treason. Unsurprisingly, then, neither side produced the letter to the jury.

This suppression of underlying fact was by no means the only one in the trial of Roger Casement. As we shall see, the version of events given to the jury, both by Casement and the Crown, was at best highly selective and at worst deeply misleading. Both the prosecution and the accused, for different and opposite reasons, colluded in a process of distorting the facts to suit their several political ends.

IV

We are fortunate that Casement during his period in Germany kept a diary for substantial periods and that he entrusted his papers, including his German diary, to a third party, a Dr Charles Curry, for safekeeping immediately before his departure by U-boat for Ireland in April 1916.

The German diary was clearly written with an eye to posterity. In its pages, we see Casement as a rather excitable and volatile character coping with illness, frustrations, and a growing realisation that the Kaiser's government was dealing with the Irish separatists' project as a diversionary nuisance rather than as a rebellion with German political commitment to bring about an independent Ireland. Germany, he discovered, was not interested in a military invasion and defeat of the UK or Ireland; it sought military victory on the continent which it hoped would lead to a peace with the British.

Casement describes his first encounter with the German Foreign Office at Wilhelmstrasse in Berlin on Monday 2 November 1914. As he waited there to meet Arthur Zimmerman, the Under Secretary of State, he reflected on his mission, and recorded that reflection in the following terms:

Strange thoughts were mine, as I sat on a big sofa in the centre of policy of the German Empire. No regrets, no fears – well – yes – some regrets, but no fears. I thought of Ireland, the land I should almost fatally never see again. Only a miracle of victory could ever bring me to her shores. That I did not expect – cannot in truth hope for. But, victory or defeat, it is all for Ireland. And she cannot suffer from what I do. I may, I must suffer – and even those near me and dear to me – but my country can only gain from my treason. ...

'Home Rule' must indeed become home rule – and even if all my hopes are doomed to rank failure abroad, at least I shall have given more to Ireland by one bold deed of open treason than Redmond and Co. after years of talk and spouting treason have gained from England. England does not mind the 'treason' of the orthodox 'patriot'. She took the true measure of that long ago. She only fears the Irish man who acts; not him who talks. She recognises only action, and respects only deeds. Those men have killed England with their mouths time and time again – I am going to hit her with my clenched hand. It is a blow of sincere enmity, based on a wholly impersonal disregard of consequences to myself. Sure alone that it is in truth a blow for Ireland, I should be a traitor did I not act as I am doing.

There can be no doubt that Roger Casement subjectively viewed his actions as treasonable towards the United Kingdom of

The trial of Roger Casement

Great Britain and Ireland and towards the Crown. His actions in Germany amounted to a premediated treason against the Crown and, despite the fact that Casement was to grow increasingly disenchanted with the Kaiser's government, Casement never doubted for a moment that his actions would be viewed as treason in the eyes of Britain and that his actions would, in the ultimate, lead him to the gallows if he fell into the hands of the British government.

From the foregoing, it seems clear that Casement never envisaged as a realistic possibility a German invasion of Ireland but strongly believed in a negotiated end to the Great War which would entail the granting of independence to Ireland.

Casement's dual purpose in Germany – (i) to secure German support for an independent Ireland with a view to discouraging recruitment of and participation by Irish soldiers on the British side, and (ii) the recruitment of Irish prisoners of war into an Irish brigade which would eventually be used to support the cause of Irish independence – must be judged in the light of his clear statement at his first meeting with Zimmermann that his 'efforts with the soldiers must be strictly defined as an effort to strike a blow for Ireland – not an attempt merely to hit England.'

Casement pointed out to Zimmermann that 'any Irishman might commit treason against England for the sake of Ireland, but that he would not do anything mean or treacherous. He would put his neck in the noose, as I had done, for the love of Ireland; he would not "desert to any enemy" or forsake his own colours merely to assail England.'

Some of these themes emerge in Casement's defence at his trial of the charge of high treason put against him. While he could not by way of defence admit that he had engaged in 'one bold deed of open treason', and while he could not put in evidence his acknowledgment that he had knowingly 'put his neck in the noose' for love of Ireland until his speech before sentence, his case was, nonetheless, to insist that his actions had to be judged as being taken for Ireland and not against Great Britain.

Viewed from the perspective of an Irish nationalist, Casement was drawing a fine distinction between supporting the cause of Ireland in arms and assisting in making war on Great Britain. But from the perspective of the government of the United Kingdom of Great Britain and Ireland, it is hard not to agree with Casement's subjective description of his own actions as 'open treason'.

Casement's German diaries also make clear his total opposition to the military rising being plotted for Easter 1916 by Devoy, Pearse, Clarke and others. On St Patrick's Day 1916, Casement reflected on his growing disillusionment with the German government's policy since 17 March 1915 in the following terms:

Even then hope had gone from me – for I realised then, already, that those I trusted here were little to be trusted and that their only interest in me lay in exploiting me, and the Irish cause in their own supposed interests.

Since then a hundred proofs have accumulated – and yesterday the climax came, and as now but little is left I begin, today, a hurried record of things that must be stated in order that some day the truth may be known.

In three weeks' time I shall probably be at sea in the maddest and most ill-planned enterprise that the history of Irish revolutionary efforts offers. But it is not of my own choosing, of my planning, or undertaken with my approval. I go because honour calls me to go – and because to stop it now (even if I could stop it) would involve others and perhaps bring greater grief. Moreover by going with the tiny band (twelve men probably) that is to sail on 8th of April I may save them – and perhaps Ireland too from a dreadful fate. To stay here, in safety, while those others go would do no good to Ireland – and would leave me a prey to eternal regret.

Thus while I strongly disapprove what is being attempted, and so wretchedly attempted with a foregone assurance of failure, I must lend it my countenance and accompany the forlorn hope.

On that day, Casement's German diary expresses his profound disillusionment in relation to the planned Rising and the manner in which Germany was making a token offer of support providing 20,000 captured Russian rifles instead of the 200,000 weapons promised to Casement. He described the mission to import those arms to Ireland in conjunction with the Rising as 'stupendous idiocy', having 'fundamental falsity' and destined 'for doomed failure'.

He also confided to his diary his fear that he himself would be 'held to all ages in Irish history as a "traitor", as the man who, at the moment of destiny, failed his country's cause and prevented the great German empire from extending "military help" to revolutionary Ireland. My God! Was ever sane man in such a position!'

On Tuesday 11 April 1916, Casement wrote his final entry in his German diary expressing his revulsion at the manner in which he had been treated by the Germans in the following terms:

My last day in Berlin! Thank God – tomorrow my last day in Germany – again Thank God. An English jail, or scaffold, would be better than to dwell with these people longer. All deception – all self interest – all 'on the make'.

V

It was in these circumstances that a sick and demoralised Roger Casement staggered ashore through the surf at Banna Strand in the early morning of Good Friday 1916. His sole aim at that point was to communicate with Eoin Mac Néill in the hope of calling off the

Rising. After his arrest, he attempted to communicate that message through a priest.

Casement was quickly brought to London and interrogated by officers of MI5, one of whom, Major Frank Hall, had played a central role in the organisation of the Ulster Volunteers and the running of German guns into Larne for the UVF in 1914. In the course of three interviews over the Easter weekend, Casement pleaded with his interrogators for an opportunity to communicate with Mac Néill to call off the Rising but was refused, being told: 'It's a festering sore, it's much better it should come to a head.'

Thus British intelligence was content to allow the Rising proceed and to keep the civil administrations in London and Dublin in the dark, as they had done in relation to decrypted German telegrams informing Berlin that the Rising was planned for Easter. It suited the cause of the United Kingdom and the Empire, they thought.

On one view, they were successfully undermining their masters' interests in the most thorough-going act of treason. These highly political spies were calmly watching a burning fuse that would destroy the United Kingdom in five years and start the destruction of the Empire itself.

VI

These events, then, form the factual background to the trial of Roger Casement on a charge of high treason. Much has been written about Casement's trial.

E. Montgomery Hyde published his excellent account of the trial in 1960 and revised it in 1964.

In addition, there are three papers, in particular, which stand out as excellent considerations of the trial proceedings themselves. These are the paper by Frank Callanan SC, 'Between Treason and

Blood Sacrifice: the Trials of Roger Casement'; Conor Gearty's 'The Casement Treason Trial in its Legal Context'; and Owen Dudley Edwards' 'The Trial of Roger Casement: A Study in Theatre Management'. These papers are happily published together in a Royal Irish Academy volume entitled *Roger Casement in Irish and World History* edited by Mary Daly, first published in 2005.

Taken together with the published proceedings of the trial edited in 1917 by George H. Knott, we have a very full account and expert assessment of Casement's trial from a number of perspectives, technical, political, and historical.

The charge read to Roger Casement by the king's coroner on the first day of the trial, Monday 26 June 1916, was one of high treason 'by adhering to the King's enemies elsewhere than in the King's realm – to wit, in the Empire of Germany – contrary to the Treason Act 1351, 25 Edward III, Statute 5, Chapter 2'.

It alleged against Casement that between 1 December 1914 and 21 April 1916 'being then ... a British subject, and whilst on the said several days an open and public war was being prosecuted and carried on by the German Emperor and his subjects against our Lord the King and his subjects', Casement, by 'traitorously contriving and intending to aid and assist the said enemies of our Lord the King', had 'traitorously adhered to and aided and comforted the said enemies in parts beyond the seas without this realm of England – to wit, in the Empire of Germany'.

The overt acts of treason set out in the indictment centred upon allegations that Casement had attempted to induce prisoners of war in Germany to forsake their duty and allegiance to the King and to aid and assist his enemies. Curiously, one of the overt acts related to the circulation of a recruitment leaflet of the Irish brigade, which included the following sentence: 'The object of the Irish Brigade shall be to fight solely the cause of Ireland, and under no circumstance shall it be directed to any German end.'

The evidence adduced at the trial clearly demonstrated that Casement had attempted to create an Irish brigade in Imperial Germany by recruiting prisoners of war in the service of the King to take part in a military force to be deployed in support of Irish independence.

The Lord Chief Justice, in his summing up to the jury, directed them as to the meaning of adhering to the King's enemies. He said that giving aid and comfort to the King's enemies included the act of any British subject which strengthened or tended to strengthen the enemies of the King in the conduct of the war against the King. He stated that this included acts which weakened or tended to weaken the power of the King and of the country to resist or to attack the enemies of the King. The test, he said, was:

Were the acts done such as would strengthen the German Emperor or such as would weaken His Majesty the King?

He added:

It does not need a very vivid imagination to see that if Germany could introduce arms and ammunition into Ireland for the purpose of helping to create a rebellion there, or strife of a serious character, so as to occupy the attention of the British Executive, and also to necessitate the maintaining of a considerable number of his Majesty's soldiers in Ireland, that would be assisting Germany.

Summarising the defence case he said:

The defence says that Sir Roger Casement only asked persons, these soldiers, to become members of the Irish Brigade for the purpose of assisting to resist the Ulster Volunteers after the war had concluded. The whole importance of this for the moment is whether it is right to say that that is the true effect of the evidence. The Crown says to you that that is not the true effect; that every fact that you examine points to the contrary; and that what was intended was that at the first sea victory Irish soldiers should be landed, and that the Irish Brigade should then be introduced into Ireland; and the comment is naturally made that until there had been a sea victory of Germany it would be impossible for Germany to land, at any rate, any considerable number of Irish soldiers ... Those are the two contentions.

Having regard to the terms of a treaty, not produced in evidence but negotiated by Casement with the German authorities, and, in particular, the provisions of Articles 6 to 10 of the treaty, there can be little doubt that Casement had, in fact, given aid and comfort of a treasonable kind to the King's enemies, when viewed from the perspective of the law of the United Kingdom of Great Britain and Ireland.

In these circumstances, it is difficult to resist the conclusion that the trial was conducted in a manner which was reasonably fair insofar as it dealt with issues of law and fact within the parameters of relevance laid down by the trial judges.

Reading the transcript, the presiding judges were at pains to be courteous and to appear even-handed. The Crown's witnesses and evidence were strong, and the issues were fairly and impartially set out for the jury to decide. Given that Britain was at war with Germany, the trial was remarkably free from passion or emotion.

Much has been made of the arguments advanced by the defence concerning the meaning and interpretation of the Norman French wording of the Treason Act of Edward III. The words of the statute, as paraphrased by the Lord Chief Justice, were as follows:

It shall be treason if a man levy war against our Lord the King in his realm or be adherent to the King's enemies in his realm giving to them aid and comfort in the realm or elsewhere.

The defence argument was that the words 'or elsewhere' only governed the words 'aid and comfort in the realm' and had no application to the words 'be adherent to the King's enemies'. As the offence charged was one of adherence to the King's enemies, if the words 'or elsewhere' did not apply to the adhering, no offence was committed under the statute.

The Crown's contention was that the words 'or elsewhere' governed adhering to the King's enemies and that it was plainly an offence to adhere to the King's enemies by an act committed outside the realm.

Even the somewhat obsequious George Knott had this to say about the argument made by Serjeant Sullivan for the defence:

As a matter of common sense as an effective law treason for the present day this may appear to the reader as not at all satisfactory but if the question is merely what is the grammatical meaning of the sentences in the Act he will, we think, consider them very puzzling, and agree that on the face of it Serjeant Sullivan's rendering is possible or even probable. It presents a nice exercise in grammatical construction and one arrives at a very unflattering conclusion of the literary skill of the draftsmen of the Edwardian era.

The ingenious renderings of the judges and Serjeant Sullivan may be read in the arguments, where is also to be found some very interesting antiquarian lore about the MSS. of the old statutes.

The language, then, of the Statute of Treasons must be admitted to be ambiguously worded, and Serjeant Sullivan could not merely give his reading, and leave it there, without doing something more to make his reading appear to be the more probable of two or more possible ones.

It was obvious that the judges could not simply be asked to read and construe the statute as if they saw it for the first time. The principle upon which Serjeant Sullivan proceeded in his argument is one expressed in a passage from Maxwell on the Interpretation of Statutes,

Chapter 2: 'The language of a statute must be understood in the sense in which it was understood when it was passed, and those who lived at or near the time when it was passed may reasonably be supposed to be better acquainted than their descendants with the circumstances to which it had relation, as well as with the sense then attached to legislative expressions'.

As Gearty points out, however, there were few precedents to hand in the law reports on this issue of construction. Gearty opines concerning the defence argument:

But consider the result which such creativity would have produced – excoriation by the British public for having contrived the acquittal of an admitted traitor on the most technical of technicalities. The case would have been more interesting had these been the various hurdles over which their Lordships had to jump in order to secure a conviction that the authorities and the people badly wanted.

Gearty points out that success for the defence argument would have required the judges 'to distinguish both case law authority and the unanimous view of legal scholars such as Coke, Hawkins, Hale and Stephens.'

He agrees with Owen Dudley Edwards in the latter's conclusion that the 'legal principle involved in the Act of Edward III had almost certainly been resolved correctly and against Casement'.

The argument that Casement was 'hanged upon a comma' still excites legal interest today but the decision of the court of trial and of the court of appeal on the issue does not appear to be unreasonable or contrived, whatever about the infelicities of mediaeval draftsmanship.

Indeed, quite apart from the wording of the Treason Act upon which reliance was based, there was in any event arguably a common law offence of treason which criminalised adherence to the King's enemies by a King's subject regardless of whether the adherence took place within or without the King's realm. Indeed, it would seem counterintuitive to believe that the law made a distinction between treasons committed within the King's realm and those committed elsewhere.

In short, while the legal submissions put forward by the defence on the construction of the statute were strongly arguable on the basis of first principle, they flew in the face of centuries of case law and legal commentary to the contrary. And if the statute had the meaning contended for by the defence, it seems highly improbable that it would not have been amended at some time during the 500 years from its enactment.

The appeal against conviction was heard in the Court of Criminal Appeal on Monday 17 July 1916. After lengthy submissions by Serjeant Sullivan on the sole issue of the proper interpretation of the Statute of Edward III (other grounds of appeal not having been argued), the judges retired and on re-assembling indicated that they required no reply from the Attorney General. The appeal court upheld the decision of the trial court in relation to the proper interpretation of the statute and dismissed the appeal.

VII

The lawyers appearing in the trial and appeal of Roger Casement deserve some comment here.

Firstly, George Gavan Duffy was a nationalist solicitor in practice in a large firm in London. He was the son of Sir Charles Gavan Duffy, an Irish nationalist who later became prime minister of the province of Victoria in Australia.

Gavan Duffy was educated in England at Stoneyhurst and his services as Casement's solicitor were sought by Gertrude Bannister and Alice Stopford Green, two society ladies who were friends of

Casement. When he undertook the defence of Casement, Gavan Duffy was confronted by his legal partners with a choice of withdrawing from the case or resigning his partnership. He made a very considerable sacrifice in defending Casement.

He returned to Ireland and became involved in the struggle for Irish independence, ultimately co-signing the Anglo-Irish Treaty in Downing Street with F.E. Smith, who had led the prosecution against Casement. Having briefly served as Minister for Foreign Affairs in the Free State Government, Gavan Duffy resigned over the treatment of republican prisoners by that government and, having been called to the Bar, was appointed to the judiciary, eventually becoming the President of the High Court.

Gavan Duffy had difficulty in assembling a team of counsel to defend Casement and ultimately persuaded his brother-in-law Serjeant Alexander M. Sullivan to take the brief. Sullivan was a constitutional nationalist who was wholly out of sympathy with the Easter Rising and who later left Ireland to practice as a barrister in London, having prosecuted cases arising out of the War of Independence and having had threats made to his life.

That there was bad blood between Casement and Sullivan there can be no doubt. Sullivan was to describe Casement as a megalomaniac. After the dismissal of his appeal, Casement wrote to his old friend Richard Mortens, complaining that Sullivan dropped some of his grounds of appeal with no notice to Casement. He said: 'I wish I had stuck to my two Welshmen [Artemus Jones and JH Morgan] and had not brought in the other [Sullivan] at all'.

Sullivan was a man of very strong and often intemperate opinions. His famous collapse in the course of his address to the jury was probably caused by immense stress. His junior, Artemus Jones (also well known as being the plaintiff in the leading case relating to unintentional defamation), was obliged to complete the address to the jury, which he did with great competence and rhetorical vigour.

However, the strength of the case against him obviously preoccupied him as can be judged by his peroration:

I am not going to address any appeal to you based on sympathy or upon anything like an emotional plea in the way of mercy. The ancient and valiant race from which this man springs does not produce the type of man who shrinks from death for the sake of his country.

The history of Ireland contains many melancholy and sad chapters, and not the least sad is the chapter which tells and speaks so eloquently of so many mistaken sons of that unfortunate country who have gone to the scaffold as they think, for the sake of their native land.

I am not going to base any appeal to you upon emotions. If the Crown have made out their case it is your duty as lawful citizens to return a verdict of guilty; but I claim this, that the law requires that the Crown should prove their case, and prove it up to the hilt, and you must with sure judgment and with clean consciences consider if you be satisfied upon that point; and if you do that, if you approach the case in that spirit and apply that test to it, dark and heavy as the case may be as far as the defence is concerned, I do suggest to you that there is a way open to you to return a verdict which would be nonetheless just because it is humane.

The technical defence mounted in relation to the interpretation of the Treason Act was, as far as can be judged, largely developed by JH Morgan, his other junior counsel. While Casement admired Morgan's ingenuity, he nonetheless felt that the technical defence was unlikely to succeed and, if made, ran the risk of adulterating and compromising the effect of his intended speech from the dock before sentence.

F.E. Smith, prosecuting as the Tory Attorney General in Asquith's coalition, was, of course, deeply compromised in the eyes of many by the fact that he had between 1912 and 1914 taken a leading role in the establishment of armed resistance to Home Rule.

Along with Carson and Craig, that movement had involved the creation of an armed force determined and pledged to resist Home Rule by force if necessary. It even involved the creation of a 'provisional government' in Ulster, a close parallel to the establishment of a provisional government by the signatories of the 1916 Proclamation.

Taking into account the massive importation of UVF arms from Germany on the SS *Clyde Valley* in early 1914, and the events described as the Curragh Mutiny – in which British officers stationed in Ireland violated their duty of loyalty to the Westminster Government by a collective decision to refuse to use force against the UVF – Smith, who was in many respects one of the chief instigators of all these actions, was hardly in the strongest moral position to credibly allege treason against Sir Roger Casement. But that did not trouble him.

Smith himself was to be the subject of an explicit and telling attack in the course of Casement's speech before sentence. Comparing his own actions with those of Smith, Casement stated:

The difference between us was that the Unionist champions chose a path they felt would lead to the woolsack; while I went a road I knew must lead to the dock, and the event proves we were both right. The difference between us was that my 'treason' was based on a ruthless sincerity that forced me to attempt in time and season to carry out in action what I said in word, whereas their treason lay in verbal incitements that they knew need never be made good. And so I am prouder to stand here today in the traitor's dock to answer this impeachment than to fill the place of my right honourable accusers.

In the words of H. Montgomery Hyde:

At this point the Attorney General was observed to smile ironically and murmur in an audible aside: 'Change places with him? Nothing doing.'

Then as if to show his contempt for the prisoner he got up and ostentatiously walked out of court with his hands in his pockets.

An ignominious lapse for an Attorney General, I think.

VIII

It is noteworthy that throughout the trial Roger Casement deliberately avoided raising in any way by way of defence his own intention, when landing at Banna Strand, to have the Easter Rising called off. All of the content of the German diary demonstrating Casement's total disapproval of the Rising was swept under the carpet in order that Casement could adopt the position that the rebellion was justifiable and that he took full responsibility for taking part in it.

A lot of this mystery can be explained by Casement's realisation that his status in history would be completely undermined if he were to distance himself from or criticise the signatories to the Proclamation.

It is an irony that the British Government issued a statement on 4 August 1916, after Casement's execution, justifying its failure to reprieve the death sentence, which indicates that between the trial and his execution the Government had come into possession of conclusive evidence that Casement intended to use the Irish Brigade against the British Crown in Egypt.

This suggests that a copy of the treaty negotiated by Casement with the German Government had by then fallen into the hands of the British Government. Curiously, the same Government statement includes the following:

The suggestion that Casement left Germany for the purpose of trying to stop the Irish Rising was not raised at the trial, and is conclusively disproved, not only by the facts there disclosed, but by further evidence which has since become available.

The German diary disproves that assertion categorically.

The Government statement makes a veiled reference to the content of the Black Diaries in the following terms:

Another suggestion, that Casement was out of his mind, is equally without foundation. Materials bearing on his mental condition were placed at the disposal of his counsel, who did not raise the plea of insanity. Casement's demeanour since his arrest, and since the trial, gave no ground for any such defence, and indeed was sufficient to disprove it.

Clearly the Government was referring to the offer by F.E. Smith made to Serjeant Sullivan of access to the Black Diaries with a view to mounting a defence of insanity based on the sexual behaviour disclosed therein. The likelihood of such a plea succeeding was plainly nil.

Although Casement clearly decided to conceal from the court and from the public his total opposition to the Easter Rising in order to secure his place in history as an Irish patriot, his decision as to how he would conduct his defence was greatly influenced by the suggestion by George Bernard Shaw that he should use his trial as a stage from which to make a totally disarming defence of his actions in terms of his nationalism, his patriotism, and the rights of the Irish people to independence and self-determination.

In one sense, Casement took, with some reluctance, an each-way bet on the outside possibility of acquittal. However, he was acutely aware that as a matter of probability his guilt would be established and that he would be judged by history by the rhetorical defence he made of his own actions.

IX

Much has been written and said about the use, or abuse, of the Black Diaries of Roger Casement by the Attorney General, and by the British Government, both before and after the trial.

A central issue has always been whether the Black Diaries, which contained explicit accounts of homosexual activities by Casement in every corner of the world, were indeed written by Casement or, on the other hand, were clever forgeries by British intelligence agents engaging in the blackest of black arts.

For my part, I am completely persuaded of the genuineness of the diaries not least by the reasoned analysis set out by Seamas Ó Síocháin in an appendix to his 2008 biography of Casement, *Roger Casement: Imperialist, Rebel, Revolutionary*. The case for the diaries being a forgery is, in my view, very weak indeed.

As I have pointed out earlier, the British Minister to Norway alerted the Foreign Office to evidence that Casement was an active homosexual in late 1914. He cited the statements of Adler Christensen and of certain other Norwegian sources confirming Casement's homosexual activity. The forgery theory would have required the deployment of very substantial resources between Casement's arrest and his trial if the diaries had been concocted in 1916.

Internal evidence, as Ó Síocháin's analysis shows, strongly suggests that the diaries were not forgeries. For instance, the typescript versions of them erroneously transcribe phrases in Irish and other names and places which appear in the manuscript diaries. One would imagine that if the typed transcripts were drawn up within weeks of the forgery of the diaries that these mistakes would not have occurred as the forger would have been in a position to identify and correct such errors.

Perhaps most telling, however, is the unsuccessful attempt by F.E. Smith, the Attorney General, to have Serjeant Sullivan read the

The trial of Roger Casement

Black Diaries in their original form prior to the commencement of the trial. F.E. Smith even threatened to report J.H. Morgan for professional misconduct for his alleged failure to give a copy of the diaries to Sullivan.

If the diaries were complete forgeries as alleged, and if Serjeant Sullivan had in fact agreed to inspect and read them with a view to examining whether a plea of insanity was available to Casement, as the Attorney General strangely hoped, it is inconceivable that Sullivan would not then have discussed them at length with Casement and, if they were forgeries, that Casement would not have immediately pointed out as much to his counsel.

In those circumstances, the fact that there were forged versions of his diaries in existence would have been clear to Casement and, presumably, his denials would have given rise to very major controversy and to allegations that he was the victim of an enormous Crown conspiracy to blacken his name.

Thus, it is hard to see why, if the forged diaries had been available prior to the commencement of the trial they would have been offered for inspection to Casement's counsel since their authenticity and provenance could have caused an incendiary dispute which, in turn, could have entirely derailed the trial itself and the motive, if any, for their forgery and production pre-trial.

In addition, the diaries were made available to a number of English and American journalists by one of the intelligence officers who interrogated Casement, Reginald Hall. Mary Boyle Reilly, an American news agency representative, supplied Gavan Duffy with details of the showing of the diary to her on 3 June 1916, long before the commencement of the trial on 26 June 1916.

The diaries in question had been supplied by a Mr Germain to Scotland Yard on 25 April 1916, four days after Casement's arrest. Reginald Hall had shown photographed extracts of the diary to journalists, to politicians, and they were even reportedly viewed by the King himself in May 1916.

Undoubtedly propaganda use was made of the diaries to discredit Casement and to undermine his credibility and the credibility of those who were championing his cause or, at a later stage, campaigning for a reprieve from the death penalty. But it appears to be beyond contradiction that the existence of the Black Diaries in their present state predates significantly the Casement trial and the preponderance of evidence lies on the side of their authenticity.

X

The transformation of social attitudes towards homosexuals and homosexuality since the 1960s, and, in particular, since the marriage equality referendum in Ireland, raises the obvious question as to why it is or was relevant that Roger Casement was or was not a gay man.

However, the allegation that he was gay if made in Edwardian times and in post-independence Ireland right up to the 1970s was considered a grave slur on his integrity and reputation and, consequently, on his standing as an Irish patriot.

For that reason, the issue as to his sexual orientation became one on which passionate opinions were ranged on either side. Books were written claiming that the Black Diaries were clever forgeries concocted by British intelligence for their nefarious ends. Herbert Mackey, a leading Dublin consultant, wrote a number of very elaborate works in support of the forgery theory. In independent Catholic Ireland, the forgery theory easily rhymed with the general view that Casement was a heroic martyr who had given his life for Irish freedom.

The issue of the authenticity or forgery of Casement's diary was hotly debated, insofar as public decency would permit such debate, from the establishment of the Irish Free State onwards. In the 1950s, the issue again arose in the letters columns of the *Irish Times* arising from the publication of a book by a journalist, Rene McColl, claiming that the Black Diaries were genuine and that Casement had been homosexual. This led to an extraordinary controversy within the Irish legal profession.

His leading counsel, Serjeant Sullivan, by now retired and living in Terenure, joined in this debate and pointed out that if the diaries had been forgeries, he would have expected to have been instructed by Casement that he had not written them, given that they had been shown to journalists while Casement was still alive and was aware of their circulation. This had not happened, Sullivan claimed.

This, in turn, caused two leading barristers, Seán Hooper and Felix Sherry, to write their own letter to the *Irish Times* claiming that Sullivan had breached a basic rule of his profession by disclosing confidential client instructions without express authority.

All the usual suspects waded into the correspondence column debate with great trenchancy and some with little regard for the truth. Not content with criticising Sullivan in letters to the newspapers, leading members of the Irish Bar went on quite a witch-hunt against the elderly Sullivan, presenting a memorial to the Benchers of King's Inns on 13 April 1956 calling for the removal of Sullivan as an honorary bencher and for his disbarment for gross and dishonourable professional misconduct.

This action was all the more remarkable given that it was Sullivan himself who in 1950 had taken the first steps in the process that ultimately led to the Lavery painting of the Casement Appeal being lent to King's Inns, where it was unveiled by President Seán T. O'Ceallaigh on 1 November 1951, and where it hangs to this day.

The Benchers in turn brought the matter to Sullivan's attention with a view to permitting him to defend himself. Ultimately, Sullivan requested that his name be removed from the roll of honorary benchers in a rather querulous letter sent on 14 July 1956 in which he resolutely defended his conduct in relation to the matter, and claimed that since he had appeared for Casement as a member of the Middle Temple, that that institution was the only one which could determine whether he was guilty of a breach of its rules.

His letter totally debunked the suggestion that Casement was unaware of the sexual content of the Black Diaries and claimed that Casement had taken the view that homosexuality was a traditional characteristic of many great men in history.

Sullivan, in his autobiography, *The Last Serjeant*, had described Casement's attitude to homosexuality as evidence of insanity, a curious echo of the offer by F.E. Smith made to Sullivan before the commencement of the trial that he should view the diaries with a view to considering a plea of insanity.

XI

As for Casement's speech before sentence, there can be no doubt that it ranks – shoulder to shoulder with Robert Emmet's speech made 113 years earlier – among the world's great examples of political oratory. He now succeeded, as Shaw had hoped he would, in his goal of converting his trial into an indictment of his oppressors.

Some passages stand out for their noble defiance, such as this:

Let me pass from myself and my own fate to a far more pressing, as it is a far more urgent theme – not the fate of the individual Irishmen who may have tried and failed, but the claims and the fate of the country that has not failed.

Ireland has outlived the failure of all her hopes – and yet she still hopes. Ireland has seen her sons – aye and her daughters too – suffer from generation to generation always for the same cause, meeting always the same fate, and always at the hands of the same power;

and always a fresh generation has passed on to withstand the same oppression.

For if English authority be omnipotent – a power, as Mr Gladstone phrased it, that reaches to the very ends of the earth – Irish hope exceeds the dimensions of that power, excels its authority, and renews with each generation the claims of the last. The cause that begets this indomitable persistency, the faculty of preserving through centuries of misery the remembrance of lost liberty, this surely is the noblest cause men ever strove for, ever lived for, ever died for.

If this be the case I stand here today indicted for, and convicted of sustaining, then I stand in a goodly company and a right noble succession.

And has there ever been a more impassioned plea for or hymn to the liberty of Ireland and the right of its people to struggle for that liberty than the following?

We are told that if Irishmen go by the thousand to die, not for Ireland, but for Flanders, for Belgium, for a patch of sand on the deserts of Mesopotamia, or a rocky trench on the heights of Gallipoli, they are winning self-government for Ireland. But if they dare to lay down their lives on their native soil, if they dare to dream even that freedom can be won only at home by men resolved to fight for it there, then they are traitors to their country, and their dreams and their deaths are phases of a dishonourable phantasy.

But history is not so recorded in other lands. In Ireland alone in this twentieth century is loyalty held to be a crime. If loyalty be something less than love and more than law, then we have had enough of such loyalty for Ireland or Irishmen. If we are to be indicted as criminals, to be shot as murderers, to be imprisoned as convicts because our offence is that we love Ireland more than we value our lives, then I know not what virtue resides in any offer of self-government held out to brave men on such terms.

Self-government is our right, a thing born in us at birth; a thing no more to be doled out to us or withheld from us by another people than the right to life itself – than the right to feel the sun or smell the flowers, or to love our kind.

It is only from the convict these things are withheld for crime committed and proven – and Ireland that has wronged no man, that has injured no land, that has sought no dominion over others – Ireland is treated today among the nations of the world as if she was a convicted criminal.

If it be treason to fight against such an unnatural fate as this, then I am proud to be a rebel, and shall cling to my rebellion with the last drop of my blood. If there be no right of rebellion against a state of things that no savage tribe would endure without resistance, then I am sure that it is better for men to fight and die without right than to live in such a state of right as this.

Where all your rights become only an accumulated wrong; where men must beg with bated breath for leave to subsist in their own land, to think their own thoughts, to sing their own songs, to garner the fruits of their own labours – and even while they beg, to see things inexorably withdrawn from them – then surely it is a braver, a saner and a truer thing to be a rebel in act and deed against such circumstances as these than tamely to accept it as the natural lot of men.

By any standard, these are noble, compelling words spoken from the dock to posterity by an Irishman, especially one who could so easily have avoided his fate by surrendering to the voices of doubt and of reason and by distancing himself from the enterprise of the Rising, but who felt compelled by honour, loyalty and circumstance to lay down his life for the love of his country and its freedom.

Who then can deny Casement the status of hero?

Remembering Willy McDowell and the futility of the so-called Great War

11 November 2018 (Armistice Day)

On the day that's in it, much will be written about the futility of the so-called Great War, and the struggle between the great European imperial powers to survive and dominate each other. Much also will be written about the senseless slaughter of those who joined the colours, particularly here in Ireland, and lost their lives in the mud of Flanders and the baking heat of Gallipoli. And of course it would be totally wrong of this generation on the centenary of Armistice Day not to remember and honour those Irish men, Green and Orange, who never came home or who came home injured in mind and limb to a rapidly changing Ireland.

It seems strange that within six weeks of Armistice Day, the course of Irish history was totally changed by the result of the 1918 general election, an entirely peaceful affair. It is, perhaps, stranger still that a few weeks later the Sinn Féin MPs elected to Westminster (or as many of them who were at liberty) met in the Mansion House to constitute themselves the duly elected parliament of an Irish republic. Curiously, that Dáil described the Irish republic as Saorstát Éireann rather than Poblacht na hÉireann, the name adopted by the draftsmen of the 1916 Proclamation.

Woodrow Wilson, the President of the United States, had at the beginning of 1918 promulgated his plan for a post-war world. That plan included recognition of the right of the European nations to self-determination, a cause of great hope for those who believed that an independent Irish state might peaceably emerge from the defeat of Germany.

Of course, as readers of the late Ronan Fanning's *Fatal Path* will know, the Tories in England were in no humour to concede Irish independence. Their offer of home rule, which was radically different from the outcome of the Treaty negotiations, was predicated on there being two Irish local and subordinate parliaments – one for the 26 counties and one for the six counties.

In the same few weeks after Armistice Day 1918, a group of Irish Volunteers, now members of the Irish Republican Army, planned secretly to ambush RIC men escorting a delivery of explosives from a barracks to a quarry in County Tipperary.

Dan Breen, Seán Treacy and Seán Hogan carried out that ambush at Soloheadbeg in early January 1919, believing that they were acting on behalf of the newly declared independent Irish republic. In the event, they shot and killed two RIC men (although they expected that the escort party would be six strong).

And thus commenced the War of Independence which would lead to the Truce, the Treaty, the establishment of Saorstát Éireann, an independent Irish state within the Commonwealth having the same status as that of Canada, and ultimately to the fully independent Irish Republic.

On Armistice Day 1918, the British Empire regarded itself, with some justification, as a victor of the Great War. But, as we now know, the outcome of the Great War was that the Empire had 'won the battle but lost the war' for its own survival. Its decline and fall had started.

It is also clear that the Great War played a critical role in the success of the movement for Irish national self-determination.

The British Government's insistence on conscription in Ireland produced the perfect tinderbox for violent revolution. National revulsion against conscription electrified the Irish people and drove the Catholic Church in Ireland into an alliance with the separatist movement which would have been unthinkable five years earlier.

John Redmond's vision of a Home Rule Ireland that would have been a vigorous proponent of the British Empire at home and abroad came crashing down when it appeared that his party had, in effect, conceded the principle of military conscription.

Among my own sons' eight great-grandparents, three were to serve terms of imprisonment in the aftermath of 1916 and two women were to play roles in the emerging Cumann na mBan. Another of their great-grandparents was to have his home and business in Cahirsiveen dynamited by Crown forces in 1920 as an official reprisal for the shooting of RIC men by the local IRA. They were the separatists.

The remaining man among those eight, John McDowell, a Dublin solicitor, was a staunch Redmondite, very close to the IPP leaders, Redmond and Dillon.

In his household, two of my father's first cousins were raised, having been orphaned around the turn of the century. One of them was Kay McDowell, who was destined to become a leading women's trade union activist and secretary general of the Women Workers' Union of Ireland. She was an active member and candidate for the Labour Party. She is remembered in the *Dictionary of Irish Biography*.

Her brother Willy, on the other hand, had enlisted as soon as he turned 18 in the 7th Battalion of the Leinster Regiment, and had gone to the front as a private soldier.

Among our family papers is a small series of letters home giving his account of life in the trenches and asking for news, including whether the reconstruction of Dublin city centre had yet started in the wake of the Easter Rising.

On 9 September 1916, Willy's guardian and my grandfather, John McDowell, wrote his nephew an affectionate letter wishing him well and sending him home news.

That letter was returned, its envelope marked 'killed in action'. It transpired that on the very day my grandfather wrote to him, Willy's battalion had been cut to pieces in one of the grimmest slaughters of the Somme offences, mown down in an advance on Guillemont, near Ginchy. The regimental history describes the scene in terms, even with the passage of 100 years, almost unbearable to read.

Willy, as his company sergeant related to my uncle by a letter replying to an inquiry as to how he had met his death, was 'shot through the heart' and 'suffered no pain'.

These well-intentioned, consoling, if formulaic and clearly fictional, words belied the savage carnage in which his last moments were spent. His dismembered body, in fact, was never recovered and his name, on that account, is carved only on the sides of the Thiepval Arch at the Somme. Forgive me if I use this column to give Willy some slight degree of personal remembrance and public honour today.

In years to come he, like the two RIC men killed at Soloheadbeg, James McDonnell and Patrick O'Connell, will be forgotten while many of those who participated in the entirely justified armed struggle for Irish independence will still be commemorated by the historians.

Uniting the Irish

The meaning of and means towards Irish unity

11 August 2019

One of the advantages of the silly season days of August is that it gives us space in which to stand back from the trench warfare of conventional political and social discourse and to reflect on other long-term and strategic issues.

In that spirit, I make this week's column Trump-free and Brexit-free.

I was asked recently to speak briefly to a mainly foreign audience on the subject of Ireland's independence. My audience was due to visit Belfast the following day and to hear presentations about the current state of play in Northern Ireland.

Gathering my thoughts on the subject of Irish independence 100 years on from the establishment of Dáil Éireann and the start of the armed struggle called the War of Independence, I reminded myself that, in the census of 1891, Belfast had a greater population than Dublin. Dublin had in the previous 100 years declined from being the second city of the British Empire to a ghost of its former self.

Northern Ireland, as it currently exists, was then far more industrialised and more prosperous than what is now the Republic. One hundred years of Union had been favourable to the North while leaving the South to be a backward, poor and emigration-gripped region of the then United Kingdom.

Political independence, I reminded my audience, did not halt the decline of the South's population, That decline persisted until the 1960s. The very project of Irish independence was itself brought into question by the failure of the 26 counties to provide even a basic means and standard of living for its young population born into very large families.

Economic recovery, population growth and a resurgence in self-confidence only took root south of the border in the 1960s and yet, by the end of that decade, the Troubles in the North were re-igniting. Notwithstanding economic crises in every decade since, the South has been on an ascending escalator ever since. And in many ways, the North has appeared to be passing us on the descending escalator during the same period.

It is true that the Republic's health services are in some respects less effective – euro for pound – than the NHS in the North. On the other hand, the education system in the South seems to out-perform that in the North in many respects, including far lower drop-out rates, higher attainment levels and greater third-level participation.

Garret FitzGerald, by no means a narrow nationalist, always argued that independence has been good for the Republic. Such economic and political autonomy as we have, and have had, has given us the means to reverse decades of decline as an economic backwater.

Perhaps it was recent news of the threat to Harland and Wolff and to Bombardier that brought home to us the extent of the transformation of the North from an industrialised and integrated part of the United Kingdom in the nineteenth and twentieth centuries into a marginalised and under-performing region of the UK in the twenty-first century.

While southern England and greater London have prospered in the near half-century of the UK's membership of the EEC and later the EU, the north of England, Scotland, Wales and Northern Ireland have lagged far behind.

Without breaking my pledge to keep away from the B-word this week, the half-century from 1970 to 2020 has witnessed the emergence of stresses which threaten the very existence of the UK as we know it. Fissures which may or may not portend the end of the Union are widening and deepening before our very eyes.

Arch-revisionists once argued that the political separation of the Republic from Britain was an unnecessary and unjustified act of political violence that lies at the bottom of many of our woes – political, economic and social.

Redmond's Home Rule, they argue, was sufficient for Irish needs.

One perusal of the Home Rule Act discredits that view. Devolved government as agreed by Redmond was no great triumph. The very limited autonomy envisaged for the Parliament to be recreated in College Green could never have reversed the decline in Ireland's economic prospects. A Home Rule parliament in Dublin was fated to fail.

In a moment of exuberance, Redmond addressed a pre-Great War St Patrick's Night dinner in London. He stressed to his audience the limited domestic nature of the envisaged Home Rule parliament's powers and laid great emphasis on Ireland's future role in the Empire which would, on foot of Home Rule, become 'our Empire' in which Ireland's manhood would join the ranks of Empire armed forces across the globe.

My point is this – even with limited devolution for Scotland, Wales and Northern Ireland, the Union has failed them badly in comparative terms. And it is hard to believe that this failure will be reversed by anything that will happen at Westminster in the short, medium or long term.

Of course, unionism is not purely an economic frame of mind. A sense of being on the down escalator economically or politically does not mean that the voters of Northern Ireland or Scotland will automatically jump off and opt to leave the Union. In the North and in Scotland too it is undoubtedly true that unionism is identitarian as well as economic in character.

But just as radical economic integration in the EU would now leave member states at the periphery at a huge disadvantage in the absence of those member states having political independence to off-set centripetal forces, the same principle has been clearly demonstrated in the UK. Economic well-being has haemorrhaged towards southern England. The devolved governments and assemblies in the rest of the UK lack the fiscal and economic independence to protect or grow their regions.

The counter-factual of Ireland having remained in the UK really bears little consideration.

Ireland – the entire island – truly is approaching a crossroads.

To demand a border poll in these circumstances is putting the cart before the horse. Nobody now knows what the poll would be about. We have seen just how chaotic a referendum can be if the consequences have not been considered.

The wisecrack that 'a referendum is a process by which you get an answer you didn't expect to a question you didn't ask' is no mere joke.

Those – like myself – who favour Irish unity will have to work out the meaning of that term. And then – and only then – we will have to work out how it could come about. Only then could the people – north and south – make any kind of informed choice on the issues arising.

I think that those who shout loudest on the subject of Irish unity are those who have done least to enable it happen and done most to prevent it from happening.

I will be putting forward my own views on the meaning of and means towards Irish unity at the forthcoming Kennedy Summer School in Wexford early next month.

But we all have a lot of thinking to do.

What exactly do we mean by Irish unity? How could it come about?

Paper presented at the John F. Kennedy Summer School

7 September 2019

The meaning of Irish unity will decide if it can be agreed

There are two major issues in relation to 'a united Ireland' or 'Irish unity'.

The first is as to what these terms mean. The second is as to whether or how 'Irish unity' or a 'united Ireland' could come about by consent. But these two issues are not separate. In reality, they are inseparable.

There is simply no point in holding a border poll on Irish unity if the people taking part in such a vote do not know what they are voting for. You only have to look at the post-Brexit referendum in the UK to understand that putting a simple binary decision on an abstract proposition to the people without affording them the right to understand the consequences of their choice is fraught with danger.

The options broadly stated

If by a vote for Irish unity or a united Ireland, you mean a decision for Northern Ireland to leave the UK and to become part of a single, unitary Irish republic under its existing constitution (with or without amendment) or to become part of a single, unitary Irish republic with a new constitution to be adopted (Option A), that is one thing.

If, on the other hand, you mean a decision for Northern Ireland to leave the UK and become a part of an agreed Irish confederation between two parts – Northern Ireland and the Republic (Option B) – that is another thing entirely.

The events, steps and processes required to achieve Option A rather than Option B are entirely different.

A unitary state?

The Taoiseach, Leo Varadkar, recently stated that a united Ireland would be a 'different state'. Presumably he was realistically accepting that the 1937 constitution of the Republic, which was framed on the basis that it would be the constitution of an all-Ireland republic (with provision in Article 15.2 for a 'subordinate legislature', presumably in Stormont), would not be the constitution of a future, united Ireland.

Put bluntly, while some may wish for a unitary Irish state, it remains the form of Irish unity least likely to come about in the short- or medium-term because it is the least acceptable form of Irish unity to a substantial majority in Northern Ireland (and perhaps too in the Republic).

Problems with a new unitary state

Asking Northern Unionists and many Catholics who regard themselves as Northern Irish to abandon the Union in a border poll seems very problematical unless that choice is seen by them, all in all, to be in their political, social and economic interests.

To join a unitary Irish republic seems the least attractive choice for any Unionists – especially compared with a confederal form of

Irish unity which would leave Northern Ireland, with which they are familiar, intact as a jurisdiction.

In terms of practicality, a unitary state is also the most difficult to negotiate. It would entail amalgamation of institutions, courts, police, the judiciary and an entirely new constitution – to be drafted by whom?

Drafting a new, unitary constitution in the course of a negotiated process of persuasion is fraught with difficulty and danger.

Who would the drafters be? On whose instructions would they act? Would Unionists be reasonably expected to sit down around a table to draft such a document? Would there be a constituent assembly to approve the draft? Would it be put to the people of the entire island in separate referendums? What would its content be? Would it end up a collage of current popular concerns?

Would it be accepted by a separate majority in each jurisdiction?

The confederal alternative

Does it not make much more sense to develop and put forward a confederal form of unity which would leave both jurisdictions largely intact and in which, as distinct from a federal solution, only limited powers would be devolved by each part of the confederation to its institutions?

Under such a model, powers devolved to the confederation would relate to its membership of the EU (presuming that both parts of Ireland would be part of the EU) and to other aspects of international relations, and to other matters only where it was agreed that authority needed to be shared at a confederal level.

Confederal institutions of this limited kind would probably have to include some balanced form of joint ministry and some elected body to which the ministry would be accountable. There would have to be some form of tribunal or court to decide on confederal matters in dispute.

Each part of the confederation would have its own constitution, parliament, government, laws and institutions including local government, and its own social welfare system, educational system, police force, etc.

A treaty of confederation could also be a framework for future development on a consensual basis.

It is possible, for instance, to consider a situation where the Republic remains as it is, and Northern Ireland could have some continuing connection to the Crown – in the same manner as Canada and New Zealand do – but for both parts of Ireland to share sovereignty on matters – including international relations – devolved to the confederation institutions.

Such a form of Irish unity would be non-threatening, consensual in character, and mutually respectful.

If approved by a majority of people in Northern Ireland, it would not constitute a danger or a threat or a provocation to those reluctant elements in either community who might have voted against it. It would demonstrate to those who value their British-ness that the Irish-ness of others is no threat, and vice versa.

Daily life could continue as normal in the absence of any constitutional 'Big Bang'. And such a confederal relationship between the two parts of the island would largely defuse the 'existential threat to identity' dimension that bedevils Northern politics and recasts every mundane issue as a part of a greater constitutional zero-sum game.

I argue that both parts of Ireland and both main traditions on this island would be best served by a settlement characterised by evolution rather than revolution. It is clear that the practicability and likelihood of achieving a majority vote in favour of Irish unity almost certainly depends on the shape of the proposed new order rather than on any vague, aspirational or conceptual proposition.

The well-known political slogan 'If you don't know, vote No' is very powerful in any referendum debate.

It is noteworthy that Fine Gael proposed a confederal form of unity many years ago. Mary Lou McDonald has stated that she would consider a confederal form of unity. Professor Brendan O'Leary has argued for confederalism for a long time and has elaborated on its potential. Claire Palley has advised the DUP to consider it as an option instead of drifting into a unitary Ireland.

Apart from Northern Unionist opinion, it might be the form of unity with which most people in the Republic would feel most comfortable.

A second forum?

That brings us to the issue as to how a package or proposition for consideration in plebiscites held north and south of the border might be developed.

We hear talk about the government of Ireland establishing a second forum open to all in the island to consider and debate and formulate a model or a number of models of what might amount to Irish unity or a united Ireland.

The problem with such an approach is that those who at the moment do not want to end the Union as it currently exists and who are disposed to reject a united Ireland as they presently understand that idea have little or no incentive to participate in such a forum and might well reasonably consider that any such participation on their part would imperil or damage their cause, and, in the case of elected politicians, imperil or damage their own political interest.

Why exactly should we expect a Unionist politician of whatever hue to attend and participate in a forum whose terms of reference include a possible or probable recommendation for the establishment of a single, unitary Irish republican state having the existing Irish constitution or a replacement constitution?

Would such a Unionist be there to 'argue his or her corner' for the Union, or to negotiate a compromise report, or simply to fly the flag of opposition to any form of Irish unity?

Short of participating with a mandate to attempt to negotiate a compromise report, the short-term political interests of most Unionist politicians would be equally or much better served by steering well clear of such a forum and remaining disengaged from any such structured dialogue.

In short, have we any real reason to believe that a new forum established by the government of Ireland would not have the same outcome or non-outcome as the Forum for a New Ireland, which reported in 1984?

New realities

Of course, things have changed radically since 1984. There are new realities. We have had the Good Friday Agreement; we have had the St Andrews Agreement; we have had de-militarisation; we have power-sharing; we have had an open border; we have had an all-island economy; we have had economic prosperity; and we have had some progress on reduction of sectarian consciousness and tension in Northern Ireland.

We also know so well that none of these realities can be taken for granted – especially if the fabric of the present settlement begins to fray, un-ravel or tear in the context of Brexit. We must add to these realities *three further important realities*: demographic change, particularly in Northern Ireland; social, constitutional and political change in the South; and economic change.

The first new reality: demographic change

Demographic change must be considered carefully and with a good deal of circumspection.

The population of the Republic, which was in decline (due to emigration) from 1921 up to 1961, when it stood at 2.9 million, has rapidly expanded to 4.9 million, just short of 5 million.

In Northern Ireland, the population has also grown, from 1.4 million in 1961 to about 1.9 million today (3% of the UK population, 30% of the population of the island of Ireland).

The entire island's population is now approaching an expected 7 million by 2025. That figure would put the island's population ahead of eleven EU member states, including states such as Denmark and Finland.

In Northern Ireland, the internal demography is rapidly changing too. Latest figures show how quickly the religious balance in the North is evolving.

Catholics now account for about 46% of the population and will, on present trends, outnumber all other Christian denominations (currently 48%) by 2021.

Among those of working age, Catholics constitute 44% while all other Christian denominations are 40%. Of school children, 51% are Catholic while other Christians are 35%. By contrast, Catholics number only 35% of those over 60, while all other Christians in that age group are 60%.

The majority of university students in Northern Ireland are Catholic and of those Northern students studying in British universities, 65% do not return to Northern Ireland.

Present indications are that Catholics could outnumber all other Christians as persons entitled to vote in 2028 or 2030. Belfast city is likely to have more Catholics than other Christians in the 2021 census, and only two counties out of six – Antrim and Down – will have significant Protestant majorities.

In short, the denominational demography in the North has utterly changed.

From a post-partition 72:28 ratio between Protestants and Catholics at partition, the relative size of those cohorts is approaching equality.

Northern Ireland has ceased to be a Protestant state in so far as numbers are concerned.

No point in holding a border poll now

However, it would be entirely wrong to think, on the basis of a census headcount, that these denominational and demographic changes of themselves signal the inevitable emergence of a voting majority for a united Ireland in the short or medium term.

There are evidently many Catholic unionists and there are also many Catholics who see themselves as Northern Irish rather than simply as Irish. There is no reason to believe that such Catholic voters would entirely ignore their own personal economic interests or convictions by voting to end the union.

On the contrary, any border poll for a united Ireland held now or in the next few years would, we are told by reliable opinion pollsters, be roundly defeated.

There is little reason to doubt those opinion pollsters – especially when nobody has yet articulated what kind of unity we are talking about or what the consequences would be for the North's major public sector employment cohort, and when nobody can explain how people in Northern Ireland would be able to bear a precipitate withdrawal of £10 billion in annual UK Exchequer subsidies.

In the absence of clarity on those issues, any referendum in the Republic on immediate Irish unity would quite likely founder as well.

So calls by Sinn Féin for a border poll in present circumstances are not merely very premature; they are utterly pointless and serve no useful purpose other than to heighten political polarisation, which may be in Sinn Féin's interest as they see it.

The second reality: political, social and constitutional change in the Republic

The Republic is likewise ceasing to be a Catholic state – but for quite different reasons. The institutional power and influence of the Catholic Church – once so dominant in the post-independence Free State and in de Valera's republic – has shrivelled to political insignificance.

With some exceptions, such as denominational education (which persists on both sides of the border), the South has become more liberal, open and secular as a civil society than the North.

Denominational identity has largely ceased to matter in civil society. Even at a subconscious level, people meeting in social contexts do not bracket each other denominationally – especially among the younger age cohorts.

Northern fears that 'Rome rules' south of the border are no longer justified. On the contrary, the majority of people in the Republic now wonder why abortion laws and laws on homosexual marriage are so slow to change in the North.

In short, no Christian of whatever denomination in Northern Ireland has anything to fear from the South in terms of the free practice of his or her religion.

The Republic's constitution has been amended so as to fully accommodate the Good Friday Agreement and to drop the always questionable claim that the Irish government and parliament had a right to exercise jurisdiction over the North and to impose its constitution on the people of the North.

The people of the Republic amended Articles 2 and 3 of the Constitution expressly to disavow any attempt to unite the two jurisdictions on the island without the consent of the majority in Northern Ireland 'democratically expressed'.

The third new reality: economic reality

The third new reality is that of economics. On the island of Ireland, there have been widely divergent trends in the latter half of the twentieth century and the first two decades of this century.

Northern Ireland accounted for 80% of Irish industrial output in the 1920s. Belfast overtook Dublin as Ireland's most populous city in 1891. As David McWilliams has commented, 'At partition the North was industrial and rich, the South agricultural and poor …'. The Republic's industrial output is now ten times higher than the North's and its exports are 17 times greater. In euro terms, average income in the Republic is nearly €40,000 while in the North it is €24,000.

That difference is less when distributive spending is taken into account. Even allowing for tax-driven relocation of profits in the Republic, it can hardly be argued that independence from the United Kingdom has, since the 1970s, hugely benefitted the Republic.

The capacity of the Republic to attract foreign direct investment (some £312 billion) since the Good Friday Agreement speaks for itself.

Moreover, the opening of the border to an emerging all-island economy has greatly contributed to the economic well-being of Northern Ireland. Other than the huge annual Exchequer subsidy from Westminster, which is palliative in effect, the Union is simply not delivering to Northern Ireland.

It is difficult this week to see where the Brexit process is going to end. But the likelihood is that the current political advantage accruing to the DUP from holding the balance of power at

Westminster is unlikely to survive the widely expected general election in October or November.

Whether the UK ends up with a Tory government, a Labour government, a coalition government, or with the SNP holding the balance of power, it is hard to see that any form of Brexit – no deal or soft Brexit – is going to benefit Northern Ireland significantly.

Regional disparities within the United Kingdom are unlikely to be reduced under a Tory administration.

The likely abandonment of HS2 suggests that the Tories have little appetite for infrastructural projects to equalise or integrate the UK economy in a manner that favours Northern England, Scotland, Wales or Northern Ireland.

Keeping the border open at all costs is, in these circumstances, of huge importance to the economic well-being of Northern Ireland. Avoiding becoming an economic backwater in a post-hard Brexit UK should be at the top of everyone's agenda in Northern Ireland – especially the Unionists.

Northern agriculture faces very substantial challenges which would be greatly exacerbated by a hard border.

There is a very strong argument for Northern Ireland to consider opting for the kind of economic autonomy that has been so beneficial south of the border in terms of taxation policy and FDI.

It is entirely consistent with such increased autonomy that the people of Northern Ireland – Protestant and Catholic, Nationalist and Unionist – should carefully examine whether a confederal relationship with the Republic – in or aligned with the European Union – is not much more likely to bring about the prosperity in Northern Ireland which the South currently enjoys.

Has the Union bought out the best in Northern Ireland? Will the Union improve the Northern economy post Brexit? Will Exchequer transfers from Westminster grow or diminish under a post-Brexit regime of whatever hue?

Britishness

Under the terms of the Good Friday Agreement, the Republic bound itself to recognise the right of all citizens in Northern Ireland to regard themselves as British or Irish or both, and to claim citizenship accordingly, and undertook to preserve that entitlement even if the majority in Northern Ireland opted for a united Ireland of whatever kind.

Furthermore, it was expressly agreed that the obligation on the Republic would remain to ensure that any form of unity would afford not merely equality among citizens, including the right to be regarded as Irish or British citizens or both, but also parity of esteem for the 'values, ethos and aspirations' of both communities in Northern Ireland and to ensure impartiality between those communities.

Journeying into the unknown

On the face of it, then, Irish unity based on a form of confederation between Northern Ireland and the Republic as two jurisdictions in a confederal partnership seems like the 'least worst' form of Irish unity from any unionist point of view.

It seems to me that, from a pragmatic point of view, the sensible thing for the Government and people in the Republic is now to consider in depth what form of confederal unity could be proposed.

I agree with the view expressed this week by Hugo MacNeill that it would be better for those who believe in bringing about a united Ireland to formulate and flesh out the proposition that they want to have put to the people in separate referendums – North and South.

We no longer have the luxury of simply putting forward the Republic's preferred unitary option unilaterally on a 'take it or leave it' basis. If we are serious about the pursuit of Irish unity by consent as provided for in the Good Friday Agreement, we must act in a spirit of compromise and of complete respect for those whom we seek to persuade.

Seamus Mallon's proposal

Seamus Mallon's recent work, *A Shared Home Place*, rightly calls for nationalists – north and south – to demonstrate a new generosity of spirit to unionists. He correctly identifies the need for Northern Ireland to be shared as equals by each of its traditions as part of the badly needed reconciliation process between Orange and Green.

He rejects the idea that a border poll should be held as soon as it appears that there may be a small numerical majority – even 51% – in favour of Irish unity.

His thesis is that the last thing the North – and indeed the whole island – needs is a process whereby a very significant unionist minority in the North finds itself being transferred wholly against its will into a united Ireland. That scenario, he argues, is the makings of another long period of civil strife and inter-communal division.

He examines the question as to whether a 51% majority should suffice for Irish unity. In particular, he examines the argument put forward by Richard Humphreys in his recent work, *Beyond the Border: The Good Friday Agreement and Irish Unity after Brexit* (2018), that the legal effect of the agreement is that 51% is legally sufficient.

Mallon's remedy is to review the Agreement and to introduce the requirement that consent for Irish unity should instead be a requirement of 'parallel consent', i.e. a majority both of unionists and nationalists consenting, where that majority includes at least a substantial minority of each tradition or, in other words, where, say,

25%, 30% or 40% of the Protestant/Orange tradition consented to Irish unity.

While this suggested change would undoubtedly constitute generosity in a high degree, it could arguably produce a new and harmful veto-type red line into Northern politics.

Mallon's argument concedes that it would be wrong to deny, say, 80% of Catholics (then 48% of the North's population) and 40% of Protestants (then say 46%) the right as a majority (57%) along with others (say 4%), in all, say, 61%, the right to opt out of the Union if that were their expressed wish.

That seems clear if one considers that the alternative proposition — namely holding a poll which showed a majority in favour of unity — could be ignored because it fell below the threshold of commanding a majority of non-nationalist support.

Should parallel consent be elevated to legal status?

There are two other problems with making parallel consent a legal obligation.

How does one define the unionist position? If any former unionists want a united Ireland, are they to be considered unionists at all for the purpose of ascertaining whether parallel consent exists? Does religion or religious ancestry determine the matter?

Are the stated views of politicians expressly elected as unionists to be taken as the position of their electors? Can we reasonably expect persons elected as unionists to regard themselves as mandated to take a leading role in a process to end the Union?

Surgery not needed

I would passionately argue, to use a medical analogy, that Seamus Mallon's diagnosis in *A Shared Home Place* is entirely correct.

His 'patient history' is truthful and accurate. His analysis of the symptoms of the unresolved conflict of aspirations is spot on. His prescription of political 'bed rest' – sharing the home place as equals – and nationalist generosity is correct.

But his suggestion that the Good Friday Agreement should then be admitted for surgery – for the insertion of a parallel consent requirement – risks killing the patient. After all, there never would – or could – have been a Good Friday Agreement at all if parallel consent had been a part of it. Of that, I am absolutely satisfied based on my involvement in the political dialogue between 1999 and 2007.

If it had been suggested in 1998, the Stormont talks would have collapsed. If it had been suggested in 2006 at St Andrews, those talks too would have failed. There would have been no de-commissioning and no Paisley/McGuinness joint First Ministership.

In any event, a border poll is not likely to result in Irish unity in the foreseeable future unless a substantial number of those who have in the past favoured the Union change their minds.

Generosity

Seamus Mallon has spoken and written on the need for nationalist Ireland to be generous – particularly in the emerging demographic balance between Protestants and Catholics in Northern Ireland.

I agree.

Mallon makes it clear in his book that he himself believes that Irish unity may require a separate Northern entity with a 'half-British' ethos – a 'kind of confederation'.

In my judgement, the 'nationalist generosity' that is now most needed is the stated willingness of the Republic in particular to share sovereignty in a form of Irish unity based on confederation with Northern Ireland on the basis I have mentioned – a confederal outcome that really accommodates the British dimension to Northern Ireland.

The 'generous' thing to do is to take off the negotiation table any proposal for the absorption of Northern Ireland into a unitary Irish republic.

Fear of absorption on a German model into a unitary, all-Ireland state is a real and tangible political emotion on the part of unionists which must be respected and accommodated in political discourse on this island and among those who aspire to Irish unity.

To offer a genuine partnership in the form of an Irish confederation which would demonstrably accommodate the desire of people in Northern Ireland to feel and to be British or Northern Irish or both and remain so is, I think, the only practicable and achievable form of Irish unity by consent.

I would add that while the amendment to Strand One agreed at St Andrews, which accords the position of First Minister to the party getting the highest first preference vote may have been necessary to induce both the DUP and Sinn Féin to the rest of the Agreement, it had the effect of polarising the electorate – the DUP could make the argument that voting UUP or Alliance could make Gerry Adams or his successor the titular head of the North's executive.

I would also envisage that compulsory power-sharing in Northern Ireland would be reviewed as part of a confederal arrangement. Ideally, coalition government elected by a majority of parliamentarians based on a proportional representation system should become the norm on both sides of the border.

Compulsory power-sharing should give way to voluntary coalition power-sharing in any stable democracy. That prospect should be put on the table in any discussions on Irish unity.

No sudden post-Brexit clamour for unification in the North

24 July 2016

As someone who is by conviction a republican and aspires to live in a united Ireland, I have to say that I have found the sudden outbreak of 'unification' chatter in the aftermath of Brexit a bit far-fetched and, alas, counterproductive.

There is absolutely nothing apart from the grossest wishful thinking to suggest that the decision of the UK to leave the EU betokens a present desire among the majority of people in Northern Ireland to leave the UK and to be unified with the Republic.

Under the terms of the Good Friday Agreement, the British Government are obliged to hold a formal poll on unification only if it appears likely that a majority of the people of Northern Ireland would favour such an outcome.

There is simply no logical connection between a Unionist farmer having voted 'Remain' and any likelihood that he or she favours Irish reunification at this point. The same applies to many Catholics in the North who voted 'Remain'.

In November last, RTÉ carried out opinion polling on both sides of the border. Support for Irish unity 'in your lifetime' was 66% in the South with 14% opposed. North of the border, 30% of all voters would like to see a united Ireland in their lifetime but 43% were opposed. The 'don't knows' were 20% in the South but 27% in the North.

Those figures could change but they clearly show that there is a long way to go before a majority in Northern Ireland would vote for Irish unity.

Brexit is an important ingredient in the mix. The demographics of Northern Ireland are changing quite rapidly. A majority of school children in Northern Ireland are now of Catholic background.

Within 20 years, Catholic voters may well outnumber Protestant voters. Differential migration rates among undergraduates may well accelerate the achievement of 'confessional equality'.

A clear majority of university undergraduates in the North are already from Catholic backgrounds.

But welcome as such a new equilibrium would be in terms of creating a climate for equal partnership among the people in Northern Ireland and ending the dynamic of religious majoritarianism there, it does not foretell a sudden see-saw movement towards unification in the short, medium or long term.

The political case for a united Ireland (in which I believe) must be preceded by a lengthy period of mutual reconciliation. That process is the task and vocation of true republicans on this island.

The tricolour is not 'a flag of green, white and gold'; it is a flag of green, white and orange. And the orange panel stands for something we have got to value, if we aspire to unite the Irish people under that flag.

I do not see a 'hard border' as a possibility – now or in the future. An irony of Brexit is that it may see the introduction of migration monitoring and control between Northern Ireland and Britain rather than between North and South. The same may apply to hard customs controls.

Can Northern farmers trust the UK to support them to the same extent as the EU does at present? Is EU funding for cross-border and cross-community initiatives and EU Social Fund support for the North going to continue at current levels? Is Erasmus funding going to continue for undergraduates?

Is Northern Ireland going to be an attractive place for FDI post-Brexit? Is low corporation tax now dead as an option for Northern FDI policy?

Are single-nation Tories going to concentrate infrastructural investment on post-industrial northern England to the exclusion of post- Belfast Agreement Northern Ireland?

All these 'known unknowns' are real issues. They are deep worries for all decent people in the North – Orange or Green. And they should be worries for all decent people in the South too.

The most important aspect of Brexit for North-South relations and for Green–Orange relations on this island is how we conduct ourselves now.

Gerry Adams's call for a unification border poll was cack-handed, weak political playing to his own constituency. It was not statesmanlike.

Enda Kenny's failure to consult Arlene Foster about his All-Ireland Brexit Forum proposal was equally cack-handed, weak and incompetent. The DUP leader could easily have been quietly approached to partake in a less threatening, more unstructured dialogue. That would have shown respect.

Trust and respect are the basic building blocks of reconciliation and partnership on this island. Any other approach amounts to opportunist, counterproductive rhetoric and posturing.

And then there are economics. We southerners often assume that the Orangeman is led by his nose for prosperity and that his loyalty has the thickness of a large denomination banknote.

But just imagine if the voters of the South were asked to take up the UK's massive cost of subvention of Northern Ireland as the price of raising our flag over the fourth green field. It hardly bears thinking about.

Aspirations are cheap and 'low-maintenance'. Leaps of imagination unaccompanied by action and commitment may provide column inches for the silly season.

Martin and Mary McAleese showed respect, courage and empathy in building bridges to the Orange.

Now is the time for respect. Now is always the time for respect.

The Definite Article: UNITING THE IRISH

Republicanism is about reconciliation and inclusiveness – not violence between the Irish

18 February 2018

The tragedy of the present impasse in Northern Ireland is that the great majority of people, whether unionist or nationalist, are, or appear to be, decent, sensible, well-intentioned women and men who want to get on with their lives and with their neighbours.

But is that really true?

How come that picture does not seem to feed into the politics of the North, which remain septic and raw?

The truth, alas, is that bigotry and sectarianism lie below the surface of society in many cases. Tolerance and mutual respect are but a top veneer of a social discourse that deeper down is polarised and mutually suspicious in many cases.

Why would any decent society paint itself into an electoral corner where, despite the fact that the multi-seat proportional representation system affords every opportunity for moderation to assert itself, the ultimate choice for voters is between the likes of Gerry Adams and Arlene Foster?

Why would Mary Lou McDonald finish her acceptance speech with 'Tiocfaidh ár lá. Up the rebels'?

No genuine republican in the tradition of Tone and Davis could have done that. Especially at the delicate moment when the words were spoken. It was the language of defiance and confrontation. Mary Lou is not a republican precisely because, at a crucial moment, she forsook the language of reconciliation and inclusiveness and spat out sectarian words of enmity and threat.

It wasn't that she didn't think about those words; it was because she didn't care about those words. She didn't care about the message she was sending to the wider community. She doesn't really accept that there is a wider community to which she must address herself and for which she must measure what she says.

Let me make one thing clear – no genuine Irish republican party leader has any business these days organising or attending the graveside commemorations of bombers and gunmen who died in the recent Troubles. And anyone who does so in present circumstances is simply no republican.

Just as that those who lined up and machine-gunned the Protestant workers at Kingsmill were not republicans but betrayers of republicanism, the MP who tweeted and posed with a Kingsmill loaf on his head on the anniversary of that massacre has not even a smidgen of republican blood in his veins.

There are a lot of phony 'letty-on republicans' on this island – people who, at heart, despise the appeal of Thomas Davis for reconciliation of Orange and Green. They seek conquest – not conciliation. They try to arrogate the tricolour to their sectarian view of politics, just as they try to hijack the 1916 Rising to bookend their sordid history of killing and maiming.

They have no moral right or title to the term 'republican' and the media are foolish to use that term to describe their violence and their divisive brand of politics. Separatism and republicanism are not the same. You can be a violent separatist and still be no republican.

Real republicanism has nothing to do with the glorification of the 30 years of violence. The real republicans were those who, like Séamus Mallon, sought to stop the violence, who endured the graffiti calling them touts and traitors and the death threats from all sides, and who sacrificed everything, except their integrity, in pursuit of peace. The real republicans were the architects of Sunningdale – not those who brought it down.

None of the foregoing excuses the political weakness, would-be supremacism and political sectarianism that increasingly seem to fuel the DUP's behaviour since the departure of Paisley. But it must be said that Sinn Féin is great at demanding respect while being extremely ungenerous in showing respect.

Here is the litmus test. If the DUP leadership were to attend at the graveside commemoration of one of the Red Hand commandos or UVF killers, what would Sinn Féin say? What message would that send to the nationalists in the North? Can you imagine the outcry? And yet similar behaviour on their own side is supposed to cause no offence and show no disrespect!

While it may well be that Sinn Féin are using the Irish language issue as a battering ram in their ongoing siege politics, it is undoubtedly the case that the UK government conceded that the legal status of the Irish language would be provided for in the context of the St Andrews Agreement.

And apart from expense, what exactly is the problem of giving legal recognition to the Irish language in Northern Ireland in the same way as Gaelic is recognised in Scotland or the Welsh language in Wales? Each of those devolved UK jurisdictions has adopted laws recognising official status of Gaelic and Welsh respectively.

Is Scotland or Wales less British on that account? Are Welsh or Scottish unionists diminished or offended by such recognition?

Or is this yet another instance of the zero-sum theory of Northern politics – to give to one side is always to take from the other? Looking at a TV vox pop broadcast from East Belfast this week, it appears that there is a visceral backlash to the recognition of Irish among DUP supporters. But that form of political reaction is no reason not to reinstate the executive and assembly at Stormont.

It is the equal and opposite reaction to Mary Lou's 'Tiocfaidh ár lá. Up the rebels' peroration.

Will direct rule bring gay marriage and abortion to the North? Or will Nigel Dodds save Ulster from sodomy by holding the balance of power in London for a few more months while the roof comes in on the North's post-Brexit economic future?

Are we to despair?

Brexit turns more threatening by the day. And yet the main protagonists in Northern politics seem content to engage in attritional trench warfare while Boris Johnson and Michael Gove light an economic house fire that portends disaster for all sides in the North – not to mention for us in the Republic.

Nationalists in the North now have no political voice or forum. In the Seanad this week there were exchanges concerning the wisdom of Sinn Féin leaving the nationalist voice in Northern Ireland wholly absent from the debate on Brexit at Westminster.

De Valera adopted the 'empty formula' approach to the Oath of Allegiance in the 1920s, and abolished the oath on assuming office. Sinn Féin were offered alternatives to the oath if they would take their seats at Westminster. They declined – but they still draw their remuneration as MPs.

Abstentionism was fine in the 1918 to 1921 period because there was an alternative assembly – namely Dáil Éireann. But now those elected as Sinn Féin MPs and MLAs in the North have no assembly at all.

Sinn Féin changed their minds about abstaining from Stormont and Leinster House in the past. When their voters need representation on Brexit in the debate in London, they are to be found posing with loaves on their heads, or cutting off clamping devices, and parading at the graves of those killed in the Troubles.

Do Sinn Féin think, as they used to think, that things must get far worse before they get better? Who will bear the blame for the consequences of that kind of politics?

The ceasefire is largely about military capitulation disguised as a political transformation

16 April 2017

In an intriguing recent radio discussion on BBC last week, John Ware, presenter of a *Panorama* programme on Stakeknife and Kieran Conway, a self-described former Provo intelligence officer and author of *Southside Provisional,* discussed the significance of the now accepted belief that Freddie Scappaticci was simultaneously a British spy and the IRA's chief counter-intelligence interrogator, torturer and executioner in respect of persons suspected of being lower-level informants within the IRA.

Strikingly, Conway, who is now a lawyer practising in Dublin, advanced the view that the British had, by their dirty war, 'defeated' the IRA.

That, in his view, explained why the IRA called a ceasefire in the aftermath of the Downing Street Declaration in December 1993. He personally had opposed the IRA's 1994 ceasefire and the subsequent endorsement by the IRA of the Good Friday Agreement in combination with the abandonment of the 'armed struggle'.

The deep penetration by British intelligence of the IRA's central structure, as evidenced by Denis Donaldson's and Scappaticci's enlistment by MI5, is remarkable by any standard.

I have no reason to assume that they were by any means the only British 'assets' at the core of the IRA; on the contrary, I strongly suspect that the British penetration went higher and deeper in the Provo command structure. Otherwise, greater efforts would have been made to protect Donaldson from exposure in the course of the Stormontgate affair in 2002.

Scappaticci deserves close consideration as a phenomenon.

Here he was, violently interrogating suspected touts in the Provo ranks. When their 'operations' were foiled or went wrong or

The ceasefire is largely about military capitulation disguised as a political transformation

when senior Provos were arrested or arms caches seized or arrested members were released from police custody, a debriefing process would follow. Volunteers and sympathisers suspected of 'grassing' were detained by Scappaticci's Internal Security Unit (the ISU or colloquially the 'Nutting Squad') and the truth was coaxed or tortured out of them.

Scappaticci was at the centre of this process. He knew what lesser Provos knew. He reported ISU findings to those at Army Council level. He could protect valuable British 'assets' and sacrifice other informants to the bullet in the back of the head. He had 'access all areas' in the course of his ISU 'duties'. He could identify those Provos who were innocent of informing as much as he could choose life or death for those who were not.

While reporting to the Provos' top brass, he was also reporting to his MI5 handlers. Whether and to what extent his reports to these bodies differed we will never know. But he was an astonishing catch and a valuable asset for British intelligence.

Scappaticci was later implicated as a weak link in the Provos by giving his 1993 interview for a programme called *The Cook Report*, an interview he did not realise was being recorded. In that interview, he implicated Martin McGuinness in the infamous killing of Frank Hegarty.

It is not clear when the Army Council first suspected or fully believed that Scappaticci was a double agent. But it must have become an issue for them in or about the ceasefire in 2004.

Once his double role became known to the Army Council's members, they must have known that the game was up.

That is not to imply that the British handlers knew everything. One has to assume, for instance, that the Army Council somehow kept the later 1996 Canary Wharf bombing secret from MI5. The bombing could hardly have been permitted to happen just to protect sources. But some of the British sources within the Provos may nonetheless have known of the Canary Wharf operation and kept it back from their handlers as a form of self-protection.

On Kieran Conway's view, the peace process was in reality an acceptance by the IRA of their 'military defeat' and the coldly calculated 'exit strategy' for the Provisional movement into politics.

The ultimate imperative from the British point of view was to ensure that Adams and McGuinness 'took the IRA with them' largely intact and that the armed struggle would effectively end by a decisive option in favour of the ballot box over the Armalite. That was what the 1998 Good Friday Agreement and the St Andrews Agreement in 2006 were all about. Adams and McGuinness shared that British aim.

Assuming, as I do, that there were other very senior Provos in effective collaboration with the British in pursuit of that goal, the peace process must now be seen to a large extent as Kieran Conway describes it – a military capitulation disguised as a political transformation. And it is hard not to see it as a sort of parallel with the pragmatic 1921 compromise that led to the Irish Free State – however unpalatable that parallel may seem to modern Sinn Féin supporters. Collins saw himself as having delivered the substance of an Irish republic in 1921 – albeit within the framework of the Commonwealth. So did the then Supreme Council of the IRB.

The maximum that could be achieved in 1998 without an Orange–Green civil war in the North was traded by the British in exchange for giving the Provisional movement a share in the executive power in the North. Whether, to use Collins's phrase, the settlement amounts to the 'freedom to become free' is as yet unknowable.

It must also be remembered that the destruction of the Twin Towers in New York in 2001 sealed forever the impossibility of continuing the armed struggle in Ireland. Terrorism and urban guerrilla warfare anywhere in the West in pursuit of separatist causes was doomed by the actions of Osama bin Laden. There was no prospect of success for the Provos' armed struggle. It was proven, in Kieran Conway's words, to be a 'waste of time'.

All of it – the armed struggle, the dirty war, the killing, the maiming, the bombings, the economic destruction, the MI5 double agents, the kidnappings for ransom, the financial extortion, the torture, the hunger strikes and the appalling misery – was devoid of moral value at best and the pit of depravity at worst. There was nothing heroic or brave or patriotic to be found there.

Did stopping it from within amount to statesmanship or did it betoken the crudest and most selfish instinct for power and self-preservation?

Were any of those who 'ran' Scappaticci – whether Provos or MI5 – any better than the rest or better than him?

We will never know the truth – or the half of the truth. And investigating these matters with a view to criminal prosecutions as is currently happening, is also, to borrow Kieran Conway's phrase, 'a waste of time'.

Who is less worthy of office – those who ran Scappaticci's Nutting Squad or those who bungled the 'ash for cash' affair?

Can we not just restore power-sharing? Especially as Brexit looms larger and larger.

A message to the Easter marchers – take the road of reconciliation

21 April 2019

A republican Easter Message this weekend to those who use or who glorify fifty years of violence in the North.

You are not republican. You are not creating the Republic of Tone or Davis. You are defiling their memory and their patriotism. You are damaging their ideals and undermining their goals. You are not an army. You are a network of twisted haters. You are a band of very petty criminals, community bullies and heartless thugs.

You will fail in your attempt to shop-lift the bright clothes of genuine republicanism to cover the pitiful black berets, black balaclavas, black polo necks and slacks, and your black sectarianism hearts.

You are on the road to nowhere – politically, morally or historically. You will never be commemorated; the best that you can hope for is to provoke a shudder in the unlikely event that your actions come to mind in future times.

There is only one road for republicans to travel.

It is the road of reconciliation. It is the road of generosity and inclusiveness. It is the road of respect for those who have different loyalties and values. It is also the road of atonement for wrongs done.

You may murder a young journalist, Lyra McKee, or some man or woman in the PSNI. But you can't murder the truth.

There will be no republic without reconciliation. There will be no reconciliation unless there is no violence.

What part of 'no' do you not understand?

When I say that such a message is due to those 'who use or glorify violence', I also have in mind those who spend their weekends parading and speechifying at gravesides and before monuments to the perpetrators of sectarian violence.

If you glorify such deeds, you re-enact them and exploit them in the minds of the victims of those deeds and their relatives. You re-open the wounds. You exhume the bodies.

Real republicans must understand that glorifying paramilitarism and reconciliation are now opposed to each other.

The Good Friday Agreement was based on the idea that the political and cultural and religious identity of everyone on this island must be respected and should co-exist rather than compete for dominance of one over the other.

By adopting those values, the space for reconciliation can be created. By asserting the claims of one side alone, the chances of reconciliation are put on hold and soured.

The fact that the Good Friday institutions have lain unused for years now is a scandal. The responsibility lies with the DUP and Sinn Féin in equal measure. Both parties posture as if they want the institutions to work. But neither party really wants the Good Friday settlement to succeed.

The DUP and Sinn Féin have another thing in common; neither deserves to hold seats at Westminster. Abstentionism on the part of Sinn Féin and parliamentary wrecking tactics on the part of the DUP mirror each other in contempt for the best interests of the people of Northern Ireland.

Calls for a border poll by Sinn Féin are dishonest and cynical. They know it would fail badly. But they relish the thought of increased polarisation and regression to binary non-choices in the politics of the North bereft of middle ground.

Likewise, the DUP has been utterly dishonest in not putting forward the position of the great majority of people in Northern Ireland – namely that an open order and a soft Brexit, if contrary to their expressed wishes there must be a Brexit at all, is not merely the least-worst but the best that can be done.

The DUP have betrayed the people of both traditions in the North by falsely elevating the back stop to the status of an existential threat to the union. By making common cause with the Tory right in a visceral rejection of the EU, the DUP have jeopardised the union to an extent that no unionist politicians have ever done before.

The people of Northern Ireland are wretchedly served by Sinn Féin and the DUP – parties that seem to thrive in symbiotic mutual revulsion.

At some point, the truth will dawn on voters.

The Republic's media have abjectly failed to put the spotlight on Sinn Féin. It is not a normal political party. It is a political construct in which an obscure politburo located in Belfast rigidly controls an organisation that masquerades as being a conventional political party.

It has lost about 30 elected members of the Oireachtas and county councillors who have left citing bullying and organised defamation as the means of exercising discipline in the party.

Their TDs and senators in Leinster House do not have parliamentary party meetings to decide policy. These matters are decided at politburo level in the sanctum of the Felons Club in Belfast and communicated to public representatives through small team meetings controlled by commissars.

The same modus operandi applies with a little tweaking at county council level.

When Peadar Tóibín resigned from the party, he says that he found empty crates in his Dáil office. He claims (and it has not yet been denied) that an unelected person he describes a 'political manager in the Dáil' (code for a Belfast-appointed commissar) came into his office and shouted at him to 'f**k off' out of his office and off the floor 'before something happens'.

That incident neatly sums up the fact that the party is controlled by a ruthless and nasty inner circle which makes the real decisions about who will be de-selected and who will be nominated. The testimonies of those who have been forced out consistently point to a darker reality.

While individual SF public representatives can be affable and plausible, no dissent is tolerated. The elected members of the Oireachtas are controlled as to whom they must employ and what they may say. They are not permitted to go on radio or TV without permission. One can sense their growing realisation that they are more in the line of 'useful idiots' of a hidden hierarchy than autonomous public representatives.

The very nature of their party means that they are not suited to participate in government.

It has emerged in the 'cash for ash' inquiry being conducted by Sir Patrick Coghlin in Stormont that elected ministers in the power-sharing executive receive political dictation via their 'advisers' from an inner clique of unelected veteran republicans including former senior IRA figures.

So it's not enough for us to express utter abhorrence at the cruel killing of Lyra McKee by dissidents who wanted to celebrate Easter by killing PSNI officers in the Creggan.

Genuine republicanism demands that our Government does everything to re-start the political process in the North and to get ordinary cross-community democratic politics working again. Wreckers in Sinn Féin and in the DUP need to be faced down.

Reconciliation cannot wait and wither in the face of Brexit and those who are itching to fill the vacuum with violence and distrust. Handwringing is no substitute for political courage and risk-taking.

When extortion and murder were their stock in trade

3 September 2011

A few weeks past, a newspaper story caught my eye. A stamp collection was to be sold this month by Sotheby's in London and it is anticipated that it will realise £4 million sterling.

My immediate reflection, probably that of most people, was that we live in a very strange world where insignificant pieces of paper designed and used for the most mundane purpose, could, by reason of rarity, achieve a colossal value in the highly rarefied philatelic marketplace. All the more so when we consider that stamps are a relatively modern invention with a history of less than 200 years. While diamonds, gold, and fine art also command great prices in rarefied marketplaces, stamps are unusual because they had such a negligible value when first printed and sold.

I then set to wondering what kind of person could amass a stamp collection of such value and noted that the particular stamp collection being sold at Sotheby's was part of the estate of a life peer, Lord Steinberg of Belfast. His family had decided to donate proceeds from the sale to a number of causes and charities with which he had been associated during his lifetime, including a fund that he had started with the aim of helping to rebuild Old Trafford, the celebrated Lancashire County Cricket Club grounds.

The very name, Lord Steinberg of Belfast, surprised me. As somebody with a reasonable grasp of current affairs, I have to confess that I knew little of him.

It turns out that Leonard Steinberg was born in Belfast in August 1936. His grandfather had fled the anti-Jewish tsarist pogroms in Riga for the safety of Belfast. By doing so he saved his children from the Holocaust. As a member of the small Belfast Jewish community, Leonard was brought up by his father, who ran several small businesses, including a dairy shop and an optician's. Before his father died in 1954, young Leonard, aged 18, was running a small unlicensed betting business at the back of the dairy shop in Belfast.

By 1977, when this business had grown to sixteen licensed betting shops in Belfast, the Provisional IRA shot Steinberg five times on the doorstep of his house on the Antrim Road.

His 'crime' in the eyes of the IRA was that he was a businessman, he was Jewish, he was a unionist, and, most heinous of all, he would not pay protection money to the IRA, which, in those days and right up until very recently, quietly extorted vast sums from businesspeople under threat of violence.

Having survived the shooting attempt in 1977, Leonard Steinberg understandably left Belfast to live in northern England. But he remained at heart and in accent a Belfastman.

His betting business went on to become one of Britain's largest – Stanley Leisure. Following his move to Manchester, Steinberg bought 100 betting shops from Ladbrokes and he grew a gambling business which came to include 45 casinos and 500 betting shops, employing about 7,000 people. His resulting wealth financed his passion for philately.

Predictably, Leonard Steinberg in England gravitated towards the Conservative Party in Britain and eventually became a party deputy treasurer as well as president of Lancashire County Cricket Club. When the Tories duly made him a life peer in 2004, Leonard Steinberg adopted the title 'Lord Steinberg of Belfast'.

Leonard Steinberg was not the only Belfast Jewish businessman targeted by the IRA. Three years after Steinberg's shooting, his good friend, fellow Jew and antiques dealer Leonard Kaitcer, a married man with two children, was abducted from his Belfast home. The IRA demanded £1 million ransom for his return. An American cousin flew to Ireland to conduct negotiations for his release but the IRA panicked, shot Leonard Kaitcer in the head, and dumped his body in West Belfast.

Of course, neither Leonard Steinberg nor Leonard Kaitcer was targeted simply because they were Jewish. But it probably helped. They were targeted by the IRA for murderous extortion because they were both wealthy and socially vulnerable. Many others were targeted in a similar fashion. Don Tidey, Galen Weston, Tiede Herrema and Ben Dunne are some of the lucky, better remembered southern survivors of the cruel policy of kidnapping and murder of businessmen by the IRA. Garda Gary Sheehan and Private Patrick Kelly were murdered while trying to rescue Don Tidey in Derrada Woods.

Extortion by the IRA became so commonplace (and the loyalist thugs were at it too) that the payment of protection money came to be regarded as a legitimate business expense even for tax purposes in Belfast. Apart from those businessmen, many more modest targets for extortion paid with their lives for refusing to pay money to the Provisional IRA.

All this reminds us that in the cracked mirror of their crazy, warped ideology, the Provisional IRA had convinced themselves that the IRA Army Council somehow was itself the legitimate government of Ireland and the sole repository of the powers of the Republic established in 1916!

That madcap theory, as set out in the Provos' volunteers handbook, depends in turn on a meeting on 8 December 1938, between some former members of the Dáil and some members of the IRA. The IRA claims that at this meeting an obscure minority of the many surviving former backbench members of the long-defunct Second Dáil elected in 1921, who in 1938 now claimed to be the 'Government of the Republic', in some manner 'delegated' their 'sacred trust' to the Army Council of the IRA until a 32-county republic was finally established, 'confident ... that in their every action towards its consummation they will be inspired by the high ideals and chivalry of our martyred comrades.'

Perhaps there is still, unbeknownst to us, another rival government composed of people who have in total secrecy inherited directly the sacred trust of Robert Emmet's republic of 1803 or the Fenian republic of 1867. Who knows?

On top of that nonsense, one has to add a layer of savage, revolutionary Marxism espoused by the core IRA leadership from the 1970s onwards. A Marxist worldview convinced those grim-faced, beret-wearing coffin-carriers that murdering businessmen who would not hand over their money to the IRA was not merely legitimate in terms of this so-called 'republican' theory of governmental succession but also justified in terms of Marxist revolutionary theory. A potent cocktail of madness and evil very far removed from 'high ideals and chivalry'.

Anyhow, on such ludicrous, demented ideology rested the justification some forty years later for killing Leonard Kaitcer and shooting Leonard Steinberg. The Irish Republic was 'entitled', the Provos believed, to exact taxes and revenues from the well-to-do – by extortion under threat of murder and arson. Needs must! Or, as Lenin would have put it, it was all part of 'what is to be done'.

These actions, of course, could not be 'crimes' – because they were economic actions authorised by the Army Council who, of course, as custodians of the 'sacred trust' embodied the legitimacy and exercised the authority and powers of the Irish Republic.

We are led to hope that the Mahon Tribunal will report in the coming months. There will be justified breast-beating and angry, if ritual, condemnation when that tribunal enunciates that which we now know to be true, namely, that a small but sizeable minority of Irish public representatives behaved corruptly in relation to the planning process over many decades.

To the fore among the breast-beaters will be household names, now elected to the Dáil and to the Assembly in Northern Ireland (and some of them to Parliament at Westminster). They will claim that they themselves weren't ever into bribes. They hope that we will forget that their politics were financed by murder-based extortion of fellow Belfastmen like Steinberg and Kaitcer.

It would be a salutary thing if, while listening to post-Mahon 'politics of condemnation' (something to which Gerry Adams, for instance, was at one time notoriously averse), we listen carefully for the voices of those who were personally actively engaged in directing the campaign of murder and extortion-base fundraising that killed Leonard Kaitcer and nearly killed Leonard Steinberg.

Those paragons of virtue, remarkably, now have the neck to pontificate on corruption and misconduct in public life, confident that amnesiac media sheep will have long since forgotten that they, personally, directed a movement financed by the murder of innocent businessmen, threatening of their families, stealing or destruction of their property, and extortion of vast sums of money from a great number of people, all to further their political ends, to feather their own nests and to provide themselves with 'walking around money'.

Above all, perhaps we should remember that some of those who wish to be respectable household names in our new political order still have the blood of Leonard Kaitcer on their hands and have never apologised for taking *his* life – while demanding and extracting apologies from all around them.

Perhaps some in the media will bring home to the public on both sides of the border the immense moral gulf which separates the Marxist thugs in the Provos who directed the murder for his money of Leonard Kaitcer from the patriotic founders of our State. Perhaps some brave, enterprising broadcaster or journalist will now make a 'lift the lid' documentary on the Provos' fundraising campaign of extortion and murder. Don't hold your breath.

Adams' post-factual parallel universe

11 December 2016

The phrase 'living in a parallel universe' is often used to describe the mindset of people who inhabit a different moral space from most people and have created their own moral and factual order. This week it has been used about Gerry Adams as he wriggles and twists in an attempt to reconcile his membership of the elected parliament of a modern Irish democracy, on the one hand, and his central role in the IRA, on the other hand.

Adams' post-factual parallel universe

Living, as we all apparently do now, in a 'post-factual' world, Adams is entitled to be regarded as a pioneer explorer of that new order; he saw the light many years ago. Like Trump, he understands that truth is less important than gut feeling.

He was, he claims, never a member of the IRA. Well, you know, that might just be true. Why? Because there is no such thing as 'membership' of the IRA, as IRA members see things.

People who join the IRA become 'volunteers' or Óglaigh – not 'members'. And volunteers can rise to high rank within the IRA but they never cease to be 'volunteers'.

'Membership of the IRA' only exists in the criminal law books of the oppressor states – the Offences Against the State Act 1939, and so on.

So, you see, he is right – and you are wrong. Silly you! You only imagine that you remember him donning the black beret at funerals. Or if you find a photo of a beret-clad, youthful Adams, why can't you accept that it was just a youthful fashion statement? All his Provo colleagues who remember him acting as OC of the Belfast IRA are 'getting on' and no longer reliable.

The Stack family were told that an IRA volunteer shot their father without IRA sanction. They were told by the IRA that it was done in the context of a 'brutal' prison regime in Portlaoise jail. That was to provide the Stacks with a little 'moral context'. They were assured that the volunteer was 'disciplined' – whatever that meant, it didn't mean killed.

How do the IRA know that the shooting was unauthorised? Well, we must assume they carried out an inquiry among their members – oops! – their volunteers. The inquiry must have happened fairly recently because they spent decades denying any involvement in the murder. So a relatively recent inquiry led to a relatively recent imposition of 'discipline'.

Who has been in charge of the disciplinary arm of the IRA in recent years? We don't know. But the disciplinary measure can't have been physical because the IRA have forsworn violence.

If you are confused by all of this, don't trouble your little head. It's all history now! Part of a dark and troubled past! The 'peace process' means that we have all moved on, doesn't it?

Well, not quite. You see, certain crimes committed against nationalist and republican people still need to be investigated. And Sinn Féin are constantly campaigning for this. And for a Truth Commission. Those crimes are in a different category. They were committed by the State. IRA crimes are not really state crimes.

Why not? Because the IRA, by definition, never committed a crime. Why is that you ask?

Again, you are simply not thinking straight! The Army Council of the IRA is – and has been for decades – the 'legitimate government of the Irish Republic'.

How do we know that? Because in 1938, a group of seven people conferred that status on the Army Council. It was all official and done in writing!

What power had those seven ageing people to transfer the powers of the Republic to the Army Council?

It's so obvious that I need hardly tell you. But let me spell it out for the slow learners among you.

The seven signatories of the 1938 handover document, you see, were all members of the Second Dáil elected in 1921. They may all have contested a number of later Dáil elections up to 1927 and then lost their seats. But that doesn't matter; they, as a tiny fraction of the Second Dáil, somehow kept their Jedi status for another 18 years as holders of the legitimate power of the 1916 Republic – long after the Second Dáil's term had expired and long after they had been rejected at the polls.

Adams' post-factual parallel universe

If you find this confusing or dubious or ridiculous, that's your problem.

Every volunteer takes an oath of belief in this magical chain of legitimacy. They swear allegiance to the IRA and its Army Council as the legitimate government of the Irish Republic precisely because of that little ceremony in 1938.

On enlistment as volunteers, they are given the IRA's Green Book, which sets all of this out for them like a catechism. Look it all up on Google, if you doubt me. It says:

The moral position of the Irish Republican Army, its right to engage in warfare, is based on:

- *The right to resist foreign aggression,*
- *The right to revolt against tyranny and oppression,*
- *The direct lineal succession with the Provisional Government of 1916, the first Dáil of 1919, and the second Dáil of 1921.*

In 1938, the seven surviving faithful Republican Deputies delegated executive powers to the Army Council of the IRA, as per the 1921 resolution. In 1969, the sole surviving, Deputy Joseph Clarke, reaffirmed publicly that the then Provisional Army Council were the inheritors of the first and second Dáil as a Provisional Government.

These are the core beliefs of Adams, McGuinness, Ellis and Ferris and all the other Provos – to this day. Their Army Council is 'the legal and lawful government of the Irish Republic'.

So 'authorised' operations involving murder, torture, robbery, mutilations, and bombings cannot be crimes. They are legitimate acts of our 'legitimate government'. If only we had known!

Therefore, the murder of Brian Stack falls to be judged by one criterion alone — was it properly authorised by the inheritors of the powers of the Second Dáil?

And the Stack family must be hugely reassured that their father's death — unlike Jerry McCabe's and so many other gardaí — was 'unauthorised' by the true Government of the Irish Republic and can therefore be described not merely as 'wrong' — but also, maybe just, as a crime.

This is the parallel universe in which Gerry lives. Those of us who have been slightly taken aback by his radio description of naked workouts on the trampoline with his dog and by the slightly wacky tweets he sends at bedtime, can take some comfort in knowing that his parallel universe is all legally and constitutionally above board.

Could Disney yet film another *Star Wars* episode in which R2-D2 rather than Deputy Joe Clarke hands over the secret powers of the Republic to do battle with the Empire to Gerry Adams on the trampoline high up on Skellig Michael? The mind boggles.

Religion and Social Affairs

Tuam is a by-product of the deeper scandal of a religious and social culture that seems so cruel, and yet so recent, to the modern world

March 2017

One of the less edifying aspects of politics is the tendency of some practitioners to engage in the rhetoric of competitive moral outrage. The Tuam Mother and Baby Home scandal is a case in point. The Oireachtas has heard in each House genuine and moving personal accounts from survivors of the Irish system of dealing with unwanted pregnancy in the first half of the twentieth century. That was good and wholesome.

But we also witnessed this week the self-indulgent rhetoric of competitive outrage – the subtext being 'Look at me. I am more morally appalled than most others, and I am better able to express my outrage than anyone else.'

There was something toe-curlingly awful about the Taoiseach's contribution in the Dáil on the subject of Tuam this week. Not for the first time, he came into the Dáil armed with a cleverly written, mordant condemnation of appalling Roman Catholic double standards. Somewhere in Government Buildings there is a gifted script-writer from whom this topic brings forth great lines.

The problem on this occasion was its delivery – which was just awful. In auditions for an amateur dramatics society, the director would have stopped it halfway through with an emphatic 'Next, please!' The Taoiseach, alas, came across as phony, contrived, forced and false – as a ham actor feigning instant emotional outrage.

Which was a great pity – because the work of the Commission of Investigation chaired by Judge Yvonne Murphy has a difficult task to perform – which task needs to be carried out in a calm, truthful and careful way. Survivors and relatives of those in these homes need confidence that the task will not be enlarged to the point where we will wait many years for conclusions. Overblown rhetoric adds nothing to the process of uncovering the truth – still less to the process of learning from that uncovered truth.

Part of that truth is this.

In 1934, the Archdiocese of Tuam held its annual Clergy Conference. Among other topics discussed and minuted was the 'scandal of illegitimate births'. The minutes of the Conference had this to say:

Whenever an illegitimate birth occurs in a parish, and is publicly known, the scandal ought to be denounced without mentioning names, with a view to calling the guilty to repentance and as a deterrent to others. The denunciation ought to be in sorrow more than in anger and the preacher ought to point to the scandal as:

A grave sin against the sacrament of matrimony and against the sixth commandment,
A degradation of the soul,
A disgrace to the family,
A sin against the good name of the locality.
Not only is the general permission given, but a direction is also given, to make this denunciation. In a special case, after consultation with His Grace the Archbishop, the matter may be deferred for a time. But in every case the scandal is to be immediately referred to the archbishop.

> Tuam is a by-product of the deeper scandal of a religious and social culture that seems so cruel, and yet so recent, to the modern world

As Kieran Waldron, an astute clerical historian of the Tuam archdiocese, commented in 2008, this procedure 'would create horror to modern sensibilities' but remained in common use in Ireland until the 1950s.

A 'letter of denunciation' from the Archbishop was accordingly read at local masses, which, while using no names, effectively presaged the expulsion of the mother from the local community.

To avoid this public obloquy and the personal and family disgrace, pregnant unmarried girls were quietly banished with clerical assistance to mother and baby homes for their confinement and often for a post-natal period of work service which sometimes extended into a lifetime of utterly lonely servitude.

Cruel and utterly wrong to our eyes is the very idea that the preservation of church and social morality in those days required not merely those steps, but also ordained the destruction of the relevant mother–child relationship – the extinction of the natural relationship of love and nurture of a mother for her child – and all to serve and preserve the supremacy of the Church's version of Natural Law in relation to sexuality and marriage.

Apparently the avoidance of 'scandal' simultaneously demanded the public denunciation of defenceless unmarried mothers, on the one hand, and the systematic concealment of clerical sexual abusers, with their victim sworn to secrecy on pain of excommunication, on the other hand.

This we all know – and this we all have known.

Mortality rates in the Tuam home and disposal of the babies' bodies are not the only scandal – they are also the by-product of the deeper scandal of a religious and social culture that seems so cruel, and yet so recent, to the modern world.

The irony of the situation is that such injustice and such contradiction of the contemporary understanding of the core of Christianity is based on a Thomist view of sexuality and marriage which has in the meantime crashed the contemporary Roman Catholic Church onto the rocks – and appears to have made it into an institutional shipwreck in Ireland.

That navigational error was not just the result of Humanae Vitae – the 1968 reiteration of the papal condemnation of birth control; the broader celibate Church's utter failure to comprehend sexuality – and its age-old obsession with its own misunderstanding of sexuality – seem to guarantee that no-one can now drag it off those rocks.

The same moral force and authority – the magisterium if you like – that enabled the social and moral hegemony of a Jansenist Roman Catholicism to hold such sway in Ireland between 1850 and 1960 – now seems intent on devouring the goodwill and beliefs of an entire generation of would-be Christians in Ireland.

A far cry, I think from Tom Kettle's poetic, 'For a dream born in a herdsman's shed, and for the secret Scripture of the poor'.

Ministers who lost their positions and the consequences of opposing reform

27 October 2013

It is a strange irony that Lucinda Creighton and Derek Keating, both Fine Gael TDs, who voted in opposite lobbies on the Government's Protection of Life in Pregnancy Bill, should, on that account, each face the loss of a ministry that was dear to their hearts.

Lucinda Creighton, as is well known, lost her ministry, her membership of the Fine Gael parliamentary party, her Dáil office, and was informed that she would be deselected as a Fine Gael candidate for the next general election, because she voted against the legislation.

Meanwhile, Derek Keating, a backbench TD for Dublin Mid-West, was informed by his parish priest that by reason of

Ministers who lost their positions and the consequences of opposing reform

his vote for the government legislation he was to stand aside as a minister of the Eucharist in his local parish church.

Each erstwhile 'minister' had, it seems, gravely offended the relevant political or ecclesial magisterium to the point where forfeiture of ministry was the condign and inevitable consequence of his or her vote.

While the fate of Lucinda Creighton attracted a good deal of media coverage and a fair share of public sympathy, Derek Keating found himself receiving no sympathy in the editorial column of the *Irish Catholic*. He was criticised there for bringing his loss of ministry to the attention of the public via the media rather than attempting to discuss the matter with his parish priest.

The *Irish Catholic* editorial also made the point that Derek Keating should hardly be surprised if he was removed from Eucharistic ministry for opposing Catholic teaching when he apparently accepted without any difficulty the sacking of his colleague, Lucinda Creighton as a consequence of her vote.

The editorial also stated:

The last thing that practising Catholics who cherish the sacredness of human life want to see when they attend Mass is the spectacle of those who vocally support abortion distributing Holy Communion.

Vocal support for abortion? Deputy Keating? Truth? Christian charity? Hmmm.

Meanwhile on an ultra-orthodox Catholic blog called *Protect the Pope*, contributors were exulting in the fate of Deputy Keating's ministry. Compliments were abundant for the parish priest, Father Reilly, who had taken the step of removing the TD from his ministry.

That blog makes very interesting reading. It even features on its homepage a clock-type box in which the time which has now elapsed since when Enda Kenny, in the view of the blog master, 'should have been excommunicated' is continually calculated in terms of months, days, hours, minutes and seconds.

In his recent major interview, Pope Francis seems to be opening up the Church to new directions and priorities. He said:

We cannot insist only on issues related to abortion, gay marriage and the use of contraceptive methods. This is not possible. I have not spoken much about these things, and I was reprimanded for that. But when we speak about these issues, I have to talk about them in a context. The teaching of the Church, for that matter, is clear and I am a son of the church, but it is not necessary to talk about these issues all the time.

The dogmatic and moral teachings of the Church are not all equivalent. The Church's pastoral ministry cannot be obsessed with the transmission of a disjointed multitude of doctrines to be imposed insistently. Proclamation in a missionary style focuses on the essentials, on the necessary things: this is also what fascinates and attracts more, what makes the heart burn, as it did for the disciples at Emmaus. We have to find a new balance; otherwise even the moral edifice of the Church is likely to fall like a house of cards, losing the freshness and fragrance of the gospel.

These comments, however, are a million miles away from formally abandoning the Church's well-known positions on abortion, gay marriage, and the use of contraceptives.

To the old rhetorical question, 'Is the Pope a Catholic?', the answer is and remains undoubtedly 'Yes'.

But nonetheless the Pope's statement concerning the 'likelihood' of the moral edifice of the church falling like a house of cards in the absence of a 'new balance' is, in my view, of huge significance. This Pope clearly understands that the strident and obsessive concentration by elements within the Roman Catholic Church on reproduction and sexuality is a very real threat to the survival of the church as an institution.

Unless that new balance is struck soon, the Roman Catholic Church is quite likely in my view to simply mutate into a narrow, highly centralised orthodoxy commanding an ever-dwindling membership practising an atavistic faith in an increasingly isolated space. Without the new balance, the road to implosion is plainly open.

It seems to me that the starting point in Church renewal must be a fundamental reconsideration of the disastrous course taken by the papacy in *Humane Vitae*. That encyclical not merely wounded the Church; it caused an infected wound which simply will not heal. It is poisoning the Church. It discredited – and still discredits – the Church as a moral community.

Confession of the error of that encyclical would not weaken the Church; it would strengthen it. While such confession might cause a problem for those who are tied to a nineteenth-century view of the Church's magisterium, it could do wonders for the revival of the Church as a community of the people of God.

Likewise, the obsessive preoccupation of the papacy with securing a totally phoney external conformity within the Western Church's ranks on the issue of priestly celibacy is, I think, repugnant to the great majority of thinking Catholics.

How priestly celibacy squares even with Paul's First Letter to Timothy is one of the great mysteries of faith. How the Church survived for a millennium without priestly celibacy is another mystery. Why it can still do so in certain eastern parts of the Church is yet another.

That obsession is also part of a piece with the other obsessive doctrines on sexuality and reproduction; these obsessions not merely alienate the would-be faithful, they undermine the credibility and integrity of the institutional Church itself. They are surely the 'cards' of which much of the 'house of cards' of the Church's 'moral edifice' is now composed.

The attitude of churches and of religions to women is also part of a wider context. Change is afoot.

So perhaps, as in the case of the two former 'minister' TDs, there are some striking parallels between politics and religion. The term 'house of cards' is apt in both contexts. A new balance is possible in both arenas. Reform is not a dirty word any longer. The consequences of opposing reform become clearer as time passes.

There can be no ambiguity over 'crime' of blasphemy

25 January 2015

You have to make some allowances for the apparent clumsiness of Pope Francis's remarks about the *Charlie Hebdo* murders in which he pointed out that if you insult someone's mother you can expect a punch. If he meant that there was no need to be gratuitously offensive and no call for gratuitously provoking those who are easily provoked, then his words were nothing more than plain old common sense, civility and even Christianity in practice.

But if he meant more than that, it raises some interesting and serious questions.

Going back to the Salman Rushdie fatwa, we should not lose sight of the fact that the constitutionally powerful Iranian ayatollahs who effectively dominate a modern state, Iran, were seen by the world to instruct such of the Muslim faithful as pay attention to them that it was their right and duty to kill Rushdie wherever in the world they could find him on the basis that they had adjudged that certain parts of his *Satanic Verses* were blasphemous.

Either that is tolerable or it is not. Either Islam, or some parts of Islam, claims the moral and legal right for its followers to kill blasphemers or it doesn't. Put another way, either Islam and all parts of it, accepts that it is a grievous crime to kill any person who exercises his right of free speech in his own democratic state by uttering a blasphemy against Islam or it doesn't. This is something on which there can be no ambiguity. Full stop. There is no wriggle room on this issue.

If there is doubt on these matters, a wholly unnecessary question mark thereby hangs over the relationship between Islam and our modern democratic states.

For my part, I would not avail of these pages to mock the religious beliefs of others. That said, I do feel it is my right to freely express my own views on the validity, credibility or falsity of any religion or religious belief without any expectation of a 'punch' from anyone I may have offended.

Mormons have to put up with the West End musical *The Book of Mormon*, which satirises their heartfelt faith. Christians had to put up with *The Life of Brian*, even though it deeply offended the likes of Malcolm Muggeridge and Mary Whitehouse. Devout Irish Catholics may resent *Father Ted*. Muslims may not like, but may not stop, the depiction of the Prophet or the satirising of aspects of their faith.

Nobody forces any of us to see or watch any of these satires. And I think I have a right to see them and enjoy them. It is an entirely different issue when those who are offended by what they consider blasphemy seek to prevent anyone else from seeing that which they consider blasphemous or to punish or harm the blasphemer.

We have all seen in recent years that Christians in Pakistan, Sudan and elsewhere live under the threat of denunciation and execution for blasphemy and apostasy. That is what Sharia law means today in some Islamic states. It was the same in Christian Europe up until the Enlightenment. The savagery of the Inquisition and the torture and burning of heretics was a characteristic of the Christian equivalent of Sharia. So also was the orthodoxy of antisemitism.

We in the West have been spoon-fed a history of Christianity that sometimes bears little or no relation to reality. Far from being noble, the crusades were a shocking, evil episode in the history of the Roman Church. It was not only in the Holy Land that violence, slavery, torture and burning was the means of bring Christ's message to the heathen and the pagan. The natives of the newly 'discovered' Americas were also savagely converted to the love of Christ.

One way or another, every single one of us is an 'infidel' in the eyes of someone, somewhere. Since that is axiomatic, we should, I think, reflect on what it means for our own society now.

In Ireland, North and South, we seem at long last to have moved on from oppression, hatred and violence against our own infidels. We are well down the road to the creation of a tolerant, secular republican state and society where the religious and philosophical liberties of all citizens are respected and guaranteed. There is a way to be travelled yet – North and South – on the road to tolerance, respect and inclusion.

We should always remember our own recent and distant history in our dealings with others. Aggressive secularism today may in future be seen as equally oppressive as the aggressive sectarianism and confessional-ism of the past. Respectful secularism threatens nobody.

On the gay marriage referendum, I think there is also need for tolerance and honesty. I support the referendum as a means of bringing about a culture of respect and inclusivity. I personally cannot see how in reality – as opposed to theory – gay marriage 'weakens' marriage for everyone else or the individual marriage of anyone else. I do not see how civil partnership has done any harm at all to marriage and I am glad that I was able to push-start the process that led to civil partnership when I was in government.

I have, however, feared and felt that the opponents of gay marriage would ultimately fasten on a concern for the 'interests of the child' as a ground for rejecting marriage equality for gays. And so it is turning out.

As respectfully as I can, I want to express my sincere doubt that 'concern for the child' is the real issue for many moral conservatives. I think it is more of a construct designed to win an argument rather than a real, heartfelt concern for any individual child.

The 'ideal' of a child being raised by a father and a mother is that – an ideal. Many children are raised in circumstances which are far from ideal. But there are many, many children who are given a loving childhood in a family where both of their parents are not part of their family.

Many moral conservatives might also ask themselves whether they themselves were as 'concerned for the interests of the child' when they opposed the legalisation of contraception or the ending of illegitimacy or the referendum to allow for the adoption of the children of married people.

It was, by the way, striking to hear Pope Francis expressing – again rather clumsily – his concern about people irresponsibly multiplying like rabbits but still defending the generally discredited doctrine on birth control found in *Humanae Vitae*. Something has to give – some day.

It seems to me that we need to be respectful and generous to each other in our social and political discourse. But that does not mean self-censorship. Honesty and tolerance are not enemies.

Conservative and reactionary forces in the Roman Catholic church wonder whether the Pope is a Catholic

12 August 2018

Pope Francis, despite his unflappable, affable demeanour, is locked in a bitter struggle with conservative and reactionary forces in the

Roman Catholic Church who have since conducted a sometimes mutinous campaign to curb him.

While hundreds of thousands of Irish Catholics are eagerly and enthusiastically awaiting his visit, a vociferous minority of Irish church traditionalists, egged on by American reactionaries, are also waiting for him – but in the long grass.

Just as 'birthers' questioned whether Barack Obama was an American-born citizen or a Muslim, these reactionaries use social media and blogs to question not merely the orthodoxy of Francis, but whether some of his statements and actions are actually heretical.

For them the old humorous question 'Is the Pope a Catholic?' is no longer a joke at all. They really wonder whether he is in fact a Catholic.

Last year, four cardinals, Carlo Caffarra, an Italian, Raymond Burke, an American with Irish roots, and Walter Brandmüller and Joachim Meisner, from Germany, had written five *'dubia'* – formalised doubts on whether the Pope's recent encyclical document on love and the family, *Amoris laetitia*, is conformable with the Church's immutable teaching.

In essence, they claim that a divorced and remarried Catholic who maintains a conjugal relationship with his or her second spouse is committing adultery, that such sex is therefore intrinsically evil and a mortal sin so as to exclude that Catholic from receiving communion.

The Pope, on the other hand, had written that it was not a simple 'black and white' issue; he urged pastors to address the subjective complexity of the situation of such Catholics, and suggested that there should be no absolute exclusion from the Eucharist for such persons.

The *dubia* are but the visible manifestation of a deeper battle for the 'soul' of the Catholic Church. Pope Francis understood that and wisely decided to ignore the *dubia* – much to the doubting cardinals' chagrin.

The same Cardinal Burke rejects nearly all of the *aggiornamenti* of the Second Vatican Council. He keeps company internationally, including here in Ireland, with Catholics who reject the use of the vernacular in the liturgy, who disapprove of the priest facing the congregation, who prefer the Latin mass, who disapprove of women acting as ministers of the Eucharist and girls as altar servers, who disapprove of receiving the host in the hand, and who basically want to revert to the pre-conciliar rites, sacraments and teachings of the Catholic Church.

For them, the rot set in when the post-conciliar Vatican failed to deal firmly and swiftly with the intellectual rebellion by theologians, clergy and faithful against *Humanae Vitae* which affirmed that artificial birth control for family planning purposes was intrinsically evil and sinful, while the use of thermometers and charts was not.

Far from being content just to defend the status quo against demands by Mary McAleese and many others for the ordination of women and for married clergy, and for the acceptance of LGBTI persons as members of an inclusive Church, these reactionary Catholics want to turn back the clock completely, to re-establish the Church of their youth, and to have little or nothing to do with modernism, another heresy.

So the Pope's visit to the World Meeting of Families in Dublin is not simply an occasion for debating demands of liberal, progressive Catholics for a change in the Church's attitudes to issues of sexual morality and gender equality; Catholic conservatives are running an alternative conference in Dublin for 'Catholic Families' to be addressed by video-link by reactionary prelates such as Cardinal Burke, a conference which will condemn liberalism in all its manifestations.

Lumen Fidei, the organisers of the alternative Catholic Families conference in Dublin, have been using their well-produced fortnightly newspaper, *Catholic Voice*, to fan flames of dissatisfaction with the World Meeting of Families.

The *Catholic Voice* recently revealed to its readers that the 'first liberal' was none other than Lucifer, and that his doctrines have been espoused by a series of well-known figures including Nero, Genghis Khan, Stalin, Hitler and, wait for it, Hillary Clinton.

The Catholic Families conference will also be addressed by John Smeaton of SPUC who has openly accused Pope Francis's *Amoris laetitia* of propagating heresy.

When the Pope has returned to Rome, the galactic battle will resume. Conservative and reactionary Catholics across the world, not least in the US, regard Francis as a temporary aberration into heterodoxy, error and heresy which will mercifully end with his death or resignation, which can't come soon enough.

They confidently believe that the next conclave of cardinals will not make the mistake of electing someone in the mould of Francis or John XXIII. And it is probable that their expectations will then be rewarded.

Francis, by the way, is no radical intent on a second Reformation. He is, in reality, quite conservative. But he wants to save the Roman Catholic Church from the clutches of reactionaries and absolutists who are intent on driving it over a cliff on a policy of 'making the Vatican great again'.

His reactionary opponents, when he is gone, will probably find it far easier to bully the Vatican establishment into going backwards than Mary McAleese will find it easy to drive the Church forward to the changes she articulates.

It was, after all, John Paul II who, as Karol Wojtyla, Archbishop of Krakow, in 1967 privately implored the then pope, Paul VI, from behind the Iron Curtain to reject the report of a papal commission that had recommended the church to change its position on contraception. He later wrote after the publication of *Humanae Vitae* urging the pope to crack down on dissidence among the clergy and the faithful and to explicitly elevate the doctrine as infallible teaching.

Thus, when, as John Paul II, he visited Ireland ten years later, the damage done was already beginning to show through the cracks. The innocence and naivety of the young so graphically recorded at his Ballybrit event, where Eamon Casey and Michael Cleary were his unforgettable warm-up act, seems like a different world.

Francis, apparently, has also established a 'study group' on *Humanae Vitae* which will almost certainly not reverse it but will seek to create an interpretative moral flexibility on family planning.

It is exactly that possibility which the absolutists are determined to prevent.

They see the whole Church edifice threatened by any acknowledgment of previous doctrinal error or by any acceptance of conscience-based moral relativism.

It is a dogma (or an error itself, as many think) which has simply made prisoners of the entire clerical Church – from Pope down to priest – but not of the laity.

When Bishop Kevin Doran of Elphin ran the standard of *Humanae Vitae* up the flagpole again last week, Simon Harris implored him to 'stop it'. Fat chance.

These clerics are waging an existential, spiritual battle in a different dimension from the merely 'transient' issues of child abuse, married or female clergy, or contraception.

They are fighting a destructive all-out civil war for control of ideas and dogma while their all-too-human institution disintegrates before our eyes.

The Definite Article: RELIGION AND SOCIAL AFFAIRS

The worst is not over for the institutional Church in Ireland

4 January 2023

A friend commented that there was a remarkable difference in the amount of media attention devoted to the death of Pele compared with the death of Pope Emeritus Benedict XV. In modern times the idea of a pope resigning the see of Rome was unheard of until now.

Time was when Radio Éireann would suspend normal programming and play solemn music instead to mark the death of a pope. There was huge interest and widespread public understanding in Ireland of the detailed process of succession to the papacy. Schoolboys would collect special *sede vacante* postage stamps issued by the Vatican post office.

But now that is all changed. The vast majority of the younger generation have little or no interest in or knowledge of the Vatican's affairs except perhaps what they might glean from watching *The Godfather III*'s unflattering depiction of ecclesiastical scandal in Rome.

On the ground, the Irish Catholic Church is visibly withering. Mass attendance has slumped and the Covid pandemic added to the rate of decline in overt religious practice among Irish Catholics. In rural Ireland, parishes are being grouped together so that Sunday masses are shared on a rotating basis among grouped parish churches. Decline in the number of priests and vocations seems irreversible.

And it seems that the worst is not over for the institutional Church. Recent exposure of sexual abuse of pupils by priests and teachers in schools run by religious orders has given rise to a political commitment to establishing some form of public inquiry.

It is thought that a scoping exercise on the nature and extent of such an inquiry will commence soon. That scoping process will itself be interesting. How many other religious orders than the

Spiritans should be within an inquiry's scope? Can there be any case for excluding Christian Brothers, Jesuits, Carmelites, Franciscans, Dominicans, Salesians and other orders from inquiry? Will it extend to lay teachers? Will it extend to children abused abroad where known or suspected abusers were exiled to the missions to prevent abuse and scandal in Ireland? Will it extend to religious redeployed from education to other functions?

Will such an inquiry deal with the issue of knowledge of such abuse by the Irish and Vatican hierarchies? What about state knowledge – departmental and prosecutorial? Will its proceedings be held in public or in private?

One thing is clear; any prospect of providing a report within two or three years will depend entirely on the architecture of any inquiry.

The Commission of Investigation into clerical abuse by the clergy of the Dublin archdiocese's report was widely seen as a great success. But Judge Yvonne Murphy was required by its terms of reference to inquire in private into a small sample of cases where priests were accused of abuse.

A newspaper recently reported that the Jesuit order in Ireland had already paid €6.4 million to victims of abuse. Presumably that sum cannot all have been paid to the ten victims of the only named abuser, the deceased Father Joseph Marmion, who came forward. It suggests many more victims and some more perpetrators.

Will all victims want to go public in the same way that some brave victims of Spiritan abuse have done? Can an inquiry held in public name perpetrators – suspected or proven – while affording complete privacy to victims?

The Mother and Baby Homes Commission of Investigation became controversial precisely because it deviated from the purpose of the Commissions of Investigation Act to provide for a confidential committee process to enable all comers without limit to put their experiences as victims on record, while dealing with a sample of homes for the purposes of the main inquiry. Judge Murphy and her fellow commissioners were criticised – I think unfairly – for not conducting some form of remedial process for the cruelly treated women and children cast out from a hypocritical social community.

People demand a rights-based approach to inquiries. People propose a victim-led inquiry. If inquiries are designed to bring closure and healing to victims, and if they are victim-led, are they in some sense drifting into social theatre rather than wholly impartial ascertainment of truth?

The Commissions of Investigation Act 2004, which I introduced as justice minister, was never intended to be a social theatre or a healing mechanism for historical wrongs.

That is why we need clarity now. A massively lengthy, comprehensive and expensive inquiry into all sexual abuse of religious secondary school pupils may be less useful than a focused, sample-based inquiry. That is a banana skin decision for politicians.

For the Catholic Church in Ireland, and for all the decent religious who gave their lives to doing good, there seems to be no good news on the horizon.

Will the visit of Pope Francis actually change anything?

26 August 2018

When Francis returns to the Vatican, will he leave behind a different Ireland? Will he be returning to a changing institutional Church? Does his visit amount to some form of watershed in the relationship between the Irish people and their State and the Roman Catholic Church?

Or will his short visit amount to a brief episode in a long-term, irreversible historical process of transformation both within the Catholic Church and between that Church and the Irish people?

Will the visit of Pope Francis actually change anything?

The first question is whether this papal visit will have any greater outcome for Ireland than the visit of Pope John Paul II in 1979. To answer that question, one must first consider whether the 1979 papal visit actually had any significant lasting effect on Ireland and the Irish.

In truth, it is very difficult to argue that the 1979 visit changed Ireland or that Irish history would have been significantly different if John Paul had decided not to come to Ireland.

Did the youth meeting at Ballybrit halt the decline in religious practice among the young – a decline that had started well before the visit? Was there a surge in vocations? Did religious practice rebound? Did the Irish Catholic Church itself change? The answer to these questions must, in truth, be in the negative.

So it is very difficult to see how this Pope, a very different man from John Paul, is going to change Ireland, the Irish or the Irish Catholic Church by this visit, or even to see how the World Meeting of Families in Dublin can have any lasting transformative effect.

With Irish Catholic bishops openly predicting a contracting role for the institutional Church – a 'smaller Church' – in Irish society, there is little or no optimism for any form of recovery in the political or social status of the Church.

But that is only half the question. There is another more important issue.

Accepting that the Church will be smaller, what kind of smaller Church will it be?

Is there within the male, clerical, institutional church any real appetite or capacity for reform? Is Church teaching or doctrine going to change? Or is the male hierarchical Church as we know it condemned to fossilisation as an institution and as a set of beliefs?

A shrinking Church may, on one view, refuse reform and see itself as needing to get 'back to basics', reverting to the doctrines, beliefs and practices of a century ago, content to weather the storm.

On another view, the Catholic Church, confronted with what appears to be an inexorable decline in the developed world, may choose to migrate spiritually to the developing world – a less sceptical audience – as its future theatre of operations.

While the various scandals have rocked the institutional Church in the eyes of the developed world, we should recall that the process of decline started before these scandals came to the fore. In Quebec, for instance, the decline in Catholic religious practice started in the 1960s and progressed just as far as it has later done in Ireland in the last few decades.

The scandals are perhaps catalysts which boost the speed of decline; the decline cannot be wholly or even mainly explained by them.

Strangely, it may be the case that it was the decline in practice and belief that brought the scandals out into the open rather than the reverse. After all, the community served by the Magdalene laundries knew all about them but averted its gaze because it readily accepted the 'morality' that placed women there.

While the Catholic faithful subjected themselves unquestioningly to the authority of the clerical Church, the scandals could remain hidden.

As the Church saw it, the greater sin by far – the sin of scandal-giving – lay in bringing the depravity, the corruption, and the wrongdoing to the attention of the innocent faithful in a way that might damage or imperil their innocence, and their faith in, and their obedience to, the Church itself.

Secrecy and '*suppressio veri*' were viewed as virtuous if deployed in the interests of the Church itself and for the avoidance of scandal.

So while the growing mass of evidence of the Church covering up its scandals now dominates the horizon, not least in the recent Pennsylvania Grand Jury report, the Catholic Church's problems run deeper than the scandals and the cover-ups; the Church's difficulties stem from the intrinsic nature of the institutional, clerical Church itself.

What chance has Francis of reforming the institutional Church?

To answer that, we need to look at a few issues that stand in the way of reform.

Perhaps the biggest stumbling block or what may turn out to be the millstone around the neck of the institutional Church is its self-idolatry as expressed in its claims to being the exclusive means of salvation and its claims to be infallible. This proud self-image prevents it from humbly admitting and addressing institutional error and sin.

Rome thinks it cannot do a U-turn on contraception because of the papal encyclicals *Casti Connubii* and *Humane Vitae*. Any thinking person can see that there is no logical connection between Christian belief and prohibiting contraception. But two popes solemnly pronounced that 'artificial' contraception infringes God's law and the natural law and is intrinsically evil and sinful.

Only a male, celibate and entirely fallible institution could have made that mistake.

Can a male, celibate and self-professedly infallible institution now humbly admit that it got contraception wrong?

Can such a male, celibate and self-professedly infallible institution humbly admit that a believing Christian may be fully part of that institution although divorced and happily remarried?

Interestingly, I recently discovered that the members of the powerful political lay body, the Catholic Committee, in Dublin in the 1790s not merely repudiated the idea of papal infallibility but secured the concurrence of the then Catholic archbishop of Dublin in a formal rejection of the theory.

The promulgation of papal infallibility in 1870 was controversial even then. It seems indefensible now just as it did to Dublin's Catholic Committee in the 1790s. It is a doctrinal claim that hangs from its own bootlaces and one which is seriously damaging to the Catholic Church in its behaviour and attitudes.

Reformists such as the We Are Church movement and Mary McAleese make an almost unanswerable case for ending the discrimination against women in the institutional Church. Surveys suggest that most Catholics agree with them.

But that also raises the question: 'Exactly what would persuade the institutional Church in Rome to treat men and women equally?'

It seems to me that the present existential threat to the Catholic church's survival is not yet seen in Rome as a reason to consider such a reform. Many members of the male hierarchy would, it seems, prefer to do down with the ship than allow priests to marry or women to become priests.

The Catholic doctrinal obsession with sexuality, sexual morality, and their exaltation of celibacy, purity and virginity are all part of a piece with the circumstances that have given us the abuse scandals, the cover-ups and the self-destructive behaviour of the hierarchical Church.

I find it hard to believe that a non-celibate hierarchical clergy could condemn contraception as intrinsically evil and sinful.

Even Paul the Evangelist, who seems to have preferred a subordinate role for women in the early churches, wrote in his First Letter to Timothy urging that the bishops in those churches should be married!

But the Roman hierarchy prefers to ignore both scripture and the views of the laity and many brave clergy by insisting not merely on clerical celibacy – well, at least in the Western Church – but in prohibiting the clergy from discussing the issue at all!

It is all very well for a liberal priest, Father James Martin SJ, to point out at the World Meeting that the Catholic Church is treating gay people like lepers. But does the Catholic Church in Ireland require of teachers that they instruct pupils in Catholic secondary schools that their gay classmates are disordered and that acting on their orientation at any point in their lives will be intrinsically evil and merit eternal damnation? Or do they realise that such a doctrine is absurd and unchristian in the eyes of those pupils?

And will anyone in Rome listen to and respect and respond to those who applauded Father Martin's speech?

Irish views of what is right and wrong, tolerable and intolerable, and Christian and unchristian, are in many respects diverging from the views of the Roman Catholic institutional Church. The State and the people no longer see the institutional Church as holy and authoritative in the way their parents and grandparents saw it.

Francis is one human being. He is surrounded by a hierarchical institution of men who are not attracted to reform, who believe that they collectively are guided by God in their decisions and practices, who believe that they are entitled to the obedience of the faithful, and believe that they are axiomatically incapable of collective error.

Francis seems a kindly and intelligent man. He wasn't invited here for a dressing-down. He wasn't invited to be confronted with disbelief or disputation. He knows some of the problems. His critics don't know many of his problems.

There are profound questions for Ireland too.

Is the contracting, smaller future Church going to abandon its role in education, welfare, and health? Are these areas to be the theatre of operations for the all-powerful State alone? Is social voluntarism and philanthropic initiative to wither and die with mass religious practice? Is social morality to be the mere ghost of religious morality?

These few days bring these issues into focus. But resolving them will take more than a few days.

———

The Definite Article: RELIGION AND SOCIAL AFFAIRS

Sex education shouldn't be taught on a take-it-or-leave-it basis

2 October 2024

A controversy is brewing over the content of the Social Personal and Health (SPHE) curriculum and materials intended for use in the Junior Cycle post-primary years for young teenagers. Some commentators are extremely concerned about the underlying value system that is or is not present in the teaching of the subject.

The SPHE courses are closely connected with Relationships and Sex Education (RSE). Early adolescents are undergoing profound peri-pubertal development, physically and psychologically. The SPHE programme is stated to be one which is non-judgemental, supportive and empowering.

Inevitably, the whole area of what is now termed 'gender ideology' is engaged. What early adolescent children are taught or not taught in this area is a matter of legitimate concern. The perspective of such education is important. Are there values involved? What are those values? Can such a programme of education be value-driven and non-judgemental at the same time?

Is gender identity a matter of choice in whole or in part? Are early adolescents in a good position either individually or in educational groupings to evaluate their choices? Is pedagogical affirmation of choices being considered a necessary or helpful aspect of school education?

Is group study of sexual activities in the context of classroom SPHE needed? Are 12- to 15-year-old children sharing a single classroom all in the same position of maturity to address such issues? What should they be told about gender identity? Are there, as the Department of Justice now seems to believe, if the hate speech Bill is proceeded with, a multiplicity of genders? Are children to be taught that such a multiplicity of genders exists and if so, what are the main genders other than male and female? One government spokesperson suggested that there were nine genders, but nobody has defined or described rather than enumerated them.

These are areas where parents have a legitimate concern and interest in relation to their children's education. That much is stated to be part of our fundamental law – in the Constitution. Article 42 of the Constitution lays down some important principles which need to be borne in mind.

Parents are stated in that article to be the 'primary and natural educators' of the child and to have an 'inalienable right and duty' to provide for the religious, moral, intellectual, physical and social education of their children.

Since parents are also assured under Article 42 of their constitutional right to provide for the education of their children 'in their homes or in private schools or in schools recognised or established by the State' and not to be obliged 'in violation of their conscience and lawful preference' to send their children to state schools or to 'types of school designated by the State', it seems to follow that they have a right to be consulted, at the very least, as to the nature of SPHE programmes to be followed in relation to their children.

Of course, there is an irony that such constitutional guarantees co-existed with a virtual Catholic monopoly for most families in post primary education for a century of post-independent Ireland. There many were taught of the very graphic nature of an eternity in hell for adolescents who died in a state of mortal sin because of their impure thoughts or actions.

The terror and shame that posed as SPHE education in those days was undoubtedly deeply harmful to young adolescents. Catholic parents had no real choice to protect their children from such harm.

The issue, as I see it, is not one where schools must either say or do nothing in the areas of SPHE or RSE, on the one hand, or teach a curriculum to which many or most parents profoundly object, on the other hand. As I see it, schools receiving state assistance do owe parents a constitutional respect as to what is or is not taught to early adolescent children in the SPHE or RSE areas.

It cannot be that one family can veto what is taught to the children of all other families. But it does seem sensible, and, indeed, constitutional, that schools reach out to parents to seek a broad consensus on the approach adopted in these matters. If individual families wish to opt out of such programmes, their reasonable wishes should be accommodated or respected.

That is why we must be careful that an agenda is not set by activists or ideologists on a 'one size fits all' basis for schools across the nation. The State is not all-knowing or authoritative in these matters in the twenty-first century in the way that church educators claimed to be in the twentieth century.

Parents arguably wrongly abdicated their inalienable constitutional duties for the most part in relation to their children's RSE teaching to religious denominations in the past. In an increasingly post-denominational secular society, there is a need for parental involvement to reassert itself and be respected.

A level-headed public debate on these issues is badly needed.

Trans rights: a case for reasonableness and common sense

20 July 2022

I have nothing but complete empathy for any person who finds themselves having to confront a deep-seated conviction that their ostensible physical sex does not correspond with their gender. That self-understanding or conviction is not a matter of sexual orientation – conveniently divided by some into heterosexual, bisexual and homosexual. Orientation or attraction varies among people with gender dysphoria as much as it does with all other people.

Moreover, I also accept that many trans people endure a great deal of profoundly painful rejection and/or suspicion from those who neither understand nor empathise in any way with their situation. They naturally see such rejection as a form of discrimination and, moreover, an unjust discrimination that infringes their human rights.

And that is where things become complex. Current thinking favours elimination of all forms of discrimination on the ground that it necessarily involves inequality.

But that raises the question as to whether society or the Irish Constitution is bound by anti-discriminatory principles to regard everyone for all purposes simply as a human citizen with an innate human right to self-identify as male, female, fluid, transgender, or, indeed, non-gendered.

I incline to the view that for the vast majority of citizens, distinction based on ostensible physical sex is very important in many but not all aspects of our social existence. Sex cannot simply be wished away as a concept or as a social reality. The growth of women's equality as a strong anti-discriminatory movement in the last hundred years demonstrates that distinction between ostensible physical sex is hugely important. While legal and economic inequality for women is being tackled with varying degrees of success, the demands from within the trans community for the large-scale dismantling of distinction based on ostensible physical sex is not necessarily a common cause with feminism.

Take, for instance, sport. In some, but not all, areas of competitive sport, women wish to compete separately from men. This is not a relic of outdated ideology but is based on an obvious truth – that men are physically more likely to win than women in sports like running, rugby, all kinds of football, swimming, wrestling, boxing and many others.

To require people with objectively male physiques to compete against other such people and people with objectively female physiques to compete with other such people is only fair if that is the way that the great majority of competitors want. Achieving such objective athletic fairness and justice, I think, trumps any sense of injustice that a person born with a male body and identifying as a woman may feel if excluded from competing in an all-women's event.

Does that mean that we prohibit gender self-identification for all purposes? I don't think so. If a person I previously assumed was male tells me that he wants to be dealt with as she or her, perhaps good manners and empathy requires me to do that. Those who wish to signal their preferred mode of address should be free to do so.

But it does not, in my opinion, mean that we all must adopt gender-neutral language such as 'chest-feeding', 'men with wombs', 'people who menstruate' and the like, in order to spare the feelings of some of those with gender dysphoria.

In the end it is a question of reasonableness and common sense. I think that the great majority of people would happily legislate to ensure that identity documents can easily be changed to accommodate the genuine wishes of people with gender dysphoria. By the same token, many people may not want to end gender-based changing rooms and bathroom facilities in all cases or to legally require further such facilities for transgender people.

For the great, great majority, gender-based language, thought, concepts and social convention are really part of what we are – just as central to our personalities as the identity convictions of trans people are to them. It isn't a question of thoughtlessness.

That trans people experience rejection as a consequence of our civilisation's social recognition and distinctions of sex and gender does not confer on them an absolute human right to erase gendered thought and language on a widespread basis.

While anyone can cite statistics, studies tend to suggest that adult dysphoria is very rare, and much rarer in people born women than men.

I sense that there is a real danger for transgender people that ideological activism by a tiny minority may lose them the goodwill and empathy of the great majority. That would be a pity.

A caring consensus on gender issues requires broad national discussion

8 March 2023

The HSE now proposes to develop a new policy in relation to gender dysphoria, transgender issues and the availability and access to gender transition counselling and medical treatment.

This raises the immediate question as to who or what the HSE is at present. It is an executive agency of the State with wide responsibilities in the provision of public health services. But it is by no means clear that the board of the HSE is competent to evolve national policy on gender issues.

There have been repeated calls for proper parliamentary consideration of these issues based on reflective debate. That seems more urgent than ever.

The great majority of Irish people are not activists in relation to gender issues. But the airwaves and newspaper columns seem to be dominated by activists who seek to frame the discussion in terms of the denial of human rights and discrimination against the small minority who have dysphoria or who consider themselves to be 'gender fluid' or who argue that the conventional male/female binary gender distinctions in society are oppressive or unjust.

For my part, I am very sympathetic to anyone who is experiencing gender dysphoria. I think most people are.

That does not mean discussion of these issues must be conducted only in the vocabulary or with the conceptual understanding of those activists. I have difficulty accepting that there are many genders; I readily accept that there are shades of gender.

Gender is important. Maleness and femaleness are realities for the great majority of people, including gay and lesbian people. The great majority is not obliged morally to simply discard fundamental social and psychological concepts such as masculinity or femininity because a minority find those concepts limiting, challenging or even offensive.

The linguistic chaos of using the plural pronoun to describe a single individual is, I think, contrived. Most people have no problem with addressing someone by their chosen name or dealing with them on the basis of their chosen gender identity. But using a plural pronoun with a single verb stretches, confuses and distorts meaning.

The idea of a broad LGBTQI+ coalition is fine. But I have been struck by the number of gay men and lesbian women who privately dissociate themselves from some of the demands of trans activists. One can readily appreciate a sense of mutual loyalty among members of the broad LGBTQI+ movement, which has won huge advances in equality for gay and lesbian men and women. One can sympathise with the idea that these successes should leave no one behind. But surely there is at the same time nothing wrong with straight, lesbian or bisexual women wanting to pursue feminist agendas on the basis of gender as they see it.

Particularly, as regards dysphoria among minors, we must be very careful and protective of children. Pre-pubertal, peri-pubertal and post-pubertal children are transitioning into adulthood. Adolescence is a psychologically challenging time for many children. We cannot simply expose children to a random lottery of ideologies or treatments in the light of what went wrong at the Tavistock clinic.

A caring consensus on gender issues requires broad national discussion

The emergence of transgender issues on social media in the last decade seems to have created a much greater interest among adolescent children in gender identity.

There is little evidence that there has been significant use of conversion therapy in Ireland for children with homosexual orientation, and all children must be legally protected from conversion therapy as we have seen it in the US.

At the same time, children may or may not be experiencing long-term gender dysphoria. They may be experiencing different temporary uncertainties about their gender orientation or about their own personalities or identities.

The Tavistock clinic experience highlights the risks and dangers of irreversible and inappropriate interventions, from puberty blockers to reconstructive surgery, for highly vulnerable minors and for their parents.

At a recent highly informative briefing in Leinster House, Irish experts from the National Gender Service reported a very high correlation between adolescents and young adults seeking to transition and autism. It is not simply good enough to dismiss that correlation by saying that young people with autism have the same rights as anyone else. Of course they do. This correlation needs to be explored and understood.

In developing policy on trans gender health services, we badly need a fact-based objective approach which is firmly rooted in care, consultation, and counselling. We need a national, inclusive debate.

This is not just a matter for the HSE. Nor is it a matter only for activists. It is a matter for all citizens and all politicians to devise good policies.

For that to happen there must be a broadly based national discussion where nobody fears condemnation or cancelling and from which, hopefully, a caring and careful consensus emerges.

The Definite Article: RELIGION AND SOCIAL AFFAIRS

Quidditch falls to earth in a show of intolerance

22 December 2021

It being the festive season and goodwill abounding, I have decided to skate out on thin ice and to raise the alarming news that the powers that be in the sport of quidditch have apparently decided to consider renaming their game in an attempt to distance themselves from what they consider to be transphobic utterances by J.K. Rowling, the author of the Harry Potter books.

Quidditch, for the small minority who need to be told, is an imaginary game played in Hogwarts school by its pupils – young magicians – and features players swooping about on magic broomsticks and scoring points by derring-do – a little like aerial polo players. Rowling has elaborated on quidditch in a separate book entitled *Quidditch through the Ages.*

Apparently, youngish adults across the world – mostly college students – have adapted the imaginary game into a faintly ridiculous form in which they play an earthbound version on a pitch and must at all times carry a broomstick between their legs as they canter about competing for points. This terrestrial form of quidditch is sometimes known as muggle quidditch – muggles being Rowling's term for humans who lack magical powers.

Quidditch players – like their imaginary Rowling characters – play a mixed game, open to both genders. A bit like tag rugby games, I suppose. However, they have a 'four maximum rule' which prohibits a team from having more than four players of either gender (excluding the 'seeker') on the pitch at any time. This rule is complicated by other rules that entitle a player to choose either gender or none. The quidditch sport compliments itself for its gender inclusivity.

So far, so good.

But then Jo – as J.K. Rowling is known to her friends – went and spoiled it all. She queried online the use of the phrase 'people who menstruate' as a woke term for biological women of a certain age.

Suddenly, she was engulfed in torrid controversy. She stood what she considered to be her ground and stated:

If sex isn't real, there's no same-sex attraction. If sex isn't real, the lived reality of women globally is erased. I know and love trans people, but erasing the concept of sex removes the ability of many to meaningfully discuss their lives. The idea that women like me, who've been empathetic to trans people for decades, feeling kinship because they're vulnerable in the same way as women – i.e. to male violence – 'hate' trans people because they think sex is real and has lived consequences – is a nonsense.

Many people might have thought that this clearly and adequately explained her views in inoffensive terms and that that might have been the end of the matter. Nobody had to agree with her, after all.

But it wasn't the end of the matter. The Maya Forstater case in which Ms Forstater successfully appealed a decision of a tribunal employment judge for holding that her dismissal for a series of tweets questioning government plans (which were not proceeded with) to let people declare their own gender was unacceptable, became another battleground for J.K. Rowling and her critics.

The tribunal judge had held that Ms Forstater was 'absolutist' in her view and did not have the right to ignore the rights of transgender persons and the 'enormous pain that can be caused by misgendering'. In the High Court, however, it was held that Ms Forstater's views 'did not seek to destroy the rights of trans persons'.

Rowling now reiterated her position. One of her online critics tweeted as follows: 'Do NOT read #JK Rowling's transphobic manifesto. I already did it for you. Every line is misinformation, fearmongering, misgendering, othering, ignorance, far-right language/

dog whistles, and pure hate. It's not just ugly. This is HATE. Don't ingest this BS. I beg you.'

Last year, by contrast, the conservative newspaper *Catholic Voice* was warning Irish parents against the malign anti-religious influence of Harry Potter books. This year, woke activists are shunning Rowling because she has stood by her own views on the reality of gender and on the limits of concepts such as self-identification in gender for many areas of life, including language and sport.

The faintly ridiculous decision of the international quidditch community to rename their gravity-bound broomstick sport in order to demonstrate gender inclusivity is but another instance of the growth of caustic intolerance and cancellation in our social and political debate.

Many people are empathetic to their fellow citizens whose lives are deeply affected by transgender and gender fluidity issues. But should those who consider themselves to be victims of social indifference or discrimination also have the sole right to proscribe language in which other kind-hearted citizens carry on conventional life as offensive or unlawful?

There is, after all, a large difference between giving offence and taking offence. Free speech is important for us all – not just for those who would decide the rights of others while bestride their broomsticks.

Why stop with Berkeley? Cicero was a slave owner too

3 May 2023

Trinity College is an independent university and is as free to name, rename or de-name any part of its campus as any other Irish university.

Given that the Berkeley Library was only built in the 1960s and was quite recently described by the college on its 50th anniversary as a 'brutalist gem' in architectural terms, its name is hardly one of the institution's ancient items of heritage. The other modern libraries in Trinity are named after Ussher and Lecky.

James Ussher, a scholarly bishop historian, wrote in 1626: 'The religion of the Papists is superstitious and idolatrous: their faith and doctrine erroneous and heretical ... to give them therefore a toleration, or to consent that they may freely exercise their religions ... is a grievous sin.'

Lecky, a nineteenth-century historian and opponent of Home Rule, was a deal more tolerant of Papists but nevertheless wrote that Catholicism was 'on the whole a lower type of religion than Protestantism, and it is particularly unsuited to a nation struggling with great difficulties'.

That George Berkeley owned a small slave plantation in New England in the early eighteenth century and felt no moral qualm is hardly a startling revelation for a student of history. George Washington was a slave owner at the end of that century.

And even if the library is de-named and renamed, the name of Berkeley is still going to apply to the Californian city and university called after him.

The problem with zealous cancellation of historical figures is that it is completely unhistorical in a broader sense. Do we think less of Cicero because he, like most prominent Romans, was a slave-owner in a slave-owning society? Or do we simply say that most historical figures must be judged in their historical context?

I think that there is very good reason to connect contemporary attitudes to slavery with modern racial discrimination against Black people.

Nobody now cares much about papal galleys in the Mediterranean being rowed by Muslim slaves four centuries ago. Indeed, Christianity had a long-lasting philosophical discourse about whether the enslavement of Christians was morally defensible while ignoring the moral issues in relation to the enslavement of people they regarded as heathens or pagans. Outright Christian condemnation of all slavery took a long time to emerge.

There is a real difference, I think, between Americans adorning their cities with statues of Confederate generals and the decision of the Fellows of Trinity sixty years ago to name their 'brutalist gem' library after George Berkeley.

The difference is the message that was intended. I doubt anyone in Trinity intended to cause offence to Catholics or to approbate the injustices of the Penal Laws when commemorating Berkeley, Ussher and Lecky. Nor were any Catholics offended by commemoration of Trinity's liberal, Protestant origins and heritage, I imagine. If anyone wants to go prospecting for offence, they will find some nuggets in the writings of Berkeley, Ussher and Lecky.

But commemorating and glorifying the American Confederacy by monument in the post-Civil War era of reconstruction and Jim Crow laws had – and still has – an unmistakable message and meaning for Black Americans. It is about current racist attitudes and discrimination.

What about the UK? The whole British imperialist project was based on subjugation of other peoples justified by a theory of racial superiority and entitlement. The 'guilty few' are not just those who ran slave ships or slave plantations. The entire British economy depended for its few imperial centuries on racial subjugation, of which the Atlantic slave trade was just one very barbaric example.

Distancing Sinn Féin in 1919 from John Redmond's stated ambition to make the British Empire 'our empire' for the Irish, Eoin Mac Néill described imperialism thus:

It takes to itself a body made up of predatory feudalism and predatory capitalism, of oligarchies seeking to dominate the earth given to the millions to inhabit and the industry exerted by the millions to make the earth inhabitable – in short to enslave the world.

Fintan O'Toole rightly drew our attention this week to repugnant racist and pro-slavery writings of the Young Ireland patriot John Mitchel, which have been hiding in plain sight across a century of his commemoration and deification in Ireland. Even this paper (then strongly pro-Unionist) wrote on his death in 1875 that Mitchel 'descended into the grave without bringing the shadow of a stain on the fair name of his ancestors'. But asking young Black Irish GAA members today to join a club bearing Mitchel's name could be seen as cruel.

I side with Diarmuid Ferriter in questioning Trinity's wisdom in de-naming the Berkeley library. Arguments for cancellation of some names and monuments may have validity in the US but may lack it in Ireland.

The removal and later reinstatement of the Shelbourne Hotel statues on the erroneous suspicion that they were slaves should cause us to take a long-term reflective view of history.

Sanitising Britain's imperialist past would require collective amnesia

24 June 2020

Many people will find themselves somewhat emotionally torn by the sight of statues being toppled and defaced by angry, if self-appointed, modern iconoclasts.

On the one hand, George Floyd's cruel murder has started a long-delayed and hugely needed confrontation by America with the reality of its shameful anti-black political, economic, penal and social discrimination and subjugation, a process that has sent ripples across the world.

Removing monuments to the Confederacy and its politicians that proliferate in America and ending the provocative use of their flag is, I think, a justifiable symbolic reaction and expression of pent-up sense of injustice in relation to the cruel mass relegation of American blacks to second-class citizenship and social inferiority. The erection of those statues in the past and the use of those flags in the present represent an implied approbation, in some way, of the Confederacy's legitimacy. For most black Americans, they connote white ambivalence about racial equality, given that the South fought for the retention of enslavement of American blacks.

On the other hand, the rictus of self-examination occurring in Britain raises questions as to how far a society can or should go in sanitising its public spaces and institutions of traces of its history that commemorate or even acknowledge Britain's imperial past, including British involvement in slavery.

The whole idea of empire, after all, is based on subjugation. Imperialists and the colonists have always clothed subjugation with the moral mantle of bringing civilisation and redemption. Rome gave the English its blessing on that account to subjugate and colonise Ireland.

Reading the excellent *Handbook of the Irish Revival*, edited by Kiberd and Mathews, I came across a piece written by my grandfather, Eoin Mac Néill, in 1919 during the Irish War of Independence, which he passionately supported, describing imperialism:

Imperialism is something more than the glory of dominating over lands and seas and subject peoples. To the pride of life, it adds the lust of the flesh and the lust of the eyes, the appetite for luxury and gain. Its pride, being contemplative, needs to be sustained by these active forces; and whenever you find the Imperialist spirit, you will find that it takes to itself a body made up of predatory feudalism and predatory capitalism, of oligarchies seeking to dominate the earth given to the millions to inhabit and the industry exerted by the millions to make the world inhabitable – in short, to enslave the world.

That judgement has some relevance to the present British examination of conscience over racism. Toppling Edward Colston's statue in Bristol or removing Cecil Rhode's statue in Oxford is one thing; facing up to the fact that Britain, as a new political entity distinct from England, only evolved over three centuries into Great Britain by a sustained process of imperialism, involving enslavement, subjugation and colonisation, is another matter. Mac Néill might well have added that one aspect of imperialist pride was a penchant for monumental self-glorification.

If all traces of its imperial past are to be carefully sanitised or removed or covered up to create space for a new inclusive British political narrative, a collective amnesia bordering on historical dementia will be needed. You simply can't eradicate these traces and be true to history; they are woven into the tapestry of British history as permanently as the events of 1066 are woven into the Bayeux tapestry. By all means, it is open to every generation in any society to take its own view of its collective history and to interpret it anew. But it can't be falsified or denied. Leaving the traces of history is qualitatively different from waving the Confederate flag in today's America.

Any person wandering in Parliament Square will see statues of Churchill, Gandhi and Cromwell. A well-informed Indian will look at Churchill and see a man who private despised the Indian people as a race and publicly argued for their continued subjugation in the British Empire. A well-informed Irish visitor will, at the very least, have deeply ambivalent views about both Churchill and Cromwell. A black South African might remember the racial prejudices of

Gandhi in his younger days in South Africa – as might any lower-caste Indian who remembers Gandhi's earlier defence of the caste system.

Others might think that the three statues stand in that square as physical monuments to very diverse figures from Britain's imperial history which should cause no offence to reasonable British people of all colours and nationalities. They shouldn't have to be boarded up – let alone be 'defended' by a self-appointed gang of racist thugs.

I think the answer is more statues, not fewer. I don't mind Prince Albert lurking in the bushes at Leinster House, long after his wife was removed from there and transported, like her Young Irelander rebel felons, to Australia.

Perhaps, in Pride Week, Dublin might acknowledge the glaring truth that Roger Casement was gay and give him a decent statue to commemorate his struggles for Ireland, against imperialism, and for the cruelly enslaved people of the Congo and Amazon basins.

Islamic extremism is incompatible with our liberal society

31 July 2016

The cruel murder by ISIS adherents of a defenceless, elderly Catholic priest celebrating Mass in a small Normandy church is by no means the first of its kind. Jihadists waging 'holy war' have been doing similar cowardly acts to Christian clergy and laypeople here and there across the Maghreb, the Middle East and in Saharan Africa for twenty years now. The 1996 slaughter of Trappist monks at Tibhirine in Algeria by extreme Islamists was a foretaste of what has now become a commonplace event.

When it happens close to home, the media impact is greater; but the horrific reality has largely been under-reported by Western media.

Islamic extremism is incompatible with our liberal society

The Al-Nusra Front in Syria (which has been backed by Erdoğan's Turkish regime and financed by Saudi Arabia and Qatar without any effective protest by Western governments) has been committing similar atrocities against Christians and other vulnerable religious minorities for the last six years.

ISIS or Daesh is only the latest manifestation of extreme Islamist fundamentalism which wants to wage religious war in the name of Islam.

As I wrote here a few weeks ago, the great irony of the Blair–Bush war on Iraq justified by the need to eliminate non-existent 'weapons of mass destruction' was that the real WMD that existed in the Middle East was Saudi Salafism which has been exported worldwide by despotic regimes, including the Saudis and the Qataris.

It is all very well to say that Islam is a religion of peace; Salafism is not. And the proliferation of Salafist Islam across the world is dangerous. The danger has been long appreciated. I was personally briefed on it by US security services during my time as Minister for Justice.

Right across the Islamic world, madrasas preaching Wahhabism have been established, expanded and funded by Saudi Arabia, directly and through Saudi-funded 'charitable' foundations. The result of all of this fundamentalist activity can be seen from Bali to Timbuktu, from Glasgow (where an 'apostate' shopkeeper was murdered) to Los Angeles to Nairobi, from Nice to the Twin Towers.

While the vast majority of Muslims are good, law-abiding people, there is a very real vein of extremist Islamic fundamentalism which is being fed and nurtured by Saudi Salafism.

We need to face it down. We need to challenge the Saudis and the Qataris about it.

We need those who claim to be moderate Muslims and their religious leaders to state unequivocally that nothing in the Quran can justify the killing, imprisonment or oppression of any man or woman on grounds of heresy, apostasy, or blasphemy, and to state unequivocally that such treatment of human beings for their beliefs is wrong wherever it happens in the world.

If Islam is to be accorded the status of a religion and given charitable status in our society, there can be no ambivalence on these issues. Either a religion teaches that no person or state has the right to kill a human for apostasy or it does not.

If a religion cannot be unequivocal on that simple issue, it must exclude itself from social recognition in a modern secular democracy. If it teaches ambivalently on that issue, it is a menace which must bear responsibility for all the consequences of such ambivalence.

Our constitutional guarantee of the free practice and profession of religion is expressly made subject to public order and morality. Any religion that advocates, defends or teaches a doctrine that its adherents may kill other humans here or anywhere in the world because of what they say that they believe or have ceased to believe, does not enjoy constitutional recognition or protection because that doctrine fundamentally flies in the face of public order and morality.

Of course, non-Muslims are not immune in this respect. If any extremist fundamentalist Christian or Jew preached biblical authority for killing 'infidels' on the basis of what the Book of Joshua claims God ordered by way of genocide (and it makes gruesome reading), we would have to act against them decisively too.

Our values are inconsistent with many aspects of traditional fundamentalist Islam. We do not condone chastisement within marriage. We do not condone forced, arranged marriages. Every Muslim girl and woman must be accorded the rights and freedoms accorded to every other woman. No imam, mosque or sharia tribunal has temporal authority in our State. It is not intolerant to say so.

Those who believe that we in Ireland are centuries ahead of the Islamic world would do well to reflect on the relatively recent abandonment of many social injustices against women, ranging from criminalisation of family planning, sacking of women public servants who married, and the condoning of matrimonial rape to the Catholic doctrine of male superiority and womanly obedience in the family as set out in the encyclical *Casti Conubii* (another eye-opener easily available online!).

In many respects the attitudinal time-gap between the Western world and the Islamic world is much shorter than we care to think. Before we look down on Islam or Muslims, we should reflect on how narrow that difference is.

There are signs at last that the appalling folly of backing the replacement of Syria's secularist regime by an Islamist coalition backed by the Turks, the Saudis, and the Qataris is being abandoned by the naive policy-makers in the US State Department. That is good. The illusion that the West can export pluralist, multi-party democracy delivered by smart bombs to the Arab world is now shattered.

The West (including Obama, Hollande, Erdoğan and Cameron) came within days of using air warfare to blast away the Assad regime and making way for an Islamist repression in Damascus. The idiocy of thinking that there was a moderate government-in-waiting that would face down the Saudi-backed Islamists seems hardly credible now.

In the meantime, Ireland has to get real about Salafism and Wahhabism. These forces are not going away. In a firm but understanding way, we have to identify and assert our own values at home and abroad.

Opposing such forces is an attribute of Irish citizenship. Clarity on these matters is not intolerance – quite the opposite.

The Definite Article: RELIGION AND SOCIAL AFFAIRS

Profound issues at stake over free speech and Islam

4 November 2020

Our Constitution guarantees freedom of religious belief to all citizens and provides that the State will not endow any particular religion.

In the 1960s our Supreme Court developed a theory that the Constitution guaranteed unenumerated rights to citizens in addition to those rights explicitly mentioned in the 1937 text. The court held that these unenumerated rights fell to be identified by the courts by reference to what was implied by the 'Christian and democratic' nature of the Irish State. What the term 'Christian' meant in that context was never tied down. Whether it involved basic Christian philosophy concerning the equal worth of all individuals and the moral imperative of charity in all human dealings was never clarified.

Whatever about theology, it still seems that the great majority of Irish people would consider themselves to be philosophically Christian in the foregoing sense. That raises questions about the relationship of Irish society to non-Christian cults and beliefs, whether ancient or comparatively modern.

In that context, the decapitation of Samuel Paty, the French secondary school teacher, for showing his pupils Charlie Hebdo cartoons of the Prophet Muhammad to explore issues of freedom of speech and thought and any limits on the right to blaspheme in the eyes of some of the community, also raises questions about the meaning of republicanism and the status of religion in a secular republic.

French political culture places enormous value on what they term *laïcisme*, a doctrine which affects total blindness as to the theological and metaphysical beliefs of the citizens of their republic.

French society and indeed many in Europe were simply horrified that a young Chechen might feel entitled by what he saw on social media to seek out and behead a man whom he had never met on the grounds of blasphemy.

The robust stance of Emmanuel Macron against such barbarity and for the right of Charlie Hebdo and Samuel Paty to use cartoons of the Prophet Muhammad for satirical or educational purposes excited a wave of anger across the Islamic world from North Africa through Turkey, South Asia and Indonesia directed against Macron and the French Republic.

Is Macron wholly sincere in championing the use of these cartoons? Or is he, perhaps, issue-surfing? The Muslim minority in France feels itself to be the subject of economic and cultural discrimination by the French Republic. Notwithstanding laïcisme, many Muslims believe that French society is not blind to their ethnic origins or religious beliefs. After all, it is hard to believe, in these days of facemasks, that the French Republic sought to penalise Muslim women who wore facemasks in public or who went bathing in full body attire just a couple of years ago.

Bitter words exchanged between the French government and Erdoğan's Turkey in recent times raise questions as well. France now charges Erdoğan with attempting to re-establish an Ottoman Empire. This is a bit rich for the French state, which spent a considerable portion of the early part of the last century trying to dismember Turkey itself. It is a great irony that France should believe that it still has some moral right to intervene militarily in the Middle East, given its previous desire to extend imperial control over those lands without any entitlement, good, bad or indifferent.

Some Quranic experts argue that nothing in the Quran itself (as distinct from other statements attributed to the Prophet Muhammad) requires or justifies killing any person for what Muslims consider to be blasphemy, apostasy or heresy.

And yet Ayatollah Khomeini and his successors have kept a fatwa and a massive reward promised to any Muslim who kills

Salman Rushdie on account of his allegedly blasphemous work *The Satanic Verses*, his apostasy, and his atheism.

Should a liberal, democratic republic afford any special protection or charitable status to any religion which seeks to justify, or fails to condemn outright, killings, judicial or extra-judicial, imprisonment or flogging of humans anywhere in the world for apostasy, blasphemy or heresy? Does any group in our society which justifies the deprivation of religious freedom to others anywhere in the world really deserve protection under our Constitution at the same time?

There are profound issues at stake here. On the one hand, many in the woke generation are demanding that hate speech laws be enacted to prevent free speech from being used to cause profound offence and hurt to others in the community. On the other hand, many of the same people are wearing 'Je suis Charlie' T-shirts.

For Ireland, which recently removed a constitutional reference to the crime of blasphemy by referendum but left in place provisions stating that 'the homage of public worship is due to Almighty God' and undertook to 'hold His Name in reverence' and to 'respect and honour religion', there is a debate to be had as to whether we pursue *laïcisme* or simple pluralism.

Britain and France have different approaches but both have very poor records in dealings with the Islamic world.

Vienna, on the other hand, has not been throwing its weight around for a long, long time now. And yet terrorism has come calling there.

———————

International Affairs

It is easy to see parallels with the late 1930s, as truth and integrity are being displaced by cynicism and absurdity

7 July 2019

When the Nazis finally invaded Poland in 1939, a number of things happened in terms of truth.

First, the invasion was a carefully concealed plan in furtherance of the Molotov–Ribbentrop pact between Hitler's regime and the Soviet communist regime of Stalin. Hitler and Stalin had carefully pre-planned the invasion by the Germans in a manner that allowed the USSR to stab the Poles in the back and to divide Poland between them along a pre-agreed line of demarcation.

But it was essential that this evil agreement remained secret. The USSR had to appear as responding to a German–Polish conflict which had nothing to do with Moscow.

From the German point of view, the co-ordinated destruction of Poland had to appear as an act of self-defence against Polish aggression against Germany. For that reason, an evil deception was concocted to make it appear that Polish forces had invaded German territory and had killed innocent Germans.

To that end, innocent prisoners of the Reich were dressed up in Polish uniforms and executed in order to provide 'proof' of the alleged Polish invasion.

Hitler and Goebbels worked out this cynical outrage in minute detail. The Russians watched on as the deception was planned and mounted.

All this is well known. The two most powerful military states in the world deployed 'fake news' to disguise their mutually agreed plan.

Now it may be said that few in the Western democracies had any illusion as to what the Nazis were up to. But the depth and cynicism of the deception involving the Soviets was not so clear.

The average German accepted the deception without question. The Poles were the aggressors. They were mistreating Germans in Danzig. They wanted to invade Germany. And they did so.

The average Russian was led to believe that the wrong of the Brest–Litovsk Treaty between the Kaiser and the Russians was being righted and that the eastern part of Poland was being rightfully restored to the USSR.

Britain and France knew differently. They saw through the lies. They realised that the dismemberment of Czechoslovakia in 1938, in which they had acquiesced because of weakness and dishonesty, was now but a stepping stone to the Nazi domination of Western Europe.

And so the world again went to war. Drawing parallels with that awful period may seem over the top. But there are parallels that we cannot ignore.

We have watched the Russians lie and then invade Ukraine in support of Russians in eastern Ukraine and the Crimea. They did the same in Georgia. Putin claims that he wishes to protect all the citizens of Ukraine.

We have watched the Americans encourage the gradual annexation of the West Bank by Israel. We have watched the Americans and the British arm and encourage the murderous Saudi–Emirati alliance in the Yemen civil war.

> It is easy to see parallels with the late 1930s, as truth and integrity are being displaced by cynicism and absurdity

We have allowed the Trump regime in the White House to whitewash and ignore the brutal abduction and killing of Jamal Khashoggi without comment or criticism.

Oh yes, our government is 'concerned'. 'Concerned' to the point of doing absolutely nothing, even at the EU level.

A UN investigation has pointed to the truth; but the EU has done damn-all to sanction Saudi Arabia and its young tyrant prince.

He is received at the G20 conference as though he were an innocent man.

Trump is forging a tri-partite alliance of Israel, Egypt and the Gulf emirates against Iran with a view to toppling the Islamic Republic of Iran.

He is wandering the world's capitals pursuing his 'deal-based' policy of bullying and blackmail.

The Huawei controversy is but the tip of the Trumpian iceberg of hypocrisy.

It was a matter, a few weeks ago, of US national security that Huawei should not supply its IT infrastructure to any countries in the Western world. Now that has become utterly negotiable.

The dishonesty and opportunism of it all is breath-taking.

His son-in-law, the laughable Jared Kushner, a man whose father was once successfully prosecuted and jailed by Senator Chis Christie for infamous deeds in relation to his own brother, is ludicrously posing as a peace broker between the Israelis and the Palestinians.

Kushner is touting a ridiculous plan in which the Palestinians are expected to trade in their nationality for the dubious 'beads' of economic prosperity supplied – not by the US – but by the oil-rich corrupt autocracies in the Gulf.

Meanwhile, Kushner's wife, Ivanka, pathetically attempts to pose as some sort of international personage at the G20 summit. The YouTube pictures of her attempts to obtrude herself into the company of world leaders at G20 were just excruciating to watch.

And yet Trump went on the record as regretting that he had not made her head of the World Bank.

Is America a republican democracy in any sense of the word?

The military parade in Washington was a ridiculous and very damp squib.

Is there any country in the world that would allow its elected president to attempt to accord official representative status on the hapless and utterly unqualified offspring of his second marriage?

This is all the stuff of the most ridiculous of banana republics.

But it passes without official comment throughout the Western world – presumably because while it may be grotesque it is not technically criminal.

Maybe too, we should just laugh at this week's Jeremy Hunt threats of UK sanctions against China arising out of the Hong Kong demonstrations.

It was plain to me that the invasion of the Hong Kong assembly by masked students waving the Union Jack while the police abandoned their posts and permitted their vandalism was the result of Beijing's agents provocateurs' plans to discredit the peaceful protest of 500,000 Hong Kong citizens elsewhere in the former colony.

Between Gavin Williamson's absurd threat to send the UK's only aircraft carrier (still awaiting aircraft) to the South China Sea and Hunt's threat of sanctions, we are now seeing the depth of the post-imperial delusion that is driving the Brexiteers in the Tory party.

Are we not really witnessing the playing out of a grotesque fantasy or charade which rivals the Marx Brothers' Ruritanian farce of Freedonia or Peter Sellers' famous *Mouse That Roared* depiction of the Duchy of Grand Fenwick?

As I said, truth and integrity are being displaced across the world by untruth, cynicism and absurdity. There really are echoes of the late 1930s.

> It is easy to see parallels with the late 1930s, as truth and integrity are being displaced by cynicism and absurdity

The Democrats in the US have only one duty now. Beat Trump!

To do that they must select a candidate that will win back middle America to their side. I don't mind whether that candidate is stale or exciting. I am only concerned with that candidate's capacity to beat Trump.

Implying falsely that Joe Biden is soft on racism may win a debating point before party activists in Florida for Elizabeth Warren, Kamala Harris or Bernie Saunders.

But if, as I suspect, they can't individually beat Trump, they should back a candidate that can.

We should value our freedom and stay out of conflicts or a common EU defence alliance

15 April 2018

Donald Trump, Theresa May and Emmanuel Macron directed their military forces to launch missile strikes on certain installations in Syria, which, they claim, have some role in the manufacture or use of chemical weapons, as a response to reports of such usage in Douma in the last hours of the subjugation of the Eastern Ghouta rebel enclave.

This operation is asserted to be a deterrent to the future use of such weapons by the Assad regime, and a form of retribution for their past use and for the breach of commitments made by the Syrians and the Russians that chemical weapons would not be used again in the Syrian civil war.

What are we to make of this missile strike?

First, General Matthis has described it as a one-off event. This suggests that the missile strikes are not part of a rolling programme of degradation of Assad's military capacity. Theresa May has stated that the strike is not intended to affect the outcome of the Syrian civil war or to bring about regime change. Speaking about the missile strike on BBC radio on Saturday morning, Lord Richards, a former general, and Frank Gardner, a security correspondent, both accepted that the Assad regime had effectively won the Syrian civil war, and that the priority now was to re-establish peace so as to allow the rebuilding of Syrian society. Gardner went further, by stating that, in retrospect, the Russian intervention in the Syrian civil war had prevented the establishment of an ISIS/jihadist Islamist regime in Damascus.

Second, while I am wary of appearing to be a 'useful idiot' or of lapping up Russian fake news, there is something about the Douma incident that somehow does not make sense. Discounting completely the Russian suggestion that some foreign power carried out the chemical weapons in an attack in Douma, there still remains the possibility that the incident was contrived to provoke military intervention by the Western powers. It seems almost absurd, in terms of the Assad regime's short-, medium- and long-term self-interest to have used chemical weapons, especially when the Eastern Ghouta operation was almost complete and bound to succeed. It even raises the question as to whether Assad would have contemplated taking this step when it clearly doesn't suit his Russian allies or his Iranian supporters to bring things to a head at this time. When victory was at hand, why should they turn it into an opportunity to snatch a defeat?

Third, even assuming that the chemical attack was carried out by Syrian state forces, we must ask what practical purpose has been served by retaliatory missile strikes on Assad's installations? Unless they have the effect of toppling Assad and his regime, they would appear to have served little or no purpose. As a moral statement, perhaps they have some value in underlining the abhorrence of chemical weapons. They may serve Donald Trump's domestic political purposes, in that he heavily criticised Obama for not taking military action when the chemical weapons red line was transgressed in the past. But opinion polls in the UK suggest that Britain's participation in the operation had only 20% support.

Furthermore, it is difficult to see how missile strikes launched from aircraft supplied by the UK and the US to the Saudi government, which killed scores of people attending a wedding in Sana'a, in Yemen, two years ago, are radically different or morally more tolerable.

The fourth question we must ask is whether missile attacks are likely to be effective. Given that Theresa May has disavowed regime change or altering the outcome of the civil war, the Western intervention appears to be limited in scale and even more limited in impact.

The irony of the situation is that Donald Trump had appeared last week to be hinting at his intention to withdraw all US forces from the Syrian theatre of engagement. Apart from the shameful unspoken decision to allow Turkey a free hand in dealing with Trump's erstwhile Kurdish allies, who bore the brunt of the casualties in eradicating ISIS from northwestern Syria, there is something very strange about Trump's flip-flopping on America's strategic aims.

The fundamental question that can never be answered by a fusillade of missiles is as to what kind of regime could replace the Assad regime and what kind of Syria could arise from the ashes of the present civil war if Assad is defeated.

Ask any Syrian Christian, Alawite, Druze, or Shia, or even any republican secularists, and you will hear what they think of the installation of a Sunni-dominated Islamist regime supported by the likes of Saudi Arabia.

Indeed, it was Qatar and the Saudis, acting back then as joint sponsors of an Islamist Sunni revolution, that started the Syrian civil war. It was Britain, France and the US who tacitly supported that Islamist revolution as part of what they termed the 'Arab Spring'.

The immeasurable suffering, displacement and economic damage which flowed from the unsuccessful attempt to replace Assad's secular regime with a Sunni-dominated Islamist regime must be the responsibility of the Western powers who did nothing to stop the Saudis and the Qataris in their failed attempt to overthrow Assad.

The damage done to Europe by the resulting wave of immigration and the cack-handed response of Angela Merkel with her open-doors policy for migrants coming from the Near East and the Maghreb are all directly attributable to external interference in Syria by international players pursuing very different agendas.

Behind all the hypocritical posturing of the 'Western powers', and Turkey and Israel too, lies a theory that the greatest threat to Western interests stems from the existence of the regime in Iran. The Shia majority in Iraq has disappointed the western powers by siding with Tehran since the end of the Anglo-American intervention in Iraq. That means that the attack on Saddam Hussein was not merely counterproductive inside Iraq but has created the circumstances in which Iran is almost obliged to pursue its own interests across the Middle Eastern region as a response to Saudi muscle-flexing.

Readers of this column will remember that I have consistently predicted that Trump's dysfunctional personality would move him towards war-making as a distraction from his own internal political failures.

Ask yourself this: exactly what threat does Iran pose to the western world? If you can't answer that question easily and convincingly, the next obvious question is as to why it has suddenly become accepted orthodoxy among the hawkish elements in Washington, Paris and London that containing Iran is an almost existential imperative for our political, economic, and strategic wellbeing.

All of the foregoing suggests that Ireland would be very foolish to abandon our constitutional prohibition on participation in a common EU defence and military alliance. The four Fine Gael MEPs have recently suggested that Ireland should participate in creating a common EU defence and consider amending the Constitution to permit that.

When the world can be brought to the brink of major military hostilities by the likes of Trump, Putin, Assad, May and Macron, we should value our own freedom and stay out of such conflicts.

By equivocating on the cruel fate of Jamal Khashoggi, Washington is effectively dipping its hands in his blood

21 October 2018

Last week I wrote here about the horrible fate of Jamal Khashoggi. I ventured to suggest that these events, horrific as they are, could be the beginning of the end of the grotesque and arbitrary character of what passes these days for US foreign policy under Donald Trump.

Nothing in the last week has diminished my belief that the United States must bear a degree of moral blame for the Khashoggi incident – in that the US and Israel uttered no words of condemnation when Saad Hariri, the Prime Minister of Lebanon, was summoned by the Crown Price to Riyadh, arrested and forced into making a broadcast resigning his premiership while held hostage in the desert kingdom.

The Israelis were clearly complicit in that effort to destabilise the ruling coalition in Lebanon. They mobilised their international diplomatic service to exploit the expected crisis in Lebanon. But the whole plan failed when the Lebanese kept their cool and when Hariri returned to Beirut.

Now we are to believe that Trump and Pompeo are awaiting the result of a Saudi inquiry into what transpired at their consulate in Istanbul before deciding what, 'if any', further action they will take.

The Definite Article: INTERNATIONAL AFFAIRS

Only a fool could avoid the obvious truth of the butchering of Khashoggi. Only an idiot, and a bad-minded idiot at that, could articulate the absurd proposition that Jamal Khashoggi may have been the victim of a 'rogue' killing.

It is abundantly clear that the hit squad which butchered him was sent by Crown Prince Mohammed bin Salman. The Saudi consulate at Istanbul made itself available to the butchers. The Turkish staff there were given the afternoon off. The consul was threatened by them as to the consequences of any failure to cooperate with them. He was told he would be dealt with in Saudi Arabia.

The personnel involved in the hit squad included the closest personal security team of the Crown Prince. They have paced beside him in public in all the capitals of the world. The team also included a forensic practitioner equipped with a bone saw to dismember Khashoggi's body, but not before pulling off his fingers while they interrogated him. If they do that abroad, only Allah knows what they do in the desert kingdom.

Any suggestion that the 'reformist' Crown Prince's security detail could commandeer Saudi jets, fly to Istanbul, and take over the consulate there to butcher Khashoggi without the actual knowledge and authority of the Crown Prince is simply absurd.

Nor could what happened be likened to the medieval death of Thomas à Becket at the hands of knights who (so we were told) misinterpreted their monarch's words 'Who will rid me of this turbulent priest?' Henry II covered up for that hit squad.

The Saudis may even be tempted now to decapitate the killers (or innocent substitutes) to cut off the line of responsibility.

That process called 'direction by indirection' – plausible deniability.

Even if the Saudis disavow their earlier protestations of innocence and ignorance of the murder, and acknowledge that Khashoggi was indeed murdered in their consulate, but proffer the face-saving excuse that the murder was carried out without the knowledge or authority of the Crown Prince, any such fictional formula designed to save the faces and the pockets of the Saudis' western allies will amount to the most grotesque creation of 'fake news' that we have seen since Trump assumed the presidency.

Unless the Americans clearly and emphatically denounce Crown Prince Salman as the author of this barbaric murder and impose personal sanctions on him, and impose economic and political sanctions against the Saudi Kingdom until his father, the doddering King Salman, removes him from office, any remaining credibility of the Trump regime will be absolutely zero.

While Pompeo and Trump desperately seek time, diplomatic space and fake news to give them room for manoeuvre, the world is looking on and increasingly identifying Trump, Pompeo and the US administration with the puppet kingdom that they sustain.

Trump cannot say that there is no point in his imposing sanctions or demanding the removal of the Crown Prince.

As I pointed out last week, he had told one of his red-neck rallies in Mississippi earlier this month that the Saudi royal family wouldn't last a fortnight without US support. He can't claim on the one hand to be keeping King Salman and his butchering son in power while at the same time suggesting that he is helpless to prevent them from carrying out murders such as that of Khashoggi or sanctioning them when such murders come to light.

Of course, there are geopolitical strategic considerations in play.

The Saudis are conducting a brutal war in Yemen which the UN believes is in imminent danger of creating the single greatest mass famine of the twenty-first century. Apart from the tens of thousands of people already killed by the Saudis in confident air warfare using American and British armaments, the UN has warned there is now a very real possibility, over the next few months, that millions of people will starve to death because of the Saudi blockade of the Yemeni ports.

The Definite Article: INTERNATIONAL AFFAIRS

None of this would be happening without the direct encouragement of Washington, London and Paris. While Trump's elephantine commentary on the Khashoggi murder attracts the limelight to Washington, foreign office officials in Whitehall and on the Quai d'Orsay are smugly congratulating themselves on their success in keeping their heads down and washing their hands of moral responsibility for the Yemeni war.

It is by no means clear that keeping the House of Saud in power in the Arabian peninsula is in the strategic interests of the Western powers or their peoples. Saudi oil is no longer of such strategic importance to the West. Accumulated sovereign wealth funds have nowhere but the Western economies as safe investments.

Right across the Muslim world, the influence of the Saudi royal family over the last 25 years has been malign. Across that world, it is the Saudis who have propagated reactionary Islamic teaching through a network of madrasas and other institutions and funds.

The result has been an upsurge in Islamic extremism from the Philippines to Indonesia, to Bangladesh, to Pakistan, to Afghanistan, to Kenya, to Somalia, and right across the Sahara to Mali, not forgetting ISIS, Al-Nusrah and the European Islamic jihadis.

When you consider it, all of the foregoing, including the activities of bin Laden and the 9/11 terrorists have been centred on the 'desert kingdom' and the values that it has spawned and propagated.

One of the great myths is the suggestion that it is the Shia, including the Iranians, which threaten the West. Iran, curiously, is the only major Islamic state where the government is chosen by the people in elections, even if the Ayatollahs circumscribe and dominate their democratic process. And yet Iran is supposedly the deadly threat to Western democracy.

One of Crown Prince Salman's closest confidants in the international sphere, apparently, is Jared Kushner. The Americans have been pushing the idea of economic cooperation between Israel,

Egypt and Saudi Arabia. Jared Kushner's wife, Ivanka Trump, has even been considered by Trump as a possible successor to Nikki Haley, the retiring US ambassador to the UN. To use Trump language, that possibility is 'sad'.

How the world's greatest democracy could have lowered itself so far in the minds of right-thinking people across the globe beggars belief. There is something morally and intellectually repugnant about Trump. Khashoggi would never have been killed and dismembered if the US had stood up to the House of Saud and its Crown Prince before now. By dissimulating and equivocating on the cruel fate of Jamal Khashoggi, Washington is effectively dipping its hands in his blood. London and Paris are little better. Cancelling visits to investment conferences is no substitute for elementary decency in international affairs.

Alas, as long as Trump is there, we can expect little better. As Trump-speak might put it: it's 'sad'. But it's also mad and bad.

Afghanistan was not and could never be the forward bastion of liberalism

25 August 2021

In retrospect (which is of course always wiser), it might well have made more sense for the NATO forces which expelled the Taliban from Kabul in 2001 to have settled for a regime of regional and tribal warlords with a weak central government rather than aspire to the creation of a unitary liberal parliamentary democracy there. From 1996, the civil war between the Taliban and the Northern Alliance, in which the Taliban received support from Pakistan, Saudi Arabia, the UAE and Qatar, was a protracted struggle in which the US eventually intervened (in the aftermath of 9/11) and drove the Taliban from power in 2001.

The period of Taliban power was not simply a period of subjugation of women (as you might think from some present-day coverage) but was a regime of extreme brutality against both men and women utilising starvation and massacre against their opponents, political and religious. When the Taliban enjoyed Saudi backing, Osama Bin Laden brought thousands of Al-Qaeda fighters into the country; and it was from there that he organised 9/11.

Many have written in recent days of the difficulties, if not futility, of seeking to sow the seeds of liberal democracy in stony cultural soil. Assuming that liberal democracy is the natural or inevitable outcome of human political development or civilisation is, I think, a major error. It can never be taken for granted. It must be guarded, nurtured and cultivated. It depends, like many forms of plant life, on irrigation and soil conditions to survive or prosper.

Religious fundamentalism is one of the soil conditions that threatens the existence of liberal democracy. So too do extreme ideologies of nationalism and Marxism. It is difficult to identify any state where liberal democracy has taken root and thrived in a society dominated by Islam of whatever denomination. Indeed, liberal democracy has largely emerged in the countries where it exists after a protracted struggle against Christian fundamentalism described as the Enlightenment.

This reflection raises a number of questions. Are Western Enlightenment values exclusively Christian in origin or in inherited character? Some writers claim that the demise of organised ecclesial Christianity in Europe poses an existential threat to the existence of European civilisation as we know it. In that school, a small but vocal minority point to the threatened Islamisation of Europe by migration and replacement. Is a secular society inherently weak or vulnerable if it is not possessed of historic religion-derived antibodies to fight off alien illiberal and undemocratic political and religious ideologies? Do we risk throwing out our vital political immune responses if we instal a politics based solely on sterile secularism?

The conventional answer is that a truly liberal, democratic society must accommodate diversity – that the fabric of a coherent liberal society is woven from multi-strand fibres and is not a monofilament weave. And with that I agree. A problem with the extremes of 'woke' culture is that they seek to impose a code of thought and speech instead of acknowledging the right to differ and the right to see the past and, indeed, the future differently. In that regard, hardline 'woke' culture tends towards totalitarianism of thought.

While we ponder the decline of religious ecclesial practice among European Christians and its likely long-term effects, we will have to reflect on issues of cohabitation with the Muslim world. Irish people don't mind if Muslim women cover up in public so long as that is their free choice. They do object to young girls being made subject to arranged marriages in Ireland where their parents are of South Asian origin precisely because that is not their free choice.

Will we accord Irish constitutional protection for religion to preachers in Ireland who defend the killing of blasphemers and apostates abroad – not to mention stoning gays and adulterers? Does advocacy of killing become legitimate just because the victim lives elsewhere or because it is justified or supported by verses in the Old Testament or the Quran?

We face a future of friction between the civilisation equivalents of tectonic plates. A good deal of Islamic activism has been financed by oil wealth. Much of the Islamic world is facing into a darker post-hydrocarbon world where increased desertification threatens their homelands. Climate change is a challenge for more than the liberal West.

Afghanistan was not and could never be the forward bastion of liberalism. But the contest between liberalism and religious or ideological fundamentalism seems permanent.

The Definite Article: INTERNATIONAL AFFAIRS

Each day of Netanyahu in office prolongs suffering of 2 million people

20 March 2024

What is happening in Gaza is entirely predictable. It was not inevitable, however. As far back as 11 October last, I wrote here of the need to avoid the destruction of Gaza and its people. The dangers of letting Netanyahu pursue his unforgiveable plan to match the Hamas-led atrocities of 7 October with his own atrocities must have been equally obvious in Washington, London, Paris and Berlin.

The governments of the US, UK, France, and Germany utterly failed to prevent what is now happening, mostly for their own internal political reasons. They embarked on a campaign of irresponsible rhetoric and military support calculated to bolster the position and intentions of Netanyahu, instead of imagining what he would do and stopping it.

By doing so, they must now accept the responsibility and the blame for the outcome. Tens of thousands of innocent people – men, women and children – have already died. No one can count the casualties – mental and physical – who have survived until now. Disease, starvation, and famine have been unleashed on more than two million people by Israel. There was another way.

Handwringing is now the common reaction of those who never cried 'stop'. But it is not good enough from Biden, Blinken, Sunak, Cameron, Macron or Scholz. What does Biden mean when he now says that a military assault on Rafah by Netanyahu's army would cross a 'red line'?

Destruction of Hamas, the movement that Netanyahu deliberately nurtured to weaken the Palestinian Authority and the aim of a two-state solution, means in reality what we have already seen happen in northern and central Gaza. There we have witnessed all males of military age who fall into the hands of the IDF being stripped, handcuffed, blindfolded, and trucked away to interrogation centres where they are abused like the 'hooded men' were in Northern Ireland.

And if there are at the end of such a winnowing process, say, 5,000 captured identified Hamas fighters, what will happen to them? We are not going to see a formal court process such as was done in the case of the Holocaust architect Adolf Eichmann. Will they be summarily executed or detained in prison camps back in Israel for the rest of their natural lives?

The accidental killing by the IDF of the hostages who tried to escape under a white flag suggests that summary execution is probably the preferred way of dealing with Hamas prisoners.

Netanyahu chose the course which he is following with the support of his allies – domestic and foreign. I agree with Senator Chuck Schumer, the most senior US Jewish political figure, that the continuation in office of Netanyahu is an obstacle to peace. Many, many Israelis know he is right and many, many others must suspect that it is so. I would go further than Schumer. Every day that Netanyahu remains in office conducting his war of extermination against the odious Hamas movement and ideology is a prolongation of the inhumane and barbarous treatment of more than two million innocent people.

Cynically choking off food, water, and medical supplies for those two million defenceless, vulnerable and suffering people is utterly unforgiveable. If the people of Israel continue to countenance such barbarity, they will leave an indelible stain on the character of an enlightened and civilised state that their parents sought to create and defend. It must stop. And Joe Biden must stop it – given that he helped start it and failed to avert it.

An all-out military assault on Rafah using US-provided weapons and materiel of war is now planned. Can the Western states not even now indicate that Israel has seen the last veto card played at the UN Security Council? Can the Western states not even now defend UNRWA from the gross defamation unleashed on it by Israel and restore its full funding? Is there a whit of moral courage in their diplomacy to match the destructive military might which they have created and deployed to be used against innocent Palestinians?

The Israelis are sending a delegation to Washington to argue for their plan to smash Rafah and its swollen number of inhabitants whom they have herded there from the other killing zones in Gaza. The matter should not now be one for debate, argumentation or persuasion either way. They should bring that message home.

The US government has handled the Hamas atrocity of 7 October very, very badly. Now it must show steely determination to do the right thing for two million other innocent people. Israel's government must be told 'Enough is enough' in no uncertain terms. The people of Israel must hear that message and bring Netanyahu's atrocious campaign to an immediate end.

The fate of the surviving hostages should not be forgotten either. Total destructive war in their name seems like madness.

Growth of Hamas was observed and encouraged by Israel's government

9 October 2024

It is natural that the public's attention should, on the anniversary of the barbarous Hamas attack on Israeli men, women and children, refocus on the killing of 1,300 people, and the brutal hostage-taking. The unforgivable viciousness of 7 October 2023 can easily be forgotten in the maelstrom of cruelty that has followed.

About 45,000 Palestinians have perished in the Gaza Strip and on the West Bank, the great majority wholly innocent non-combatants

– men, women and children who pose no threat to anyone, and who cannot assist any initiatives for peace.

In addition to the Palestinian dead, few have counted those who have lost limbs, eyesight, sanity, loved ones, families and homes. If, at a crude estimate, there have been two awful life-altering injuries for every death, it is by no means inconceivable that more than 120,000 people have sustained death or dreadful injury to date at the hands of the Israel Defense Forces.

Physical destruction of homes, buildings, infrastructure, schools, hospitals, and businesses in Gaza is simply colossal. Perhaps half of built Gaza has been pulverised and there is no end in sight for the people who are herded from one bombing zone to another in pursuit of the destruction of Hamas.

Likewise, what has happened in the West Bank has been barbarous. Apart from the killings, casualties and destruction of urban infrastructure, economic subjugation of West Bank Arabs has neared totality.

Now we have ongoing war in Lebanon with mass expulsions and uncounted civilian deaths and serious casualties in pursuit of Hezbollah who have rained aerial destruction on northern Israel.

All this is truly shocking, and all this could have been avoided if decency and statesmanship existed in adequate measure on either side of the Israeli–Palestinian historical dispute.

Those in Tehran and Tel Aviv, and those in Hamas and Hezbollah, who spent 25 years frustrating all international efforts to bring about a just and peaceful compromise based on a two-state solution, bear joint responsibility for all that has happened in that quarter-century.

Words spoken by Ireland's chief rabbi, Yoni Wieder, at the 7 October massacre vigil in Dublin need to be carefully examined. He claimed that Israel was not waging a war of retaliation against

Hamas, 'whatever some politicians in this country might have us think'.

As I understand the Israeli government's stated policy, the war against Hamas in Gaza is one of elimination, the 'destruction of Hamas's military and governing capabilities'. Precisely how one eliminates Hamas has never been clarified. Does it entail the destruction of everyone who participated in the Hamas administration of the Gaza Strip?

It must be recalled that growth of Hamas was not merely observed by Israel's right-wing government; it was actively encouraged because it weakened and divided the Palestinians and undermined pretensions of the West Bank PLO (Palestine Liberation Organisation) movement to represent Palestinians internationally.

The apparent success of the current Israeli campaign against Hezbollah has undoubtedly increased the morale and sense of solidarity of pro-Israel supporters. Many had been flagging in the face of international revulsion at the destruction of Gaza and its population, and the manifest failure of the Israel Defense Forces and their government to secure the release of the hostages.

Few neutral observers felt much compassion for most victims of the remarkable deployment of exploding pagers in the hands of Hezbollah operatives. Statements issued by Hezbollah and their allies, including the Iranian theocracy, still insist that their aim is the destruction of the state of Israel.

Ireland's position is, always has been, and I think always will be, that we recognise the right of Israel to exist in security and peace within the boundaries determined by international law specified under Resolution 242 of the United Nations. Creeping annexation of the West Bank territories is, in the eyes of Ireland and the International Court of Justice, wholly unlawful.

Every adherent of the International Court of Justice is bound, as a matter of international law, to take all reasonable steps to prevent the unlawful expansion of the territory of Israel by the campaign of settlement encouraged by extreme Zionists and their supporters in Israel, the United States, and everywhere else.

Calls from members of the Israeli government for military action against the Iranian government in the form of aerial destruction of its military and petrochemical infrastructure are massively dangerous in present circumstances.

The hope of Israelis that the anniversary of 7 October will mark a turning point, and that international sympathy will strengthen if the Middle East is embroiled in regional warfare, are misplaced.

The majority of Europeans and of the world beyond the US have had enough of the savagery and barbarity. They demand a just peace based on a two-state solution. I hope that is the view of the chief rabbi in Ireland – because it is also the stated view of many courageous Jews who live in Ireland.

Respect for truth is being hacked to pieces

26 May 2021

I am reading the recently published *Surviving Katyn* by Jane Rogoyska, a riveting account of the lead-up to and aftermath of the liquidation by Josef Stalin and Lavrentiy Beria of 22,000 Polish officers captured by the Soviet Union in the 1939 carve-up of Poland with the Nazis. As is well known, some of their mass graves were uncovered by the Nazis in 1943 after the tide had turned for Operation Barbarossa.

After the discovery, a grotesque propaganda war ensued between the Nazis, who were all the time engaged in the horrific mass exterminations of the Holocaust, and the Soviets, who had only recently completed horrific mass exterminations of their own citizens during Stalin's reign of terror. Sad to say, liquidating 22,000 Polish prisoners was small beer to both the Nazis and the communists.

After the fall of the Soviet Union in 1990, papers in the Communist Party archive in Moscow (which I have had the pleasure of visiting myself) revealed that the massacre of the Poles was fully and personally authorised by Beria and Stalin, down to the exact numbers of men to be shot in the head.

This did not prevent Beria and Stalin from waging a relentless propaganda war to attribute the liquidation to the Germans. Nor did it prevent the Soviet's allies, Britain and the US, from going along with that monstrous lie, notwithstanding their suspicions as to the true perpetrators.

This week we witnessed the same propensity on the part of the Belarus regime of Lukashenko and his Moscow puppetmaster, Vladimir Putin, to issue a flurry of lies for home consumption, claiming that the hijacking of the Ryanair flight from Greece to Lithuania was caused by a bomb scare generated by Hamas, of all people. That grotesque lie serves the odious regimes in Minsk and Moscow in their relentless campaign of repression and violence towards anyone standing for democratic values.

The apparent detention and beating up of Lukashenko's quarry, journalist Roman Protasevich, is as brazen as the hijacking of the aircraft. Some commentators in Moscow have praised Lukashenko's criminal behaviour – forgetting the official Kremlin position that what happened was a well-intentioned intervention to avert a bomb threat to the Ryanair flight.

Protasevich and Navalny now rot in jails as human reminders of the lengths that Moscow and its puppets will go in the suppression of free speech and dissent. Protasevich had fled Belarus; Navalny had bravely returned after Putin's goons tried to murder him by nerve agent.

The apparent involvement of the same team of Russian agents in the Salisbury poisoning of Sergei Skripal and the destruction of a

Czech Republic ammunition store reminds us that Russia remains as happy to kill its exiled opponents as Stalin was when he arranged for the pre-war axe murder of Leon Trotsky in Mexico.

Totalitarian regimes share utter contempt for bourgeois notions of truth. That contempt is sewn into the fabric of the Marxist–Leninist worldview today. It does not matter how outrageously unlikely the big lie may be or how powerful contradictory evidence may be. Regimes that believe in maintaining the dictatorship of the proletariat and the authority of the Party rank loyalty to the party line as the supreme virtue practised by their Marxist adherents.

Thus, we have the brazen denial by the Chinese communists of both the intent and extent of their cultural liquidation and demographic suppression of the Uyghurs. Uyghur men have been loaded onto cattle trains to serve as slave labourers in distant parts of China; Uyghur women are rounded up for compulsory sterilisation. Their ambassador in Dublin blandly denies this as Western invention.

Obviously communist and post-communist regimes have no monopoly on war crimes, stealth assassinations and modern barbarisms. The Iraq war and the cruel fate of the Palestinians in Gaza and the West Bank show that even those who trumpet righteousness sometimes have hands steeped in blood.

But there is a fundamental difference in the approach of liberal democracy and that of the communist and post-communist regimes as regards allowing the truth to be known and disavowing propagation of brazen falsehoods as politically convenient truth.

Apart from the rule of law and the ballot box, there is the additional differentiating factor of a free press and media.

That is why the present craven, repugnant conversion of the American Republicans to propagating the big lie of a stolen election is such a serious matter. That is why Murdoch's Fox News was, and is, so malign.

That is also why we must wake up to the online threats Ireland faces. It's not only the HSE that being hacked or Ryanair hijacked – truth and respect for the truth are being hacked down.

We ignore these events at our extreme peril.

A weak response to Russia's threat to invade will jeopardise the international order

26 January 2022

As I write, Vladimir Putin has massed a very substantial Russian army in areas including Belarus, Russia, and areas of Ukraine the subject of de facto annexation by Russia in a manner which suggests that a full-scale invasion of Ukraine is in contemplation. This is the first time since the end of the Cold War that any major European state has threatened to invade another sovereign state which is a member of the United Nations and which is internationally recognised, since it gained its independence in 1991, as a fully-fledged member of the international community of nation states.

We should remember that Ukraine declared itself to be a neutral state and, indeed, formed a sort of military partnership with other former Soviet states in the early 1990s. Russia subsequently attempted to draw Ukraine further into its military and economic sphere during the presidency of Viktor Yanukovych until mass protest ended in his deposition. Since 2014, Russia has annexed the Crimea and has established military control of a large section of Eastern Ukraine in the Donbas region using Russian armaments and proxy military formations.

Ukraine, for its part, sought to deepen its economic relationship with the European Union to avoid total political, military and economic subjugation by Putin's Russia.

Many commentators have advanced the view that Putin is not concerned with any military threat to the security of Russia but is more concerned that a functioning and successful liberal democracy should emerge so close to the Russian heartland without being a demonstrable part of its sphere of influence.

Russia has a long record of subjugation of nation states lying to its west and south in the form of the Warsaw Pact and, in addition, has sought to politically neutralise other states such as Austria, Finland and Georgia as part of its general desire to extend its sphere of influence.

One doesn't have to have a 'reds under the bed' or political paranoid frame of mind to see that Russia and China are currently pursuing a coordinated strategy to challenge the hegemony of the so-called Western powers.

Clearly, the West is not in a position to intervene militarily by the deployment of military forces in the defence of Ukraine. Accordingly, the only deterrent available to Putin's threat of invasion must be the prospect of massive, severe and sustained crippling sanctions against Russia and Belarus by the members of NATO, the EU, and Western allies in the Pacific region.

The nature of such sanctions is not clear at this point. It seems that they would have to be much more severe than those deployed on Iran if they are to have any serious credibility or deterrent effect.

They could entail total severance of economic links, not merely in the realms of banking and high finance. Suspension of international air traffic rights and freezing of financial assets held outside Russia are also a possibility. Massive reduction of diplomatic relations (reducing embassies to skeletal staff) and bilateral cultural and economic relations could also form part of a credible deterrent. The US has a long record of using extra-territorial reach in respect of its sanctions regime, including penalising any third-party sanctions-busters.

It appears that Western Europe could survive interruption of gas supplies if Putin seeks to weaponise them as part of his subjugation or counter-sanctions strategy.

While Russia may think that it can weather a prolonged period of political, economic and cultural isolation, its wealthy elites, the types who flock to the Mediterranean sunspots and Western cities, would probably find that suspension of visa and residence rights on a sustained basis would be a price too big to bear for a large-scale and bloody invasion of Ukraine.

All this is a very major problem for President Biden. His dreadful predecessor, Donald Trump, sent Putin all the wrong messages for reasons still murky. Trump also brought about the Afghan fiasco by his disgraceful agreement to the Doha accords with the Taliban. The Afghan debacle raises pressure on Biden to reassert his and America's soft and hard international power to re-energise America's allies who were left befuddled by Trump's foreign policies.

If Russia invades Ukraine, the entire international order will be jeopardised by a weak or incoherent response by the US, NATO, the EU and the Pacific region democracies. Of course, there is probably room for a middle way to emerge in the coming days. Whether Ukraine really wants to become a NATO member must be open to doubt. Whether NATO wants it as a member is likewise doubtful.

It may well be that the price of real Ukrainian independence and security will eventually include cession of the Crimea and the Donbas region in eastern Ukraine to formal Russian control in one form or another.

But a Putin invasion, if left effectively un-penalised, would be catastrophic for liberal democracy worldwide.

Ukraine needs more than feather-duster sanctions

23 February 2022

On 26 January, my piece here assumed that Putin probably intended to invade Ukraine and that the only response available to the West was a package of massive, severe and crippling sanctions against Russia. And so it has turned out to be. Any lesser response by the US, NATO, the EU and Pacific region democracies, I wrote, would jeopardise the entire international order. Putin never intended compromise.

Now that the Russian invasion is a reality, such a response must follow. The sanctions regime on Iran is severe; Putin must endure at least the same. What has been initially announced is wholly inadequate, as Bill Browder, the champion of Magnitsky laws, has already pointed out.

The West has leverage of a massive kind. The issue is whether it is disposed to use that leverage in a united and concerted way. Sanctioning named senior figures in the extended Russian kleptocracy will not hurt Putin or his domestic popularity.

Serious sanctions, including exclusion from economic, banking and currency markets and institutions would hurt. So would freezing of Russian-owned assets, including deposits, shares, property and investments. Revocation of travel and residency rights for expatriate oligarchs, their families and their associates will bite. Prohibition of trading in strategic goods and commodities backed by extraterritorial sanctioning of sanction-busters can have a real effect.

The feather-duster approach apparent so far seems ineffectual. We have seen weakness and timidity in Western responses to poisonings and assassinations. The UK's noisy but weak response to Skripal and Salisbury was clearly influenced by the City of London's appetite for Russian capital and investments.

Massive reduction in diplomatic engagement, and reduction of embassy staffs to skeletal proportions seems appropriate. The Russian embassy in Dublin should be severely cut back – not expanded.

After the hijacking of the Ryanair flight to Minsk and the shooting down of the Malaysian airliner over the Donbas region

– both done by Putin's glove-puppets – reductions in international air traffic are more than justified.

The Ukrainian democracy deserves such a response. Nothing less will do. Even now, clarity on such matters might yet prevent widespread slaughter and mass evacuations by refugees.

As I wrote in January, this is the ultimate test for Joe Biden. Is he up to this challenge? Is the US willing to lead? Is NATO willing to follow?

If not, the outlook for Georgia, the Caucasus, the Balkans, the Baltics and Poland and Romania is clouded.

Listening to Putin's rambling exposition of the arguments for the non-existence of an independent, sovereign Ukraine, I had to pinch myself. Ukraine, a soviet socialist republic, was, along with the Byelorussian SSR, made a founding sovereign state member of the United Nations in 1945 on the representation that each of those states enjoyed sovereign freedom to secede from the USSR!

Ukraine has remained a separate, sovereign, founding member state of the United Nations from the inception of that organisation for nearly 75 years exactly on that basis. That suited Russia under Stalin, Khruschev, Brezhnev, Gorbachev and Putin.

Now Ukraine has no right to a separate democratic existence – because its elimination now equally suits Russia – Ukraine has now been relegated to an invention of Lenin and Stalin – a fiction. It is now a Russian land – as Russian as the Baltic states, Finland and Stalin's own birthplace, Georgia. The implications of Putin getting away with this invasion are obvious for them.

The consequence of the Putin invasion must be a re-commencement of the Cold War freeze-out of Russia. The Russian economy is fundamentally weak. Its supplies of natural gas and oil can be obtained elsewhere. Ending Nord Stream is only a start.

Diplomacy has signally failed. The era of perestroika and Deng's economic transformation of China have yielded place to monstrous totalitarianism and brazen kleptocracy in close alliance. We have got to get this picture into clear perspective.

If that alliance is to be the coming world order, we are entering a dark and dangerous phase of history – with many echoes of what our parents' and grandparents' generations beheld in its frightening reality.

It is no consolation remembering that the politically ugly Donald Trump emboldened Putin and Xi by his politically illiterate approach to his allies, to NATO, Canada, and the EU. His re-election would solve nothing.

The Democrats in America must prove what they are made of now. In Europe, we must show real unity of purpose. Macron was used by Putin to test Western resolve. Boris Johnson and Liz Truss were sidelined by events. Germany now seems to grasp that energy dependence on Putin comes with a terrible price.

The EU has economic strength which can be used to impose sanctions with real teeth and withstand retaliation to persuade all Russians that invading Ukraine comes with a heavy price for their short-, medium- and long-term wellbeing and happiness, and that Putin is the person who will make them pay that price.

I am gobsmacked at the ambivalence of Irish Marxists to Putin

23 March 2022

We must be clear on a few things. Ukraine was not, is not, and never could or will be a military threat to the Russian Federation. Likewise, Ukraine is not governed by a Nazi government and is in no need of de-Nazification. The excuse used by Putin for invading and annihilating a democratic sovereign state which is a member of the UN is an outrageous lie designed to conceal a base bid at crude conquest and annexation.

The only sense in which a democratic Ukraine threatens the Putin regime is that the Russian people have before them an example of a neighbouring democratic state which is not a kleptocracy and which does not imprison its dissidents, poison and assassinate its citizens, and does not suppress all protests against a corrupt feudal clique of oligarchs entirely subject to the whim and extortion of a dictator turned warlord.

That is why Belarus is tolerated; it is the weak mirror image of Putin's regime. It is a puppet in the same way that all the member states of the Warsaw Pact used to be.

Putin wants to hold power in all the former USSR's territory by the threat of subversion or invasion. Those parts of that territory that freely sought membership of NATO did not do so to threaten the Russian Federation; they did so to avoid the current fate of Ukraine or Putin's envisaged future fate for Ukraine.

It is an irony that the great majority of Irish people aged forty or less have forgotten the name or fate of Alexander Dubček, a reformist premier in Czechoslovakia (more exactly the First Secretary of the Praesidium of the Communist Party of Czechoslovakia) who sought only to liberalise the cruel Soviet regime that had held sway in his country. In August 1968, the Warsaw Pact under the Kremlin's command sent in its tanks and removed Dubček. It was an almost bloodless invasion that deposed Dubček in hours rather than weeks. A puppet regime was re-established in Prague and Dubček was briefly taken to Moscow but left in his nominal role without power. It took twenty years for real democracy to return to Prague.

Such a short, sharp surgical strike was envisaged last month for Ukraine. Putin believed that his massive conventional army could crush Kyiv in the same speedy way as Soviet power had extinguished post-war movements for democracy in Warsaw, Budapest, and Prague.

I am gobsmacked at the ambivalence of Irish Marxists to Putin

He has received a bloody nose that the Soviets never received since their pre-war mauling at the hands of the Finns and later from the Afghani mujaheddin. His infantry will not fight; his armour is ineffective; only his weapons of annihilation – missiles and long-range artillery – are working to order. And that order is the destruction of civilians and their communities.

I am gobsmacked at the ambivalence of our domestic Marxists and their fellow travellers about what is happening. Somehow the attempted annihilation of a democratic sovereign member state of the United Nations is the fault of the West. If only the West had left all democratic former Warsaw Pact countries out of NATO and left them open to invasion and subversion by the Kremlin, this war would never have started.

Damned right too. There would be no need for war. States like the Baltic and Balkan democracies, Ukraine, Poland, Moldova and Georgia would be peaceful satellites of the Kremlin kleptocracy.

The threadbare character of that worldview now has one Irish political party purging its archives of pro-Russian material. And that is very apt. The Russian communists were past masters of deletion, photo-shopping and correction of the public record to suit the needs of the present moment. In a totalitarian mindset, the record is entirely subservient to what is needed now. It's not just a matter of truth being the first casualty of war; truth is the indentured servant of the Marxist agenda. Embarrassing pro-Kremlin and anti-Western publications have been deleted; we all support (however mutedly) the Ukrainians now. Out with their old friend – bleach. The embarrassing votes in the European parliament are simply availing of that dubious online concept – the right to be forgotten.

Next, we will hear that the Ukraine should surrender because the cost in civilian lives is too great to bear. The useful idiots will parrot that view, citing humanitarian grounds for extinction of democracy in Ukraine. Resistance will be described as useless. It mirrors the Cold War useful idiots' mantra: 'Better Red than Dead'.

We need to be clear on one more thing; all the guilt and responsibility lies with Putin. This war is what he freely chose. The cruelty is all his. The dead are all his victims. It is unforgiveable. And there must be accountability.

The innocent dead cannot avail of any right to be forgotten.

Ukraine's defence cannot fail. Putin must be heavily defeated

14 June 2023

If the Ukrainian counteroffensive bogs down in a slow-moving ground campaign aimed at retaking one semi-abandoned village after another, there will be very serious consequences not only for Ukraine but also for the NATO member states and for the wider Western world.

If by the end of the summer or early autumn this year there has not been a forced withdrawal of Russian forces from the greater part of the territories that they have stolen from a UN member state, it is hard to see how that end will be accomplished in 2024.

Classic military theory of conventional warfare tells us that a ratio of three to one in favour of attacking forces is required to capture territory and to expel well dug-in defenders. In terms of manpower, such a ratio is beyond the capacity of the Ukrainian armed forces along the entire frontline of occupation.

In those circumstances, Ukraine's strategy will have to concentrate its forces in narrower spearheads aiming at breakthroughs, encirclement and destruction of static defending units. Hoping to rout demoralised defenders in strategically important locations by these means is the most obvious plan of campaign for Ukraine.

The big problem, of course, is that these considerations are equally obvious to the Russians. If they can motivate their defenders to wage a slow, defensive battle of attrition everywhere the Ukrainians concentrate attacking formations, they will defeat the counteroffensive.

While motivation and morale are hugely important factors, the great bulk of Ukrainian forces are recent recruits with limited combat training; the same applies to the Russian forces. The Ukrainians need sophisticated satellite and drone intelligence to identify Russian defensive positions and points of concentration vulnerable to attack by drones, rocket systems and artillery in order to spare their advancing infantry and armour from excessive casualties and damage. Up to now the Ukrainians have had the advantage of superior intelligence, presumably with Western assistance. The trick is to use that intelligence to sustain concentrated axes of advance to break through the frontlines and capture strategic targets or cut off Russian strategic supply lines.

Verdun-like struggles to capture or re-capture centres like Bakhmut are pointless if they involve heavy fighting in ruined built-up areas. The defender has a wholly disproportionate advantage in those cases. The battle for Bakhmut proved how pointless and wasteful full-on frontal assaults on trophy positions can be. There are clear indications that the Wagner forces learned a very bloody lesson at Bakhmut which they will never allow to be repeated anywhere else.

It is impossible to see how this counteroffensive could result in the recapture of the Crimean Peninsula. The most the Ukrainians could do in the southern theatre of operations would be to make a major advance towards the Sea of Azov, cutting or rendering unusable the land corridor to Crimea.

Of course, media armchair generals and commentators are not privy even to the outline aims of the Ukrainian counteroffensive.

It may well be that probes and feint attacks will first be deployed in order to flush out Russian countermeasures and to launch later concentrated attacks once intelligence is to hand that demonstrates points of weakness. We may only be witnessing such a preliminary phase at this point.

But the political reality remains that the West's appetite for massive assistance to Ukraine will ebb if this year's counteroffensive bogs down or makes only limited territorial advances. That is Zelenskyy's dilemma.

There is obvious Western reluctance to tool up the Ukrainian air forces with state-of-the-art F-16 fighter aircraft. If recently supplied Western tanks and armoured vehicles are combined with advanced weapon systems such as the American HIMARS rocket launchers to punch significant holes in Russian defences leading to major advances by the autumn, it will be possible to sustain public opinion and political confidence in support of continuing the war.

It was noteworthy recently that Anthony Blinken, the US Secretary of State, spoke in terms of a dual purpose for the Ukrainian counteroffensive – both recapturing territory and putting Ukraine into a much stronger position in any negotiations to end the conflict.

The fact that such negotiations are seen as inevitable does not mean that the counteroffensive is wholly redundant or unjustified. Everything depends on the circumstances in which such negotiations start.

Unless Russia is seen not merely to have failed in its earliest war aim, which was to occupy and subjugate the entirety of Ukraine (and it has failed completely in that aim) but also to have lost on the battlefield to a major extent, the outcome of those negotiations will be very grave for Ukraine, the Balkans, Georgia, Moldova, and the Baltic states in the short to medium term.

Putin's global strategy for Russia must be heavily defeated. His greatest global partner and admirer, Donald Trump, is hovering in the wings, stage right.

The next twelve or fourteen months are critical for us all.

Trump wants to divide, subjugate and destroy the EU into a continent of economic vassal states

5 March 2025

To call the Zelenskyy meeting in the Oval Office a 'shouting match', as many timid commentators managed to whitewash it, is a lie. It was a unilateral, vicious, premeditated political ambush – a mugging aimed at the political destruction of Volodymyr Zelenskyy in the eyes of the world – and in the eyes of his own people. It was as disgusting as it was shameful.

Trump is publicly showing what many of us have for years now discerned in him – sociopathic, bullying, ruthless, selfish and destructive traits – all clearly identified in the perceptive pen portrait of him written by his own niece, Mary Trump. He has a dangerous and dark personality which feeds off the fear of others.

While his first term in office fizzled out electorally in a clownish orgy of sackings of nearly all those whom he had appointed to hold high office, he has now surrounded himself with a circus of super-wealthy, unqualified sycophants whose fulltime activity is competitive adulation of their ringmaster's folly.

When I wrote here last year that the world was entering into a dark age redolent of the late 1930s, some acquaintances suggested that I was being unnecessarily pessimistic and alarmist. All our worst fears are being realised one by one. Trump's engagement with Putin has all the evil potential of the Molotov–Ribbentrop pact for the people of Europe – all Europe, not just the eastern bloodlands.

Trump has set his sights on the destruction of the European Union, a body that has brought peace and prosperity to a continent ravaged by war and the post-Yalta carve-up. That is not a charge or speculation; it is his stated aim. He has openly claimed that the EU was established to 'screw' America, later apologising for using that rude term 'if I said it'.

Make no mistake, Trump wants to divide, destroy and subjugate the EU into a continent of economic vassal states dominated by the US and the Russian Federation. Everything he says and does, and has said and has done, points to that strategic purpose. The words of his acolytes – Vance, Musk and Rubio – all point in that direction.

Under the guise of demanding that Europe pays for its own defence (in which case it would need its own power and deterrence equal to that of the US and Russia), he is pursuing an entirely different aim – that Europe should be weak and vulnerable, and accessible to bullying pressure from the US and Russia.

Trump does not want to create a democratic and secure Ukraine and is no longer a reliable guarantor of the integrity and sovereignty of, say, the Baltic states. They cannot by themselves fend off Russian aggression no matter what they do. The US alliance is being rapidly transformed into a Trumpian geopolitical protection racket in which vassal states like them must bend the knee to America's every whim.

Consider the US political assault on the economy, sovereignty and status of its longest-term ally, Canada. Under a manifestly fraudulent Trumped-up pretext of wishing to control illegal immigration and smuggling of fentanyl, he is seeking to impose crippling tariffs in gross violation of the North American Free Trade Agreement which he himself negotiated with Canada and Mexico.

Calling for Canada to be absorbed into the US as a state and referring to the Canadian premier as a 'governor' is no joke. It has badly backfired if Trump really did hope that right-wing Canadians would be seduced by such a prospect. That behaviour is deeply offensive and wrong. So is proposing the annexation by military force, if necessary, of Greenland. How does it sit with protecting Taiwan – an ally now being bullied into relocating its core economic activity – chip-making – to the US?

Do thinking Americans not cringe with shame as statesmen like Keir Starmer have to play out an idiotic diplomatic charade of waving a 'beautiful letter' in the Oval Office – apparently obsequiously signed in large marker inviting Trump to come and dine with King Charles? Starmer played a veritable stormer by keeping a straight face and bat during his shrewd encounter with the crude, loud and volatile Trump.

The suggestion made by Vance that Zelenskyy had never thanked the US for all the support it received under Biden's administration was patently false. So also, the ludicrous claim by the Trump administration that Zelenskyy does not want peace and only wants to continue the war was as contrived as it was false.

Most revealing was Trump's claim that Zelenskyy was risking World War Three. Just who has rattled the nuclear scabbard? Ukraine surrendered its nuclear arsenal in solemn exchange for a US security guarantee. If continued defence of its own existence by Ukraine risks World War Three, is Trump himself reacting to such a threat from Putin?

And if MAGA Man is cowed by such a threat now, God help the Baltic states. Because Trump's America won't.

The rise in anti-Semitism and other forms of racism must not be ignored and must be countered

27 January 2019

Today is Holocaust Memorial Day. In Ireland the official Holocaust commemoration takes place today in the Mansion House. It has taken place each year with the help of sponsorship of the Irish Government, initiated by me, since 2003.

As Minister for Justice, Equality and Law Reform in that government, I took the first opportunity to publicly and formally apologise, however belatedly as far as the Irish State was concerned, for the abject and dismal failure of the pre-war Irish Government to offer any refuge to those Jews who were desperately seeking refuge for themselves and their families from the vile Nazi persecution and for the begrudging attitude shown to the post-war Holocaust survivors.

I pointed out that the Irish State's failure was explained to a significant extent by the prevalence in Irish society of casual but widespread anti-Semitism. The Jewish community in Ireland, although almost uniquely in Europe granted explicit recognition in our Constitution enacted in 1937, were nonetheless subjected to very serious anti-Semitic prejudice and discrimination in the day-to-day social life of the State. Attacks on Jewishness and on what was termed the Masonic–Jewish–Marxist conspiracy and its influence in politics, the media, and the economic life of the country were commonplace, emanating from lay and clerical sources.

In the days of strident Catholic political hegemony, clerical authors not infrequently used books and pamphlets to warn the laity of the dangers of Jewish influence as the visible face of a satanic threat to faith and morals.

Such attitudes persisted well into the 1950s and 1960s.

It was in that historical context that I delivered a comprehensive apology on the authority of the Government and on behalf of the Irish State in 2003.

So the Round Room of the Mansion House will see today the 17th Irish Holocaust Memorial Ceremony in the same week as it hosted the Dáil 100 Commemoration.

Irish attitudes have changed dramatically over those 100 years. Dáil Éireann itself heard anti-Semitic speeches from some of its deputies; others doubtless held anti-Semitic views but refrained from uttering them on the floor of the House.

The immense barbarism, inhumanity and pure evil of the Holocaust is now well known. Children learn about if from an early age at school. The Holocaust Educational Trust helps hugely in that vital educational process.

We can say that it must never happen again – to the Jews or any other minority. But we must soak ourselves in that value to ensure that it does not happen again.

In today's world, the whole issue of anti-Semitism is again at the heart of public controversy and debate. In Britain, the issue was in the political spotlight until it was eclipsed somewhat by the Brexit crisis. Across Europe, there is evidence of a rise in anti-Semitism in many forms, from murders to terror incidents to vandalism and abuse.

The rise in anti-Semitism and other forms of racism is not imaginary and must not be ignored. It must be countered.

A hugely complicating factor is the ongoing crisis in Israel and Palestine and the failure of the world powers to devise and put into operation a two-state basis for peace in that region.

In Ireland, there is a groundswell of sympathy for the Palestinians. But that does not mean that there is any significant sympathy for the idea that Israel is illegitimate or must be destroyed.

The vast majority of Irish people acknowledge the existence and legitimacy of Israel and of its right to security and self-defence.

Where most Irish people have a serious problem is with the process of creeping annexation of the territories occupied by Israel after 1967 – a policy that is seen as one driven by a right-wing expansionist element in Israeli politics.

The fact that this element holds power on foot of elections in Israel and therefore claims a democratic mandate does not, for most Irish people, legitimise its policy of annexation, expropriation or expulsion. That policy must be judged in just the same way as it would be if Israel, like its neighbours, were not a democracy. There is no right to annexe territory deriving from democracy as distinct from any other form of government.

For those of us Irish who have always opposed and condemned anti-Semitism, who strongly support the rights of Jews both here and elsewhere to live as part of our communities free from anti-Semitism in any shape or form, and who strongly believe that Israel is a legitimate state, and who hope for a secure and safe Israel in a secure and safe Middle East, there is nothing inconsistent in seeking to prohibit the economic annexation of Palestinian territory by legislating to prohibit the importation and sale of goods produced on foot of illegal settlement in that territory in Ireland.

Either Ireland and indeed the EU believes in the illegality of territorial annexation of territory contrary to international law or we do not. The same applies equally to Ukraine and the West Bank.

Ireland regards the West Bank as occupied territory; Israel wants us to regard it as 'disputed' territory. Most Irish people and their government refuse to accept the 'disputed' label for the West Bank. It is properly described as occupied and, as a matter of international law, cannot lawfully be settled or annexed.

All of the foregoing is relatively trite stuff.

But when the Israeli government summons the Irish ambassador to a dressing-down on the basis that the Occupied Territories Goods Bill, which passed the Seanad with overwhelming support and is now being considered by the Dáil, is anti-Semitic, a line has been crossed.

There is not a line in the Bill which is anti-Semitic or anti-Israeli. In fact, Israel is not mentioned in it at all. It may be 'anti' the policies of the Netanyahu-led government but its content and purpose have received support from some Jews and Israelis internationally who can see nothing anti-Semitic in it at all.

Without getting self-important, I have to protest at being labelled anti-Semitic by the likes of Benjamin Netanyahu for supporting the Bill. When the likes of Michael McDowell, Ivana Bacik, and David Norris, to name but a few, can be publicly insulted by Netanyahu as anti-Semites for supporting this legislation, either language has lost all meaning or the present government in Israel has decided to pervert the meaning of anti-Semitism to smear anyone who stands up for decency and against the cynical usurpation of international norms and law. Nor are we liberal dupes or useful idiots being manipulated by racists or anti-Semites.

Netanyahu is busily backing Duterte in the Philippines, Crown Prince Salman in Saudi Arabia, Bolsonaro in Brazil, Orbán in Hungary and Trump in Washington.

When the Irish parliament is accused of anti-Semitism by the head of a government that exults in such company and wishes to unlawfully annexe the West Bank, unopposed and by stealth, Israel is badly betrayed. When he lets loose the charge of anti-Semitism against people who fairly consider themselves to be friendly both to Israel and the Jewish people across the world, he goes far too far.

Immigration and Asylum

No workable alternative to some form of Direct Provision

6 November 2019

There is a world of difference between economic migration and asylum seeking in national and international law. Ireland, as a member state of the EU, has certain obligations to permit EU citizens to migrate to Ireland to pursue economic activity in the state. We have entirely different and separate obligations under EU law, international law and domestic law in respect of those who seek international protection from state persecution.

The horrific death by asphyxiation of Vietnamese migrants in a sealed refrigerated container which people smugglers were cruelly using to traffic them into the UK has rightly evoked a rictus of revulsion and pity, especially here in view of the suspected Irish connection.

The coincidence of that awful event with protest in some rural communities related to the possible opening of Direct Provision centres raises questions about Irish attitudes, values, and social morality in relation to immigration generally.

That combination of news stories has also evoked some degree of virtue signalling among certain commentators, many of whom chose not to draw much distinction or to blur any distinction between asylum seeking on the one hand and purely economic migration on the other hand.

We have a common travel area with the UK which has existed since independence, and we and the UK accord to each other's nationals full right of migration, economic establishment and even the right to participate in parliamentary elections.

The common travel area will undoubtedly require us in a post-Brexit era to ensure that Ireland does not become an uncontrolled means of access to island of Britain. It is naive to think that Ireland's open land border, immigration laws and border controls can exist without regard to their implications for the UK.

It may not be fashionable to draw much distinction these days between genuine asylum seeking as a protection against state persecution and economic migrancy to escape poverty.

The historical fact of Irish famine-era and later emigration to America, Britain and Commonwealth states is deeply ingrained in our collective memory and values. We even refer to our illegal migrants in the US by the euphemistic term 'undocumented'.

But it is simply neither xenophobic nor racist to have legal barriers on inward economic migration or to enforce them. To fail to do so would be chaotic and unlawful. Where migration masquerades as asylum seeking, we must have laws, systems, controls and enforcement measures to counter such abuse effectively.

We are bound by EU law and international conventions to give asylum protection, including the full right to work and live normal lives, the same entitlements to social welfare, housing, education and health as are enjoyed by Irish citizens, to genuine refugees; we are not bound to afford those rights to persons who come to our state posing as refugees from state persecution when in reality they are economic migrants. It is utterly unsustainable, socially and financially, to treat all would-be economic migrants as though they were refugees. Worse still, to do so would inevitably tend towards racist unrest and disorder.

Take Direct Provision for asylum applicants as an example. In a period of acute domestic housing shortage and sky-high rents, the State cannot simply provide family homes directly or through rent subsidies for everyone who applies to be recognised as a refugee. Ireland is not alone in this matter. The UK also has huge problems accommodating asylum applicants in temporary housing provided by Home Office contractors.

Nor can the State pay social welfare payments at domestic levels to everyone who claims to be a refugee. The same applies to work permits. A simple claim to be a refugee cannot put every migrant on the same footing as a recognised refugee.

If it were legally possible to work in Ireland simply by coming here and applying for asylum, our entire system of immigration controls and employment permit regulation would collapse.

There is no workable alternative to some form of Direct Provision for asylum seekers.

Where the State has failed is in relation to processing applications for asylum status. There has been massive delay in establishing a system that decides on such applications. The International Protection Act 2015 took almost a decade to be enacted.

Coupled with under-resourcing of the decision-making process and accumulated backlogs in the courts' judicial review list, the delay in deciding cases and implementing decisions on such cases has become massive and indefensible.

Many people spend years in Direct Provision as a result. The Supreme Court invalidated permanent legal prohibition on work permits for unresolved asylum applicants. But the greatest problems of unfairness stem directly from the length of the process itself.

Virtue signalling is no answer to the very real issues which arise from conflating economic migrancy and asylum seeking.

Programme refugees from the Syrian conflict are human beings; so too are would-be economic migrants from Georgia and Albania. But that does not mean that they must be treated by Ireland in the same way.

And it is wrong-headed to condemn the Taoiseach for pointing out the difference.

Danger of far-right politics exploiting asylum issues

28 December 2022

The Tánaiste, Micheál Martin, recently spoke of the attempts by far-right groups to seek entry into our parliament by the back door, encouraging some members to adopt racial replacement rhetoric in their contributions to debates in the Oireachtas. And his observations have some substance, even if those contributions have gained relatively little traction in the public's mind.

The notion that Ireland is, or could become, a soft touch for uncontrolled economic migrancy posing as asylum seeking is a potent political weapon if used in the wrong hands.

While some ideologues tend to ignore the distinction between economic migration on the one hand and seeking asylum from persecution on the other – or to minimise that distinction – it remains important for the purposes of international law and for Ireland's national policy development in relation to migration. Ireland offers protection to refugees from persecution and offers subsidiary protection to some persons who, although not refugees, are at risk of serious harm if repatriated.

The 1951 UN Convention on Refugees originally applied only to historic refugees in the aftermath of the Second World War, but its ambit was later extended to all potential victims of state persecution.

The Definite Article: IMMIGRATION AND ASYLUM

In an era of cheap mass air travel, the protection right accorded to would-be applicants for asylum is massively expanded in practice. Developed countries find it immensely difficult to deal with the volume of asylum-seeking arrivals in a manner and time frame that is both fair and effective. It is that inability which creates an opening for economic migrancy posing as asylum-seeking and for international trafficking of economic migrants.

Despite the terms of the Dublin III rules, would-be applicants for asylum in Ireland find little difficulty in transiting through the EU to seek asylum in Ireland.

This paper reported in October that 40% of asylum seekers at Dublin Airport appear to have lost or destroyed their travel/identity documents between boarding a flight for Dublin and presenting at immigration control. The Department of Justice has acknowledged that the volume of would-be asylum seekers has grown very significantly when compared with pre-pandemic levels. The rate of undocumented applicants is 225% higher than it was in 2018.

Quite apart from the 50,000 Ukrainians who were rightly given temporarily refugee status here this year (including rights to work, welfare and education), we already have 10,000 other asylum seekers in state accommodation.

In the months January to June 2022, 7,760 non-Ukrainian persons applied for asylum in Ireland (an annual rate of more than 10,000); the number of undocumented applicants at the airport was 40% of that figure.

Almost 20% of asylum-seekers at Dublin Airport came from Georgia, a country with visa-free access to the EU but with no direct flights. Other main countries of origin are Somalia and Algeria.

While the Department of Justice surmised that the growth in post-pandemic asylum seeking in Ireland could be explained in part by less sympathetic protection regimes in other countries, minister

Helen McEntee stated her belief that this higher rate of asylum seeking is likely to continue.

All of this is thrown into sharper focus by the crisis in emergency accommodation arising from Putin's savage invasion of Ukraine, increased reliance on extended Direct Provision facilities, and an underlying failure to ensure that home-building matches overall growth in our population.

The number of genuine asylum-seekers from Georgia must be tiny. Destroying travel documents is designed to make the Irish international protection legal process longer and less effective. While some may think that air carriers should be obliged to scan and keep records of passengers' passports, that may be difficult to implement in practice.

As if the present emergency accommodation crisis were not enough, we must recall the vital need to keep the common travel area between Ireland and the UK in proper working order. We cannot afford to become a revolving back door for illegal migrants to Britain.

It is unreasonable to expect that the UK government establishes full immigration border controls between the North and Britain – not to mention from the South. No government at Westminster, even a Labour-led government, can be indifferent to the possibility that transit through Ireland succeeds the Channel boat crossing route as a means of illegal entry.

We must face up to these issues honestly, reasonably, and, most of all, effectively if we are not going to play into the hands of extremist would-be politicians trading in xenophobia and fear.

International protection applications must be processed far more quickly. Destruction of air travel/identity documents must become a negative for applicants. Judicial review should be simplified and take a different form, perhaps, in lower-level summary immigration courts. All areas of delay need to be tackled urgently.

So Micheál Martin was correct to warn us about the dangers of far-right politics exploiting this crisis. But words of warning are insufficient; action is also required.

We have a national right and duty to determine migration policy

18 January 2023

Like it or not, Ireland is part of what is called the West. While we may not be part of any military alliance with other Western states, we are a member state of the EU and we depend on the West for our security, our prosperity, for our freedoms, and, in some respects, for our value systems and our cultural life.

That is not to say that we are a mere province of some Western empire; we have a considerable degree of autonomy – culturally, politically and economically – based on our status as a sovereign, independent political state.

The very notion of an independent nation state is questioned by many, particularly on the far left, which views the nation state as an essentially bourgeois concept inconsistent with their internationalist socialist ideology.

Nationalism is no longer seen as a fashionable political ideology. Taken to extremes, it develops a repugnant character, both internally and externally.

But the notion of nation state must be considered in the round. Unless we aspire to a single world democracy (whatever that could be, if it could exist at all) or some Orwellian world such as that imagined in his 1984, in which vast totalitarian empire blocs – Oceania, Eurasia and Eastasia – make war in pursuit of world control, it is difficult to see an alternatives to a world order based largely on the nation state as the granular component of international order.

The United Nations and the earlier League of Nations recognised this fundamental reality. So does the EU, when it is not as viewed by its federalist extremists such as Guy Verhofstadt and Daniel Cohn-Bendit, who in 2012 published a manifesto 'For Europe!' demanding a 'postnational revolution' for the EU, to start in 2014 by a decision of the EU parliament to unilaterally declare the EU a sovereign entity from which all dissenting states would then have to exit.

That brazen bid to extinguish national sovereignty for member states was published four years before Britain's disastrous Brexit referendum decision and fed into the climate of English public opinion that brought about Brexit. As Verhofstadt told his readers: 'the world will be organised from now on around poles which can be described as empires' and he called for the creation of the EU as a 'good empire'.

But ridiculous and dangerous as such rhetoric may seem to most people in Ireland, judging by opinion polls, it equally raises the valid question as to why we value, as we do, the existence of independent nation states.

Without nation states as building blocks of international order, humanity would be condemned to a totalitarian future based on Orwell's image of 1984.

The EU cannot become a single democratic sovereign entity any more than the ill-fated Hapsburg empire of Austria-Hungary could aspire to that status. EU-wide elections where most voters could not even speak or understand the language of candidates would be grotesque mockeries of democracy. France, for all its problems, is not merely as described by Verhofstadt: 'Who are the French? They are Europeans who live in the French area.'

My point is this. We are not in the business of creating empires – good or bad. Nation states are valued as the basic components of international order precisely because they each enjoy a level of coherence and common interest. Viewing the EU as a largely intergovernmental partnership of member states is not merely truthful and realistic – it is sensible and sustainable. It is much more democratic in outcome than the neo-Hapsburgian good empire wished for by Verhofstadt could ever be.

Holding that view of the EU does not make one less a supporter of the EU than Verhofstadt or the federalists. Arguably, it is their view which poses a much greater threat to the EU than that of realists who accept the intergovernmental partnership model.

We have agreed to the right of EU citizens to come and live in Ireland to participate in our economic life. And that has worked well for us. While it has changed our demography, it has not undermined cohesion or common interest which underpins the rationale for our status as a sovereign state.

The foregoing implies a very careful path to be trodden by Irish politicians. Immigration may be a novelty for a state that spent its first eighty years haemorrhaging its population; but immigration has been good for us, I think.

But apart from the EU right to reside and work in other EU states, we have a national right and duty to determine migration policy. Our government must exercise that right carefully. Half-thought-out proposals to extend asylum rights to climate refugees are not helpful.

If we want to avoid creating a space for far-right politics in Ireland, we need our elected politicians and government to respect and value the people's sense of cohesion and common interest.

No time for consultation in the middle of a crisis

8 February 2023

In the middle of a crisis, there is very little sense in attacking the Government for failing to consult local communities about the selection of places to accommodate refugees or asylum seekers. Who in the community would you need to consult if you were minded to use, say, the disused Baggot Street Hospital or the vacant Jurys Hotel for that purpose? Local traders? Local public representatives? Residents or community associations?

If there were no such crisis it would be nice, respectful and sensible to conduct a relaxed prior consultation with all of those categories. But we have a crisis on our hands. Finding emergency accommodation is no easy task. And it is not going to be any easier as we approach the tourist season and entire regional economies need hotel accommodation for tourists to sustain restaurants, bars, music venues and festivals. Livelihoods are at stake if tourism dries up.

Added to our underlying shortage of domestic accommodation, high rents, stuttering home-building, planning disputes, gross under-provision of social and affordable housing by housing authorities, the Ukrainian refugee wave and increased non-Ukrainian asylum-seeking reaching record levels, we have a perfect storm.

It is now accepted that we cannot end Direct Provision in the present circumstances. In fact, one problem with Direct Provision is the inability of people with leave to remain to leave their Direct Provision accommodation.

The war in Ukraine is not likely to end soon. A mass return of Ukrainian war refugees is a long way off, as best one can judge.

The Government can do some things to avoid having a semi-permanent situation of people forced to live in the streets, in tent camps, or in field hospital-style accommodation in halls, arenas or warehouses. We need emergency legislation to empower a specialist agency to acquire, lease, or take on compulsory licence property such as Baggot Street hospital, disused hotels, under-used religious institutional buildings, vacant buildings and the like.

We also need to face up to the failures being encountered in the administration of the International Protection Act 2015. Ireland is not alone in buckling under the strain of migration posing as asylum-seeking. We need clarity in this area.

Delays in adjudicating on claims for asylum have not been dealt with since that Act was commenced. The Cabinet was told that Gardaí have resumed a skeleton spot check twice weekly to attempt to deal with asylum-seekers boarding flights to Ireland from safe countries and claiming to have lost or destroyed their ID and passports when presenting at immigration.

The excuse offered for this is that asylum-seekers might want to protect the identities of persons supplying them with such documentation. That cannot be allowed in the real world except in the most limited of cases. It massively delays any fair adjudication of the great majority of cases of missing documentation. And that is no accident. Garda checks carried out randomly twice a week is not the answer.

We were told that such checks were discontinued after Charlie Flanagan left office. Why? And why are they only now being reintroduced? I suspect that it was thought to be pointless in the context of an ongoing obligation to deal with all missing documentation cases.

Forty per cent of asylum seekers from places such as Georgia and Albania arriving undocumented demonstrates that the system is broken and is being abused. Georgians have visa-free access to EU states. Georgia and Albania are 'safe countries'.

Why do Georgia and Albania account for 20% and 13% respectively of recent asylum claims in Ireland? Why are they not dealt with by a summary process and returned if they fail to produce immediate and cogent evidence of a real likelihood of state persecution?

We are not told what percentage of all asylum claims are successful at the end of a process that is now normally taking two and three years in ordinary cases. We need to know that figure. And we need to know by country where applications are succeeding.

This paper reported that a 'fast track' procedure has been commenced since November to deal with safe country cases, resulting in 352 interviews having occurred. That is not really a fast track at all. applications.

Even if the Government's stated intention is to reduce the period for 'safe country' adjudications from two years to three months, it will be ineffectual if applicants simply disappear at the end and avoid deportation.

Apart from the Ukraine refugees, we are now heading back to the record levels of asylum-seeking that we witnessed twenty years ago.

Ireland needs migrants and we should warmly welcome them when they come here legally. They have made a massive contribution to our society in many, many ways.

Dealing fairly and effectively with migration posing as asylum-seeking is difficult. But it must be done if we are to avoid playing into the hands of political extremists for whom failure to do so is manna from heaven.

Irish Politics

The Lowry tapes

5 April 2013

The secretly taped conversation between Michael Lowry and Kevin Phelan, which occurred apparently in 2004, tells us a lot about what happened behind the scenes between some of the dramatis personae inn the Moriarty Tribunal.

While Michael Lowry now insists that the payment of almost £250,000 to Mr Phelan which features in the conversation was a payment that was 'fully declared' (whatever that means), he has been careful not to dispute that the voice on the tape is his, and he has not suggested that the tape was doctored in any way, or that he did not use the words attributed to him in the transcripts of the tape which were published in the *Sunday Independent*.

It was only when excerpts from the tape were broadcast in their original form on the Vincent Browne programme on TV3 that the penny dropped in the minds of the Irish public that they were actually listening to an expletive-laden, foulmouthed plea by an elected Irish public representative to an obscure land speculator not to take any steps which could link him in any way with the Doncaster Rovers land deal then being investigated by the Moriarty Tribunal.

That investigation formed part of its enquiries as to whether Denis O'Brien, who had an interest in the Doncaster development

The Lowry tapes

(which, we hear, he has finally disposed of just this month), was using, or had used or had intended to use, the Doncaster land deal to enrich Michael Lowry, whom the Tribunal found had wrongfully intervened as Minister in the interests of Mr O'Brien in a competitive licensing process in which Mr O'Brien's consortium had been successful.

The taped phone call also suggested, to many peoples' minds, that Mr Lowry seemed well-acquainted with the manner in which Denis O'Brien proposed to deal with the ongoing investigations of the Moriarty Tribunal.

The details and the intricacies of the Moriarty Tribunal's enquiries were only understood by a small minority of the Irish public when they were ongoing, and the exact significance of the evidence tendered to the Tribunal was quite difficult to follow at the time (in part due to the lamentable failure of the Irish media to keep the Irish people in the picture).

Once the transcript of the tape was published in the *Sunday Independent*, and once the tape itself was broadcast on TV3, the exact implications of what was said on the tape became clear to those few who had the time and the industry to revisit the evidence that had been given to the Moriarty Tribunal concerning the alleged involvement of Michael Lowry and Denis O'Brien in English property transactions.

Michael Lowry had told the Tribunal that he had made only one payment in the amount of £65,000 to Kevin Phelan and that this payment related to a land transaction in Wigan. The tape suggests that there had been an additional payment arranged by Mr Lowry to Mr Phelan in the sum of £250,000. The tape suggests that Mr Lowry was confident that this larger payment would not be discovered by the Moriarty Tribunal. The tape also suggested that Mr Lowry was very fearful that the £250,000 transaction would be linked by the Tribunal to Westferry Ltd, a company involved in the

Doncaster Rovers land deal in which Denis O'Brien was involved. If that linkage were found, Mr Lowry believed that he would be 'f*****g ruined'.

It is important to put these matters into context.

Kevin Phelan would not testify at the Moriarty Tribunal and could not be compelled to do so because he resided in Northern Ireland.

The Tribunal concluded (at paragraph 16.125 of its final report) that the admitted payment by Mr Lowry of £65,000 to Mr Phelan 'was for the principal purpose of presenting a contrived falsehood to the Tribunal'. That contrived falsehood entailed the withdrawal of assertions previously made by Mr Phelan against Mr Christopher Vaughan, a Northampton solicitor, in connection with the provision to the Tribunal of falsified correspondence, and, at the same time, the furnishing by Mr Phelan to Mr Vaughan of an untrue, innocent explanation for doctored correspondence tendered to the Tribunal by Christopher Vaughan when it was known to be untrue.

The Tribunal further concluded (at paragraph 16.126) that a wholly separate and distinct payment of £150,000 to Kevin Phelan made by Denis O'Brien through Westferry Ltd had a similar motivation, in that it was 'primarily intended to ensure that Mr Kevin Phelan would not further undermine the false version of Mr Lowry's involvement in the U.K. properties already tendered in evidence to the Tribunal in 2001, and the false explanation already presented, with the complicity of Mr Kevin Phelan, for the existence and provision to the Tribunal of the falsified "short form" correspondence'.

Although Michael Lowry and Denis O'Brien strongly denied (and continue to deny and reject) the Tribunal's findings in respect of the use of UK property transactions as a channel to enrich Michael Lowry using funds owned or controlled by Denis O'Brien, the Tribunal came to the conclusion that in respect of two of the transactions – Mansfield and Cheadle – Denis O'Brien had caused a very large payment, or benefit equivalent to a payment, to be made to Michael Lowry in circumstances giving rise to a reasonable inference that the motion for making the payment was connected to a public office held by him or had the potential to influence the discharge by him of such office.

As regards the Doncaster deal, the Tribunal found that, contrary to the denials of Michael Lowry and Denis O'Brien, Michael Lowry did have an involvement in the Doncaster transaction. It found (at paragraph 16.127) that this connection was one 'which it was intended would entail a payment to, or the conferral of a pecuniary advantage on him, the source of which was the ultimate beneficial owner of Doncaster, that is, Denis O'Brien.'

That the recently disclosed tape would have been of profound importance to the enquiries of the Moriarty Tribunal there can be no doubt. Its publication, in my mind, provides confirmation that the Moriarty Tribunal drew the correct inferences from the limited evidence it had in relation to the UK property transactions.

I use the word 'limited' in relation to the evidence on the UK property transactions in a charitable way. Anyone who reads the report of the Moriarty Tribunal will not fail to notice the extent and duration of what the Tribunal found was a sustained campaign to throw the Tribunal off the scent by the provision of false testimony and false documentation in relation to those transactions.

The Tribunal found that Michael Lowry, Kevin Phelan, Aidan Phelan and Christopher Vaughan were all complicit in a plan to mislead the Tribunal by supplying it with false evidence and false documents designed to conceal the truth concerning the UK property transactions (see paragraphs 8.104 to 8.110 of the Report).

What the Tribunal could never state with certainty was the *exact* nature of Michael Lowry's involvement in the Doncaster deal or the *exact* amount by which he was intended to gain by his involvement. Why not? It found that 'having regard to the concealment, suppression and deliberate falsehoods encountered by the Tribunal in endeavouring to conduct its inquiries into all of the UK properties, both on the part of the principals, and on the part of their associates and representatives', further inquiry on that matter would be fruitless (paragraph 10.121).

However, the Tribunal found that the motive for the deception strategy deployed against it in relation to the Mansfield and Cheadle properties was 'because of the acute sensitivity engendered by unwanted disclosure of that connection', and it found that 'experienced and respected professional persons involved, including the solicitor who remains retained by Mr O'Brien in the Doncaster transaction, set about and implemented a cynical and mendacious course of furnishing to the Tribunal a materially false documentary record of those transactions' (paragraph 8.112).

Happily, the massive report of the Tribunal is still available to every citizen of this Republic via the internet, so that each and every one of us can consider not merely the report but also the oral testimony on which the report is based.

While I don't expect that many people will plough through the report of the Moriarty Tribunal from beginning to end, it is easily accessible to those who wish to do so. No one, I feel, should criticise the report or discount its findings without taking the elementary step of reading it – or at least reading the executive summary.

In a related, but distinct, context, judges of the Supreme Court have very recently remarked as to the unprecedented nature and gravity of the plaintiffs' claims based on findings of the Moriarty Tribunal which in substance are being relied on in litigation by disappointed competitors in the mobile phone licensing competition which they claim was vitiated by the interventions by Mr Lowry. The Irish State, as one of the defendants in that litigation, while denying liability, is now claiming to be indemnified by its co-defendants, Mr Lowry and Mr O'Brien, in respect of any judgment for damages if the plaintiffs succeed.

It will be interesting to see whether Kevin Phelan is a willing witness in those proceedings or whether his testimony will be secured in the UK by means of mutual legal assistance in civil proceedings.

On any view, the very suggestion that a Minister of the Irish State, after allegedly wrongly intervening in a public competitive licensing process in favour of one applicant, could later become the beneficiary or object of a series of transactions or payments amounting to €1,000,000 at the behest of that applicant is a matter of the gravest public importance.

That is why the Moriarty Tribunal was established. That is why its findings to that effect are so important and cannot be ignored or discounted.

The publication of the Kevin Phelan tape is therefore in itself a matter of huge public importance. Its implications are very far-reaching. While no one believes that its contents should not be treated with care and circumspection, that is no reason for ignoring it or for treating it as 'too hot to handle'.

That only one newspaper (the *Sunday Independent*) and only one broadcaster (TV3) has put serious resources into the publication of the contents of the tape, and that only a few brave analysts have attempted to give the public some sense of the significance of the tape in the media, raises concerns about the decision by RTE, our national broadcaster (which has not merely the right but the duty to report on matters of public importance in a fair and impartial way), to steer clear of the issue and, largely speaking, to ignore it. That failure is mystifying and worrying. RTE's silence, in effect, is genuinely a 'deafening silence'.

It is bad enough for Ireland that the Moriarty Tribunal had to make the findings that it did. If we have reached the point at which our national broadcaster is too frightened to deal thoroughly, impartially and objectively with an issue which goes to the heart of our standards as a democracy, as a community, and as a sovereign state, we have reached a pretty pass.

The law of libel has recently been amended to facilitate careful and fair journalism and broadcasting on issues of public importance. Provided RTE is fair and careful, it could easily present the Irish people with a fair and clear picture of the issues involved without defaming anyone and without infringing its own duties of impartiality. Our libel laws are not the problem. Absence of will appears to be the problem.

We are constantly bombarded on RTE with the message told that 'there are many ways to pay our TV licence but that feng shui is not one of them'. On the Lowry tape, all we are getting from RTE is feng shui.

If the national broadcaster can pay its programme presenters multiples of the Taoiseach's salary without blushing, as it can, it should be able to find the funds to pay a modest wage to programme researchers who are not invertebrates and who have the skills and the drive to examine and explain the true significance of the Lowry tape for the Irish public.

Let us remember that it was precisely because the civil and criminal courts were not appropriate venues for the making of the enquiries to which the Moriarty Tribunal relates that the Tribunal itself was established. Our courts are adversarial, not inquisitorial.

Tribunals should not be necessary in a society in which ordinary standards of transparency and accountability are functioning properly. The print and broadcasting media are vital organs in keeping the body politic healthy, functional and democratic.

In the UK – the land of Mansfield, Cheadle and Doncaster – the Kevin Phelan tape would already have probably resulted in a vigorous police enquiry centring on whether the discrepancies between its contents and sworn testimony given to the Moriarty Tribunal disclosed any criminal offence.

In Ireland, by contrast, an Irish version of Chris Huhne MP would never have resigned and would be preparing to top the poll at the next election by portraying himself as a victim of his wife, the Establishment, and the media.

The Government is feigning unconcern in the hope that 'this too will pass'. The present Government's attitude to what was found against Michael Lowry may mystify some people – but not me.

Our media seem to be cowed and the 'authorities' seem to be paralysed in their responses to matters of serious public importance.

Must we wait for *Panorama* or *Spotlight* or *World in Action* or *Dispatches* to inform the Irish public about major issues as was required in the past. Maybe the cynic who famously proposed that our national symbol should be changed to the harp with broken strings above the motto 'T'will Do' was not so far off the mark after all.

The whip system is too severe – conscience votes should be permitted

24 July 2024

The Oireachtas is the name given by the Constitution to our national parliament. Article 15.2 states that it 'shall consist of the President and two Houses, viz.: a House of Representatives to be called Dáil Éireann and a Senate to be called Seanad Éireann'.

Using American terms such as House of Representatives and Senate was a deliberate choice in describing a bicameral parliament. In 1937, the desire was to signal the republican nature of the Irish State, even if the State was to remain part of the Commonwealth until 1949.

But ever since the foundation of the Irish Free State in 1922, there had been in Dáil Éireann a culture of firm imposition of a party whip on TDs. Dáil majorities were tight enough to lean heavily against individual TDs breaking ranks occasionally to vote with the other parliamentary side.

There were historical exceptions – but those exceptions were so rare as to prove the rule conclusively. Liam Cosgrave, as party leader, broke ranks with his own party to support the Offences Against the State Bill in 1972 and Micheál Martin pragmatically allowed his party a free vote on the abortion issue.

Leo Varadkar, as the late Noel Whelan wrote here in 2018, had described in 2013 the idea of a free vote on conscience matters as 'hogwash' and his party's whip warned against opening the 'the flood gates' on free votes.

I found it very strange, therefore, that when I went to the Taoiseach's office to discuss the progressing of the Seanad Reform Bill in early 2019, Varadkar suggested that he would offer the Bill no support but allow a free vote in the Dáil if it was moved in the Dáil. That was the intended cynical kiss of death to any prospect of reform – and it tore up solemn, clear commitments he personally had publicly made to the Seanad.

In Germany, members of the Bundestag cannot be penalised for voting in accordance with their conscience. Article 38 of the Basic Law provides that Bundestag members are 'representatives of the whole people, not bound by orders and instructions and responsible only to their conscience'.

While there is de facto party discipline on mundane matters, Bundestag members cannot be penalised for following their conscience.

The rules of the Progressive Democrats uniquely had a similar conscience clause for TDs and senators, which was availed of on at least one occasion.

The whip system is too severe – conscience votes should be permitted

But the party whip in Ireland is the most severe regime among modern liberal democracies. Conscious breach of the whip, even in conscience matters, has resulted and will normally result in forfeiture of membership of a representative's parliamentary party membership and chairmanship of parliamentary committees, together with all but vestigial rights to participate in time-limited debates, or suspension or deselection.

The British system and the American system, for all their flaws, do not quake at the thought of governments losing votes at the hands of their own supporters who disagree with the majority in their own parties.

Whatever about the Dáil, there is little or no excuse for imposing such a rigid whip system in the Seanad. The Seanad cannot vote down a budgetary measure. It can initiate and pass Bills and it can amend Dáil Bills.

But if the Dáil does not agree with those amendments, it can, after a mere 90 days, override the Seanad, and deem its Bill to have been passed by both Houses. Where that happens, there is a theoretical right for half of the Seanad and one third of the Dáil to petition the President to refer the Bill to the people by referendum (a power never yet used). Even then, it requires a majority of voters consisting of at least one-third of the electorate to stop a Bill from becoming law.

So there is very little reason for the Dáil to keep the Seanad in permanent subjugation by the indefensible system of Seanad election imposed by self-serving laws enacted by the Dáil or by the use of a rigid party whip system in the Seanad.

During the 'confidence and supply' FG government from 2016 to 2020, the Seanad majority was not under any rigid government whip, and the Occupied Territories Bill, although opposed by the FG government, was passed by the non-government parties and independents in the Seanad. The roof didn't fall in. That Seanad behaved responsibly and the Dáil minority FG government functioned reasonably well.

Why should a democratically elected Irish legislator need to imperil or lose his or her entire career by standing by his or her conscience?

The forthcoming general election allows an opportunity for a newly elected cohort of allied independents to insist that any government elected with their participation and support relaxes somewhat the vice-like grip of the whip in the Houses of the Oireachtas – at least to the same extent as happens, without calamity, in other European democracies.

Such change would enhance public respect for our democracy – not diminish it further.

Unforced error from Gerry won't bother Northern supporters

8 December 2013

There is a general delusion that Gerry Adams was in the IRA at some point in his life.

Grainy footage of him walking beside a coffin wearing his favourite 'men in black' outfit and a natty little beret entirely misses the point that this was purely a rebellious young man's fashion statement long before *Men In Black* came into vogue. Nothing more. Funerals were a place to see and be seen in West Belfast in those days. So studying such old footage and photos in a search for Gerry wearing dark outfits is really as pointless as reading a tattered *Where's Wally?* book.

Of course this delusion was widespread.

The recent recollections of many former Belfast IRA men and women that Gerry the Beret was their OC are just signs that they are getting old and forgetful – probably a symptom of post-traumatic stress syndrome related to the armed struggle.

And, in fairness, the delusion was shared by the Brits. They even thought that he was secretly released from Long Kesh to negotiate with them on behalf of the IRA. The 'beret photos' must have taken them in as well.

Those negotiations, come to think of it, must have been a bit confusing; the Brits offering Gerry terms for a deal and a baffled and confused Gerry replying: 'I keep telling ye, ye've got the wrong mon', which, in fairness to him, is probably what he said the day he was locked up in the first place.

No wonder those discussions were kept secret. Imagine the embarrassment if the media discovered that Her Majesty's Government had spent weeks talking to Gerry the Beret under the delusion that he was in the IRA. Anyway, the failure of the negotiations supports the obvious conclusion that they had selected the wrong man to talk to.

If you look at the IRA rules, by the way, you will find no mention of a 'member' of the IRA. There were volunteers or 'oglaigh' – never 'members'. The only people who used the term 'member' were chief superintendents giving opinion evidence in prosecutions under the Offences Against the State Act.

Since the IRA rules don't provide for 'members', Gerry couldn't have been a 'member'. Silly us! Missing the obvious again!

If there was indeed no such thing as an IRA 'member', Gerry couldn't have been a member, and it's only right and proper that he should put that denial on the record. Talk about 'slow learners'! What part of 'No' do we, the public, not understand, as Gerry the Beret himself often asked.

And he was only pointing out the obvious when he made his 'laissez-faire' explanation for the shooting of two RUC officers, Bob Buchanan and Harry Breen, this week. How careless could they get – driving around the South Armagh heartland unarmed? It was all bound to happen – even if it was 'tragically for them' as Gerry the Beret so thoughtfully put it this week.

And if the volunteers in the ASU that killed them had asked Gerry at the time, I am equally sure he would have told them that the double murder was a tragedy – a tragedy in which they were only doing their 'duty' as IRA volunteers – oops, I nearly said 'members'.

The *Smithwick Report* concluded on the balance of probabilities that an unidentified garda's tip-off played a central part in the Breen and Buchanan murders.

For some daft reason, Gerry the Beret decided to lead Sinn Féin charge into a public repudiation of that tribunal conclusion. The Sinn Féin position is that there was no garda tip-off involved.

Exactly why they should blunder into this debate is mystifying.

If an unknown garda gave them a tip-off, the IRA would have to deny it anyway. To 'out' the presence of a mole in Dundalk Garda station would be treacherous. What useful purpose would be served in exposing the facts?

And we know that the Provos went to very considerable lengths to concoct a very elaborate, different, false version of what happened involving a claim of a major telephone tapping operation in Dundalk telephone exchange – all in an effort to put the public off the scent. And the *Phoenix* magazine published it all as fact.

That decoy version was Provo disinformation – just like the 'Jean McConville is alive and living with a British soldier' story disseminated after her disappearance. But who came up with that story and why? Cui Bono?

To describe and justify the IRA terrorist campaign as a 'war' is to mangle language. The IRA terror and British counter-terror was a vile, useless campaign of inhumanity. Intelligence-gathering using moles was par for the course. Counter-intelligence was part of what the IRA Army Council did.

Fred Scappaticci is a symbol of all that was vile in the IRA. He, in his role as the IRA's chief enforcer and 'nutter', tortured and had shot 'volunteers' to extract confessions of treachery, and then shared his intelligence both with his paymasters in the IRA Army Council and with his paymasters in British intelligence. Anyone who thinks Denis Donaldson was the most senior mole in the IRA is very, very naïve. The way in which senior Provos steer clear of mentioning Scappaticci even today speaks volumes. Just think about it. And then think about it again.

No tribunal, truth commission or truth process will ever uncover the extent of Provo espionage or, for that matter, the extent of infiltration by intelligence in the Provo leadership. Nothing in that area which appears to be true can be taken at face value. And nobody – however senior or plausible – is innocent or trustworthy.

I doubt that the 'laissez-faire' episode will damage Gerry the Beret in his political heartland. But his colleagues in Sinn Féin who are trying to get into government soon must wonder why he made this unforced error.

At a time when our Government appears to have seriously violated the provisions of Article 28 of the Constitution by tabling a totally phony health estimate to the Dáil (an Estimate is not a vague statement of upper limits of expenditure), and at a time when the Government is trying to distract the media and the public from the real health budgetary fiasco with the top-ups controversy, Gerry the Beret seems to be intent on snatching defeat from the jaws of victory.

Sinn Féin's leaders are glove puppets for unseen controllers

23 October 2024

In the last few weeks, there has been much publicity concerning internal disputes and disciplinary processes in Sinn Féin. Now that we are in an election run-up, some consider that these controversies are sure to damage the party's prospects on election day.

But the cause of a major decline in SF support is longer and deeper than these recent problems. After the 2020 election, SF were preparing for the role of leading party in the next government. Buoyed up by the results of that election, the party began a campaign that took its voter-share dominance for granted.

It began to interact with financial, commercial, and professional business organisations. Meetings were sought with the major legal and accountancy practices. TDs were directed to wear jackets, collars and ties. The aura of a government-in-waiting was assiduously cultivated, with opinion poll ratings consistently hovering around 30%.

But suddenly the bubble burst. In the European Parliament elections this June, Sinn Féin secured 11% of the first preference vote compared to 20% each for Fianna Fáil and Fine Gael. In the local elections held the same day, they again secured only 11% of the first preference vote with FF and FG each getting 23%.

What had happened? Not the recent scandals. Something deeper happened to the party's public perception and support base. The departure of Leo Varadkar may have been one factor. Likewise, the party's wobbly and ineffectual support for the ill-fated Yes side in the Family and Care referendums in March, despite its difficulties with the wording and its promise (or threat?) to rerun the vote, damaged its credibility.

Add to these factors the failure of the party to capitalise on the Government's mishandling at Irish and Europe level of the refugee/immigration issue (which is a matter of real concern to the Sinn Féin voting base as distinct from party ideologues) and you have some insight into the possible causal factors in the slump in Sinn Féin support.

On the issues of housing and health where the current coalition is vulnerable, Sinn Féin just isn't scoring points – let alone knock-out blows.

Its housing policy proposals, which end up with the state owning an ever-increasing proportion of Irish houses as ground landlords with diminished rights of home occupiers to dispose of their homes, smack of thinly disguised far-left socialism. They reflect the ideology of the leftists in Belfast rather than addressing the actual aspiration of Irish people to really own outright their own homes.

There is still an open political battleground on matters such as childcare services, disability services, GP services and hospital services. No party has as yet managed to stake out the high ground on such matters in the minds of the public. And all these issues could be game changers between now and polling day in late November.

My own take on Sinn Féin's apparent blowout is that the public are increasingly sceptical of the party's core agenda. It aspires to establish a 32-county socialist republic. And when it says socialist, it means far-left socialist.

Its connections and sympathies with FARC, the Colombian Marxists, with the Cuban government, with ETA, the Basque Marxists, and other world revolutionary movements, as well as its far-left fellow Left group members in the European Parliament all speak of a movement out of tune with the centre ground of Irish politics and thinking.

Post-Brexit, most voters in the Republic want Northern institutions to bed down rather than polarise the North with a border poll for which there still is no likelihood of a majority for a decade at least. Rekindling smouldering constitutional and sectarian questions in Northern Ireland at this point is counterproductive; slow and steady reconciliation and positive mutual engagement in the North is what is needed by both parts of the island.

It is now four years since Colm Keena's admirable exposition in these pages of the true nature of Sinn Féin. That fine piece of journalism needs constant rereading. The facts have not changed. The

Army Council still exists. Sadly, none of our broadcast media has the courage to deal with the realities uncovered by Keena.

Sinn Féin is not a conventional political party; it is a tightly controlled revolutionary movement still in the grip of a very small group, many of whom were active in the IRA's campaign of violence.

It brooks no open dissent. It controls its TDs, senators, councillors, MLAs and abstentionist MPs with a vice-like grip. Its elected public representatives take policy and instruction unquestioningly from its Coiste Seasta and Ard Chomhairle. They are all liable to arbitrary deselection by the unelected party centre. TDs and councillors are notified of their political fates by backroom messages – not by voters. Their leaders are not really leaders but more like glove puppets for unseen controllers.

Their recent controversies and cover-ups are but the symptoms of their underlying reality – not the cause of their decline. Or the real reasons to be wary.

Middle Ireland can end the stalemate in our politics

20 August 2017

In a world in which this last week has seen the terrorist outrages in Spain, the departure of Steve Bannon as Trump's strategy adviser, the flip-flopping of Trump on whether American neo-Nazis are to be condemned, the temporary cessation of Kim Jong Un's plan to fire ICBMs at the seas surrounding Guam, the almost-instant collapse in popular support for Emmanuel Macron, and the exposure of the UK Tory government as naive and clueless on the post-Brexit implications for the Irish border, it might seem a little petty or introverted to lift the carpet and closely examine the possibility that Sinn Féin is edging closer to participation in a coalition government here after the next election.

But the prospect of an FF–SF coalition is now being considered by a number of FF frontbenchers if this week's news reports are to be believed. This reported development is probably unwelcome news for Micheál Martin who has, until now, consistently rejected the idea of coalition with Sinn Féin out of hand.

But there are two identifiable strands to Fianna Fáil – one is urban, middle of the road, pro-business, while the other hankers after the radicalism of Dev's pre-war politics. These two strands have been held together by the party's sense of loyalty and self-image as a single, continuous national movement.

While FF rural traditionalists might see an alliance with Sinn Féin as the healing of an old rupture in republicanism and a mathematically realistic path for re-entry into government, the urban, pro-business wing of the party can only see a collapse in middle-class electoral support in such a scenario.

Micheál Martin knows that any chance of FF overhauling FG in the cities and becoming the dominant party of the middle class would be ended by a whiff of suspicion that Gerry Adams and his colleagues would devise the next programme for government.

Both strands are resolutely opposed to coalition with Fine Gael – especially such a coalition under a FG Taoiseach. The latter scenario would, they believe, utterly destroy the party and see it being supplanted by Sinn Féin. Some of them fear an FF-led grand coalition almost as much, thinking that FF would be the ultimate losers if Sinn Féin became the major opposition party

Having stayed out of a grand coalition, most FF deputies now want to put their posteriors on seats at the cabinet table, the chairs of Oireachtas committees and the back seats of ministerial cars. They want a more direct say in how Ireland is governed. They see themselves as a 'natural party of government'.

Above all, Fianna Fáil do not want to be in opposition for a third consecutive term. And if avoiding that entails coalition with Sinn

Féin, then so be it. Hold your nose and take the plunge. So much the better if Gerry Adams stands down in the meantime. And if Micheál Martin has to go as the price of such a deal, well, that price may have to be paid as well. Three terms in opposition is too much to accept. And handing the republican mantle to Sinn Féin is simply a form of political suicide.

Some readers may take the view that the foregoing analysis simply means that middle Ireland will be forced to re-elect Fine Gael to lead a disparate coalition based on a constellation of independent groupings and micro-parties. That is what FG strategists are hoping for. But things are not that simple.

Leo Varadkar will publicly keep the door open to a grand coalition with FF. But if he is asked whether he will bring FG into such a coalition as the smaller partner, he will have to say 'no'. To make such a concession before polling day could deflate the FG campaign and become a self-fulfilling prophesy.

And so the problem with either scenario – governments led by FG or FF without participation by the other – is that Ireland will be governed by a coalition in which the hard left tail wags the centrist dog. The availability of non-ideological independents to make up the number will not survive into the next Dáil if polls are to be believed.

Middle Ireland does not want to be governed by the policy demands of the hard left. But if the two largest parties for which middle Ireland votes – Fine Gael and Fianna Fáil – are dead set on not coalescing with each other, no other outcome seems possible.

Middle Ireland is, in international terms, centre-right. It has created a political order in which its policy goals are frustrated by the FF-FG 'non-cooperation pact'. We have a stalemate in which normal democratic choices for government are effectively denied to the electorate. Short-termism has been enthroned as a paralytic normal. Even the 'permanent government' of civil servants has been largely stymied by the icy grip of the 'new politics' on the legislative process.

So what is wrong with Sinn Féin entering government here the next time? There are many reasons why it would be wrong.

Sinn Féin, first, is not a normal democratic party. It is under the thumb of the old Belfast Brigade who decide everything and control everything through a network of provo cadres and commissars liberally sprinkled though the party at every strategic point.

Sinn Féin does not accept the legitimacy of the State or its institutions. It still lives in a parallel universe in which the last legitimate Dáil was elected in 1920 and in which the powers of Republic were vested in the Army Council of the IRA by members of that Dáil in the 1930s.

Sinn Féin's ruling elite subscribe to a Marxist worldview in which Raul Castro and Nicolás Maduro are their poster boys.

Their economic outlook would destroy Ireland's prospects as a small open economy in which foreign investment is welcomed.

Their Northern policy is confrontational and incompatible with reconciliation between Orange and Green.

Their taxation policies would cripple the private sector in Ireland and end our attractiveness as a place to do international business.

They are intent on mopping up the remains of the Labour Party in their remaining vulnerable seats.

These considerations might cause some in middle Ireland to ask themselves whether it would make more sense to elect thirty or forty TDs to the next Dáil who were collectively committed to breaking the stalemate imposed on us by the narrow self-preservation priorities of the old war-horse parties that have betrayed the interests of middle Ireland, and who collectively committed to forming a coalition with one or both of those parties to restore the capacity of the majority to govern this state in an effective way.

If one in five or one in six voters saw their way to supporting such candidates, each constituency would send a deputy to Dáil Éireann guaranteeing the end of the politics of paralysis. Middle Ireland needs hope. Young Ireland needs a plan for the future. Even the support of one in eight or one in ten voters for such candidates would end the stalemate.

The great symbol of the 'new politics' must be the Irish Water saga, which will see those of us who paid our lawful debts being reimbursed while Drogheda went dry.

What is going on in Irish politics is not sustainable. We deserve better. If the outcome is not to be the entry into government of Sinn Féin, an undemocratic, Marxist party which contests the legitimacy of the very State itself, middle Ireland has to end the stalemate in our politics.

State is now turning its guns on private landlords

22 March 2023

I wrote here some time ago about the issue of private landlords exiting the market. I raised the question as to whether this really mattered, insofar as every house being sold by a private landlord would either end up in the hands of an owner-occupier or in the hands of another private landlord.

And the answer to that question is not as simple as some might think. There is a demand for rental accommodation as distinct from owner-occupation. There are many, many people who, for a variety of reasons, cannot or do not want to become owner-occupiers.

To take some simple examples, there are highly mobile employees who want to live in Ireland temporarily. There are people who want to take up employment temporarily away from their family homes, such as junior doctors and nurses. There are technicians and skilled tradesmen and women who need to live in a particular area for the duration of a project. There are visiting academics. Many are single; some have families.

There are recently qualified younger people who do not want to tie themselves to a mortgage and who prefer to move out from their parents' homes to share houses with other similar people for a number of years. There are many people whose circumstances have changed for a variety of reasons, including family breakups and parental death. There are immigrant construction workers and bus drivers whose families live elsewhere in Europe or further afield. There are care workers supporting families in the Philippines. There are students, apprentices, and trainees.

None of these people can realistically expect that the State can provide them with instant social housing in the form of a single permanent home wherever they want to live. In an era of population growth and immigration, there will always be a permanent need for private rented accommodation no matter how many new houses and homes are provided for long-term tenant or owner occupation by the State through social housing, affordable housing development or by private home developments.

It does matter whether we have an effective private rental sector and it does matter whether that sector is expanding or contracting.

But there are also many, many people, including families, who are trapped in the private rental sector because they cannot obtain social or affordable housing and cannot purchase homes due to spiralling prices. They are trapped in a world of ever-increasing rents in a sector where small private landlords will no longer invest because of a series of legislative and policy blunders.

Our biggest problem is that a single department of government has horrifically failed in its primary area of responsibility. However its name may have changed, the department in the Custom House has utterly failed in its home building and provision functions on almost every front.

As the department in charge of local government, it is supposed to oversee the functions of local councils both as housing authorities under the Housing Acts and as planning authorities under the Planning and Development Acts.

Far from providing homes as its priority, the department seeks as a priority to rigidly control local authorities in acquiring land and buildings, designing social housing, enforcing wholly outdated and counterproductive building standards, preventing the zoning of residential development land, and even requiring through its agency, the Office of the Planning Regulator, local authorities, such as Dún Laoghaire-Rathdown Council, to de-zone development land, thereby increasing the costs of development.

It has failed in so many whack-a-mole initiatives such as its strategic housing development and shared accommodation experiments. Its Land Development Agency has been ridiculously slow and limited in its efforts. The department has effectively stopped compulsory purchase of unused or underused development land. There is no reason in law, statutory or constitutional, why planning and housing authorities should not use compulsory purchase, site assembly and development leasing to ensure major urban renewal in obsolete urban and suburban locations.

While home completions last year reached record levels, they are due to decline this year. Why? Home building and home provision is simply not increasing at a rate that will satisfy effective demand. That failure means ever-higher rents and higher house prices.

We need to approach housing policy with effective and reasoned proposals. The Irish State relied on the private rental sector to make up for its massive abdications and misadventures in housing policies for decades. Now it is turning its guns on private landlords as the problem. Tax breaks won't halt the damage that has been done to lessors of private accommodation by outlawing even four-year leases and substituting permanent tenancies of indefinite duration coupled with tenant-substitution rights, rent freezes, and taxes.

The War of Independence witnessed the physical destruction of the Custom House. But what we need now is the political end of the present Custom House regime. We need fundamental change.

Our 'New Politics' caused a lurch to the left

5 June 2016

The reality of the 'new politics' is slowly emerging. Let's look at some important issues.

The Irish Constitution divides the powers of government into three categories – legislative, executive and judicial.

These categories are not completely watertight; but what is termed 'the executive power of the State' is required to be 'exercised by or on the authority of the Government', which is 'responsible to Dáil Éireann'. (Note that the Government has a different relationship with the Seanad.)

Does Enda retain the support of a majority?

Article 28.10 of the Constitution obliges a Taoiseach who has ceased 'to retain the support of a majority in Dáil Éireann' to resign unless the President dissolves the Dáil on the Taoiseach's advice. It is noteworthy that Enda Kenny was nominated for appointment as Taoiseach by a minority of the Dáil members voting. But those who abstained in the vote on his nomination must be taken as 'supporting' him to remain as Taoiseach.

So, if Fianna Fáil at some point cannot be counted as 'supporting' Enda Kenny as Taoiseach, he and his government are constitutionally obliged to resign, unless they have won the support of the remaining members of the Dáil.

That does not mean, however, that he is obliged to resign simply because his government loses a series of Dáil votes.

It does mean that he must resign if he and his government is defeated on a confidence vote. And it does mean that he and his government must resign if they can no longer perform the budgetary functions reserved to the government under the Constitution because they lack the support of a majority in the Dáil in the exercise of those functions.

On other issues, such as day-to-day legislation and motions on policy matters, a Dáil defeat does not carry with it any obligation to resign. It is within these constitutional parameters that the 'new politics' can properly operate.

Nobody but the Taoiseach can recommend any Bill or resolution to lawfully appropriate exchequer funding. And only the Government can present annual estimates of receipts and expenditure. So the present minority government retains a constitutional veto on budgetary matters. That means that in order to survive the Government must create and sustain a majority budgetary consensus in the Dáil.

No executive dominance of the Oireachtas

While any party can still operate a rigid internal whip system, the government whips no longer control either House of the Oireachtas by virtue of their office.

The 'legislative power of government' vested in the two Houses has broken free from the 'executive power of government' and the State is, for the first time, being governed by parliamentary consensus in most matters.

In principle that all sounds good. The traditional overweening power of the Irish Government is over for the time being.

Constitutional vigilance

But the 'new politics' is not quite that simple.

The traditional role of the Attorney General as constitutional watchdog over government legislation is seriously compromised if non-government legislation in the form of Bills or amendments is free from such scrutiny. The Attorney is adviser to the Government – not to the Dáil or the Seanad. If the Government has lost its whip hand, who keeps an eye on what non-government legislators are doing? The President has a role under Article 26 to send suspect Bills to the Supreme Court for examination of their constitutionality. Does the Supreme Court's role under Article 26 extend to constitutional validity arising from our EU membership?

Bearing in mind EU legal obligations in making our own laws, who is going to keep an eye on that area of validity? This is not academic. The water charges issue is likely to be a very immediate area of controversy. Who will hear and pay attention to the views of the Attorney on such legislation?

The Seanad

Another interesting constitutional angle to the 'New Politics' is the role under Article 27 and Article 29 of the Seanad where the Government only has about twenty members of the FG parliamentary party out of a sixty member House.

If the Dáil uses its constitutional power to over-ride the Seanad's position on any ordinary Bill coming from the Dáil, a simple majority of the Seanad can, with the support of one third of the Dáil's members, petition the President to refer such Bills to the people for approval in a referendum on the grounds that it is of such 'national importance that the will of the people ought to be ascertained'.

Likewise, the Seanad can now realistically veto the exercise by the Government of certain EU powers in relation to enhanced cooperation, the relaxation of the requirement at EU level for unanimity and in relation to Schengen, justice and home affairs matters, and on certain other EU measures. So can the Dáil.

Each House of the Oireachtas makes its own rules. Mandatory pre-legislative scrutiny of Bills under Dáil standing orders does not apply to Bills, whether Government or non-Government, in the Seanad as things stand. The Seanad is free to take a different approach now that it is freed from government control.

With power must come responsibility and accountability

But each House remains part of our parliament (along with the President). The country has to be run. Any giddiness arising from the collapse of executive dominance in parliament must be tempered by the assumption of collective responsibility resting on the parliament under the Constitution.

Watching the 'new politics' from a distance for the last fortnight, it strikes me that there has been an effective lurch to the left as Fianna Fáil seeks to reposition itself as a left-of-centre party in its competitive struggles with the other opposition parties and groupings.

How long is Middle Ireland content to have a left-wing tail wag the dog in pursuit of party advantage?

Is there not now a need for new choices and voices to allow the views of Middle Ireland to find expression in the political process. Is that a 'gap in the market' we see? Is there a 'market in the gap' under the 'new politics'?

We'll see.

The President is not bound to silence on all matters of public interest

22 September 2019

The President, Michael D. Higgins, raised some eyebrows by making comments recently on the issue of soldiers' pay and in relation to the beef dispute. It wasn't the first time he has done so.

He had in the past made political comments, including comments on the values and ethics of neo-liberal economics in 2013 and comments on the wisdom of promising tax cuts in the run-up to the 2016 general election. More recently, in 2017, he offered the view that the State must face up to the issue of homelessness.

His two predecessors, Mary McAleese and Mary Robinson, had, on occasion but to a lesser degree, caused a flutter in the political dovecotes with remarks and actions that some commentators thought transgressed an unwritten line relating to the presidency.

Given that the President is not answerable to either House of the Oireachtas or to any court 'for the exercise and performance of the powers and functions of his office', there is a parliamentary convention that there is no criticism or debate on the President in either House. Whether that convention is necessary or overly generous is a matter on which more than one opinion exists.

But there are a few constitutional points which should be borne in mind before adopting an overly restrictive view of the capacity of the President to comment on matters in the public sphere without prior government approval.

First, the Constitution provides that the President is actually part of the national parliament – the Oireachtas. He is elected by the people. The people, in the Irish constitutional order, are the sovereign power.

In the United Kingdom, the 'Queen in parliament' is sovereign in legislative matters. The people, even when consulted by referendum, are not the UK's sovereign power.

Second, the President makes a solemn declaration on entering office promising three things:

1. To maintain the Constitution of Ireland and to uphold its laws, and,
2. To fulfil his duties faithfully and conscientiously in accordance with the Constitution and the law, and
3. To dedicate his abilities to the service and welfare of the people of Ireland.

This last solemn commitment seems to ask of the President something more than the simple fulfilment of constitutional functions and duties in a quiet and passive way. It suggests that a President is not condemned to Trappist silence and inaction unless the Government authorises the making of every public utterance, statement or action. It demands an energetic and active service to the people.

Nothing in the Constitution actually obliges the President to speak in accordance with the Government's wishes on a topic of the Government's choosing.

The President must, however, receive the prior approval of the Government for any formal address or message to the Houses of the Oireachtas on any matter of national or public importance or to address a message to the nation on any such matter.

It follows that the President should not attempt to communicate messages to the nation on matters of national or public importance without the express or implied approval of the Government. He has solemnly undertaken not to do so.

The President is not bound to silence on all matters of public interest

Does that mean that he is sworn to silence on all matters of public interest unless he has Government approval for the expression of his personal opinion or belief? I don't think so.

Indeed, I welcome the major contribution made by the President to the recent centenary celebrations and commemorations of the 1916 Rising, the Great War and the establishment of Dáil Éireann.

I look forward to his similarly thoughtful expression of his own take on the War of Independence, the Treaty negotiations and the Civil War in due course.

He was elected by the people partly, if not mainly, on the basis of his personal talents to play a leading role in the national discussion of such issues and events.

To take an example, it would be very strange indeed if a speech by President Higgins on the Civil War depended for its content on whether it reflected the views of a government led by Fine Gael or Fianna Fáil in 2022. Frankly, there would be plenty of opportunity for the Taoiseach and the leader of the opposition in two years' time to express their own views on matters such as, say, the Civil War.

While I am sure that the President would take pains to speak on issues with care and consideration, I would be disappointed if I felt that every word he spoke on the subject had been handed to him from government for recitation to the people.

In matters of history and culture, I enjoy hearing the perspective of President Higgins, even where his opinion might not be shared by myself or some others. As long as they are considered and worthwhile opinions, there is no point in demanding that everyone who hears them must agree with them.

Article 45 of the Constitution sets out Directive Principles of Social Policy but states that the application of those principles in the making of laws shall be the 'care of the Oireachtas exclusively' and not justiciable in court.

As a part of the Oireachtas, the President is, by his inaugural declaration, bound to uphold those principles because he has committed to upholding the Constitution.

While some may say that the Article 45 directive principles are reflective of early twentieth-century Catholic social theory (and they are), their validity is not, by that alone, undermined.

So, for instance, it remains a matter of constitutional obligation on the State and on the Oireachtas to favour 'private initiative in industry and commerce'.

By the same token, the State is obliged under Article 45 to ensure that private enterprise is conducted so as to ensure reasonable efficiency in the production and distribution of goods and so as to protect the public against unjust exploitation.

Article 45 also obliges the State to 'safeguard with especial care the economic interests of the weaker sections of the community' and to direct its policy towards ensuring that all citizens have the right to an adequate means of livelihood to make reasonable provision through their employment for their needs.

The article, in its Irish version, also obliges the State to pursue a policy which favours the establishment of family farms to the greatest extent practicable. Recent indications that the wealthy are buying up thousands of acres of farmland as trophy hedge investments seem to fly in the face of the State's constitutional policy, and we should not lose sight of that value simply because the Land Commission has been abolished. The family farm is a constitutional value

So commenting informally on the State's need to address homelessness and the State's need to ensure that members of the Defence Forces are paid sufficiently to meet their domestic needs or that the State must be conscious of the need to uphold the interests of farm families is merely the expression of constitutional values which the Oireachtas – including its President – is bound to uphold.

Admittedly, when the President eulogised the deceased former President of Cuba, Fidel Castro, his choice of words would not have been mine. Castro's repressive regime may have been more just than his corrupt predecessor, Batista's, but that did not make it any the less repressive.

But I am not such a snowflake as to take umbrage or offence at his expression of what I would always have believed Michael D's opinion to be when I voted for him to be President seven years ago.

Five-year national programme needed in new reality of Covid-19

11 March 2020

Just as we thought that the general election had created a perfect political storm in which no combination of two of the three largest parties could form a government unaided, we now have a national crisis superimposed on the political crisis.

As crises go, the common coinage of politics right through the election campaign was 'health crisis' and 'housing crisis' and 'home-building crisis'.

If we had thought that the annual wave of influenza admissions likely to land in emergency departments at our hospitals amounted to a crisis, we now have to recalibrate the term 'crisis' to describe what is happening in Italy and what may happen here.

The chronic shortage of intensive care beds in Irish hospitals must now be seen in the light of what the Italians are doing – converting hospital corridors into intensive care units. At Boris Johnson's press conference on Monday, it was stated that the UK Government were taking steps to buy up respirators. What prospect is there that Ireland will be able to match that effort?

On Sunday I went to have a regular coffee with a friend in south Dublin. It seemed to me that footfall had shrunk to 30% or so at the venue. Anecdotally, it seems that hotels and restaurants are experiencing a similar fall-off in business. Service industries such as cafés, restaurants and hotels depend on cash flow to pay their wages, their suppliers and their VAT, PRSI and PAYE bills.

A continuation of the customer famine for such businesses threatens their viability in a way that a week's snowstorm would not.

The Government announced a large package of big-figure measures to deal with the economic consequences of the Covid-19 crisis. High level fiscal stimulus is not sufficient by itself. Some relaxation by way of postponement of tax liabilities for highly exposed service sectors will be required as well.

The cancellation of large parts of the St Patrick's Day Festival will be a body blow to many commercial enterprises, including travel, accommodation and entertainment.

More broadly, Covid-19 has the potential to cause a delay or postponement of many other financial transactions.

Those making public health policy decisions inevitably affect our economic wellbeing as well. Their responsibility is a very heavy one and the capacity to overreact is as fraught with danger as the capacity to underreact.

Cancelling large-scale events will have negative economic and exchequer effects. Not doing so may be seized upon as evidence of nonchalance. In short, we are in a bind.

While it is fortunate that the last Budget was predicated on making provision for the economic consequences of a no-deal Brexit, the much talked about envelope of fiscal space to finance tax cuts or public expenditure increases has evaporated before our eyes.

The political landscape has changed utterly, not merely because of the election result but because areas of disputation about economic and expenditure policies have become irrelevant in the face of the likely financial consequences of Covid-19.

Into this mix comes the suggestion that we should form some kind of national emergency government – presumably on an all-party basis.

The idea seems radical, but the question remains whether it is plausible. Would a cabinet of all the senior political figures from across the ideological spectrum be any more adept at good decision-making than a majority government with a narrower political base?

Economic wellbeing depends to a significant extent on the vital element of predictability. A short-term national government would hardly bring predictability into our affairs. The notion that we might have such a government with a short-term mandate to be followed by a general election might simply put everything on hold in large swathes of economic activity and decision-making on investment.

On balance, it seems that the case for a government composed in the main of Fianna Fáil and Fine Gael is now transformed into an imperative. Whether such a two-party arrangement needs the addition of a third party or a number of smaller parties is not yet clear. Fine Gael and Fianna Fáil could put together a national plan and seek to have it supported by a number of the recently elected independents with which such parties are ideologically compatible.

Independent TDs don't like early general elections, especially in a climate where their seats would be vulnerable. That fact is part of the laws of physics of representative politics.

My hunch is that there is a workable majority for a government with a national programme, provided that the leaders of Fianna Fáil and Fine Gael acknowledge political realities and their own responsibilities. If Covid-19 is likely to bring about a difficult period in terms of economics and the public finances, the need for a five-year programme is all the more obvious.

Apart from the political firefighting entailed in handling Covid-19, the groundwork has to be done in other transformational policy areas including home building, health reforms, and urban planning.

The credibility of such a government will depend completely on its capacity to signal to the electorate that it would be united on short-, medium-, and long-term policy goals – and on taking immediate steps to implement their achievement.

Challenging, yes – but unavoidable.

Voters need more choices than a hard-left coalition or the status quo

12 June 2024

Last Friday's vote by Irish voters demonstrated, as many commentators have remarked, that the broad centre of Irish politics is not as fragile as those on the hard left and hard right imagined and calculated.

Those, including Stephen Collins and myself, who have consistently argued and written that the entry into government by Sinn Féin was neither inevitable nor desirable can breathe a sigh of relief that our view has been corroborated by the outcome of the local and European parliament elections. But the magnitude of that corroboration was, it must be admitted, not foreseen by anybody.

Sinn Féin's collapse in support over the last year from opinion poll levels in the low to mid-thirties to just below 12% in the local elections is dramatic. Explanations are probably as diverse as they are difficult. And they will not permit any public post-mortem or inquest. No elected representative is allowed to criticise the party's strategy or leadership. They appear to have lost the protest vote – even if the twin topics of housing and health on which they have waged political war since 2020 have not 'gone away'.

At both local and European level, they implemented a strategy of fielding a multiplicity of low-key candidates in the hope that buoyant national support levels would lift their boats in the same way as relative unknowns floated into Dáil Éireann on a high tide in 2020. But the political tide turned on them and left very many of their candidates beached in shallow water.

This loss of momentum contrasts strongly with their carefully orchestrated strategy of politically grooming themselves for government – a process involving two-way briefing sessions with banks, financiers, law firms, government departments and agencies and other political stakeholders over the last nine months as well as imposing shirt, suit and tie dress code for TDs and senators. If there is a general election this autumn, as most believe quite likely, the time for Sinn Féin to turn their political tide and refloat their fortunes is very limited, as we are now in the run-up to the summer break and the pre-budget political silly season.

As a party, they have aspired to be political chameleons. In reality they are driven by the hard left socialist ideology of James Connolly and still adhere to the proposition that they are the moral and political heirs to the 1916 Republic vested in the IRA Army Council since anti-Treaty extremists in 1938 handed over the powers of the second Dáil to the pre-war IRA.

The Belfast leadership of Sinn Féin still denies the legitimacy of the Irish state and still aspires to establish a 32-county socialist workers' republic. Mary Lou McDonald is not a leader vested with leadership control over a conventional political party. Their elected TDs and senators in Leinster House do not collectively decide anything, and receive rather than decide their policy from outside party bodies.

Local party members have little or no autonomy. Every member is bound by Leninist principles of 'democratic centralism' to publicly uphold without hesitation the policy line decided in private on pain of suspension or expulsion for deviation.

The grim prospect articulated by many political commentators until now that the next Dublin government would probably be a coalition consisting of Sinn Féin as majority and Fianna Fáil as minority partners suddenly seems less likely than it did three months ago. It was never inevitable.

Anyone who, like me, was present at the initial tally of Dublin Euro ballot papers and witnessed the massive cross-voting patterns between Fine Gael and Fianna Fáil supporters would realise that last Friday marked a political watershed. A seasoned former politician remarked to me that it was strange indeed to see the former civil war parties congratulating themselves and each other for reaching 23% support levels each in local elections. Who would have predicted that mutual backslapping five or ten years ago?

But does all this fightback by the centre mean that the people will be confined to a non-choice of re-electing the present government in the autumn or choosing a hard left coalition dominated by a winded but recovering Sinn Féin? Will there be centre options other than a re-election of the present coalition?

Which part of the fragmented left mosaic in Irish politics would hold itself out to voters as a potential coalition with the centre ground parties? Political scientists struggle to discern any real difference between Labour and the Social Democrats. I can't see the need for competing parties in their limited collective space.

The Social Democrats had a poor outing last Friday considering their slick branding and wide candidate spread. They were dismissed by one veteran politician as 'SUV socialists'. Ivana and Holly badly need to talk.

Somehow, I find it difficult to believe that a general election in the autumn will be a simple repetition of last Friday's outcome. There are important choices to be made on our future.

Can directly elected mayors really make a difference in improving our cities?

22 June 2022

Directly elected mayors (DEMs) have been proposed as the solution to the general malaise in local government. But it is arguable that the problems with local government run deeper than can be resolved by giving someone chosen by the electorate a five-year term as mayor.

In the case of Limerick city and county, a plebiscite was held to approve the principle of directly electing the mayor. The idea was very narrowly approved by a margin of 52.4% (38,122 votes) to 47.6% (34,573 votes). Voters in Cork and Waterford rejected the idea by narrower margins.

An Implementation Advisory Group, chaired by Tim O'Connor, has produced a very impressive plan for legislating for the election of a DEM for a five-year term from 2024 to 2029. The areas of competence proposed for the Limerick DEM are huge in scale — almost daunting. The responsibilities to be cast on the mayor are so varied that it would probably take a year for the office-holder to get on top of the job. He or she would probably need a personally appointed cabinet to function effectively.

But the elephant in the room is the money problem. It is all very well getting powers equivalent in scope to a government minister. But unless a DEM can get the resources to implement policies, the results will be disappointing. If resources are largely determined and allocated by national ministers and departments, the DEM will be little more than a local administrator.

It has often been said that Ireland has local administration rather than local government. The county manager system (now described as chief executives) is a system of prefectures which has largely emasculated local democracy. Local authority members have little or no effective control over the great bulk of their revenues or expenditures.

Unlike English councillors, Irish local authority members have no role in decisions on individual planning applications. Their functions in relation to city and county development plans are now heavily circumscribed by directives from the minister and by the new powers conferred on the Office of the Planning Regulator.

Irish councillors have to play an elaborate game of secret deference to their chief executives in order to progress their personal agendas on local matters. The balance of power lies with the executive; councillors who disregard that balance lose their capacity to appear effective in the eyes of their voters.

Perhaps we should consider making the office of councils' chief executive officers less permanent and powerful by providing that it is held at the pleasure of the elected members or a qualified majority of them. That could be done in tandem with the extension of DEMs across our system of councils.

If DEMs are going to be leaders of their local authorities, they will need to tackle the housing crisis. If you open a legal textbook on Irish local government, you will see elaborate provision in statute for the discharge by local authorities of functions as planning authorities and housing authorities. They have a legal duty to plan and provide for adequate housing under the Planning and Development Acts and the Housing Acts.

Corresponding with those duties are huge powers of compulsory acquisition, construction project initiation and oversight, zoning and control.

These powers exist on paper but seem to be too burdensome for council executives to exercise them.

Dublin City Council seems to concentrate its efforts on demolishing and redeveloping its own housing schemes as in the sagas of Ballymun, O'Devaney Gardens, St Teresa's Gardens, Fatima

Mansions, etc. And the term 'concentrating its efforts' is rather charitable in this context, to put it mildly. Ballymun was so badly managed and maintained by the council that it had to be 'regenerated' after 40 years.

Dún Laoghaire–Rathdown County Council did nothing for 18 years with more than 20 acres which it acquired at Shanganagh for social and affordable housing. Shamefully, it is only now being handed over to the Land Development Agency for development to commence.

It is pitiful to see so many homes boarded up on the ground floors of Dublin City Council's own apartment blocks. Chancery House near the Four Courts was badly neglected by the council for years but is now a secure and well-maintained social housing project. Providing and maintaining social housing requires effort and imagination, such as we see in the Iveagh Trust complexes.

We need a positive plan for supplying homes – social, affordable and private – in liveable cities. Housing authorities need to drive the process themselves and not be lazy and jaded spectators in this crisis.

If a tenth of the administrative energy that has been put into traffic management over the last two years had been put into the exercise of housing powers over the last 10 years, things would be a lot, lot better.

Will directly elected mayors succeed where managers abysmally failed?

UK and Ireland Politics and Brexit

Prejudice, not rationality, will decide #Brexit referendum outcome – the Irish have reason to be scared

15 May 2016

There is an old and somewhat cynical definition of a referendum: 'A referendum is a process whereby you get an answer you didn't expect to a question you didn't ask.'

With 39 days to go to the UK's Brexit referendum, and with an awful lot staked on the result for Ireland and the UK, that definition may be truer than we like to think.

Let's take two examples – Northern Ireland and Scotland.

In the North, there is little enough real love for the EU on either side of the Orange–Green divide. What, for instance, does a DUP voter, in his or her heart, make of the threat of border controls between the six and the twenty-six counties?

What does a DUP voter, in his or in her heart, make of Sinn Féin support for staying in the EU?

What do Sinn Féin voters make of their party's very belated enthusiasm for staying in the EU, after fifty years of solid opposition to the EEC/EC/EU?

How will the two blocs in Northern Ireland view the Brexit question? There are moderates in the North who instinctively steer a course between agreeing with anything that is proposed by either the DUP or Sinn Féin. They are now in a quandary.

Look then at Scotland. The SNP is dominant; the Tories are resurgent and Labour is in retreat. The SNP favours Scotland staying in the EU. They are talking of another referendum to secede from the UK if the Brexit vote succeeds on 23 June.

Will there be SNP voters who in the privacy of the ballot box vote Leave in the secret hope of Scotland having another referendum to leave the UK? By the same token, will some Scottish Tories vote Stay to head off another referendum to break the Union?

Now you may begin to see that the old definition of a referendum has some truth. The 'question you didn't ask' could be a more significant border between North and South in Ireland, or a more significant border between Scotland and England.

This week we have seen a flurry of arguments in England. From the lofty heights of geopolitics to the mundane trivia of day-to-day life, it is sometimes difficult to see which type of argument will resound better with the voters.

Cameron, for instance, has spoken about Brexit being a threat to world peace, the 'special relationship' between the UK and the US, and Britain's influence in the world. Heady stuff. Scary stuff. This theme was supported in the broadsheets by US governmental luminaries – past and present.

The *Daily Express*, by contrast, informed its UK readers this week that the EU is now proposing to outlaw Britain's traditional electric kettles and electric toasters as part of a new energy conservation drive, but that the EU has postponed the measure for fear of alienating UK voters. God knows what the Commission has in mind for the Aga cooker.

At which level is the 'typical voter' moved – the threat to their kettles and toasters or the threat to the UK's special relationship with the US? How do these issues 'play in Peoria' – to borrow an Americanism?

Add to all of that the issue of immigration. Angela Merkel's invitation to one million migrant refugees to come to Germany was a tad naive. It has gone pear-shaped in Germany. But her efforts to make all other EU member states open their frontiers to the migrant masses from the Middle East has created a political crisis for all of the EU as well.

The Cameron Deal to avoid Brexit was supposed to give the UK an emergency brake on immigration. But Merkel would only concede the possibility of an emergency brake on migrants' welfare. Is that enough?

Will UK voters be swayed towards rejecting Brexit by any appeal coming from Merkel, Hollande, Juncker or the Brussels establishment? Or will such appeals become counterproductive?

Do UK voters actually care about claims that Brexit poses an 'existential threat' to the EU project? Have EU federalists pushed their project so fast that it threatens the EU itself. In just over five weeks we will find out.

What exactly will work to persuade voters to vote Stay?

With the gap between Stay and Leave steadily narrowing, even among business people, it is doubtful whether scare tactics are working. Old and hoary resentments such as the Common Fisheries Policy are increasingly creeping into the media debate.

We in this state have good reason to be scared of both the known and unknown consequences of a Brexit vote.

The scariest aspect is this. The Brexit referendum outcome will probably be decided by the strength of prejudice in underlying attitudes rather than the rationality of the political arguments.

We in Ireland know very well from recent experience that the referendum process is one where intensity of feeling rather than opinion poll predictions is the important factor. And we Irish are largely spectators in that process.

Unlike the English voters who are unimpressed by scare tactics, the Irish have reason to be scared.

Brexit will not deliver a united Ireland soon, but it's a challenge that should unite us all

19 March 2017

One of the perennial problems in discussing the future of Northern Ireland is that the discussion of itself has a seriously polarising effect on the two main communities there. The underlying conflict of aspirations comes to the surface, however peacefully, and the process of normalising relations between those two communities is set back.

On the other hand, it is arguable that the long-term future of the North is the perpetual 'elephant in the room' and that a self-censoring dialogue that simply ignores the issue serves no useful purpose and encourages a dishonest, introverted kind of politics.

Those who – like me – consider ourselves to be republicans in the true sense, and who work for a united Ireland based on reconciliation and consent, have a right and a duty to think clearly about the current situation.

So let us confront two truths.

First, a border poll on a united Ireland held now would be decisively beaten by a 70:30 margin among northern voters – even in the aftermath of the Brexit referendum. This is the constant indication from opinion surveys conducted in the North.

The Good Friday Agreement or the Belfast Agreement (funny, we can't even agree on its name!) provides that such a poll should only be taken if it appears 'likely' to the Secretary of State that a majority, if polled, would opt for the North to leave the UK and become part of a united Ireland. So there is simply no basis for holding such a poll at this point – in law or in common sense.

Why, then, does Gerry Adams demand a poll that he will not be given – and a poll that he will not win? The answer is very simple – making that totally cynical kind of demand is excellent 'polarising politics'.

UUP votes that transferred to save SDLP seats are of little interest to the backroom boys in Belfast who really control Sinn Féin. Nor are the views of Alliance voters. Gerry was talking to his own constituency. Moderation on the constitutional question is simply of no interest – even when there are such green shoots on the middle ground. A poll would destroy the middle ground.

We need a border poll now like a hole in the head.

The second truth is this. There is the clearest evidence that the demographic balance in Northern Ireland is changing – and perhaps at an accelerating pace. The Catholic population is young and growing towards 45% or 46% in the next few years. The Protestant population is ageing and shrinking towards 42% to 45% in the next few years.

In other words, we are heading towards a Northern Ireland where the Catholics and Protestants will be approximate equals in terms of a simplistic headcount. Already, Catholics form a majority among school students and university students up north. That will translate into an equality of voting strength with time. The old Protestant Unionist hegemony is over.

But this demographic change does not, by any means, indicate that some see-saw switch to the North opting for a united Ireland will happen in the short term.

It does mean that the politics of Unionist ascendancy are coming to an end. The capacity of either community to dominate the other politically, socially or economically is over. Pursuit of such dominance is futile. Polarising opinion in pursuit of such dominance is likewise futile. The use of terrorist violence or of repressive violence on either side in pursuit of constitutional aspirations is more unthinkable and more counterproductive than ever.

The business of Northern politicians is to work together forwards the prosperity of everyone in the North.

Brexit – hard or soft – is not going to deliver a united Ireland in the short term.

But Brexit is a challenge that should unite us all on this island – at least in addressing its consequences and in working towards the common good of everyone on this island. No one except the real zealots can gain politically from any adverse consequences on this island – North or South.

There are very strong arguments for a special deal for North South economic relations as part of the EU–UK Brexit agreement. And there is precedent.

West Germany negotiated a protocol giving special EEC status for trade with East Germany during the period prior to reunification. Such trade was given the status of 'internal trade' within the EEC and deemed to fall within the common external tariff customs union as it then was – all subject to safeguards.

So we should now be examining special Irish arrangements for North–South, and perhaps East–West, trade and for agriculture, especially if the UK fails to win a comprehensive free trade relationship in its negotiations with the EU.

It is laughable that the North has no functioning democratic institutions at this critical juncture when its economic fate is being decided. To allow the impasse to continue could be tragic.

How likely is it that global industry or business will be attracted to a politically dysfunctional Belfast as a base for European activities or as a location for its executive management teams post Brexit?

Instead of niggling and gouging about 'respect' issues, retrospective criminal investigations, and silly demands for a border poll, the North needs all its political energy to be devoted to its own economic future – a future that is looking bleak right now.

Northern Ireland is not going to leave the UK as an immediate response to Brexit. So what exactly is its political response to Brexit to be? Arlene Foster's DUP supported Brexit as an exercise in 'British nationalism' – or should that be 'English nationalism'? But now the DUP must pick up the pieces.

Strange as it may seem, the DUP under Paisley as First Minister seemed more interested in the economic problems of the North than it has under the leadership of Arlene Foster. Now that the post-Brexit outlook for the North has become no laughing matter, we need a little of the spirit of the departed 'chuckle brothers' – in terms of a joint resolve to rescue Northern Ireland from potential ruin.

In Dublin too, there is political inertia, apathy and decay all dressed up as the 'new politics'. How right I was here last year to compare Enda's endless departure with Frodo's struggle with the Ring on Mount Doom. How can a minority government credibly function in the shadow of a succession struggle and subsequent reshuffle?

We are not being well served – North or South – by our elected leaders. We badly need statesmen now.

We need a realistic and honest debate on the type of Europe we aspire to now

2 April 2017

The draft EU guidelines for negotiating Brexit are a welcome first offer in the process by which the departure of the UK from the European Union will be negotiated.

It is, of course, a little artificial for a negotiating strategy to be developed in public and in the full gaze of the other party to the talks. And so, there is an element of a wish list and an element of posturing in the draft as published. It could not be kept secret in any event.

While lip service is paid to the phasing of the negotiating process, and the idea that the terms of departure will be decided first while the future EU–UK relationship comes later, in reality the two phases are completely inter-dependent, and 'nothing will be agreed until everything is agreed'.

The Irish interest is well flagged in aspirational terms; there is explicit recognition that the position of Ireland is 'unique' in the process and there is strong support for the Good Friday Agreement, and its aims are recognised as being of 'paramount importance'. There is express recognition of the need for 'flexible and imaginative' solutions to the problems created for Ireland by Brexit. And there is a stated aim of avoiding a hard border and preserving existing bilateral agreements and arrangements between Ireland and the UK as far as compatible with EU law.

As I have written here before, the Common Travel Area is not a huge or difficult issue. Britain simply does not propose any imposition of visa-based travel for EU citizens.

Their post-Brexit 'border' for EU citizens, as I predicted, will be based on post-arrival restrictions on remaining in the UK based on barriers in terms of access to employment, welfare, housing, healthcare, social welfare, education and public services, such as permits and driving licences for future would-be EU citizen immigrants.

Organising a formal system of overseeing the departure of overstaying EU visitors would be very complex and would probably entail the introduction of landing cards; that seems far too difficult to contemplate.

So our 'mini-Schengen' on these islands will probably continue indefinitely. Nothing very different will happen at our borders.

Irish citizens will continue to be exempt, on a reciprocal basis, from UK controls that will apply to non-Irish migrants as regards employment, healthcare, welfare, residence, voting rights, economic establishment, and education.

As far as personal travel and establishment within these islands is concerned there will be no noticeable change.

It is at the economic and trading level that the need for 'flexible and imaginative' solutions to avoid a 'hard border' between the UK and Ireland is most obvious and pressing.

Obviously, the more the British succeed in negotiating a free trade relationship with the EU, the softer will be the border as far as exports and imports of goods between the UK and Ireland will be.

But unless there is a comprehensive UK-EU free trade in goods agreement, there will have to be some form of trade monitoring in some areas either between Ireland and the entire UK, including Northern Ireland, or else between the entire island of Ireland and Britain. Could that monitoring be done on a desk-top basis or would it have to be physical?

The case for the whole island being considered a special economic zone or a special trading zone (as was once the case in EEC law between West and East Germany) could arise depending on the work-out of the free trade negotiations.

Most North-produced milk is exported south. A huge amount of Irish-produced agricultural output is exported to the UK. Preserving that trade on a tariff-free basis is a huge priority for us. The UK has to make some pretty fundamental decisions on whether it wants to pursue a globalist cheap food policy or to subsidise its own agricultural sector on an EU-compatible basis post-Brexit. Ireland has a lot at stake in that deliberation. So do northern farmers and the northern economy west of the Bann.

Non-agricultural goods exports are equally important. It is there that the promise of 'flexible and imaginative solutions' is most challenging. What are those solutions? What are the North–South implications?

The other aspects of the single market for services are not as problematic for Ireland. We can live with limitations on the UK's access to the single market for services. There may be some advantages for Ireland as a location for service providers arising from those limitations.

We will be at a loss of our strongest ally at the EU Council table. That is very serious, as I know from my days at the Justice and Home Affairs Council meetings.

The Irish interest in the entire EU project has been radically affected by Brexit. It was easy to claim that we were enthusiastic Europeans while we had our bigger, stronger British buddy at our side to resist the integrationist urges of the federalists. Now our interests are quite different.

While a few EU wonks will still blather on about the need to be at the centre of the European project, the adoption by the Brussels establishment of a two-speed Europe as a future path for the Union is probably best for Ireland. We do not want to be integrated as a tiny province of an EU superstate. We want and need to retain the maximum scope for the unanimity rule in EU affairs.

If some member states are really serious about enhanced political, defence and fiscal integration (which I very much doubt), I say 'Let them go ahead'. The newer member states are in no mood to build a German dominated sovereign Europe. The French will never admit that their relations with Germany are other than on the basis of equality. But it suits both France and Germany to pose as equals, even if the rest of us are not fooled.

Trump's attitude to the EU is already deflating, as is his attitude to NATO. There is no brooding menace to us that justifies our huddling together in an integrated EU superstate.

We need a far more realistic and honest national debate than heretofore on the type of Europe we aspire to now. I can see the opportunity to develop that debate and I hope we can all contribute to it.

No monopoly on imagination or flexibility in Ireland's response to Brexit

14 May 2017

The warm and attentive reception given to Michel Barnier by the two Houses of the Oireachtas underlined the seriousness of Brexit as an issue for Ireland and the Irish hope that the UK's departure from the EU will take place on terms that will not set back the political settlement on this island and the economic hopes of the two parts of Ireland.

Barnier's words were encouraging if you take the view that good intentions count for much in international affairs. His standing invitation for the implementation of 'imaginative and flexible' solutions for Ireland's difficulties is, however, just that – an invitation addressed primarily to the Irish but also to the British and the other 26 member states of the EU.

In truth the Common Travel Area is not a problem at all. It can easily continue to exist without in any way compromising Britain's desire to control immigration and the EU desire to maintain freedom of movement to the greatest possible extent. EU citizens will continue to travel to the UK visa-free. Such UK controls as may be implemented will happen in relation to employment, welfare, healthcare and access to public services.

So the real issue which must be addressed now is that of tariff barriers on EU–UK trade in goods. Michel Barnier appeared to favour maximising free trade in goods as part of the overall Brexit settlement.

Of course, if it were possible to have a comprehensive free trade agreement between the EU and the UK, the one remaining issue in respect of a hard border in Ireland would be largely academic. The UK is not going to be part of the 'single market' or, in all probability, formally part of the customs union itself. But free trade in goods, by necessity, entails a level playing pitch as regards state aids and regulatory provisions in respect of quality, safety and consumer protection.

Of very major significance for Ireland – North and South – is trade between the island of Ireland and Britain in agricultural and food products.

We simply do not know whether the Tories intend to retain the EU system of highly subsidised agricultural output from 2020 onwards. If the Tories have in mind a cheap food policy based on international imports, Brexit would have very serious implications for the two economies on this island. On the other hand, if part of the EU–UK Brexit deal as ultimately negotiated envisages the UK retaining something like the CAP, the high tariff barriers on trade in food imports between the EU and other countries could be avoided.

An 'imaginative and flexible' solution could involve allowing both parts of Ireland to have special status for trade in agriculture and food products with the UK. It might even entail the establishment of a North–South body to supervise and regulate agricultural policy and trade for the entire island. The Good Friday Agreement envisages the creation of such bodies and, as Micheál Martin pointed out on Thursday, the Good Friday Agreement is not frozen in its present form as regards the development of North–South bodies.

In the days of the pre-EU European Economic Community, the Germans negotiated a special status for trade between East and West Germany within the framework of the Treaty of Rome. So there is a precedent at European level for special arrangements to be made as exceptions to the common external tariff regime. Special status for trade between these islands is not unprecedented in the history of the European Union.

Another area demanding 'imagination and flexibility' is the question of where movement in goods across any tariff barrier would be monitored. Clearly the avoidance of a hard border would suggest that any actual or electronic tariff barriers between the island of Ireland and Britain would best be located at Irish Sea crossings. The bottom line in respect of tariff barriers and free trade is that the shape and implications of Brexit can only really be appreciated in the light of the outcome of EU–UK negotiations on free trade.

Clarity on these issues may only happen in two or three years' time, assuming, that is, that the Brexit negotiations do not break down completely within the 24-month period provided as a backstop by Article 50 of the Lisbon Treaty.

It is remarkable that Barnier's call for 'imaginative and flexible' solutions comes at a time when there is no functioning democratic government in Northern Ireland. It really is hard to excuse northern politicians for the suspension of their own functions at this critical juncture. Gerry Adams went through the motions of defending his call for an early border poll in the Dáil on Thursday. Everyone knows that such a poll, if conducted now, would result in a decisive defeat for those advocating a united Ireland. So why does he ask for such a poll? Surely he cannot think that the majority vote in the north for Remain somehow indicates a majority desire for a united Ireland in the wake of Brexit?

Any such poll held now would be a futile and retrograde distraction and an exercise in tribal polarisation. Sinn Féin would be better employed playing a constructive approach in the restoration of the Northern executive than engaging in divisive and futile grand-standing.

We badly need the development in both parts of Ireland of a 'coalition of the willing' which can focus on devising and evaluating options to maximise prosperity North and South and to minimise the grave risks that tariff barriers pose for the wellbeing of the island of Ireland.

Everybody has a good idea of the worst-case scenarios that Brexit could bring. There is simply no point in concentrating our attention on the worst possible outcomes while ignoring the need to develop models and special arrangements by which we can avoid those outcomes.

It was reassuring to hear Michel Barnier praising the efforts of the Irish Government and diplomats in making the 'Irish question' a central part of the EU's negotiating position.

However, the next stage is one in which wider participation by civil society North and South is necessary in order to explore, evaluate and propose 'imaginative and flexible' solutions to the Brexit problem for Ireland.

Who is talking to Ulster farmers and agri-business on these issues? Is Ibec engaging with the CBI in the North on possible solutions for avoiding tariff barriers to trade on this island? In the area of health, education and border area communities, is there any dialogue happening or planned?

Without in any way devaluing the efforts of those in the public service and State agencies who are engaged in shaping Ireland's response to the Brexit threat, Michel Barnier's invitation to devise solutions was not confined to public and semi-state institutions and agencies.

No one in Ireland has a monopoly on imagination or flexibility. Barnier's invitation extends to us all. It is marked RSVP and not 'regrets only'.

We need not feel too much sympathy for Theresa May

9 December 2018

The penny is beginning to drop with many, many British voters. There is no prospect of a hard Brexit anymore. Britain will, one way or another, have a very close economic and trading relationship with the EU. That means that the UK will not be able to negotiate free trade deals as it wishes throughout the world as though it did not have a de facto customs union or partnership with the EU.

Even as the Norwegians sharply react against the UK joining EFTA or the EEA, the headless chickens in the Tory party squawk on about 'Norway Plus'. They claim that Norway Plus would give them control over immigration. It wouldn't – it might only give them an emergency brake at best.

Just what is good about leaving the EU is now very hard for Tory voters to see. They will be rule-takers in any likely scenario. They will give up all their powers and influence in making the EU's rules to co-exist like Norway does.

Whether it is May's draft agreement or Norway Plus, Britain will be economically and politically weaker outside the EU.

The European Economic Area in which EFTA and EU states share membership is built on the famous 'four freedoms', of which freedom of movement is one.

If Theresa May's draft agreement is voted down, as looks likely, the UK will plunge into uncertainty and intensified discord.

The political eejits in the Tories' ERG (European Research Group) will advocate sending a delegation back to Brussels to 'sort out those chaps' and to knock a bit of sense into them. Just as they could do to all troublesome fuzzy-wuzzies with a gunboat in the nineteenth century; it should only take a bit of 'now look here' diplomacy to put manners on the EU 27. The 'Arish' will see sense if and when the UK threatens to bankrupt them (as Jacob Rees

Mogg suggested a number of months ago) or threatens to cut off their food supplies (as Priti Patel, the former Tory minister who had to resign for having secret meetings with the Israeli government, advocated this week).

The defeat of May's draft agreement will create a new scenario, one way or the other. The UK could seek an extension to Article 50's 29 March deadline if the EU 27 unanimously agree.

But to do what? To demand new concessions from the EU? To save the Tories' face? To avoid an election? To save Theresa May? To give Boris or Jeremy a go behind the wheel? To sell Norway Plus to the Norwegians and then to the British people?

It is plain as a pikestaff that if the British voters had really understood that the set of choices with which they are now confronted were the direct consequences of voting Leave, the narrow majority in favour of Leave would never have materialised in the first place.

It is a fatal mistake to feel or express too much sympathy for Theresa May. She is the person who is plodding doggedly onwards in the process of pulling the UK out of the EU – a course of action that is deeply damaging to Ireland, the UK and the EU. Her draft agreement is probably better than no agreement. But that is as far as its merits go.

Infinitely better would be something against which she has set her face – to go back to the British people and tell them that it is their sovereign right to choose to withdraw the decision to leave the EU if they believe that the choice to remain is better than any of the Brexit scenarios that they believe are truly available to them.

Remember that it was May who went along with the referendum proposal to thwart the UKIP threat to marginal Tory seats in the first place. She and her party put their party interests before their view of the country's interest to avoid the UKIP threat and to silence their internal minority.

It was she and her colleagues on the Remain side who failed to make convincing arguments against the dishonest Brexiteers in the referendum campaign.

It was she who, having taken over the helm and promised no early election, broke her word and gave away the balance of power to the DUP – a party determined to damage Northern Ireland and the Good Friday Agreement.

So while one might feel sympathy for her on account of those in her own party, and in the DUP, and in the Labour Party who are busily wrecking the economic prospects of us all in pursuit of an illusion based on lies that Brexit is good for anybody, and while she may be the least bad leader on offer, she remains determined not to allow the British people to avail of their right to reverse out of Brexit.

The only chance of a people's vote is if her draft deal is rejected. The ensuing chaos might, but only might, produce a second, informed and intelligent referendum outcome in which the people of the UK decided that on balance the Remain option was preferable to any other available outcome.

That is what we should all hope happens.

Obviously our government has to pay lip service to accepting the outcome of the first UK referendum, but others in Ireland should, in a friendly and decent way, publicly encourage the people's vote cause. It would be honourable and honest to do so – provided it was not done in a counterproductive way.

It would be a great help if the cross-community Remain consensus in Northern Ireland could find its voice again – and demonstrate that the DUP viewpoint is a minority viewpoint there.

When you think of it, the DUP have a lot to answer for. They helped channel illicit funding to the Leave campaign. They are now flying in the face of the Ulster farmers and Ulster business groupings' strong advice – all in pursuit of a hard Brexit.

The want to have their cake and eat it in terms of corporate tax autonomy for the North. They have accepted Irish Sea inspection regimes on food and agricultural produce. They know that an open border can be preserved with a soft Brexit. They know the advantages of doing so. They know that Michael Gove is secretly pursuing a post-CAP UK cheap food policy which will damage their farmers. They know the backstop is unlikely to come into play.

They have never looked hard at the potential advantages of EU citizenship for the North's population. In the very unlikely event of the backstop taking effect, it could give the North's economy significant advantages. The backstop could only have effect as long as the North was part of the UK, in any event.

But all of this has meant nothing at all compared with the bogus opportunity to use Brexit as an issue to prove their true-blue Britishness. Demographic changes coupled with rethinking basic loyalties and commitments and economic self-interest among Northern Ireland's voters strongly suggest that the DUP's brand of politics is on a political and historical down escalator.

I write none of this with rancour – only with a profound regret that Brexit is doing huge damage to these islands and their peoples. I hope that it can yet be undone for the good of everyone.

If you want a document which is part of the UK Constitution, look no further than the Good Friday Agreement

10 February 2019

Let's get a few things straight. There is a cohort of around 50 Tory MPs who want a no-deal Brexit because they want the UK to deal with the EU and the rest of the world on a WTO-terms basis. This aim is completely inconsistent with an all-Ireland economy which is central to the Good Friday Agreement.

This group of Tory MPs does not care about the Good Friday Agreement, the border, or peace and reconciliation on the island of Ireland.

They have convinced themselves that the integrity of the United Kingdom and its unwritten constitution requires that Northern Ireland's relationship with Ireland and the EU precludes any special economic or regulatory regime for the North.

Insofar as the United Kingdom has a constitution at all, as distinct from a series of long-standing but alterable conventions which can be changed at the will of Parliament, these Tories seem to forget that they have already elevated to constitutional status the Good Friday Agreement which, among other things, makes it clear that the continued membership of the North as part of the UK depends upon the will of a majority of the people of Northern Ireland and that the North will cease to be a part of the UK if a majority of Northerners opt for a united Ireland.

If you want a document which is part of the UK Constitution, look no further than the Good Friday Agreement. Not merely was the Constitution of the Republic amended to accommodate it, but Britain registered this solemn agreement at the United Nations.

The Good Friday Agreement, and not some Westminster statute, is now the key constitutional document defining the status of Northern Ireland and defining the terms in which the North's sovereignty can change.

So when you hear talkative MPs querying whether a majority of MPs can properly take over the conduct of the Brexit process from a government lacking a parliamentary majority on the subject, and when you hear them claim that the parliamentary business at Westminster must, as a matter of constitutional imperative, be determined by Her Majesty's Government, a rule of parliamentary procedure is being elevated above the wishes of a temporary majority in the House of Commons and is being accorded a sacrosanct status which it doesn't deserve.

Just as in Ireland, the Dáil accords the government a leading role under its Standing Orders in deciding the business agenda of its sittings, that aspect of Standing Orders is not of constitutional status and is liable to be overridden by a motion headed by the words 'Notwithstanding anything in Standing Orders …'

A majority in the House of Commons is free to take over the reins as it sees fit to ensure that its will is implemented.

The false equivalence of parliamentary procedures and conventions with the United Kingdom's constitution demonstrates a complete absence of understanding on the part of the Tory hardliners of the nature of parliamentary sovereignty in the United Kingdom.

Moreover, that false equivalence which seems to accept that Britain has no constitutional duty to uphold the Good Friday Agreement if the House of Commons prefers to allow the UK to crash out of the EU on a no-deal basis demonstrates profound ignorance of the constitutional status of Northern Ireland since the Good Friday Agreement.

All this would be very obvious were it not for the alliance of convenience between the hardline WTO Brexiteers and the DUP.

We have to remember that the DUP was not an original party to or adherent of the Good Friday Agreement. Many senior DUP members disliked the Good Friday Agreement and regard it as something which was imposed unfairly on the Unionist community in the North.

There is a strange symmetry between the DUP and Sinn Féin; both parties have a visceral antipathy to the principles of the Agreement and each of them really wishes that the Agreement would simply go away.

If Theresa May is to win the approval of any majority – cross-party or not – for any withdrawal agreement, she must either acquiesce in the ambitions of her WTO hardliners and their temporary allies in the DUP or, alternatively, find sufficient support across the House of Commons for a withdrawal agreement which does not command the hardliners' support.

While there are some signs that the Labour Party might be willing to support a withdrawal agreement which was combined with a political statement of intent to have some form of EU/UK relationship similar to a customs union arrangement, Mrs May's problem is that such a withdrawal agreement will definitely lose the support of her hardliners and may only possibly attract the support of the DUP.

It isn't clear whether the DUP would, if they were outvoted by a moderate Tory–Labour majority, withdraw all future support from Mrs May's government. If they were of a mind to withdraw their support for the Tory government, the question arises as to whether they would push the matter as far as a general election or would simply retreat into the political jungle to wage guerrilla war against a minority government from then onwards.

It is conceivable that a withdrawal agreement coupled with a political declaration committing the EU and the UK to some form of customs union relationship could have majority support in the Commons from moderate Tories and moderate Labour MPs.

It is even conceivable that such an arrangement, which could definitely avoid a hard border on the island of Ireland or some form of invisible border in the Irish Sea between the North and the rest of the UK, might be acceptable to the DUP.

If the DUP voted for or abstained on such a withdrawal agreement motion in the House of Commons, the alliance between the WTO no-deal Tory Brexiteers and the DUP would come to an end.

However, the DUP could still hold the balance of power for the remainder of this parliament's term once such a Tory/Labour compromise was voted through.

The EU 27 is not going to accept a qualification of the backstop or a temporal limitation on it if the resulting situation gave the hardline WTO Tories a new opportunity to take the Belfast Agreement hostage and to use it as a bargaining chip in extracting concessions from the EU 27 in the next phase of negotiations on the future economic relationship between the EU and the UK.

The way things are going, it does not appear that the backstop will be jettisoned, diluted or time limited. If there really is some 'alternative arrangement' which delivers the substance of the backstop and clearly prevents the Good Friday Agreement from becoming a bargaining chip in the next phase of EU–UK negotiations, we have yet to hear of it.

As I wrote here last week, Mrs May has found out the hard way from her visit to Brussels that it takes two to tango. The EU simply will not dance to the tune of the Tory hardliners.

Mrs May has her work cut out. It isn't a matter of Ireland holding its ground in some obstinate or retributive political stance. Upholding the Good Friday Agreement and ensuring that it is not shredded or damaged by a small parliamentary rump which has little or no regard for it is an existential Irish interest.

Reneging on the backstop would deliver into the hands of future UK negotiators an immensely powerful lever which the EU 27 could not resist if it seeks to preserve the character of the EU, including its single market.

The imperative of party interest has degraded Britain to a pantomime state

30 June 2019

If, like me, you regard the emergence of Boris Johnson as odds-on successor to Theresa May with a certain feeling of numbness, it may be time to examine the path that has led the UK to this nadir in its fortunes.

Let's not mince words. Britain is degrading into a pantomime state. Boris is a vacuous, amoral chancer whose appeal is based on his image as a toffish, loutish buffoon.

His likely opponent in the next general election, Jeremy Corbyn, is an unreconstructed and very thinly disguised Trotskyite Marxist.

Both of them will have emerged from electoral processes in which a small and unrepresentative minority is pursuing the interests of their party before the wishes of the great majority of their citizens.

The best that can be hoped for is that either of them (or both of them) if elected as prime minister will prove to be a disappointment as far as achieving their personal political aims is concerned.

In the case of Johnson, those who have worked with him routinely describe him as dishonest. They claim that he is simply a stranger to the truth and to decency in his personal and working life. He is very Trump-like in so many ways.

Any party that selects Johnson or Corbyn as its leader deserves to be hammered.

And the shocking thing is that both the Tories and Labour will fight the next election on the sole issue as to whether their opponents' leader is worthy of office.

And both of them will, of course, be right. Neither of them is remotely suitable for high office.

The imperative of party interest has degraded Britain to a pantomime state

In an era in which Trump, Crown Prince Mohammed bin Salman, Putin, Netanyahu and Chinese President Xi regularly rub shoulders for photo calls at international summits, vacuous, amoral Boris should fit in very nicely, thank you.

What brought us to this pass?

The simple answer is the categorical imperative of party interest. The Tories bought off the risk of losing seats because of a leakage to UKIP by promising a Brexit referendum even though the great majority of Tory MPs were remainers.

To vote to hold a referendum to decide an issue when you firmly believe that one outcome would be bad for your country is not simply amoral and foolish – it is immoral and dishonest. All the more so if your only motive is to save party seats.

But that is what David Cameron and the rest of the Tories decided to do. To stop Ed Miliband, they promised to hold the Brexit referendum. It wasn't to keep UKIP out of office. It was done to keep Labour out of office. It was cynical and disgraceful. And the great majority of Tory MPs went along with it.

Among them was Boris Johnson, a man who later tore up an article he had written explaining why he would be voting to remain in order to position himself as the candidate of the right-wing Tories for the leadership in the succession to Cameron, whenever that opportunity might arise.

His later support for Brexit was not based on conviction but on naked cynical self-interest.

And so the Tories got their quick electoral fix. They beat Miliband and caused him to resign.

The hard-left Labour party members who had selected Ed rather than David Miliband had sown the seeds of their defeat.

And yet again, some very foolish and irresponsible Labour MPs who never wanted Jeremy Corbyn to be their leader nevertheless backed his nomination in the ensuing leadership contest either out of complete idiocy or cynical tactical motives, or both.

And so, a filter mechanism designed to prevent any extremist like Corbyn from getting onto the ballot paper by requiring a minimum number of MPs' nominations was casually overridden by those MPs who dishonestly abandoned their own judgements and beliefs to nominate him.

So there is a symmetry of cynicism lying at the back of the ridiculous emerging choice between parties led by Johnson and Corbyn.

And, of course, there is also Theresa May's cynical, self-serving and dishonest abandonment of her pledge on becoming Prime Minister that she would not call a snap election.

She broke that pledge for an imagined opportunity to smash a Corbyn-led Labour party. Her cynical dishonesty backfired.

She ended up in a minority government, a political hostage to the DUP and the ERG group in her own party, and, in so doing, handed herself over to those who would use Brexit to get the keys of Number 10.

All of these political disasters spell deep trouble for Ireland – North and South.

Under Johnson, some believe, the UK is on autopilot for a hard Brexit. That means a hard border.

The only way that outcome can be averted is if the EU 27 makes it absolutely clear to Johnson and especially to the British people that there will be no 'negotiated or managed no-deal' Brexit.

There is high-stakes poker being played here. Ultimately, the UK hand is weak, and it can't afford to have its bluff called by the EU 27.

While some in the Tories are reportedly considering sending a negotiating team to Brussels including ERG and DUP members, to somehow convince the EU 27 that whatever 'deal' they agree will be passed in the House of Commons, it is hard to see the EU

27 negotiating with such a team rather than with the UK prime minister.

In any event, the threat of a no-deal Brexit would really have to be 'backed' by all remainer Tories if it were to be credible. And that can't happen.

So the UK is not going to be facilitated by the EU 27 if it seeks to use the difficulty of getting House of Commons approval as a bargaining chip.

The majority in the House of Commons is dead against a no-deal Brexit and it could, with the cooperation of Speaker Bercow, yet pass a short bill prohibiting the UK government from exiting without concluding a withdrawal agreement on pain of extending or revoking the Article 50 process, if the prospect of no deal or of Johnson proroguing the Parliament to force his no-deal strategy became real.

Ireland's advice to the EU 27 must be: 'Don't feed the unicorns'.

Ireland is collateral damage in a very English struggle between the Tory right and everyone else

1 September 2019

We are approaching the endgame in the battle between the right wing of the Tory party and Ireland. It is not a battle between the UK and Ireland. Nor is it a battle between Britain and Ireland. It isn't even a battle between England and Ireland.

Ireland and England are no longer enemies. The great majority of Irish people and English people regard each other with fondness. There is no reason to fan the embers of enmity now.

What is happening is all to do with English politics. Ireland is a potential victim of the polarisation of English politics which delivered the Labour Party to its hard left and which delivered the Tories to their hard right.

The rise of Jeremy Corbyn to the leadership of the Labour Party was a wholly disastrous event for Ireland – as was the holding and losing of the Brexit referendum.

David Cameron's decision to see off the electoral threat of UKIP by promising an EU referendum and his consequent victory over Ed Miliband persuaded Ed Miliband to resign.

Ed Miliband was unpopular with the people. He was the uncharismatic choice of the Labour left, including the trade unions. His brother David would probably have beaten Cameron but he was rejected by the left of a party anxious to shed the image of Blairism.

Corbyn had no chance of succeeding Miliband as he did not have enough MP supporters even to secure a valid nomination. But some MPs who did not support Corbyn, whom they knew to be a fairly unreconstructed Marxist and footsie-player with groups such as the IRA, decided to sign his nomination papers anyway – perhaps hoping to split the hard left vote.

With the aid of Momentum, Corbyn beat off the centrists in Labour and became the leader. Party rule changes have made it more or less impossible for the MPs to dump Corbyn as leader.

Corbyn was ambivalent or even schizoid on the subject of the EU. He instinctively opposed the EU on competition and trade policy. He saw it as a capitalist construct. He was blinded to the possibility that the social market EU was more useful to the workers of Britain than allowing uncontrolled Thatcherism to be imposed by the Tory right.

In consequence, Corbyn did not mobilise Labour against Brexit. He did not lead the campaign to keep the UK in the EU. Perhaps he even saw advantage and opportunity in getting out of Europe.

He remained ambivalent because he thought that the Brexit shambles was a possible nemesis for the Tories. Even after the demise of UKIP, he saw in Farage's new Brexit Party a further

Ireland is collateral damage in a very English struggle between the Tory right and everyone else

possible threat to split the Tory vote which could win the next election for Labour.

That same perceived threat, of course, sealed the fate of Theresa May. The Tories knew that they had to outflank Farage decisively. And they probably have done so – if Johnson can get the UK out of the EU before the next election, which is coming in the next few months. She had to go.

And so we now have Boris Johnson in Downing Street preparing for that election – and we have the Labour Party looking weak, ineffectual and unelectable.

Most English people are utterly sick of the Brexit issue. 'Get it over with!' is their gut feeling. Playing to that feeling, Johnson has fixed on an exit on 31 October, come what may. That is a popular deadline.

Brexit fatigue, the Tory press and the Tory right have anaesthetised the majority of English voters on the consequences of a no-deal Brexit. They do not know whether they are the objects of a remainer-driven Project Fear or whether there will be an economic recession if there is no deal.

As I wrote last week, relations between Downing Street and Merrion Street are at an all-time low for the last two decades. Tempers are likely to fray. Now is the time for cool heads and tight lips in Dublin.

The idea of recalling the Dáil early seems silly. There is a cross-party consensus in Leinster House. Nobody has anything very useful or original to say and I suspect that some headline-grabbers there might avail of the opportunity to say things which might not merely be far from useful – they might use the opportunity to say very unhelpful things.

We should not forget that Johnson brought into his cabinet a number of ministers who have explicitly threatened to 'bankrupt' or 'starve' Ireland into backing down on the backstop issue. In addition, Michael Gove, who is in charge of Brexit preparations, is the historic author of the most savage and reactionary attack on the Good Friday Agreement.

The EU insisted on the Irish border issue being resolved in the withdrawal agreement precisely because they knew that the UK would attempt to make cynical use of it as a bargaining tool of blackmail if it were left for resolution in the subsequent agreement on future EU/UK economic relations.

The Johnson cabinet still wants to use the Irish border issue as leverage to get other concessions. They don't give a fig for Ireland – North or South. They hope to wave the DUP goodbye after the next election. Special provisions relating to Northern Ireland's regulatory alignment simply are no threat to the union. Failure to keep the border open is, by contrast, a threat to the union.

But having used the DUP to bring down Mrs May, the Tory right will have to endure their company for the couple of months before the next election.

And so we see the people who extended the backstop to the whole of the UK to appease the DUP now in the absurd position of demanding that it be ended.

Nobody in Britain's media seems to be asking any Tory minister how they came to be in negotiation with the EU given that Johnson attempted to make EU agreement to removal of the backstop a pre-condition for any talks just three weeks ago.

Arguably that was the shortest-lived Tory red line of them all.

How will Barnier play out his hand? If the EU 27 leaders are shrewd, they will make it clear to Johnson that a no-deal exit will be very, very harsh in its immediate consequences for Britain, and thereby ruin his chances in an early election. They could simultaneously offer him a letter or protocol binding them to find an agreed alternative to UK-wide regulatory alignment within a stated period of 24 or 36 months. There will be a transition period.

Ireland is collateral damage in a very English struggle between the Tory right and everyone else

The UK would be definitely 'out of the EU' and the withdrawal agreement would have been 'superseded' by his protocol document.

He will come home and wave his piece of paper claiming victory. He will call an election after the Queen's speech which will be, in large part, his manifesto.

Once he is rid of the DUP's balance of power constraint an election, he will use the transition period either to come up with a workable technological means of keeping the Irish border open or else he will reluctantly introduce regulatory alignment for Northern Ireland and Irish Sea controls as a 'purely temporary' alternative to the backstop, or, equally likely, do a bit of both.

The only fly in the ointment is whether he will actually win the election.

If the UK is actually 'out of the EU' with such a deal, will the Lib Dem remainer-based resurgence carry through an election campaign? Will the people's vote campaign quietly die? Will the Tories wither again in Scotland? Will the Brexit Party wither, like UKIP, in England and Wales? Will Corbyn appear to voters to be a beaten docket?

Has Johnson an alternative to an early election? He has virtually no working majority. He could tell the voters that Britain needs a majority government. That would be a strong message for England and Wales. He might achieve the victory over Corbyn that eluded Theresa May.

Can his opponents stop him from following this path? Perhaps they will push through legislation under a guillotine providing that the Article 50 notification process shall stand revoked unless a deal is done by 25 October or unless the EU 27 grants an extension on the application of the UK. If such a Bill passes the Commons and the Lords before prorogation, it could complicate his life.

But even if that Bill did pass, would it stop Johnson from agreeing his protocol and coming back in triumph, as outlined above, to start his election?

Truss should not be forgiven or excused for what has happened

19 October 2022

The spectacle of political implosion in the Conservative party is no reason for schadenfreude (joy at misfortune of another) among Irish and European democrats. But the Truss premiership has turned out to be an unmitigated disaster for Britain. She cannot be forgiven or excused for what has happened.

Truss and her allies ruthlessly hunted Sunak, the MPs' favourite, into defeat at the hands of the Tory party membership. They portrayed Sunak as a Labour chancellor in all but name. They rubbished his concerns for the integrity of the UK's public finances. They sold their message of unfunded borrowing leading to dramatic growth with the zeal of true believers. They were contemptuous of any political wimps who preached caution. Their strategy was one of reckless self-belief rather than a mild case of wishful thinking.

And yet Sunak did surprisingly well to defy the pollsters' predictions of a humiliating defeat at the hands of the Tory membership. Faced with Sunak's better than predicted performance, Truss ruthlessly purged his supporters from her cabinet as if she held them all in contempt as benighted cowards whose political mettle disqualified them from the ranks of true believers.

We are in no great position to judge whether there was any substance to the Truss team's very damaging campaign press briefings which portrayed Penny Mordaunt as a gormless lightweight. But having seen Liz Truss blandly, blithely destroy her erstwhile closest ally, Kwasi Kwarteng, and show herself to be a slow-witted, inarticulate mouther of poorly scripted mantras at her pathetic press conference last Friday, one can only think that, at very best, she proved that 'it takes one to know one' if those criticisms were at all true.

And to think that Truss bemoaned her own comprehensive school for 'overlooking her potential'!

This debacle is one, like Brexit, engineered by the Tory Commons rump now known as the European Research Group (the ERG) but previously dubbed 'the bastards' by their own leader, John Major. The ERG lives in a fantasy world where trade agreements with the Commonwealth and domestic enterprise zones, coupled with welfare reductions, spending cuts and a buccaneering spirit, will ensure that Britain escapes its long-term post-industrial malaise.

The new austerity now enthusiastically espoused by Jeremy Hunt (who outbid Truss's 19% corporation tax promise with his own 15% variant) ends all talk of raising defence expenditure to 3% of GDP and much of the Johnsonian levelling-up agenda.

The ludicrous aspect of the ERG's mentality is their failure to grasp the colossal damage done by them and by Truss to Britain's standing in the eyes of the world. The result is pitiful. They endorsed the 'unfunded borrowing to growth' strategy. It blew up. And now their concern is to save their own seats from the consequences of their own misjudgements, political deafness and blindness.

In Northern Ireland, there was hope that the Stormont administration could go to Whitehall with an outstretched begging bowl to politically massage the reconstitution of the power-sharing executive. Spending cuts do not augur well for that aspiration. On the contrary, there is every sign of a looming budgetary crisis to compound the political crisis of DUP abstentionism.

That is why schadenfreude is wholly inappropriate among political observers in Dublin. The UK needs to get back on an even keel politically and economically. If Sunak or some like-minded leader emerges to rescue the Tories from immediate meltdown, he or she could face down the ERG by threatening a general election if they will not support one-nation Toryism instead of the Boris–Liz fantasy ideology.

The Western world is facing a crisis of self-belief. Trumpism in America and Trussism in Britain threaten the viability of the two major pillars of Western democracy and freedoms. We are weeks away from the likely loss of both Houses of Congress to Trump-dominated Republican politics.

This Western crisis is, in no small way, the disastrous legacy of Rupert Murdoch, a man whose pursuit of political influence at the expense of centrist democratic politics is an ongoing toxic drip-feed in the arm of democracies wherever he has cast his media shadow. Fox News and the Tory tabloids who recently noisily lauded Kwarteng's so-called mini-budget are part of a piece. They are reckless purveyors of divisive, deceptive political snake oil.

Come to think of it, who in the UK media actually supported Sunak's conservative approach to the UK economy? Are sensible media dumbstruck by the fear of being proven wrong by opinion polls. One of the Tory right's hit-list victims is the BBC, a last bastion of centrist reasonableness. Is public opinion to be informed by the BBC or led by the *Sun*, the *Mail* and the *Express*?

Britain has to learn lessons from this national and international debacle. Its centre has to be reconstructed and empowered.

Having avoided the madness of Corbyn, Britain needs to shake off the delusions of its hard right.

What is the DUP up to now? Simple answer: saving face

1 March 2023

There was a good deal of stage management in the presentation of the Windsor Framework on Monday. Sunak and von der Leyen and everyone on the inside of the negotiations maintained the pretence that the deal was not finalised over the previous weekend in order to keep its detail tight and to control its publication.

The EU has shown maximum pragmatism and flexibility consistent with maintaining Northern Ireland's status within the single market and keeping the Irish border open. Use of the green and red channel system means that paperwork obstacles to free movement of goods, pets, parcels, medicines, plants, and seed potatoes within the UK is almost completely avoided.

The EU has conceded that red/green channels and data sharing are sufficient safeguard for protecting the integrity of the North's dual status for movement of goods within the EU and the UK. From a day-to-day practical perspective, citizens in Northern Ireland will simply not encounter any adverse consequences from the operation of the protocol in their lives.

So, what is the DUP up to now? The simple answer is saving face.

Unionist farmers, shoppers, business owners, and consumers will have the best of both worlds – free access to the UK and Irish economies. The few red lanes are reserved for goods transiting to the Republic; nobody but a political extremist could reasonably object to their presence in northern cross-channel ports or ask for them to be speckled along the entire land border. They don't affect sovereignty – whether located in Larne or Stranraer.

Manufactured and theoretical objections based on alleged diminution of the North's status are bogus; the constitutional status of Northern Ireland is only alterable by the decision of a majority of its voters in a plebiscite. That remains the position. But its economic status is hugely enhanced by dual membership of the single market and the UK market.

Because the Windsor Framework will accord a right for 30 MLAs from at least two parties (not necessarily cross-community) to trigger a process in which Westminster can protect the North from any future significant and harmful changes in the single market regulatory regime, the maintenance of a general uniformity in single-market rules simply does not create any real likelihood of adverse outcomes for the unionist community.

Of course, if the DUP thinks that it cannot rely on Westminster in future to defend unionist interests, it should reflect on the fact that it has never been the case that the sovereign parliament of the UK was constitutionally bound to do its bidding. The Act of Union and the Government of Ireland Act are only effective in UK constitutional terms as long as Westminster maintains them.

An emotional Steve Baker spoke on Monday about his personal struggles with the effects of fighting the ERG and DUP battles on Northern Ireland at Westminster. His sincerity, to my mind, contrasted with the casual and opportunistic negativity in the reactions of Ian Paisley and Sammy Wilson. They seem to me to be grasping at any straw to delay resumption of power-sharing at Stormont.

Perhaps they see the prospect of rolling the electoral dice once more with a view to out-polling Sinn Féin and securing one more go at nominating the First Minister. Perhaps they think they can devour the political cadaver of Doug Beattie's Ulster Unionists and seeing off the TUV challenge. Perhaps the Tories would afford them such a chance.

Beattie now has a chance to endorse the Windsor Framework and reassert his party's claim to be the voice of moderate unionism. If he fumbles this political Garryowen, he will not escape the status of a beaten political docket. For him, it's now or never, I think.

As for Boris, Jacob Rees Mogg, Suella Braverman, and the remnants of the ERG group, one can only admire the graciousness of Sunak's footwork. He has avoided a visible confrontation with them; if they continue their muted brand of political sedition, he can simply marginalise them at his leisure.

Railing against the EU, the US, and reasonable voters increasingly disillusioned with the economic outcome of their decision in the Brexit referendum is stony ground politically; even the Tory press has copped on to the futility of perpetual warfare with the EU.

As a Brexiteer himself, Sunak now has some room to distance himself from the extremists who sold the lie that Brexit would yield £350 million a week to be spent on the National Health Service.

I don't think that the DUP will be able to meekly accept that Sunak has done as good a job for the people of Northern Ireland as anyone could. In the polarised politics of competitive grievance and victimhood that have held sway since 1998 in Northern Ireland, there is always a premium on acting with dogged irrationality and partisanship.

We can but live in hope.

The decline of the House of Windsor has implications for Ireland

10 May 2023

I have made a habit of abstaining from routine public comment about the British royal family for a number of reasons. The first is that they are human beings and are obvious targets for facile criticism and ridicule. The second is that, as an Irish republican, I consider that they have little or no significance in my life. The third is that I regard the whole British media circus of royal watchers, royal correspondents, and royal paparazzi as ridiculous.

The age of monarchy and hereditary nobility is over, and the House of Windsor is not merely an anachronism; it has lost its credibility and any prestige that it once possessed.

Yes, I concede that the British are very adept at public ceremonial centred on their royal family. But apart from its value as spectacle for tourists, most of that ceremonial is losing its previous meaning.

I watched the coronation as a once-in-a-lifetime event. I was intrigued by the massive build-up in the British media. I found the coronation ceremony itself to be somewhat stilted and awkward, rather than awe-inspiring, while the parade was elaborate and well-rehearsed.

The whole idea of the royal court, royal titles, royal orders and honours, seems to me to be an embodiment of discrimination based on status and class. The royal establishment, nicknamed 'The Firm', seems to absorb huge resources, acres of newsprint, and promote soap opera-like fetishism with personalities in a voyeuristic manner slightly reminiscent of an extended *Truman Show*.

I can quite see how Prince Harry, like the eponymous Truman, might realise the cruel falsity of his imprisonment and want to escape to North America where, to the chagrin of British media, he enjoys popular support.

Was that the last coronation of its kind? Put bluntly, if Charles were to pass away suddenly anytime soon, would the whole pageant be repeated for William? That seems far-fetched.

The House of Windsor is nearing the end of its present life. Perhaps it will endure as a Scandinavian pocket monarchy. But its glory days, such as they were, are over. The remaining Caribbean states are espousing republican constitutional status. The main dominions, Canada, Australia, and New Zealand, also seem set to become republics too.

Then why write here about the sun setting on the House of Windsor? That sunset has one or two potential side-effects for Ireland.

First, it will have an effect of the Unionist community in Northern Ireland. Loyalty to the Crown will inevitably change its meaning if the monarch increasingly resembles a very modest Scandinavian institution clad in suits, casual gear, and bicycle clips.

Second, a reduction in the role of class consciousness in British society and thinking will inevitably have backwash effects in Ireland. Social inequality is still ingrained in British culture and ideology. It is part of the notion of British exceptionalism.

Accepting foreigners as equals, the antithesis of the imperial mindset, is part of a republican ideology. Brexit was in part motivated by a sense that Britain was in some way the natural superior of other European nationalities. Ireland's relationship with Britain will be better for a lessening in a residual tendency there to subordinate others by reason of their origins.

Post-independence Ireland had its own royalty or nobility in the quasi-monarchical role we gave to the Roman Catholic hierarchy and clergy. Newsreel footage of politicians genuflecting before prelates to kiss episcopal rings reminds us that we once had an appetite for flummery analogous to that of the British.

Nobody imagines that we will see a social out-pouring like that of last week's coronation in Britain for another Eucharistic Congress in Ireland. Even papal visitation sank rapidly in terms of public participation in the last few decades. Likewise, visits from American presidents and foreign heads of state or royalty are becoming very low-key affairs.

From time to time there are calls for the establishment of an Irish Légion d'Honneur or similar body. We are better off without titles of honour or quasi-nobility.

Those with a taste for such things must make do with donning ceremonial garb to receive honorary degrees, freedoms of cities, or accepting membership of institutions such as Aosdána or medals from the President. We are spared the inconvenience of having to cancel knighthoods or revoke membership of royal orders for misbehaviour, and the annual grisly spectacle of politically inspired honours lists.

We are by no means classless, but we do not fetishise class or accord social recognition based on ancestry or preferment by a self-serving establishment.

The British codded themselves in 1953 by speaking of a new Elizabethan era. While her reign was long, Elizabeth never defined an era so much as a period of political decline. Talk of a new Carolean era is absurd.

Defence, Policing and Security

If the worst happens, who can come to Ireland's defence?

24 April 2024

It is a strange irony that the majority of EU states, including NATO members, are collectively considering how to deal with the threat posed by the emergence of a militarist Russia under Vladimir Putin which seems bent on reestablishing a dominance over neighbouring states such as Ukraine, Georgia, the Caucasus states, and on forming a global axis with China and North Korea, while Ireland is experiencing a hugely serious decline in its physical capacity to defend its territory by land and sea.

The strength of the Defence Forces including the army, naval service and air corps has been allowed to wither so that we now have a total strength of about 7,500 full-time members – the lowest number since the foundation of the independent Irish state a century ago.

The numbers of reservists have collapsed. As of last August, the strength of the reserve Defence Forces had fallen to 1,319 in the Army Reserve, 81 members in the Naval Reserve, and 280 members of the First Line Reserve – all compared with a nominal, theoretical establishment of 4,069, comprising 3,869 army and 200 navy.

In effect, the Irish state now has fewer than 10,000 trained military members which it could call up in the event of an emergency.

Membership of the Garda Reserve stands at approximately one quarter (371) of its original strength.

Over the last ten years, the size of the Civil Defence service has halved to less than 2,500.

And while we are paying lip service to the middle option plan outlined in the report of the Commission on the Future of the Defence Forces, our navy is largely tied up for want of crews, and we are experiencing serious difficulties in supplying adequate levels of soldiers to serve overseas as personnel for UN peacekeeping and monitoring activities.

We spend less than a quarter of 1% of GDP (0.24%) on defence while NATO members and other European states aim to spend 2% of GDP – eight times our fraction – on their defence.

In 1986, the actual strength of the voluntary FCA was just under 15,000. In 1980, the number of reserve forces available to the Irish state was approximately 15,000.

After the Belfast Agreement in 1998, there was talk of a 'peace dividend' – a euphemism for a reduction in the size of the Defence Forces. Right across Ireland, army barracks were closed, sold off or repurposed. FCA training bases were closed. Volunteer reservists who previously had training session held weekly on a local basis in local towns were forced instead to travel up to fifty miles to train. Such distances have proven a great burden for volunteer reservists and would-be reservists. We no longer have any equivalent of a territorial volunteer reserve like the UK's territorial army.

We no longer have a full-time Minister for Defence at the Cabinet table. We have smugly assumed that defence expenditure was rather wasteful in Ireland's circumstances. Recruiting and retaining soldiers and sailors has become more and more challenging – especially in a period of high employment.

Admittedly, the pay for private soldiers has improved substantially. But this has not resulted in the Defence Forces filling their nominal establishment ranks as was hoped for.

We need to radically alter our attitude to national security. We are acutely vulnerable to any internal or external threat, and travelling figuratively on the vapours in a near empty petrol tank. Can we be complacent about the apparent absence of immediate security threats on our domestic horizons? The point about many emergencies is that they arrive without notice or warning. Can we be absolutely certain that there are no such dangers? Where are the trained and disciplined forces to confront them? Who will deal with the consequences of major environmental events such as flooding? We are collectively ignoring the need for training, resources and numbers to back up the State in unforeseen emergencies, if things continue as at present.

There are simply far too few trained and properly equipped volunteer reservists ready to assist our civil power in the event of crisis, disaster, or a breakdown in collective security. How many young men or women have any capacity to bear arms in the defence of our democracy? Could we adequately provide armed security for our energy infrastructure as we had to do in the 1970s using the FCA?

The headlong decline in our security services and of voluntarism in support of our Defence Forces and policing has been truly frightening. Throwing pre-election shapes now about prioritising 'law and order' may attract momentary headlines. But very different long-term commitment to our collective security is now needed from the political establishment.

A quarter of one per cent of GDP for military security is a pitiful reflection of a national malaise on security that threatens the morale, capacity and number of our security services. It represents an abdication from one of the most fundamental duties of state and government.

Let's not forget the maxim: *Salus populi suprema lex.*

True extent of new powers sought by Gardaí a cause for concern

16 June 2021

An Garda Síochána has asked the Government to draw up and have the Oireachtas enact a Bill to extend its members' powers to require any person whose premises are searched under warrant or who are present to provide them with PIN number access or decryption keys to any IT device they may come across in the course of their search.

This power is contained in a general scheme of the Bill recently published by the Minister for Justice.

This legislation would, if enacted, not merely codify existing Garda powers but also extend them to cases and situations not now covered.

To take one example, under Section 9, gardaí will be given a general power to stop and search any person or vehicle in a public place who the gardaí have reasonable grounds for suspecting to be carrying a 'relevant article', and to seize it. Moreover, the searching garda may require the person to be searched to accompany them to a Garda custody facility.

What does the term 'relevant article' include? It includes anything 'stolen or unlawfully obtained'. This is worrying. A thing can be unlawfully obtained without the commission of a crime by the person searched.

For instance, something obtained by a breach of confidence or breach of legal duty such as a document obtained or leaked in breach of the Official Secrets Act might be a 'relevant article' under this definition. It might even include a Department of Health confidential contract. It might include bank records in the hands of a journalist. The category of potential 'relevant articles' is potentially vast.

From the viewpoint of a private citizen, the powers to be given to Gardaí to require access to computers, iPads, laptops, and mobile phones is also worrying. There is no new express duty to volunteer all relevant facts to the judge issuing a search warrant – merely a duty to answer the judge's questions, if any.

If a search warrant for a premises yields nothing mentioned in the warrant, the searching members may still demand the production of these items and require any person there to provide access to them by passwords or decryption keys.

With the exception of legal and other privilege for which special protections are provided, it will be an offence punishable by arrest and imprisonment for up to five years not to grant Gardaí access to such IT equipment and the information stored on it.

Private citizens have legitimate spheres of personal privacy. Your personal messages to family and friends, your opinions and plans, your political activities, your personal secrets, your friends' secrets and other diary-like information may be stored on such computers. Once they are read they are known. Once the agents of the state know them, they cannot be 'un-known'.

Is it legitimate to give such powers to gardaí searching a house for, say, controlled drugs? Can they properly ask for access to a sibling's computer to check on whether there might be information there tending to identify a supplier?

If the State's agents violate privacy and secure information that might compromise you or give them leverage over you to, say, become an informer, what can you do about it? In your own house, you may risk immediate arrest for failing to grant them access to all your private secrets.

By analogy, if the KGB had visited Aleksandr Solzhenitsyn and conducted a search of his flat and had asked him to disclose the whereabouts of diaries which they knew he had compiled and given to others for safekeeping under pain of facing five years in the Lubyanka, what would we think of that?

Or if contemporary policemen in Xinjiang demand similar access to Uyghurs' mobile phones when searching their homes, what do we make of that?

You don't get to ask a lawyer for advice during a search of your home. Is there even to be a defence of 'reasonable defence of privacy'? It's not in the Bill.

Someone failing to grant access to their devices may be arrested and charged before the District Court because the maximum penalty is five years' imprisonment on indictment.

You may be briefly reassured that there are to be codes of practice in relation to the use of these proposed statutory powers. But breach of these codes or of the terms of the proposed new law by arresting or searching or seizing gardaí does not mean that any evidence thereby arising becomes automatically inadmissible.

This Bill needs additional protections and constraints. It can't just be rubber-stamped through the Oireachtas like most Bills these days which are guillotined through both Houses using the coalition's large majority.

The constitutional privacy of the individual needs concrete expression and workable safeguards. You never know who may be directing police operations in the next few years.

Our so-called Policing Authority is a useless and ineffectual quango

September 2017

The report of the newly created Policing Authority makes alarming reading for two reasons – first, the omnishambles it describes in Garda management, and, second, the frightening picture it paints of the Policing Authority itself – a grim self-portrait.

In truth, the Policing Authority is not an authority at all; it is an ineffectual and redundant piece of political window-dressing established by Enda Kenny's government as a kneejerk reaction to the crisis in public confidence arising from the departure of a Garda commissioner who received a late-night visit from Enda Kenny's emissaries in early 2014. The establishment of a policing authority was bitterly opposed at cabinet by the then Minister for Justice, Alan Shatter, but he was overruled at the instance of the Labour Party – and within weeks he was gone himself.

Policing is one of the most central functions of the executive arm of any state, including Ireland. No common law country has made its national police force (as distinct from regional constabularies) subject to a policing authority independent of the elected government.

The Irish Constitution places the exercise of the executive power of the Irish State in the hands of the Government, which is made accountable to the Dáil. The Garda Síochána is at once a national police force, a national security service, and a national immigration service. It must be under the control of the executive in any functioning democracy. It cannot constitutionally be handed over to a non-governmental body that is independent of the Government and the Dáil.

And that is why the pretence of an apolitical policing authority has entirely failed. The litany of underperformance and non-performance by Garda management described in its third report equally demonstrates that the Authority itself is useless and ineffectual. The Garda Inspectorate set the agenda for change. But the Authority is not delivering that change and never will. A body consisting of a chairperson and seven members (none of whom has a democratic mandate) is wholly unsuited to exercise any authority over the Garda Síochána. It can't and won't.

Even its own statute admits that its primary function is 'oversight' of the Garda performance of its functions. 'Oversight' is not authority; it is nothing like authority. The Act leaves the real function of giving formal directions to the Commissioner with the Minister and Government, which must always be the case in a democratic society.

There is nothing wrong with the idea of an executive management board for the Gardaí. Such a board with a civilian majority was recommended in 2006 by the report of an advisory group chaired by Senator Maurice Hayes, a member of the Patten Commission in Northern Ireland. I made statutory provision for its establishment in 2007, but four governments came and went without appointing its members.

What is very wrong is the pretence that national policing and security can be taken away from the control of the democratically elected parliament and government. That is wrong in principle and is also wrong in practice.

We hear people point to the policing board in the North as a model. That board is composed as to its majority of elected politicians reflecting party strength – ten out of its nineteen members – with the rest appointed by their Minister for Justice. It is highly political in its composition.

It is a far cry from our so-called 'authority' from which any elected politicians with a mandate are expressly barred. And it was designed to mirror the power-sharing nature of the Northern assembly and executive in the context of a community deeply divided about policing. We have a very different constitutional order in the Republic.

Real constitutional authority and accountability in this state lies, and should lie, with the Government, the Minister and a serious all-party Oireachtas policing committee.

Your heart would sink at the impenetrable mass of management speak, pie charts, flow diagrams, acronyms, cross-references and tables that makes up the latest report of the Policing Authority. It seems so detached from hands-on governance in a real, living, breathing police service. The Garda Inspectorate could easily and far quicker assess whether its own recommendations were being implemented – if the Minister so requested.

We simply do not need a further finger-pointing quango pretending to be an 'authority' to monitor implementation of the Inspectorate's reports. If the Minister and the Chief Inspector were called regularly before an all-party policing committee of the Oireachtas, the public would have accountability and transparency. The Commissioner could not then hide underperformance or engage in management misinformation, of which the latest report complains. Nor could the Minister.

The Authority's latest report is dated July 2017. It has been on the desks of the Minister and the Commissioner for many weeks, long before the Commissioner's 'unexpected' resignation. And it was probably available to them in draft form well before that. It may very well have been the straw that broke the camel's back – both for the Minister and the Commissioner. 'Sources' were recently muttering dark tales that 'the worst was yet to come' in the wake of the breath test audit. It clearly provides the context in which the Commissioner made her resignation letter complaint of being in full-time explanation and accountability mode rather being allowed to carry out her duty.

The brutal truth that the Garda management has been allowed to deliberately neglect and run down the Garda Reserve is reflected in the report. But it has been obvious for a long time that this was so. I have received despairing letters and messages from decent reservists who know that they are receiving a humiliating slow death at the hands of Garda management at all levels.

What did Frances Fitzgerald do about that? What will Charlie Flanagan do about it? Did they issue a 'do it or else' direction to the Commissioner to build up the Reserve? I had to stand up to threats of bullying and non-co-operation to establish the Reserve in the first place. And it is worth noting that England has a fully functional volunteer reserve police with more members than our entire full-time Garda Síochána.

The report also demonstrates what has been obvious since 2008 – that Garda management were actively opposed to the civilianisation process as recommended by the Maurice Hayes report and as initiated by me.

It is the Minister's proper function to determine strategy, and to issue formal directions to the Commissioner to implement it – if necessary making it clear that non-implementation will result in dismissal. The policing authority quango simply muddies the waters of democratic control and prevents any direct exaction of accountability. It is a car crash in slow motion.

Happily, there is a chance that the latest two-year review of the policing service in Ireland initiated by the Government will conclude that the recommendation for a lay majority executive management board by the Maurice Hayes group in 2006 should not have been abandoned in 2008 and that the Policing Authority is a tragic, useless and counterproductive mistake that we can well do without.

Drew Harris reforms of Garda could have an immediate impact

September 2019

Although we are now effectively in the countdown to a general election and although the chances are that the legislation promised by the Government to implement the recommendations of the Commission on the Future of Policing may not be enacted in the lifetime of this Dáil, the very good news is that no legislation at all is needed to implement the proposals for reform of the Garda Síochána organisation recently announced by the Commissioner, Drew Harris.

It is vital that these reforms proceed now without meeting any further political or electoral roadblocks.

Minister Flanagan has written to all members of the Oireachtas seeking their backing for Commissioner Harris's reforms and has made it clear that they enjoy his 'strong backing'.

These far-reaching reforms will reduce the number of Garda divisions, increase the autonomy of those divisions, reduce centralised micro-management, increase the number of sergeants and inspectors, reduce the number of chief superintendents and commissioners, and increase civilianisation.

The Commissioner will be outlining his reforms, which come into effect immediately, to the Oireachtas Justice Committee and to the Local Policing Committees established under the Garda Síochána Act 2005 which provide a framework for consultation between local government elected representatives and local Garda management.

Long overdue

The Harris plan is long overdue. The financial crisis of 2009 to 2014 and the ban on public service recruitment which resulted from it put paid to the major process of civilianising administrative and back roles in the Garda organisation which was envisaged in 2007.

This, I regret to say, was not an entirely unwelcome reprieve from civilianisation for some within the force. Many members of the force saw advancement into administrative roles as part of their career promotion and development path.

Indoors posts were regarded as more desirable by many gardaí when compared with front-line policing roles. There were, admittedly, many others who relished the front-line role as 'real' policing.

Of course, it would be simplistic to suggest that real policing always takes place outdoors. Sophisticated policing is not all done on the street, on the beat, on surveillance, or on patrol.

But there is no case at all for filling many purely administrative office roles with attested gardaí. I was struck, in my time as Minister, by the extent to which such roles were being discharged by gardaí of all ranks.

Commissioner Conroy and I visited the PSNI support services in Belfast which included civilian crime analysts whose job it was to analyse local data in order to detect patterns which might not be apparent to local unit sergeants operating in shift duties. That was an eye-opener.

Civilians need not be confined to the clerical or administrative functions. There is no reason why civilians should not take leading roles in managing the day-to-day support of criminal investigations and preparing investigation files and prosecution files, including matters such as disclosures to accused persons.

Sophisticated policing and sophisticated crime

Crime is becoming much more sophisticated than it was when the existing Garda divisions and districts were established largely as a legacy of the RIC. Detection, investigation and prevention must match the increasing sophistication of crime itself.

Modern investigation of crimes like rape, online child porn, commercial fraud and white-collar crime requires sophisticated techniques and high degrees of professionalism. These are all part of front-line policing. They need highly skilled and experienced officers.

So it is entirely wrong to imagine Commissioner Harris's reforms as just getting gardaí out from behind their desks and on to neighbourhood foot patrols. Reducing the number of divisions should lead to improving the standard of specialist front-line policing units right across the country.

Rightly implemented, his reforms should make the jobs of gardaí at all levels more satisfying as a career, and greatly increased civilianisation should mean that the increased numbers in the force really do make a difference for our communities.

Ending churn

The Commissioner's plans for devolved autonomy to the new Garda divisions are very welcome. But it will be of little value if there is constant churn in the position of divisional commanders.

The Morris Tribunal identified a serious organisation defect in the force which allowed senior positions to be held for very short periods before onward promotion, lateral movement and retirement. Many divisional and district commanders were moved on from their positions after very short periods. The consequence was that officers did not have time to bed down and really acquaint themselves with their areas or personnel.

Somehow that promotional merry-go-round has to be halted and replaced by a policy that will leave incumbents with an expectation that they will be in a particular post for four or five years, giving them time to implement their plans.

Local roots and the Garda Reserve

One aspect of modern society is that the local garda and sergeant no longer live locally. Indeed, they are no longer really stationed in many small local stations which are open for very limited hours and days. There is much less opportunity for casual contact between a local resident and members of the force.

Communities are generally distance-policed by gardaí who may live in totally different areas and who commute to carry out shift duties patrolling in squad cars. Much of that is inevitable.

But the danger is that the Garda force is becoming unrooted in the community. Of course this can be countered in part by community police officers and by Community Alert and Neighbourhood Watch schemes.

I firmly believe that the development of the Garda Reserve can play a vital role in linking the force with individual communities. I have spoken on a number of occasions in the Seanad about the shameful way in which the Garda Reserve was neglected and some reservists were treated.

Fine Gael promised to double the Garda Reserve to 2,200 in its last manifesto. Commissioner Harris has indicated that he wants to rethink the Garda Reserve. That is good. But I hope it does not mean mothballing the Reserve.

The idea of a reserve has entirely different connotations in Northern Ireland, as Commissioner Harris well knows. He must be careful of being influenced by that.

Reserve constables work very well in Britain. It is no threat to the role or status or effectiveness of full-time officers there – it complements and supports their role.

I remember bringing Irish journalists to Chester in 2005 to see the reservists in action. One vivid memory is of a woman reserve constable whose other, full-time, job was that of nurse in an intensive care unit. That showed commitment.

It can work very well here. But it needs senior commitment to make it a success – commitment that matches the commitment shown by those who volunteer to join.

We have reason to be optimistic for the commissionership of Drew Harris. He needs support and encouragement, and, from the looks of things, he will get it at the political level.

Planning, Housing and Infrastructure

We must reimagine Dublin – it cannot continue to grow as a low-rise sprawl

17 June 2018

Instead of tabling a motion of no confidence in the Housing Minister, the members of Dáil Éireann would be far better employed establishing a forum on the future of Dublin – a forum which would consider how the city of Dublin and the neighbouring counties are to be governed in future, a forum which would look at the likely growth prospects for Dublin, and a forum which would ask itself a fundamental question – namely whether we can trust market forces and serendipity to shape the future of Ireland's capital.

Ireland's system of local government is, in reality, a sham. Local prefects, appointed from the centre and accountable in the last analysis to the centre, make all the major decisions on how their areas are administered and planned. While we have a veneer of democracy in the form of local elections held every five years, the councillors that we elect have very little power, individually or collectively. Such little power as they have is constantly under threat. We need only remember the recent failed attempt by central government to direct local councillors not to discuss individual planning applications in their areas to understand just how tight the grip of the Custom House is on what happens at local authority level.

In England, local authorities have planning committees consisting of elected councillors which consider applications for planning permission and conduct their proceedings in public. In Ireland, by contrast, the planning process is entirely closed and local representatives are denied any formal role.

While it is true that local authority members have an influence over the county or city development plans for their areas, that role is itself a limited one and the real influence of local politicians on the outcome of county development plans is far less than might appear from the planning legislation.

Dublin needs to have a single mayor instead of four county managers and four council chairmen with a one-year mandate. While central government might well fear the potential power which an elected mayor of Dublin might wield, the truth is that we badly need some means of political responsibility and accountability in respect of the future development of Dublin.

It seems almost so crazy as to be unbelievable. But €170 million has been spent planning a MetroLink project for Dublin before a public consultation process as to whether it should be built at all is conducted. Needless to say there has been no detailed cost-benefit analysis study carried out on this project. The ultimate cost is likely to be between €3.5 billion and €4.5 billion.

The project entails the construction of a metro light rail system from Swords to Ranelagh, partly surface and partly underground. From Ranelagh to Sandyford, the project involves the cannibalisation of the existing Luas Green Line. It probably involves the closure of the Luas Green Line between Ranelagh and Sandyford for between 12 and 24 months during construction. The result will be that instead of travelling, as one can now, on a Luas tram from Brides Glen the whole way to Broombridge at Cabra, a person will have to make two separate tram journeys and a metro train journey in future.

Far more important than the destruction of the Luas Green Line as it currently exists is the realisation that the cross-city Luas line recently built at a cost of €368 million will become an inconvenient and difficult to explain spur added to the MetroLink system.

Of course, deciding to spend between €3.5 billion and €4.5 billion on the MetroLink project carries with it a decision (never spoken) to abandon all ambitions for any further Luas tram lines in the greater Dublin area for the next 20 years. Suburbs such as Lucan, Terenure, and Ballybrack on the south side and their equivalents on the north side will, we are led to believe, now be the beneficiaries of a network of super bus lanes to be built along major arterial traffic routes.

While the politicians bicker over who should be Housing Minister, the real questions which face our elected representatives as to how we will remedy our housing crisis go unanswered.

In truth, we have to reimagine Dublin. It cannot continue to grow as a low-rise sprawl. We need to build a huge number of high-quality apartments in the city centre and inner suburbs.

I passionately believe that a redevelopment agency with powers to CPO lands, to assemble sites, and to grant building leases of major developments is the way forward.

The property market is left entirely to private enterprise as things stand. Local authorities play little or no role in the positive planning of development in their areas. If we want to have large-scale apartment developments such as the one currently under construction at Charlemont Street, we simply cannot confine such projects to areas of public land which have become run-down or derelict or under-used.

There are many, many areas of Dublin where the housing density is so low as to make it impossible for individual builders to develop new apartment buildings on lands which may or may not become available for purchase in one way or another over time. In the mid-eighteenth century, the Irish parliament established a body known as the Dublin Wide Streets Commission, which reimagined the city, acquired lands, reconfigured the street layout and granted builders building leases of a much greater density and to a standard pattern so as to dramatically alter the face of Dublin.

Site assembly is a slow and tedious process, as we all know. It is made even slower when rival developers play chess with small handkerchief sites so as to stymie each other's projects or to extract 'blackmail' money to buy them out. Perfecting title to the component areas of large development sites is costly and difficult. Giving such development powers to an agency which can, by stipulating building standards and designs, guarantee pleasing and sympathetic street designs has shown itself in the past to be the way forward. The real problem is that we are wedded to a deeply conservative laissez-faire process of urban renewal which plays into the hands of those who hoard land in the knowledge that its value will continue to grow even if it is under-used.

Some people wrongly claim that the Constitution is a problem and that property rights as protected in the Constitution are an obstacle to the kind of planning and development process that I am describing. But the Constitution is very clear; property rights ought, in civil society, to be regulated by the principles of social justice and the exercise of property rights can be delimited by law to achieving 'the exigencies of the common good'.

So the Constitution does not stand between us and the vision of a new and better Dublin.

Failure to radically rethink the housing market in conjunction with transport policies, infrastructural investment and energy policy is not an option that Ireland can afford. The fruits of the continuing failure of present policy which is agitating the minds of the public are rising house prices, diminishing levels of home ownership, increasing dependency on large-scale commercial landlordism and the rapid ending of the aim of owning your own home for the younger generation and for generations to come.

Things cannot go on as they are. Squabbles over front gardens and bus lanes are petty compared to the enormity of the price of our inactivity and our political indolence.

Why on earth would we need a constitutional referendum on the right to housing?

17 August 2023

The Russian president, Vladimir Putin, is now seeking to co-operate with the Democratic People's Republic of Korea (DPRK). He had previously entered into a political and economic co-operation agreement with the People's Republic of China (PRC). Russia has reverted to its traditional status of an imperial autocracy, with Putin exercising absolute personal power in succession to the tsars, Lenin and Stalin. Francis Fukuyama's optimistic thesis concerning history's ending in tandem with the Cold War is, alas, utterly confounded.

We are increasingly living in a time foreseen in Orwell's *1984* and Huxley's *Brave New World*. While wanting to remain optimistic, it is hard to see how current events are not as replete with danger for freedom and democracy as those of the 1930s.

One new phenomenon, we are told, is the rise of populism. I have a difficulty with that term; it seems to me that it is bandied about by political elites who are nervous about the sustainability of their failing political orthodoxies. Was Franklin Delano Roosevelt a populist in 1930s America? Or was the 32nd president of the United States a radical politician who understood that orthodox US politics was failing the American people?

It seems to me that use of the term 'populist' to castigate one's political opponents can be lazy shorthand for your own inability to change. To take the domestic example of the housing shortage, one need only look at the floundering attempts of our Government to square up to the consequences of a great increase in our population and undersupply of dwellings.

What are these ministers offering us? A referendum to acknowledge a 'soft' constitutional right to housing. Exactly what will that achieve? Nobody knows because we haven't seen the wording of such a constitutional amendment.

But perhaps the only change that might take place would be to dilute constitutionally protected property rights in the hope that more houses would be built at affordable prices.

The gross untruth implicit in such a referendum is that there is something in the Constitution that is holding back the Government's capacity to provide housing in greater quantity and at affordable prices. Anyone who looks at the private property provisions of the 1937 Constitution will find nothing there that suggests that the present Government is inhibited by the terms of our basic law from doing things that it actually wants to do in tackling the undersupply of housing.

Bunreacht na hÉireann, on the contrary, almost invites the Government to mobilise land and resources to serve the common good in relation to housing. Every local authority in Ireland has huge powers of compulsory acquisition, zoning and planning controls with which to perform its very clear statutory obligation to ensure that there is an adequate supply of housing in its functional area. The Constitution and the laws are already there to deal with the problem.

There is absolutely nothing stopping local authorities from compulsorily acquiring sufficient development land in their areas to meet housing needs. It does not mean that all houses built on such lands must be social housing. Local authorities could mix developments between social housing, subsidised ownership housing ('affordable housing') and private housing developments on lands acquired compulsorily by them. Compulsory purchase order (CPO) procedures could be streamlined, but the Constitution is in no way a drag factor, let alone an obstacle, to doing what we have done in the past.

Likewise, local authorities have ample legal powers to acquire and redevelop existing underused lands and buildings to increase the supply of affordable housing. Owners of land and property acquired will be liable to capital gains tax at a rate of 33% on the price of the land. The cost to the exchequer of intervention is greatly reduced in consequence. All perfectly constitutional, if done; none of it is done.

What is wrong is at the political level. We have a crazy situation that a State agency, the Office of the Planning Regulator, is actually prohibiting local authorities from making more zoned development land available. Worse still, the planning regulator is actually requiring local authority members to de-zone what it considers is excessive zoning of land for housing. This is happening across Ireland right now. That drives up the price of development land. Just daft.

I wrote here last week about the Government's recent legislative changes to drive single and small private landlords from the market. Since then, the disastrous amendments they made last year to landlord and tenant law are coming under the microscope. Government policies are killing the private rented sector, except for absentee REITS, which are being given large tax subsidies to turn us into tenants.

Can we have policies that work? Can housing authorities exercise their powers and fulfil their duties?

Can hapless ministers put away their constitutional drafting pens and do their day job properly? Or do they want to be swept aside by populists who might?

The Constitution of Ireland is no barrier to regeneration

29 October 2017

As we approach the centenary of the destruction of the Custom House, then the seat of Ireland's Local Government Board, by the forces of Dáil Éireann in 1921, it is perhaps time to consider afresh the role the rebuilt Custom House has played in the newly independent Ireland for the last hundred years as the seat of the Department of Local Government, now known as the Department of Housing, Planning and Local Government.

In a week where Dublin's city manager has publicly and controversially advocated the increased use of Dublin's open spaces as land for urban building, there is quite a deal of evidence that thinking in the Custom House and among its cohort of prefects or county and city managers is very, very conservative indeed.

I suggest that the major problems that Dublin faces in the next 12 years (when the national population is envisaged to grow by 1.1 million) is not an excess of open space; on the contrary, Dublin's problem is under-use of its existing developed space.

We cannot continue to carpet Wicklow, rural Dublin, Kildare, Meath and Louth with commuter-belt housing estates as an unthinking response to housing shortage and population growth. Already the transport infrastructure of the greater Dublin area is choking. I remember well when the members of the government in which I served between 2002 and 2007 were very worried about the potential public backlash from the likely delays resulting from the widening of the M50 from four to six lanes. Now there is a growing case for a second peripheral motorway 15 miles further out than the M50.

Even the soon-to be-joined-up but very inadequate Luas network at peak hours is groaning with commuters pressed like sardines into an inadequate number of tram-sets. As the economic recovery quickens, traffic jams are spreading across Dublin's road network.

Dublin needs to be the subject of a radical, active plan of regeneration. At the heart of that plan must be the realisation that the existing built-up city must be transformed into an area where a vastly increased number of Dubliners can live and work.

While preserving the character of many precincts and streets which are part of the city's cultural heritage, we simply have to plan for a greater density of urban development. And we have to implement that plan. The existing combination of passive urban planning with private enterprise development is not working.

Telling people what they may do and may not do and then simply hoping that they will somehow be driven to implement a plan by market forces is a dead duck. Just look at how much living space above retail premises lies empty in spite of repeated incentive programmes to encourage such use. No city has been regenerated in that way.

What is missing is active urban planning and regeneration. That involves the use of compulsory acquisition powers for major site assembly. It involves planning precincts, streetscapes and mixed land usage. It involves granting building leases to developers to build in strict accordance with those criteria. It involves implementation of policies on integrating social and affordable residential housing with private housing in city centre developments. It entails very much increased building density, much greater apartment living, combined with liveable streetscapes and communities.

As I wrote here before, Haussman in Paris and Dublin's Wide Street Commissioners owed their success to active regeneration based on compulsory powers.

The schools, shops, pubs, cinemas, theatres, colleges, libraries, parks, and cultural institutions and the roadways are already there, many of them decaying for want of use and de-population. Inner city public transport, and dedicated bicycle-only roads and laneways, and pedestrian routes, must become the pleasant, practical norm for movement in the city. These need critical mass in terms of residents to be economically viable. Private enterprise will not provide them.

One of the most disturbing aspects of our present inertia is the constant muttering from the public service and from some politicians who were suborned by the same public service about the Constitution being an obstacle to regeneration, planning, housing provision, and redevelopment. I heard it myself when Attorney General and when a minister. It is always spoken sotto voce. It is never particularised.

Exactly what part of the Constitution prevents exactly what from being done? That question is never answered.

Even existing legislation such as the Planning and Development Act 2000 envisages local authorities using CPO powers to provide lands for redevelopment by developers other than the local authorities. But such development site-assembly by local authorities is very rarely used. Hence we also have an abjectly ineffectual 'use it or lose it' Derelict Sites Act regime.

There is no constitutional reason at all why land must be derelict before it may be compulsorily acquired for area redevelopment or for the purpose of site assembly.

The only thing the Constitution requires is that existing owners' property be protected from 'unjust' attack. Where compulsory purchase is done bona fide for legitimate reasons and by reference to the public good, the Constitution only requires fair compensation for the property owner – to be judged usually by the value of the land and/or the costs consequential to dispossession.

I believe that much of the muttering about the Constitution as an impediment to CPO-based development is explained by a simple lack of appetite by bureaucrats to become involved in the

CPO process in the first place. That might also explain why their beady eye is turning to public open space or to the sites of obsolescent and neglected public housing schemes.

When you think of it, there is one common denominator to many of our current problems and the causes of urban decline, dereliction and urban sprawl – the local authorities overseen by the Custom House. Local authorities, in their planning role, decide on low densities, open spaces, maximum height restrictions, and the like.

For decades large areas of Dublin, such as the Liffey quays, suffered from planning blight due to unimplemented road plans. Dereliction followed. Much of Dublin's north inner city is run down due to the failure of the local authority to ensure balanced redevelopment. Poorly maintained public housing schemes dragged their neighbourhoods into decline and decay, as I know from my own experience in Dublin 8 in the 1980s.

Is it not strange that public housing planned and built by the local authority in the last fifty to eighty years now requires to be demolished in Ballymun, O'Devaney Gardens, Charlemont Street, Dolphin House and elsewhere, while much older public apartment housing in many city centre locations could be refurbished and are highly valued? How does that speak to the competence of the local authority as an engine of regeneration.

And anyone who looks at the bunkers at Wood Quay must still gasp in amazement that the designers of that complex now sit within it claiming to be the arbiters of urban design, street design and the need for a human scale for present and future design in Dublin city.

I weep to think that these people also gave the go-ahead to the second essay in architectural barbarism now being implemented by the ESB in Fitzwilliam Street. Could the ESB not have retired to Sandyford and allowed someone else the opportunity of restoring Dublin's Georgian mile? Why did they have to stay where they were neither needed nor loved? And spare me the functional brutalists' condescending condemnation of pastiche architecture. I know ugly when I see it. I shudder to think what the present-day centre of Warsaw would look like if sniffy contemporary views on façade-ism and pastiche held sway in the post-war years.

If Dublin is to be regenerated as a beautiful, heavily populated city, we need a new renewal agency that is neither based in the physical bunker at Wood Quay nor the intellectual bunker at the Custom House. Is that too much to hope for?

Eye-watering rents extracted from younger generation in city centres are not sustainable

28 April 2021

Most people do not bother with the directive principles of social policy set out in Article 45 of the Constitution. They are stated to be for the general guidance of the Oireachtas and their application is 'the care of the Oireachtas exclusively' and not to be cognisable by the courts.

Among those principles is the following: 'That there may be established on the land in economic security as many families as in the circumstances shall be practicable'. This aim was also to be found in the stated aims of the Fianna Fáil party.

The Irish Free State had inherited and developed the Land Acts passed in order to confer on tenant farmers the freehold of their holdings by expropriating absentee landlords or the owners of unproductive land.

Right up to the 1970s, the Irish Land Commission distributed agricultural land in fee simple to smallholders in exchange for land bonds compensation to the lands' owners.

Of course, a fundamental issue was the size of viable farms and with the passage of time it became clearer that many small farms could not lift the usually large families from poverty.

Eventually, the Land Commission was abolished and agricultural land became freely transferable.

It now appears that buying agricultural land has become a favoured form of capital investment – 'they're not making any more of it'. Some believe that some few wealthy investors are amassing large holdings of 15,000 to 30,000 acres in areas of prime agricultural productivity. These holdings are then made available for rent.

In short, the process of tenant enfranchisement which characterised the background to the campaign for Irish independence has not merely halted; it is going into reverse. Land is now regarded as capital in the hands of non-farmers. This process is happening in tandem with development land acquisition by investors hoping for capital gains consequent on rezoning.

The last decade has also witnessed the entry into the Irish housing market of property funds intent on large-scale investment in residential property development. 'Build to rent' has replaced 'buy to rent' as a policy to tackle housing shortages.

The previously established policy bias in favour of occupier-proprietorship for homes and farms is being abandoned quietly.

It is trite to state that the younger generation has been largely priced out of the prospect of home ownership by much stronger market forces.

Darragh O'Brien is battling to combat housing shortages on the boggy political battleground previously occupied by Eoghan Murphy and Simon Coveney. The Custom House has failed to deliver affordable home ownership. Eoghan, on radio yesterday, was upbeat about present policies on the basis that the housing market is now 'planner-led' rather than 'developer-led'. That is a dubious proposition. 'Investment fund-led' seems a more apt description.

With local authorities farming out their social and affordable housing provision functions to foreign 'build-to-let' investor funds (and paying through the nose to do so), the gradual rise of property-less citizens and families seems unstoppable. Even individual buy-to-let landlords are deserting the market.

Now we have the spectacle of the Planning Regulator seeking to impose uniform planning criteria across the country. Planning standards for towns of 10,000 just don't apply evenly to towns in the heart of rural Ireland and towns in the periphery of cities. The markets are very different.

Demand for different housing types and densities cannot be dictated or determined from a desk in the Custom House. Darragh O'Brien seems to understand this. His department has just issued a letter stressing the need for flexibility in applying national guidelines across the country.

We would be very naive to believe that a major transformation is not occurring in Ireland's social make-up. The political outlook of a generation deprived of any realistic prospect of home ownership will differ radically from that of previous generations. Nobody should underestimate the value of widespread ownership in any society.

It may well be that in our large cities a more continental system of apartment dwelling will assert itself. But rights of tenure available on the continent exist in a different legal and political culture.

Eye-watering rents extracted from the younger generation seeking to live in city centres are simply not sustainable. International investor funds buying two-bedroom apartments at between €500,000 and €600,000 and leasing them to local authorities at guaranteed rates of return of between 3% and 4% simply makes no economic sense.

Going back to Article 45 of the Constitution, the Oireachtas is also mandated to ensure that the material resources of the community are distributed among individuals and classes to subserve the common good, and that their ownership and control is not allowed to be concentrated in a few individuals to the common detriment.

Our Constitution is not the problem here; political willpower is.

Can we learn from the MetroLink fiasco as to how things should and should not be done?

24 February 2019

The leaking of a decision to scrap the incorporation of the Luas Green Line into the MetroLink project is welcome but raises important questions about the way in which important infrastructural development decisions are made.

We were told some months ago that the planning of the project had already cost €170 million when the so-called public consultation on the project started.

That such a vast sum could be expended on any project before its outline was even the subject of public consultation or political approval as part as part of the State's long-term capital programme is simply staggering.

While the entire sum was not by any means spent on the southern Green Line incorporation part of the project, and while some of it undoubtedly will be rescued if the northern city centre airport and Swords leg of the project is proceeded with, it is very, very clear that the NTA needs to be made accountable and amenable to prudent financial planning and control.

Instead of spending €170 million on detailed planning and then seeking outline approval from the public and the Oireachtas, it should have been possible to spend, say, one or two million euro on a high-level project plan and then to seek approval for the expenditure of €170 million on the detailed planning of the project as approved – if it were approved.

But that didn't happen. Why not?

One of the most frustrating aspects of the fiasco is that there were well-developed alternatives such as the cross-city Dart underground line and several surface Luas lines which have been shelved effectively in favour of MetroLink.

Whatever the comparative merits of those projects, you would imagine that they should all have been subject to a comparative public consultation process before one of them was chosen at the expense of the others. Capital resources are finite. To use them in an optimal way involves making choices. To make choices involves considering the alternatives. To consider the alternatives involves knowing what they are and what their implications are.

How much has been spent to date on planning the shelved cross-city Dart underground scheme?

Recently An Bord Pleanála refused Dublin City Council permission for a new Liffey bridge on the grounds that it would compromise the shelved underground Dart plan. Is the underground Dart plan dead? Or is it part of the great undead – the vampire projects lurking in the shadows and the crypts of the State sucking the blood of the innocent taxpayer?

Is there any democratic control of these infrastructural planners? If Dublin or Greater Dublin was a real municipality with elected councillors, decisions of these types would be made on the basis of an open and transparent dialogue between elected and accountable members of local and central government.

Instead we are left with a kind of organic policy development by unknown and unaccountable persons and bodies.

The so-called public consultation process that preceded the scrapping of the southern leg of MetroLink was a sham. It was a sales job for the decisions already made at the cost of €170 million.

Ridiculous estimates of the likely close-down period for the Green Luas line were peddled to the public. Three months and six months were mentioned. Buses would move displaced Green Line Luas passengers as commuters in and out of the city during those short periods.

The truth was that every Luas halt on the affected part of the Green Line would have had to be rebuilt as a metro station for high-speed, high-floor driverless trains programmed to stop at glass-walled platforms with sliding panels facing the doors on the trains.

All pedestrian crossings and access to the stations and lines would have had to be cut off.

The MetroLink service would not have gone as far as the new urban centres being constructed at Cherrywood and Brides Glen. A fragment of the Luas system would have operated between Sandyford and those destinations.

The fact that the recently opened cross-city Luas line from St Stephen's Green to Broombridge would simply not have been built at a cost of €268 million if the MetroLink project had come first should not be forgotten either.

Is it a case of our narrowly avoiding another yet public expenditure calamity on the scale of the children's hospital?

Yes and no.

The entire MetroLink project came with a €3 million price tag. Factor in delay, inflation and mission creep and you could well see a final price tag of €4 million on the entire project. That is twice the children's hospital budget at its worst.

What is the present planned cost of the cut-down northern leg of MetroLink? Does it budget for driverless trains? Are we to have a single-bore tunnel or a twin-tunnelled system?

What will happen to the tunnel-boring machine when it reaches Charlemont? Will it be left deep underground or will it be hoisted to the surface by a deep well-like structure such as we have seen in London's Crossrail scheme?

Will the underground station at St Stephen's Green be made so as to accommodate access to the cross-city Dart underground if it is ever built?

Have we abandoned all other potential Luas lines and/or metro routes to suburbs not served by anything except buses?

Is there a vision for Dublin's entire public transport infrastructure for the next 20 years?

Undoubtedly many people will welcome the decision to scrap the cannibalisation of the Luas Green Line as part of the Metro-madness. The news that the Green Line could have been out of action for four years if some of the plans were implemented is horrifying. Who was working on those plans? Who bears responsibility for even considering them?

Surely we should now have a genuine public dialogue in which the principles are outlined and decided first. Surely we should have an opportunity to evaluate all the alternative strategies and plans together with their costs and implications.

But will this be a case of the planners simply skulking away with their tails between their legs cursing the fickleness of the public, vested interests, and a craven political class – as they see it?

Or can we learn collectively from the outcome and turn a fiasco into valuable experience as to how things should and should not be done?

I am still optimistic that we will do better. But am I confident? Alas, not.

Will no one shout stop as the MetroLink bill heads past €20 billion?

12 March 2025

The scandal that is MetroLink illustrates everything that is intellectually rotten in modern Ireland. Across 30 or 40 years, hundreds of millions have been wasted on a project or, more correctly, a series of different versions of a project, to build some form of underground rail system for Dublin.

Before a shovel is put in the ground, the present version, MetroLink, will have cost us between €400 million and €500 million in planning, engineering and other costs involved in securing approval for the scheme.

The shocking thing is in the late 1990s the Mitsui Corporation, a Japanese conglomerate, told the Irish government that it would construct an 'x'-shaped Dublin underground system with a single central hub for nothing – yes, at its own expense, bar a small initial injection of funds from the State – in exchange for the right to operate it as franchisee for 25 years.

Meanwhile, we spent about €150 million on an entirely different underground project, the Dart interconnector, which was to connect a mainline rail service underground from Heuston station to the east coast railway with several tube stations at High Street, St Stephen's Green and Pearse Station.

First proposed in 1992, it formed part of a Greater Dublin Transport Strategy published in 2016 but was excluded from the National Development Plan published in 2018. A railway order for its construction was obtained in 2011 on the basis that private capital would fund its estimated €4 billion cost. The railway order expired in 2015, and with it, the Dart Underground expired too.

The quango called the National Transport Authority (NTA) had produced a draft Transport Strategy in 2015 which envisaged that Dart Underground might still be built by 2035.

The NTA took over transport planning for Greater Dublin and incorporated an earlier agency, the Dublin Transport Office. The separate Railway Procurement Agency managed to escape incorporation into the National Transport Authority. But the old CIÉ companies – Dublin Bus, Irish Rail and Bus Éireann – are legally obliged to accept NTA direction in Dublin. Transport Infrastructure Ireland is a brand name adopted for certain purposes by the National Transport Authority. You get the picture.

Anyhow, the NTA began working on an underground metro system which would connect Dublin Airport to Sandyford with fully automated trains operating in twin tunnels and which would cannibalise the Luas Green Line. That line was, at one stage, planned to go underground in the city centre but was later left with a terminus as St Stephen's Green. Eventually, it was built in a second phase on the surface between St Stephen's Green and Broombridge.

The new NTA plan was to use the Ranelagh to Sandyford surface section of Luas as part of the metro to the airport and Swords. However, this involved the likely closure of the Green Line for two or three years as the system was to be completely segregated and have metro stations constructed to replace the Luas stops. Tram services from Sandyford to Brides Glen and from Charlemont to Broombridge would continue as separate surface services.

This plan, in turn, was abandoned so that MetroLink would have its southern terminus at Grand Parade on the hugely congested canal cross-city route or via a rear entrance with setting down for four cars on the largely unknown Dartmouth Road in Ranelagh.

When Minister for Justice Jim O'Callaghan sensibly suggested that the southern terminus be left at the proposed St Stephen's Green station to leave open the possibility of its south-central extension to Terenure, Churchtown and Tallaght, he was told that even altering plans to shorten the route at this stage would costs hundreds of millions of euro and delay the project further.

When MetroLink was first proposed in its latest form (which abandoned the twin tunnel plans in favour of a cheaper single-bore model), the NTA estimated its cost to be about €3.5 billion.

That figure was generally considered to be grossly optimistic. It grew by stages to €11 billion. But the Dáil's Public Accounts Committee worried that even that figure could be a gross underestimate and suggested that the eventual true cost could be €20 billion.

Now we know that Minister for Transport Darragh O'Brien has been formally warned that the cost could exceed €23 billion. That is about five times the cost on which approval was originally sought by the National Transport Authority.

Compared with alternative transport infrastructure for Dublin, including up to five new Luas lines to be built by a public–private partnership system, MetroLink is simply bad value and destined to be a calamitous money pit. And it has not secured approval yet from the soon to be restructured An Bord Pleanála.

If you think that the children's hospital or the Leinster Lawn bike shelter should teach us some lessons but haven't, the case for blowing the whistle on MetroLink seems very strong indeed.

The difference is that we are blundering into this quango-driven catastrophe with our eyes wide open. Echoing this paper's great commentator, John Healy: 'Will no one cry stop?'

Not every streetscape is improved by a starkly modern addition

16 March 2018

I am always a little hesitant about putting my toe into the shark-infested waters of architectural taste and style. All the more so when the precise subject on which I am writing is largely moot because the project is already under way. But here goes!

The ESB is currently building a new HQ on the site of its old office at Fitzwilliam Street. In the 1960s, the ESB had occupied a long terrace of Georgian buildings which formed part of the longest Georgian streetscapes in Dublin. Instead of vacating those buildings and constructing its HQ somewhere else, the ESB secured permission to knock down its Georgian houses and to replace them with a modern office block which, although it claimed to pay some lip service to the proportions of its neighbouring buildings, was generally viewed as a disastrous error and a blot on the face of Georgian Dublin.

The architect, the late Sam Stephenson, justified the 1960s building on the basis that Georgian buildings had outlived their usefulness and that they were, in any event, designed to last only a lifetime. He was lucky that the then Minister for Local Government, Kevin Boland, who at that time discharged the role now played by An Bord Pleanála, viewed Georgian Dublin as an unwanted relic of our colonial past and had more to do with 'belted earls' than with the forward-looking republic that he wished to build in a decade that included the 50th anniversary of 1916.

Ironically, the 1960s building lasted far less than a lifetime. It was demolished last year as part of a new 45,000 square metre head office development by the ESB on the site between Fitzwilliam Street and James's Place. The new development is designed by Grafton Architects and O'Mahony Pike Architects.

The Fitzwilliam Street façade of the new ESB development is, arguably, much more or somewhat more in keeping with the Georgian streetscape than that designed by Sam Stephenson. But it is by no means a replica of that which was destroyed in the 1960s. It is taller and has modern proportions while incorporating some considerable Georgian references and motifs. Artists' impressions suggest that it will be much more sympathetic to its Georgian context and will be a substantial improvement as far as the streetscape is concerned.

The matter of its design is, as I said, somewhat moot as the development is already well under way.

But the issues raised by the recent history of Fitzwilliam Street are not moot at all. There are echoes of the famous Hume Street saga to all of this.

Without being an old fogey in the Prince Charles mode, I do wonder whether I am completely on my own in querying whether the current architectural 'establishment' has not bullied us into a phobia against what they term 'pastiche' or façade-ism. There seems to be an absolute fixation with avoiding the label 'pastiche'.

Why should that be? Why should we genuflect to the gods of functionalism and modernity in respect of all architectural matters? Why should a new extension to an old house or building trumpet its modernity or sharply contrast with the existing structure? Why is anything else considered a departure from 'good design'? Why is it somehow 'wrong' to replicate old design and old forms or to imitate them?

What exactly was 'wrong' with Edwardian houses echoing Tudor or Elizabethan architecture? Why do we not value the genius and the instincts of Sir Edwin Lutyens to imitate forms of the architectural past?

On the corner of Fitzwilliam Square and Lower Pembroke Street there is, for instance, a substantial pastiche Georgian office building dating back to the 1960s. It isn't all that bad and is probably more pleasing to the eye than an earlier infill office building on the opposite side of the street. While I entirely agree that we should seek to conserve rather than destroy Georgian and Victorian Dublin, there will be cases where infill sites need to be developed.

I simply don't swallow the architectural 'thought police' line that imitation or, to use their label, 'pastiche' is always wrong. Pastiche can be cheap and tacky, but replication of traditional forms can be very well done and can be very beautiful. This is not an area, I argue, in which there is objective right or wrong.

I have, however, the strong impression that modern planners belong to an orthodox priesthood that regards anything other than harsh modernism as morally suspect.

Façade-ism is not always suspect. Most of us love the Bank of Ireland building or Old Parliament House on College Green. But an aerial photograph of that building demonstrates that it is, in truth, quite a deceptive façade for the most part – and always was. Much of Dublin Castle was rebuilt, but the modern 1970s office building backing onto South Great George's Street is arguably out of place and less pleasing in its location that the other reconstructed components in the Dublin Castle complex.

None of this is to argue against high-quality modern architectural design – far from it. I simply believe that there is no right or wrong where there is genuine quality in architecture.

Exposing your structural slabs, joists and girders is only one way of doing things; concealing or decorating them is just as legitimate. Decoration is not wrong. Functionalism is not intrinsically right. There is no moral rule that requires architectural form and function to coincide with each other.

Imitating architectural styles from former periods or even adapting them is perfectly legitimate, especially when we have the techniques and the resources to do so to a high standard.

There is no reason at all why someone should not build a Strawberry Hill Gothic home if that is his or her fancy.

Yes, that can be described as derivative or derided as pastiche. But is it any the less slavish than dreary adherence to the canons of contemporary architectural style can be? Why, by the way, is 'contemporary' such a good thing?

Creativity and innovation in an era of huge development in building raw materials is great. Doing what was never done before is sometimes exciting and uplifting; but it may not always be pleasing.

I venture to suggest that there is such a thing in architecture as slavishly unslavish.

So while the ESB project in Fitzwilliam Street is being completed, let us reserve judgement. The real question is whether it will be seen as pleasing or whether it will be seen more as begging the question as to why the ESB were ever allowed to demolish the original streetscape in the first place. We can but hope.

There now! I'm glad I got that off my chest.

Ireland has a real problem with getting things done

1 February 2023

If we in Ireland can harness our offshore wind energy capacity, our likely energy needs could be more than met. Minister for Energy Eamon Ryan was waxing lyrical about this opportunity recently. And it is an attractive and achievable goal – provided we take it seriously and provided that we implement the steps needed to achieve it. Those are, alas, very significant provisos.

The process for licensing offshore wind farms still has not been put in place. Ryan told the Seanad last week that key positions in the Maritime Area Regulatory Authority, the new statutory offshore licensing body, are still being filled. Two and a half years into the Government's tenure, that is disappointing progress. The first licensing round is due to commence in April, but when will it result in the grant of licences? And when will the parallel planning process be complete?

Another worry is the planned involvement of An Bord Pleanála (soon to be rebranded as a commission under the Government's published planning Bill). The Minister informed the Seanad that the Government was now embarking on a programme of recruiting expert staff to handle planning aspects of offshore wind farming installations.

It wasn't obvious to his listeners that the board/commission is the most suitable body to decide on planning marine development. It has its hands more than full dealing with domestic planning appeals, major housing developments, urban road traffic developments, and major onshore projects such as MetroLink, Luas lines, railway infrastructure and a long line of other infrastructural, industrial and homebuilding developments.

The minister seemed to see that there might just be a case for a single-purpose specialist body to deal with licensing, environmental suitability, sustainability and necessary safeguards of offshore windfarms, whether fixed platforms or floating structures. It is hard to see how expertise on onshore construction translates into expertise on issues dealing with deep-sea licensing.

We need to develop port infrastructure to build, service and maintain the scale of offshore development that the minister has in mind. It's not happening yet. Locations haven't yet even been decided for such facilities. Delay in that regard will result in Ireland's offshore infrastructure being built in, and serviced from, ports in Britain and the Netherlands with consequent loss of employment.

Developing our electricity grid must be a priority now. We simply can't afford to have the controversy and litigation that delayed the North–South electricity interconnectors repeated.

Everything in Ireland takes so long to move from planning to execution. MetroLink is a case in point. If, which I doubt, the Transport Infrastructure Ireland proposals submitted to An Bord Pleanála are a good idea compared with the alternatives, the time frame for the first metro train running remains more than a decade away.

Recently Ryan was supportive of a rail link from Letterkenny to Derry and on to Dublin. Now we hear talk of a rail link from Letterkenny to Omagh and on south. The Dart underground is again shelved decades after planning was completed.

There is a world of difference between planning and execution. Sometimes I am reminded of Woody Allen's take on the Book of Genesis: 'In the beginning there was nothing. And the Lord said: Let there be light." There was still nothing, but you could see it a lot better.'

Book of Genesis politics will not do. It is all very well to set targets such as banning the sale of internal combustion engine cars by 2030. But who is going to make the electric vehicles? Who is going to instal charging points on roads and streets and how? Where is the electricity going to come from? How will it be transmitted in our grid? How many more data centres are we building? What will our population be? Are we able to build, heat and light homes for a massively increased population?

The Commission on Housing seems to think that our home-building targets are madly underestimated. Do we have an immigration policy?

What has happened to our afforestation policies? It does not look like we are anywhere near approaching our annual planting targets. And apart from commercial forestry, are we serious about reforesting mountainy areas such as Wicklow with native trees to act as carbon stores and flood attenuation to address increased rainfall patterns?

Housing for All is not the solution it claimed to be. The State must take a hands-on role in the provision of the homes we need. Buying overpriced high-rise apartments from real estate investment trusts financed by tax-driven offshore financiers is not the solution.

The time is past for wishful thinking; we need hard-headed planning and execution. We need less litigation and more action to address a growing problem.

It's not just a matter of sleeping bags and tents; it's the credibility of our democracy.

Why is our infrastructure delivery worse now than in the nineteenth century?

28 August 2024

Last week, Kevin O'Sullivan wrote here about the risk that Ireland might find itself a victim of heatwaves, droughts, and forest fires. Having spent this month in County Roscommon's Shannonside, previous expert predictions that Ireland was more likely to have wetter, cloudier if slightly warmer summers seemed a little more credible to me.

Predictions that climate change might increasingly result in continental tourists seeking cooler, cloudier and rainier refuge in places like Ireland abound in the media.

Whichever predictions are borne out in future, we shall see. But, in the meantime, there are some contingencies for which we must prepare in terms of infrastructure.

Which, presumably, explains why 13 years ago Dublin City Council, which was then responsible for water supply in the capital, published a plan to supply up to 350 million litres per day to Dublin from Lough Derg via a pipeline to be constructed.

An Olympic-sized swimming pool contains 250 to 400 million litres of water. So, what we are talking about is not exactly massive in terms of daily volume, especially when the current Government is promising to build many more such pools in the afterglow of the Paris Olympics.

Irish Water, the newly created national water utility, took over the project in 2016 and came up with a pipeline route from Parteen, south of Lough Derg, to Dublin serving anticipated water needs for the east Leinster area. The proposed abstraction represents 2% of the Shannon throughflow at Parteen.

The water would be pumped to a point near Cloughjordan in Tipperary and would flow by gravity to the greater Dublin area. As Kevin O'Sullivan wrote here in 2018, planning permission for the project was then being applied for.

Critics said that it was unnecessary as Dublin city was in 2017 losing 45% of its current water supply through mains leakage every day while most cities managed a leakage rate of less than 15%, according to a 2017 report from KPMG. Uisce Éireann has since reduced mains leakage to 37% in 2023 and plans to get that figure down to 25% nationally and to 20% in Dublin by 2030.

The latest position is that the Government finally decided in June 2024 to authorise the Parteen–Dublin scheme. The present estimated cost range for the project is between €4.5 and €6 billion and the project would have to go through the infrastructural planning process in 2025, with construction time estimated to be four to five years.

The bottom line is that what was planned as early as 2011 to 2016 is being given the green light some eight years later and will be completed, if all goes well, about 15 years later. The cost of the project will presumably be multiples of the original Uisce Éireann proposal. In 2016, Irish Water estimated a cost 'between €700 million and €900 million' and completion by 2024.

Contrast that with the construction in 1847 of the Dublin–Cork mainline railway. It received parliamentary assent in 1844 and reached Carlow and Cashel in 1846. Assent to extend the line to Cork was received in 1845 and the line reached a temporary terminus at Blackpool outside Cork city centre in 1847.

That massive project was largely done without anything more than pick, shovel and manual labour. (Railway buffs will rush to point out that the last few miles to Ceannt station in Cork city centre (involving the digging of a tunnel) was not completed until 1855.)

Assuming, as I do, that Irish Water's 2016 predictions of water needs in east Leinster and Dublin require the construction of the Shannon–Dublin pipeline, and even assuming that predictions of Irish drought risks are justified, how is it that our capacity to plan, approve and construct major national infrastructure projects always takes so very long compared with the early Victorian Great Southern Railway to Cork?

Would we be better reverting to a nineteenth-century procedure whereby major infrastructural projects receive parliamentary process approval and are implemented in quick order? Does everything have to be done through the current Planning Board process, including offshore windfarms and projects like MetroLink?

A central issue for nearly all public infrastructure and private infrastructure, including addressing the housing crisis, is the question of compulsory purchase. We need to revolutionise the system of compulsory purchase, to increase supply of land, both greenfield and brownfield, for housing. We badly need efficient and effective compulsory purchase in pursuit of that aim.

The same applies to all forms of public infrastructure. Compulsory purchase also lies at the heart of the whole issue of positive urban planning (as distinguished from the permissive zoning regime now masquerading as planning law).

It is tragic that the legislative proposals of the Law Reform Commission on compulsory purchase published in 2023 were left on the shelf while other legislation on planning and other major infrastructural projects are slowly enacted and progressed.

In pursuit of value for money and speed, the shareholders of the Great Southern Railway to Cork did a far better job than administrative Ireland can manage these days.

Rich must not be allowed to use farmland as a vehicle for investment

13 April 2022

I have been meaning to write here about ownership of agricultural farmland for a while, but other topics came first. This week I read a striking piece in the online business magazine *The Currency* which draws our attention to a large and growing transformation of property ownership in Ireland – investment in Irish farmland by wealthy people as part of their personal asset portfolios.

Let me set the scene. Ownership of Irish farmland was a central issue in the political development of Irish independence. Throughout the nineteenth century and for the first half of the twentieth century, the relationship between the Irish landlord class and their tenant farmers dominated the British government's agenda in post-Union Ireland, and the newly independent Irish state regarded redistribution of ownership of agricultural land as a key area of national policy.

British governments – particularly Conservative and Unionist governments – wrongly believed that by enfranchising Irish tenant farmers they would buy off the threat of radical Irish separatism. The Tories also believed they could also buy off limited autonomy in the form of Home Rule by programmes of land reform which would satisfy growing political agitation among Irish Catholics. Liberal governments believed that land reform coupled with Home Rule would satisfy the Catholic's political aspirations. In the end, neither approach succeeded.

The newly independent Irish state made continuation of the redistribution of land ownership to farming families a central policy goal. The Land Commission became the key state agency in that drive and every Irish cabinet had a separate Minister for Lands with personal political responsibility to drive that redistribution. The Department of Lands and the Land Commission occupied one side of Upper Merrion Street opposite Government Buildings. There were lay commissioners and a judicial commissioner to resolve disputes and confirm the actions of the commission. There were limitations on the right to sell land outside urban areas. Older deeds of conveyance were obliged to recite the consent of the Land Commission to the sale of farmland.

In short, the question of who owned and used Irish farmland was one in which the State and its political processes were centrally involved. Under-used agricultural land was liable to be acquired and redistributed among neighbouring farms. The Land Commission inspectors were as powerful as the clergy in the affairs of rural Ireland.

A central issue was the ideal size for family farms. As the years passed, it became clear that family farms of under 100 acres were economically questionable in terms of viability and development. Many believed that larger farms were the only means of developing the entire Irish agricultural sector.

From our 1973 accession to the EEC, a radical change in policy took shape. The Land Commission was allowed to wither and was formally abolished as late as 1999 (in Northern Ireland it was wound up in 1935).

Has Ireland lapsed from fervent belief in land policy to bordering on agnosticism?

The issue is re-emerging as one of potential importance. Quite apart from large-scale purchase of agricultural land by property speculators eyeing its potential for redevelopment, there is a comparatively new phenomenon of long-term portfolio farmland purchase by wealthy individuals, syndicates and investment trusts.

These purchasers want to become landlords where agriculture will be undertaken by tenants and contractors with no long-term rights or property interest in the land. The super-wealthy are building portfolios of many tens of thousands of the best agricultural acres simply as long-term stores of value on the basis that 'they aren't making land anymore, you know'.

This reverses completely what was a key national aim and social policy for a century – the distribution of land ownership among the maximum viable numbers of farming families.

This has a constitutional dimension too. The Oireachtas is still constitutionally entrusted under Article 45's Directive Principles of Social Policy with the task of ensuring that 'there may be established on the land in economic security as many families as in the circumstances shall be practicable'.

That policy goal for the Oireachtas remains part of the basic law of our land, albeit that the principles in Article 45 are for the exclusive care of the Oireachtas and not directly justiciable in our courts.

The article in *The Currency* raises the fundamental question as to whether the independent Irish State is simply to walk away and to permit Irish agriculture to revert after a century and a half to a landlord–tenant sector where the rich and powerful own the land and farmers toil to pay them rent. It's not just our urban homeowners who are being shunted into tenant status.

Maybe the time has come to reverse this unseen trend, and to use our tax systems to limit and reverse the growing concentration of farmland ownership in the hands of the wealthy few.

Hopelessness needs to be addressed for the coming generation, not only homelessness and the housing crisis

18 June 2017

One of the striking features of the marriage equality referendum in Ireland and the recent UK general election was the mobilisation of the 'young vote', where a collective sense of purpose seized the imagination of younger voters traditionally less engaged in politics and inclined to abstain from the electoral process.

A question that looms in Ireland's political consciousness is whether the younger generation in Irish society still cling to the optimistic belief that they can achieve more and be better off than their parents' generation. A growing realisation that they will be worse off is potentially the raw material for transformative change in political and economic attitudes and aspirations.

The next focus of generational discontent in Ireland is likely to be home ownership. Are we witnessing the first generation of post-independence Irish citizens who will face major difficulty in becoming property owners in their own right?

Economic and demographic forces seem to be driving up the cost of homes inexorably, widening the gap between the earnings potential of young people and their capacity to acquire property. The Celtic Tiger property bubble was accompanied by a credit bubble which appeared to preserve the prospect of home ownership from the great majority.

But now we have Celtic Tiger property prices and hugely restricted access to credit. This combination appears to challenge any sense of confidence or hope that many people can aspire to own their own homes in their earning years.

The housing crisis is not merely one of short-term 'homelessness'; demand for homes radically exceeds our economy's capacity to deliver those homes as things stand. This, in turn, demands a radically new approach from government. Simon Coveney's palliative measures, including localised rent control, and tinkering at the edges of planning law, while necessary, are by no means sufficient. The immediate focus of the 'housing crisis' was and is the political hot potato of homelessness. But the longer-term issue of 'hopelessness' for the coming generation needs to be addressed as well.

One disastrous coincidence was the well-intentioned but foolish decision by Simon Coveney's department to outlaw bedsits as part of a drive to improve housing standards. Across Dublin, the effect was to close between 8,000 and 12,000 homes available to those at the very bottom rung of the housing ladder.

The idea that it should be illegal to dwell in a home with shared bathroom or kitchen accommodation seems plausible until you remember that the more recent pattern of house-sharing and flat-sharing also involves tenants using shared kitchen and bathroom facilities.

The irony is that political pressure for abolition of bedsits was driven in good faith by Threshold, which denied that banning bedsits would increase homelessness. They were, alas, wrong.

We need a revolution in national policy on home building if we are not to have a crisis of home ownership. It is true that between 1930 and 1970 huge social housing projects were undertaken by the Irish State in and around our cities. This suggests that it is well within our political and economic capacity to build a great number of homes.

Large-scale social housing projects of the past were not, however, devoid of consequence as regards the social fabric of our society. Arguably Limerick was an example of a huge imbalance in one local authority area between social and private housing. The consequences for the social wellbeing of Limerick were very real.

It seems to me that demand for housing in our major cities, particularly Dublin, requires an entirely new approach. We need urban renewal agencies which can bring home building back into the centres of our cities rather than spreading Dublin's housing demand across most of east Leinster. It isn't enough for Dublin City Council or any other urban local authorities to devise development plans passively allowing for six-, eight- or ten-storey apartment buildings or providing special zoning for major housing projects.

We need something like the Wide Streets Commissioners with powers of compulsory acquisition, urban planning, granting building leases, and streetscape design to drive regeneration with a very significant home ownership component. We also need to restore the spirit of Part V of the Planning Act, which required the integration of social and affordable housing in all housing developments so as to prevent ghettoisation and geographic inequality.

Policies which merely 'hope' that private sector developers can assemble urban sites and thereafter build homes to satisfy future market demand simply don't work and can't work in an urban environment. A much more hands-on approach is needed.

I am not suggesting that the lumbering bureaucracies that we already have in the form of city and county councils should now become development agencies. That course, would, in all probability, be disastrous. I have no faith in the capacity of Dublin City Council or its elected members to shape or regenerate our city effectively or in a timely fashion and I do not believe that its structure or culture would justify giving it the resources to transform the city.

I have in mind an agency or commission which would look at entire areas and neighbourhoods and smaller infill sites with a view to regeneration.

To take a simple example, on my commute there are stretches of Clanbrassil Street with decaying single-storey and two-storey shops. The same applies to vast swathes of the north inner city. They have been in this condition for many years. Perhaps some developer is attempting, like a Monopoly player, to quietly assemble a large-scale development site there by a process of individual acquisition. Perhaps not. But that process, if it is happening, takes decades. Strangely, it was road-widening that drove much of the limited regeneration that has happened in those areas.

The Constitution, by the way, poses no obstacle at all to the establishment of such an agency with CPO powers and the power to grant building leases. It can be self-financing.

Dereliction and obsolescence in our cities is not just visual; it is a social injustice which spawns many other problems. It represents both harm and missed opportunity at the same time.

Half-hearted measures such as derelict sites legislation and proposals for site-value taxes and special development zones will not address these issues. The chemistry of urban regeneration requires more powerful catalysts to bring change on a scale and in a time frame that matches our urgent needs.

As Simon Coveney turns his gaze to foreign affairs, Eoghan Murphy is taking on a poisoned chalice unless there is fresh thinking. The social and political consequences of handing home ownership to real estate investment trusts (REITS) and vulture funds are very great; we are approaching a tipping point.

We need a vision for Dublin with people and agencies who will implement it

7 April 2019

Dublin's skyline bristles with cranes these days. It echoes the scene at the height of the height of the Celtic Tiger building boom. But the similarity is superficial. Most of the cranes are located on building sites for offices, hotels and tax-driven student accommodation. Home building is very much in the back seat – at least in the city centre.

Building costs are rising and trade unions in the sector are seeking 12% increases as supply of skilled building workers lags behind demand. The Government is responding by altering the immigration rules for construction workers in the hope of avoiding very serious labour shortages and consequent bottlenecks in the roll-out of its infrastructural programmes.

The Government is pinning its hopes on the private sector to address the homes shortage crisis. Its infant Land Development Agency has yet to be given statutory powers of compulsory acquisition.

One instance of the LDA's weakness is evident in its dispute with Dún Laoghaire-Rathdown Council over lands at Shanganagh Castle in South Dublin which became public this last week.

As Minister for Justice, I obtained Government approval for the closure of Mountjoy Prison and its replacement by a new prison complex at Thornton Hall in north County Dublin.

The plan included the sale of Shanganagh Castle, an open prison on about 30 acres for low-risk offenders, and the application of the proceeds (about €30 million) to buy a large campus in north Dublin where we hoped to build a large, modern prison complex more suitable for the drug-free rehabilitation of prisoners, including space for recreation and a variety of prison units with different security gradings and a separate space for a proper psychiatric hospital facility for offenders to replace the Central Mental Hospital in Dundrum.

The 150 acres at Thornton Hall are closer as the crow flies to the GPO than the 30 acres at Shanganagh.

At the time, we reasonably believed that the sale for development of the 13-acre complex at Mountjoy and the sale of the CMH lands at Dundrum would more than finance the cost of the new facilities. Outline plans for the development of high-rise apartments with water features at Mountjoy to be developed on the banks of the Royal Canal were commissioned by the Department of Justice.

What appeared to be a win–win solution for the taxpayer came unstuck with the property crash after my term as minister.

However, the 30 acres of lands at Shanganagh were sold in two parcels – one to private developers for home building and the other to Dún Laoghaire-Rathdown Council for social and affordable housing. The private houses were built. But the council's share of the lands has remained derelict and undeveloped for 14 years now. Plans to build 600 homes on those lands have as yet come to nothing.

The Land Development Agency is now engaged in a turf war with the council over who gets to develop the lands. And in the meantime 14 years of inactivity seems destined to continue. Someone should be able to knock together the heads of two public bodies so that badly needed homes are built.

And the Victorian prison at Mountjoy still occupies 13 acres of prime development land for home building in the city centre. Site development works at Thornton Hall, including a separate access road with a flyover, lie derelict too.

I have no problem with the Land Development Agency being used to mobilise the State's land resources with a view to addressing the shortage of home-building land at affordable prices. But it needs powers to achieve its ends.

And I strongly believe that proper urban planning and renewal needs the intervention of a statutory body with CPO powers.

But the idea that Dublin will be satisfactorily transformed by private developers building on private lands and public authorities building on publicly owned lands is delusional.

The powers that be in the eighteenth and nineteenth centuries realised that the right way to go was to vest CPO powers in the Dublin Wide Streets Commissioners, which could secure the rebuilding of the core of the city by a combination of prescriptive urban planning powers and the use of private developers to implement them. Most of the Dublin we admire was built in this way.

We need a vision for Dublin with people and agencies who will implement it

We badly need a vision for Dublin, and we badly need to have people and agencies that will implement that vision. We need a different model of home building and home ownership suitable to the needs of a modern sustainable city.

On the subject of home ownership, there is every indication that, for want of any public policy, home ownership is being rapidly transferred to REIT landlords. Owner occupation is escaping the grasp of the younger generation. Developers are selling apartment complexes 'off the plans' to large scale corporate investors who in turn plan to become landlords to an entire generation of tenants.

This trend will inevitably transform the economic DNA of Irish society. Part of liberal society's answer to the crude Marxist dialect has been to expand the middle class so as to subsume what would otherwise be an economic underclass. The dispersal of property across society is politically and economically significant; a society where the majority have no significant property is chemically different from a society where a majority have significant capital assets. This balance is crucial to self-perception as dependent or independent.

Of course it is possible to have two views as to how that balance should be struck. But security of tenure in one's home has been up till now a cherished value and one which is guaranteed by home ownership.

Security of tenure is hard to reconcile with the proliferation of 'buy to let' small investors in the property. The more the balance of rights swings towards the tenant the more reluctant ordinary individuals will be to becoming or remaining buy-to-let landlords.

There is a vast difference between the outlook and interests of an individual who lets out a single investment property as a fully furnished short-term residential letting with even cutlery provided, on the one hand, and those of a REIT that lets out unfurnished apartment complexes as long-term residential lettings to tenants with an expectation of medium- to long-term tenure, on the other hand.

Our models and the continental models of home ownership differ vastly. And if Dublin is to function as a sustainable thriving city, we will have to remodel large swathes of its centre, abandoning the idea that every family needs a front and back garden. If we are going to live increasingly in apartments, they will have, in many cases, to be large enough to accommodate families of five and more people.

All sorts of issues present themselves. What is the best model for home ownership in an urban context? How should a sustainable balance be struck as between owners and tenants, and as between different types of tenancies? Should we spend more money developing Dublin port where it is now (even banning cruise ships as planned) or should we relocate it to Bremore? How should transport issues such as MetroLink, new Luas lines, Dart Underground, BusConnects, be decided on?

What role has local democracy in all of this? What role would elected mayors have to play? What is the future of local property tax?

Do we plan anything or muddle along with serendipity?

Why do I get the horrible feeling that there is no one at the wheel?

Energy and Climate Policy

Ireland is drifting towards permanent energy crisis

27 April 2022

Fintan O'Toole wrote last week about the desirability of Ireland really getting serious about offshore wind farms and the possibility that Ireland might become an important exporter of energy to the EU. I imagine that few people would oppose such development and that most people would strongly support it.

That in turn raises the question as to who exactly can make it happen. It can't just be left to unnamed investors to make decisions as to where and when it will happen – if it is to happen.

At 10.15 a.m. on 25 March 2022, immediate demand for electricity on the island of Ireland was 5,124 megawatts (MW). Our installed wind generation capacity of 5,000 MW was yielding just 10 MW. The wind wasn't blowing. For the 24-hour period up to 7 p.m. that day, renewables provided 3% of our energy need; gas supplied 63% and coal 20%.

It seems that even if we expand our wind energy capacity by another 5,000 MW or quintuple that to 25,000 MW, there will be days when wind will deliver less than 1% of instantaneous electricity demand and less than 5% of demand over 24 hours. Due to the move away from other fossil fuel sources, our need for natural gas generation will last for decades and will actually increase.

I get a very worrying feeling that the Government – and particularly our energy minister, Eamon Ryan – isn't so much planning as hoping. I hope I am wrong, but all the signs are there that Ireland is drifting towards permanent energy crisis and insecurity. This could have catastrophic economic outcomes for Ireland.

The Government has the huge responsibility of preventing such a catastrophe. They are encouraging the growth of data centres. They are setting targets for electrification of cars, trains and vans. They are setting targets for ending the widespread use of fossil fuels. Ryan is absolutely opposed to building a new liquefied natural gas (LNG) plant in the Shannon Estuary for some reason. He stopped all offshore exploration for gas although we know that the Corrib field will be exhausted in a short number of years.

But there are other things that we know. We know we will need gas-generated electricity capacity for the next twenty or thirty years. Will there be a reliable supply of gas for that period? Can we afford to be wholly at the mercy of international energy markets? Is Tarbert or Moneypoint capable of meeting any shortfall in our energy needs by burning coal or oil as back-up capacity?

The Irish Academy of Engineering – a respected expert body – is currently working on a discussion paper on the implications for Ireland of Europe's energy crisis. It will undoubtedly make sobering reading – and it should ring alarm bells in Merrion Street – when published.

While the Government is to publish its own report on energy security later this year, engineers are aware that we will, one way or the other, be dependent on gas energy in the 'short and medium term'.

All of this is massively accentuated by the crisis created by the Ukraine war. The West simply cannot afford to finance annihilation of Ukraine by payments for Russian oil and gas. But we must face the realities of Europe's (and Ireland's) dependency on Russian energy exports. There are no easy solutions to the emerging crisis. But we are facing some options that Minister Ryan will choke on, I think.

Economic and social consequences for Ireland of this oncoming crisis could well overshadow the economic crisis of 2008–9. Just as our banking system collapsed in that crisis, our entire economy could be very seriously damaged again if we fail to plan now for obvious implications of what is already happening around us. We cannot afford to have extensive rationing, black-outs or brown-outs.

The Government's first priority must be to avert such damage to the maximum extent possible. I argued here last year that there was no need for Ireland to be the most ambitious in climate change policy (and I got predictable stick from predictable quarters for so doing). I suggest that the Government must now prioritise safeguarding our economy and society from immediate issues arising from the crisis rather than blindly adhere to climate-change goals that were set in a very different political and economic pre-Ukraine era.

Constraints fixed in carbon budgeting legislation cannot be allowed to become an inflexible autopilot mechanism guiding us into the side of the looming economic mountainside.

We need honest and urgent action led by a coherent government. Everything must be on the table. Do we need to go nuclear? Do we need more gas infrastructure, including storage terminals? Can we meet all our climate change goals by 2030?

These things matter much more than piffling debate about sod turf, lettuce in window boxes, or shortening our morning showers.

The Definite Article: ENERGY AND CLIMATE POLICY

Do we have a 'department of energy' or a 'department of lethargy'?

21 September 2022

The Government was due to 'unveil' its options in relation to energy supply security on Monday. But now we are told there will be a month-long public consultation process on foot of the much-delayed Centre for European Policy Analysis (CEPA) consultancy report looking at options which was published this week. And – wait for it – at the end of the public consultation process the Department of the Environment, Climate and Communications – which has responsibility for energy policy – will then consider the outcome and prepare its own proposals to be considered by the Government.

The CEPA tender consultancy contract was awarded in May 2021. This was before the Russian invasion of Ukraine this spring, although CEPA subsequently widened its research to encompass the possibility of Russian gas supplies being cut off.

CEPA proposes two gas-storage options among ten options it identified for dealing with shocks to Ireland's energy supply. There were to either create a floating liquefied natural gas (LNG) gas storage by harbouring storage ships in safe Irish waters, or build a big onshore storage facility (or a number of them) to create a strategic stockpile from imported gas supplies. Of course, both options may be pursued given that the onshore option is likely now to take four or five years to be completed.

Concluding that Ireland needs to build a gas storage facility to ensure continuity of gas supply did not require hiring consultants to look at options and then embarking on a consultancy process followed by a departmental review. It has been blindingly obvious for more than a decade that Ireland is vulnerable to an interruption of imported gas supplies, and that we have no infrastructure capable of sustaining us through a crisis caused by interruption of – or large price hikes – in gas imported via the UK.

Do we have a 'department of energy' or do we have a 'department of lethargy' – one that sees itself as a forum for ventilating options and reports rather than making and implementing policy decisions?

The energy department (by whatever name it is known from time to time) has been aware of the risks associated with Russian policy in relation to gas supply to Western Europe for more than a decade. But the tender for the CEPA options consultancy was only approved and issued six years after Russia annexed the Crimea in 2014.

It would be unfair to criticise any minister or department for failing to predict the subsequent invasion of Ukraine. But our vulnerability was clear from as early as 2009, when Russia cut supplies to Ukraine. Surely that was the time for options (if not decisions on our options) to be considered. Do we not have, among the officers and agencies responsible to the department, the necessary expertise to identify energy security options and carry out evaluation of those options?

Given that we need access to gas-generated power for the next few decades, and given that we are exceptionally vulnerable, you might be forgiven for imagining that it was, has been, and continues to be a very serious state policy function to plan for contingencies, options and strategies that reflect that reality.

The Green Party leader, Minister for the Environment, Climate and Communications Eamon Ryan, says that an onshore gas storage facility is his preference. He believes that it should be State controlled. He hopes that it could be future-proofed to become adaptable for storage of hydrogen whenever we become a hydrogen producer. The key questions are how, when, where, at what cost, and by whom such infrastructure can be built.

What do we do in the meantime? If commissioning, planning and implementing construction takes four or five years, the project is irrelevant to the present crisis. About as relevant as the ill-fated national children's hospital was to the Covid epidemic.

The floating LNG storage facility option might at least be planned to be commissioned in 12 or 18 months. So, is the Minister prepared to follow both options?

Let's not forget the debacle that led to emergency gas-powered generating station plans being abandoned almost as soon as they were announced. Are diesel-powered generators in data centres really earmarked for emergency power generation instead?

How does it make sense to ban further development of offshore gas fields while considering options for onshore LNG storage? The UK is expanding such activity.

There is talk of addressing possible power shortages this winter and next with domestic 'renewable' generation. We also hear about Ireland's huge offshore wind power potential. The department has been so lethargic that permits for such projects are simply unobtainable this year. Maybe next year?

Maybe we will harness offshore wind to electricity and hydrogen generation in future. But have we the political and administrative skills to convert wishful thinking into solid achievement? You would have to wonder.

Having a million EVs by 2030 is an illusion

30 October 2024

In certain parts of the midlands with which I am very familiar, local inhabitants are regularly in receipt of outages notices from ESB Networks notifying consumers that their power supply will be interrupted for lengthy periods (from, say, 10 a.m. to 5.30 p.m.) on a particular day.

For owners of holiday homes, including me, it means that they can plan to avoid visiting their homes on those days – a minor inconvenience for most. But for full-time households in the affected areas, these notices are quite serious. Domestic and social arrangements have to be cancelled. Family activities have to be set aside. Meal-making is complicated. Phones must be charged. Working from home is disrupted by inability to access the internet. Central heating stops. Electric gates need to be manually operated.

Add to this the fact that ESB Networks, especially in rural areas, is subject to unplanned outages caused not merely by storm damage but by equipment failures, and you sense the fragility of our modern dependence on electricity. Such blackouts in urban areas are comparatively rarer but not unknown.

Our lives are becoming increasingly electricity-dependent in so many ways. And the plan is to make us more and more electricity-dependent. Homes are being built which are wholly dependent on electricity. Fireplaces seem to be on political death row. Heat pumps and solar energy systems are dependent on power supply.

Transport of all kinds is planned to become electricity-powered in stages – even if planned transformation calendars are rapidly unravelling. All commercial activity – retail and manufacturing – requires electric power. Agriculture is increasingly dependent on electric power. Unless equipped with emergency generators, hospitals and healthcare facilities collapse without electricity.

The march towards complete dependence on electricity as the only available energy source seems to be inexorable. And yet we in Ireland have narrowed our options to a dangerous degree. Onshore and offshore wind energy is still very underdeveloped. We engaged in the gratuitous act of making all fossil fuel exploration in our waters illegal, yet we will continue to need such energy as part of our supply for the next 20 years at least.

We have made developing small-scale nuclear power technology actually illegal by statute for some reason, instead of leaving it open as a policy choice. We have politically foot-tripped the use of imported LNG for electricity generation. We have no real plans for the use of hydrogen in transport.

We are very vulnerable. Half of our electric energy is gas-generated. The great majority of our future gas is routed though one gas interconnector, Moffat, in Scotland.

We are totally dependent on maintaining the security of our energy networks from malign external hackers. While I would like to believe that they are safe, somehow I find it difficult to be confident where the security services of the State – the Defence Forces and Garda Síochána – have been haemorrhaging personnel to the point that they have never been weaker in terms of numbers compared to our population.

We have been warned about our vulnerabilities. The Irish Academy of Engineers spelled out the dangers two years ago. Luckily, we avoided the attempts by Putin's Russia to increase its throat-hold on the rest of Europe's energy needs in the last two years. I still wonder though at the almost inexplicable decision by Fianna Fáil's energy spokesman to back Deputy Bríd Smith's Dáil Bill to outlaw gas exploration in Irish waters a few years back.

In the next two months, we will have a new government. We need a new government badly. And we need a pragmatic, effective energy policy.

It was blindingly obvious the policy goals that we set for environmental change were wildly optimistic. The plan for one million electric vehicles by 2030 is simply an illusion now. The supportive infrastructure to sustain such a goal is simply out of reach. Other EU countries have realised that similar goals cannot be achieved. If we had deliberately devised an obstacle course to delay the development of offshore wind energy, we could not have done better than the ridiculous two-agency approach put in place by this government. One agency, Mara, oversees licensing projects while another, the hapless An Bord Pleanála (now to be rebranded as a 'commission'), deals with planning permission (a field in which it had no prior expertise).

It's all very well to talk about Ireland becoming the Saudi Arabia of offshore wind energy, but where are the plans for Irish port facilities to support such an industry? Have we even planned the power grid to support such developments?

Hopefully we are approaching an election that replaces mere aspiration with competent implementation.

Europe

A European army and federalist rhetoric

16 October 2016

Have you noticed that whenever federalists in Europe are feeling a little down and weary, they reach for the soother and the comfort blanket, snuggle up and drift off in a fantasy dream? Instead of accepting the EU for what it is and instead of taking pride in it for what the EU is, they prefer to fantasise about what it might become.

Their current reverie is about a European army. As an antidote to Brexit, the federalist chattering class began to prioritise 'security' at their conferences and began to speak of the need for an EU army. Mark my words, they will also soon begin talking about a European FBI as a necessary replacement for the sedentary talking shop commonly known as Europol.

Quite what a European army would do better than NATO does is never made clear. Deploying soldiers from Italy, Spain, France, and Germany (all NATO countries) under a single EU command structure somewhere in Eastern Europe seems a bit daft. And as deterrents go, who would be frightened by it if they weren't frightened by NATO?

It seems there is no limit to the silliness of federalist rhetoric. And so we have gullible European correspondents scribbling superficial and vacuous pieces to fill their quota of column inches safe in the knowledge that they will be able to recycle the piece in a year or two or else write a 'Whatever happened to the EU army?' piece in due course.

If there were any merit in the idea, it would have happened long ago under the rubric of 'enhanced cooperation'. But strangely, apart from a few low-meaning gestures, nothing has happened to suggest that an EU army is practicable, still less on the way.

The EU is not a state. It does not have a sovereign government. It cannot go to war. It cannot be at war. It has no democratic authority to control an army. So why on earth think of having one?

The perversity of the federalist mindset is that it sees the establishment of the EU army as means of establishing the 'need' for an EU government! At the time of the EU's monetary crisis, Dr Brendan Simms wrote in 2013:

History suggests that the current crisis requires the immediate creation of an Anglo-American style fiscal and military union of the Eurozone – a 'democratic union'. This would involve the creation of a European Parliament with legislative powers; and one-off federalising of all state debt through the issue of Union bonds to be backed by the entire tax revenue of the common currency zone (with a debt ceiling from member states thereafter); the supervised dissolution of insolvent private sector financial institutions; and a single European army, with a monopoly on external force projection.

This federalist predisposition to regard every shock as an imperative for armed integration has yet again become manifest in the wake of the Brexit vote. Ironically, it was arguably one of the causal factors lying behind the Brexit vote.

The federalist Spinelli Group of which I wrote here recently advocated in 2013 that the EU should by a constitutional convention adopt a Fundamental Law involving a sovereign EU state and that the new state should be agreed 'in good time for David Cameron's referendum in 2017 [sic]'.

One of the founders of the Spinelli Group, Guy Verhofstadt, has written:

The world will be organised from now on around poles which can be described as empires, with all the precautions that word implies: the United States, China or even India, these are empires, not nation states.

He added:

Europe must become an 'empire' in the good sense of the word, that is a continental pole able to include, on a voluntary basis, different nations, ethnic groups, cultures or religions ...'

and he concluded:

it is false to say that it is necessary to create a functional democracy first for European federation to emerge from it.

His alarming implication was that if only we establish a fully-fledged federal European state, democracy will somehow follow in its footsteps. That blithely wishes away the other, and more likely, possibility – that his trail-blazing federal benign 'empire' or super-state might never become a functioning, accountable democracy based on any self-aware 'demos' – but might become something far, far less accountable or benign.

Happily, Ireland has not merely secured an opt-out of any EU common defence but we inserted a term in our Constitution prohibiting the participation of Ireland in such a project. So we will not be part of an EU army.

But that is of little significance if the rest of the EU creates such an army with Simms's 'monopoly on external force projection'.

There is simply no logical connection between Brexit and the creation of an EU army. And Irish people and their political representatives should, I think, call out this silly federalist 'comfort blanket and soother' pillow talk for what it is – reactive nonsense.

The real post-Brexit future of Europe is more challenging, more pressing and more demanding of our attention than fantasies – the stuff of nightmares. In the midst of all our current political travails and governmental weaknesses, we Irish badly need men and women at the helm who understand statecraft.

Now, there's a dream!

Pressing EU countries into further integration might suit Macron but plays right into the hands of nationalists

10 March 2019

Last week Emmanuel Macron persuaded the editors of Europe's serious newspapers in 28 member states to carry an article expressing his concerns about the future of Europe.

His overt message was a warning about the threat to the European project from growing nationalist sentiment among the voters in many member states.

His covert purpose was to try to re-start a pet political initiative of his own – to persuade the governments and peoples of the member states that the EU should take a giant step in political and economic integration which would result in its becoming a sovereign world power to rival China, the US and Russia.

This ambition, in turn, is centred on a desire that the EU should be dominated by an axis of power between Paris and Berlin. France and Germany would be sitting in the pilot and co-pilot seats of a sovereign superpower while the rest of the EU performs the roles of cabin staff and passengers.

The lamentable departure of the UK from the EU makes it possible for Macron to pursue this strategy. There were never going to be three pilots in the EU cockpit. The UK was not interested in transforming the EU into a political, economic and military superpower. But now that the British are heading off into isolation, Macron senses an opportunity to advance his agenda.

He thinks that by identifying the negative force of nationalism, as he sees it, he can build an alliance in favour of accelerated integration. By warning of possible disintegration, he thinks he can make a saleable case for a major leap in integration.

Keeping the EU roughly as it is can be portrayed as dangerous. By claiming that Hungary's Viktor Orbán is somehow taking the initiative, Macron can make the argument that 'we' must seize back the initiative.

There is, of course, a huge problem with this 'logic'. Most member states are opposed to the creation of a sovereign EU superstate. Most electorates in most member states simply do not share this ambition. There is no demand for a massive cession of sovereignty to the EU.

We should recall that it was the federalists' demand for the restatement of the 'ever closer union' phrase from the Treaty of Rome in the Lisbon Treaty that created the political circumstances in which the formal right of secession was formulated as Article 50 of that treaty. If 'ever closer union' had not been insisted on in the treaty text, there would probably never have been an Article 50 at all. And probably no Brexit either.

And the rise of political parties and movements in the EU member states which are described by Macron as negative nationalists might – just might – have something to do with a perception that the EU is pursuing an integrationist path that threatens to strip the voters of their power to control the extent to which their states' sovereignty is ceded or eroded.

If, as is undoubtedly the case, immigration is an issue for those nationalist parties and a card which they can successfully play to win votes, can anyone even for a moment concede – even now and in retrospect – that Angela Merkel made a massive blunder in demanding that the member states should throw open the EU's borders as a response to the Syrian refugee crisis?

Was it wise or proper to seek to use the EU as a means of forcing member states to share the burden of inward migration just because the Berlin government felt that way at that time? Have we forgotten the Brexiteers' advertising hoardings showing the wave of migrants as a threatening horde?

My point is this – the EU belongs to the peoples of the sovereign member states. It is for them to determine the character and direction of the union. They do not want the federalist vision of a sovereign superpower in which each member state has the status and function of the individual states in the USA.

They do not want the EU, as such, becoming involved in armed conflicts in the Middle East or Africa. They do not want a European government. They do not want to trade their state sovereignty for a sovereign Europe. And they react against the pursuit of such goals at the ballot box.

Cast your minds back to Matteo Renzi, the Italian premier, who pledged the Italian presidency to the creation of a United States of Europe. What happened to him? He was swept aside by a tidal wave consisting in part of radical, right-wing Eurosceptics. His silly stunt of posing for the cameras with Angela Merkel and François Hollande on an aircraft carrier off the island of Ventotene was seen through. All three of them misjudged the moods of their electorates. All of them paid the price. Only Merkel is left and she is in the political departure lounge.

Who played into the hands of the AfD in Germany?

Who played into the hands of Salvini in Italy?

Who played into the hands of the Brexiteers in Britain?

Macron's underlying agenda is simply not shared by the Netherlands, by the Scandinavians, by the Baltic states, by the Visegrad states, by the Austrians, by the Italians, the Greeks, the Cypriots, the Maltese, or the peoples of the Iberian peninsula. Or by the Irish.

It is easy – and partly correct – to blame Brexit on a number of factors, from Cameron and the Tories to the British press and to delusions of post-imperial grandeur.

But if we are honest with ourselves, we should ask why the British and the Danes asked for Article 50 to be put into the Lisbon Treaty as a counterweight to the 'ever closer union' restatement demanded by the federalists. They didn't insist on Article 50 because they wanted to leave. They just wanted to underline the voluntary basis of EU membership and the preservation of the idea that the EU was a partnership of the willing.

It is perfectly respectable to be a pro-European who likes the EU as it is – a partnership of sovereign member states who have pooled their sovereignty for a limited and defined set of purposes – and to oppose the creation of a sovereign EU superstate or federation along the lines of the US.

Macron's strategy is to conjure up a threat from negative reactionary forces and then to sell further integration as the antidote to disintegration. Does no one ever ask exactly what are those reactionaries forces reacting against? Does it never occur to the enthusiastic integrationists that it is they who share the responsibility for the problems they are so anxious to confront?

The European project belongs to the member states that comprise it – not the other way round

1 October 2017

Scarcely had our new best buddy, Guy Verhofstadt, landed back in Brussels when his name appeared on a draft resolution in the European Parliament proposing that Northern Ireland should remain part of both the single market and the customs union after the UK leaves the EU.

This, the parliamentarians argued, was the only way in which the Irish North–South border could remain invisible and friction-free. The corollary is that there should be a de facto economic border between Northern Ireland and Britain down the middle of the Irish Sea.

This binary analysis and choice ignores a few realities. Theresa May and her deeply riven Tory government is dependent on the DUP to stay in office. The DUP cannot be seen to accept the repartition of the UK into an EU and non-EU federated economy.

Already James Nicholson, a unionist MEP, has pointed out that such an outcome would, in the eyes of unionists, rupture the Good Friday agreement by effectively ending UK sovereignty in the North without the formal consent of a majority there. Needless to say, nationalist politicians claim that the UK already ruptured the Good Friday agreement by committing to leave the EU against the wishes of a majority of the voters in Northern Ireland.

The European Parliament resolution also seems to forget that there is still one way to square this circle. If the EU and the UK conclude an agreement including a close free-trade partnership in goods – a partnership very similar in substance to membership of the customs union by whatever label it is known – there can be an invisible friction-free North–South border. But that involves the

UK seeking and obtaining a soft Brexit – an outcome that Ireland should work for.

The EU single market, on the other hand, does not affect how the North–South border will appear physically post-Brexit. Access to a single market for services, banking, insurance, freedom of establishment, public procurement rights, etc. is in no way affected by the presence or absence of a physical border infrastructure on this island.

Some people, including some MEPs, naively argue that ending the freedom of movement pillar of the single market somehow logically necessitates a form of immigration control between the Republic and the UK. That might be so if the UK were intent on imposing a visa requirement on EU member state nationals entering the UK directly from the continent. But there is no prospect of that. French and Polish citizens will be able to travel visa-free to the UK post-Brexit – as long as they have a passport (just as they will still need to do travelling to Ireland).

Control on inward migration from the EU to the UK will be most probably done by limitations of a different kind, including mandatory work permits, obligations to register for long-stay residents, and denial of rights to social security, of access to housing and rental, and to health services.

So the North not being a geographical part of the single market (as distinct from the customs union or a close analogue) is not an insuperable obstacle for the maintenance of an invisible, friction-free border. Northern Ireland residents have a right to be citizens of the UK or of Ireland, or of both. They will probably have the unusual status of being entitled to be regarded as citizens of the Union even though they are born and reside outside the boundaries of the Union. That does not create any insuperable problem either.

The Verhofstadt-signed EU parliament resolution is very probably destined for the political wastepaper basket. It is highly unlikely that Northern Ireland will end up as part of the Single Market. It is highly likely that the invisible friction-free border will be achieved in the context of a negotiated UK–EU free trade partnership which leaves the UK outside of the single market.

So what are we Irish to make of Petit Emmanuel Macron's so-called visionary speech on the future of Europe?

Very little, I suggest.

The speech itself was very similar to Juncker's State of the Union speech. Macron is in trouble at home. His domestic popularity is at record low levels for newly elected French presidents. Like the ill-fated Matteo Renzi, who claimed, shortly before he had to resign, that he and Italy would bring about a federal United States of Europe, Macron finds it consoling to indulge in soaring rhetoric about France's vision for Europe.

Discussion of a dominant Franco-German alliance leading the way in European integration is a great domestic political distraction for Macron. At its heart is the political lie that there is some form of equality between France and Germany – a lie that is convenient for both states in that the Germans can conceal their strength while the French can conceal their weakness.

The integrationist, federalist heave advocated by both Juncker and Macron in recent weeks is not going to work. Why not?

The Netherlands, Sweden, Denmark, Finland, Poland, the Czech Republic, Malta, Cyprus, Hungary and Greece, among others, are not meekly going down the road of a Franco-German hegemony in the EU, based on a closely integrated Eurozone with tax harmonisation and a single Eurozone budget and finance minister. We may not know where the Baltic states, Spain, Portugal, Slovenia and others are on that issue. But Macron's vision appears to be a minority view – just as his point of view was not shared by three out of the four candidates in the first round of his presidential election who between them got roughly three times the vote Macron received.

It isn't only Ireland that is opposed to it. We are not alone or isolated in any sense.

Nor is there anything stopping any member states who want to integrate their budgetary policies or tax systems from doing so. The same applies to those who want to create a common defence in parallel with Nato. Nobody is stopping them.

The real possibility of a Jamaica Black–Green–Yellow coalition in Germany is another obstacle. The CDU's sister party, the CSU, and the liberal Free Democrats are both strongly opposed to Macron's plans for integration of the Eurozone economy. And Merkel is less than lukewarm on Macron's rhetoric.

The apparent front-runner in this month's election in the Czech Republic, Andrej Babiš, had this to say about Macron and about Juncker: 'He should really concentrate on France. All these proposals that we'll have a minister for finance for the Eurozone and all of this further integration should make Mr Macron and Mr Juncker think of why Brexit happened.'

And EU council president, Donald Tusk, also very much deflated their integrationist balloon in his letter to EU heads of state attending this week's informal council meeting in Tallinn, Estonia, when he implicitly pleaded for progress on practicable policy agendas rather than divisive and unachievable grand plans.

We Irish have to break out of the lazy mindset that the future of Europe is all about federalism or disintegration – a mindset carefully nurtured by an influential but unrepresentative minority. Ireland's interests are well served by Europe remaining a largely inter-governmental partnership of sovereign democracies pooling some of their competences. There is nothing unsustainable about that form of EU; on the contrary, it is the federal model that is unattainable, unsustainable and undesirable.

The European project belongs to the member states that comprise it and sustain it – not the other way round.

Media

'Freedom of expression' is one thing; 'freedom of anonymous publication' is another thing entirely

8 January 2017

There is a current obsession in the Irish media with securing instant online reaction from readers and audiences. I am by no means convinced that online comment by readers of online newspapers adds anything at all to the quality of the journalism or to the enjoyment of the reader. Nor does it add revenue. But most newspapers feel compelled to pander to this dubious interaction on line. Why?

Generally speaking, I find that instant online comment is of poor quality, poor understanding, and poor judgement. The tone of much of it is cynical, dismissive, unpleasant and unkind. People seem to be more vicious, more careless with the facts, and more unfeeling when afforded online anonymity. Just because anonymity disinhibits comment does not mean that it is thereby improved. Inhibition often serves truth, civility and rationality.

In contrast with published Readers' Letters, online comment is unedited and lightly supervised. The online commentator seems so often to be angry, sour and ill-informed. Why afford parity of esteem to such comment and to good journalism and careful commentary?

Worse than all of that is the anonymity, which distinguishes most online comment from old-fashioned published Readers' Letters. If newspapers really do have self-esteem for the quality of their printed journalism, why, oh why, do they allow their online columns to become infested with anonymous or pseudonymous input?

If one of the problems of the information age is the proliferation of 'post-truth' disinformation to the detriment of reliable and accountable journalism, is there any logical reason why quality media outlets should themselves encourage such activity by affording them parity of esteem?

'Freedom of expression' is one thing; 'freedom of anonymous publication' is another thing entirely. Most quality newspapers dropped the practice of allowing readers' letters to be published using pseudonyms a long time ago. 'Disgusted, Dublin' has long been denied access to most letters pages on the basis that he or she should stand over their opinions and assertions.

Take the local example of Politics.ie. As a political chatroom, it has, despite a promising start, degenerated into a worthless exchange of cynical backbiting and abuse by a small group of anonymous insider contributors whose bile is largely matched by their ignorance. It is become so juvenile and ill-informed that it is generally painful to read. It is the online equivalent of old-fashioned graffiti on the walls of toilet cubicles. A good forum in concept has become a fetid backwater in practice – the fruit of anonymity.

There is, of course, a deep vein of self-serving hypocrisy running through the mindset of the social media world. The privacy of the user is sacrosanct. The idea that one's online activity might be open to surveillance is anathema. But, at the same time, the 'right' to anonymously propagate one's views and assertions of fact to the world is equally sacrosanct. But is that right?

The Pirate Party movement is another case in point. Its origins lie in an asserted 'right' to secretly steal copyright creative material with impunity. The mind-set of the Pirate movement is all to do with 'rights' and nothing to do with 'duties'. Online newspapers only pander to the Pirate mentality by making their content available free. Pay-walls of any kind are anathema to a generation brought up on a diet of taking things free.

Likewise, many radio programmes seem to crave instant listener feedback like a drug. Sophisticated PR practice ensures that when a personality is interviewed on radio, there is instant arranged 'spontaneous' positive commentary, sent in online to create the right overall impression of the interviewee. All anonymous, of course. Instant feedback is so vulnerable to manipulation, but it is presented as authentic.

But when you think about it, the best of radio programming on these islands has little or no instant listener feedback. Broadcasters lack confidence when they beg for instant feedback by way of affirmation. And the kind of person who gives them instant feedback is by no means to be assumed as the typical listener. When the *Late Late* show featured instant on-screen ticker-tape type feedback, it didn't really add value to the programme.

When traditional newspapers are under such a threat from online competition in social media (and they are), it is strange to see them becoming subject to a form of Stockholm Syndrome involving complete prostration before their competitors.

If you have confidence in your own editorial judgement, why spend time informing readers online that one article or another is 'Most Read'? It is useful information to the editor but it is of doubtful value to the reader.

If we truly value our print media and our domestic broadcasters, there are things that we can do to help them deal with globalised online competition.

A zero-rate VAT, as distinct from exemption, should be considered for the Irish printed media. The EU Commission opposes such measures. But right across Europe the print media are under threat. The EU Commission's ideological commitment to VAT harmonisation should simply not be permitted to assist in the annihilation of printed journalism.

Pretended concern about the emergence of the post-truth society and its implications for democracy does not sit easily with indifference to the fate of printed journalism.

Our Constitution, in its Fundamental Rights chapter, recognises expressly the role of the press as educators of public opinion and as thereby playing a role of 'grave import to the common good'. There is every reason to tilt the playing field in favour of the print media insofar as we can.

We simply cannot blithely assume that our print media will seamlessly migrate in good order from print to the internet. Online newspaper publishing is very, very difficult from an economic point of view.

But the Irish media have to face the challenge themselves.

One last comment. Is it really necessary for interviewers on current affairs radio and TV shows to show such disdain, characterised by badgering and interruption, for their local political interviewees but simpering, fawning softness to other journalists and to any representatives of NGOs and interest groups demanding more resources for 'good causes'?

The statutory duty of impartiality suggests that scepticism should be more evenly and sparingly distributed. Listeners and viewers might prefer it too.

Is Mark Zuckerberg the most modern of the evangelists?

26 February 2017

In an IT age I suppose it is almost inevitable that a somewhat binary perspective on reality should suggest itself to Mark Zuckerberg, who has just published his Facebook manifesto, as a vision of a better world.

The 'either or' or '1 and zero' underpinning of the software programmer's language is almost bound to translate into a broader philosophical approach to world affairs for the secular priesthood of internet-based human globalism and, in particular, for Zuckerberg, the prophet of the new faith.

'It's Trump or me' is the unspoken, binary subtext of Zuckerberg's latest dissertation on the choices facing humanity.

What are we, poor mortals, to make of the latest 'Book of Revelation', this latter-day gospel of Mark? Biblical scholars always knew that Mark's gospel was the oldest of the four gospels. Are we now to believe that Mark is the most modern of the evangelists?

Zuckerberg's hymn of praise to Facebook is striking in its simplicity and yet worrying in its shallowness.

We are somehow to be transformed by IT technology into members of a global community. Our neighbours are all mankind. That sounds familiar. Mutual awareness carries with it a call for mutual empathy. In turn, that call becomes the universal moral vocation. That all sounds good.

But there is a catch.

The global moral community simply does not exist. Internet culture is largely proprietary. It has become 'monetised'. Its owners are becoming richer and richer while vast swathes of the envisaged global community are becoming poorer and poorer – at least in comparative terms. Our online behaviour is not merely observed by all-seeing digital deities; it is monitored, monetised and, increasingly, manipulated by disparate forces that are rapidly becoming cosmic.

Cyber morality is, alas, imaginary; cyber warfare has already arrived. The internet brings as much division and alienation as it brings unity and understanding.

The Definite Article: MEDIA

I had the honour some months ago of launching Dr Mary Aiken's groundbreaking work *The Cyber Effect* here in Dublin. It was, I then commented, as challenging a book for this generation as Desmond Morris's *The Naked Ape* was for that of the late 1960s. Morris invited us to reimagine ourselves as we see other animals; Aiken now asks us to reimagine ourselves as participants in an IT cosmos.

Zuckerberg's vision of humanity as a web-based moral and philosophical community is, I think, offered to us as the binary alternative to Trump's introspective and chaotic 'America First' vision of how to 'make America great again'. It is a new secular faith system.

Many magazines and commentators are already majoring on the intriguing possibility that Mark Zuckerberg is positioning himself for a run at the US presidency in 2020. Is that less plausible in 2017 than a Trump presidency was in 2014?

Reinventing the bedraggled Democratic Party in the next couple of years and finding a candidate for the presidency is a formidable challenge for US political society. Is Zuckerberg the new messiah for the American left?

He has all the credentials for this role. Poor and struggling Americans always seem drawn to supporting billionaires. He has a 'new take' on community, solidarity and idealism. He embodies an entirely novel American exceptionalism. His vision is forward-looking while Trump's forlorn vision is a backward regression to fossil fuels, rust belt reindustrialisation and corny moral atavism. He is a successful hi-tech innovator while Trump is an old-fashioned property speculator.

Zuckerberg has Obama's detached air of intellectualism combined with entrepreneurial expertise. He is young and he will be understood by the young.

And yet we should hesitate. The world is not binary. History is not binary. The human imagination is not binary. Zuckerberg looks like a shallow, binary personality.

He preaches globalism but does not adequately address or value the diversity or complexity of the human experience or of the various human cultures. He aspires to simplify and to unify. His Facebook manifesto seems simplistic rather than just simple.

The great flaw with the Marxist mindset was its binary juxtaposition of capital against labour and its binary historical theory of Hegelian action and reaction. It failed – and fails – to address the non-binary complexity of history, culture and identity.

Oddly, I suspect, we Europeans are loyal to our values precisely because they are unique to our various cultures – not because we see them as universal. Community, nationality, belief, culture and individuality are part of the warp and weft of what we are – and of what we cherish and aspire to be.

We are witnessing the chaos of Donald Trump's politics in all their ugliness in these days. I keep feeling – and fearing – that his only way out of his Lewis Carroll world in the Washington swamp is to provoke a conflict somewhere in the world that is decisively winnable in his imagination. God help those who inhabit that coming battlefield as their homeland. It will probably be in the Middle East.

Trump's recent press conference embodied all that was worst in his sad, dysfunctional personality – bouncing like a demented pinball machine from crassness to rudeness, from vanity to ignorance – and back again. Making America ashamed again – and again.

If the admittedly shallow Zuckerberg manifesto is the binary alternative to Trump, so be it. If that is what American greatness is all about, so be it. Zuckerberg has the resources, the self-belief, and the drive to counter Trumpism. That is not a bad place to start. The language of his Facebook manifesto is both political and aspirational.

If he could only avoid deifying the web and if he could only acknowledge – or at least accommodate – the diversity of the human experience, he could get something worthwhile going against an otherwise darkening skyline.

Inefficient, expensive, exasperating TV licence regime needs overhaul

5 July 2023

The issue of TV licence fees has cropped up again in circumstances where it cannot be kicked down the political road in the way it has been over the last 15 years. Opinion polls suggest that the public is now increasingly determined to withhold payment of the licence fee as a protest at recent events.

So, will politicians in the run-up to an election finally and firmly grasp the nettle of funding something which we (nearly) all value – public service broadcasting, however defined? The issue simply can't be kicked past the life of this Dáil.

The statutory basis for licensing TV originates in the pre-TV era. The Irish Free State enacted a Wireless Telegraphy Act in 1926 which licensed both receivers and transmitters. Radios were usually referred to in common speech to as 'wirelesses'.

There was a general security concern that radio transmission had potential implications for the safety and authority of the state. Owners of radios had to pay £1 for a valve radio licence or 10 shillings for a crystal set in 1926. The cost of a radio licence rose to 30 shillings by 1971 and radio licences were abolished in 1972 with the advent of movable transistor and car radios.

By then a TV licence had been introduced at £7.50 in 1961 under the 1926 wireless telegraphy legislation, as amended. The cost of a TV licence (which differed for a while between colour and black and white TVs) has grown steadily to its present level of €160 per premises (with exceptions for persons over 70 and certain classes of welfare recipients below that age threshold).

A separate licence is required for each separate premises at which a TV is kept. This means that a worker who has a caravan in which his or her family spends a few weeks away from a modest home must buy two licences at a total cost of €320 (roughly equivalent to €600 in gross earnings for many workers). A wealthy family sharing a single large residence equipped with many TVs only needs one licence at €160. Is that fair?

With modern communications technology and in the era of iPhones and portable tablet devices, there is little or no reality in attempting to preserve a premises-based licensing system for TVs. This blindingly obvious conclusion has been staring the political class in the face for at least ten years.

But successive governments have done everything to avoid facing up to abandoning the TV licensing system and raising the funding for public service broadcasting in some other way. The FG/Labour government of 2011/2016 toyed with the idea of a premises-based public service broadcasting charge. The FG minority government from 2016 to 2020, with Richard Bruton as minister, also said that a 'device independent' broadcasting charge would be devised and implemented from 2024. Where is it?

The current ludicrously inefficient, expensive, and exasperating regime of licences, post offices, inspectors, scanners, court proceedings, and incessant media advertising, 'it's the law: brought to you by the Government of Ireland', seems to have run headlong into the buffers of public hostility and rejection.

It's six years now since the Oireachtas joint committee with responsibility for broadcasting policy of which I was a member reported, again recommending change. I proposed collecting a charge as part of a reformed residential property tax. I wrote here two years ago about the four-year delay in addressing that report.

The ongoing paralysis is pathetic. A cynic might suspect that the current crisis might will finally be used to break out of political lethargy to address what is really meant by public service broadcasting and how it should be subsidised.

The current licence fee is used to subsidise RTÉ and TG4. I do not begrudge its use for Lyric FM either. I wonder whether 2FM needs subsidy or state ownership to function in a crowded and highly competitive market.

I also wonder at RTÉ's advertising strategies. Compared with satellite TV channels on the Sky platform, RTÉ's ad breaks seem heavily dominated by state and semi-state advertising, by promos for their own programmes, by 'RTÉ supporting the arts – supporting us' ads, and car advertising, rather than the type of Irish-market advertising carried by other channels. Did Covid-related advertising prop up a failing advertising strategy and an uncompetitive rate card until now?

I do not want to join the political institutional and personal pile-on. I unequivocally support state subsidy for public service broadcasting as an essential input into a healthy culture and democracy. I personally worked with many fine broadcasters in documentaries I presented without payment on issues such as Church–State relations and history.

Politicians collectively share part of the blame for the present crisis. They didn't turn a blind eye to exactly what has now emerged. But they funked the issue of financing public service broadcasting for far too long.

Murdoch will do anything in pursuit of power; Trump and Johnson are the press magnate's useful idiots

9 February 2022

Max Hastings, the historian, journalist and newspaper editor, has a sharp pen and intellect. Writing about the character of Boris Johnson, he has delivered a devastating critique of the British Prime Minister's character, proclivities, and weaknesses. All his criticisms rang true, coming as they did from a man with extended dealings with Johnson over many years. Disavowing any malice, Hastings in effect warned the Tory party and the world that Johnson is wholly unsuitable to hold the public office to which he was elected.

If half of what Hastings describes as the true Boris Johnson is correct, the inescapable implication is that the United Kingdom is now governed in large part by a deeply flawed opportunist with little or no commitment to the public good – something which he is incapable of distinguishing from his own sense of ambition and entitlement.

The power of most of British print media and their slavish support of the Tory party and heretofore of Johnson himself raises the question as to whether they have led the UK into political disaster from which it will be very hard to retrieve itself.

Tory-supporting editors seem torn between their desire to keep the Tories in office and their desire to propagate the notion that the UK is still a world power. Conversely, they fear that Johnson will bring the Tories electoral defeat in the form of a Keir Starmer-led Labour government. If Johnson imperils the Tory grip on power, they will ruthlessly abandon him. If there is still some reasonable hope that Johnson will survive and stave off Labour government, they may still back him.

Nowhere is this deep-seated ambivalence more evident than in the editorial policy of Rupert Murdoch's media. So far, those papers have refrained from advocating deposition of Johnson. Murdoch's underlying aim is to leave Johnson a lifeline so long as that is remotely consistent with the pursuit of Murdoch's overall quest for influence, power, and a direct say in international affairs.

Across the Atlantic, we see the recrudescence of Trumpism in all its ugliness. Murdoch's Fox News is largely to blame for the shocking polarisation of US politics which first took the form of the Tea Party and thereafter the cause of Donald Trump. Trump, ably abetted by Murdoch, has successfully planted an enormous lie in the minds of four out of ten American voters at least that Trump actually won the 2020 election and that Joe Biden cheated his way to office by falsifying and subverting American democracy.

Trump's shameless persistence in this lie, even to the extent of condemning his Mike Pence for failing to abort the 2020 election and his recent promise to pardon the 6 January Capitol insurrectionists, is worthy only of the lowest grade politics of a third-rate tinpot dictatorship. But that is what is now on offer to American voters as the alternative to the faltering Biden presidency.

The malign influence of Rupert Murdoch cannot be doubted, as manifest in the US and in the UK. We should not forget that Trump, supported by Murdoch, set out to destroy the European Union politically and economically. Nor should we forget that the current protestors' occupation of Ottawa is inspired, financed and justified by the Trump movement in the United States. Murdoch must bear serious personal responsibility for plunging the free world into an existential crisis in which he and his friends offer crude and dangerous populism as the only way out for anxious voters. It's Ottawa or Portland, folks.

Murdoch, Trump and Johnson share a predilection for division, polarisation and cynical exploitation of political fear rather than loyalty to civic cohesion, solidarity and the rule of law.

Murdoch knows as well as anyone that Johnson's decision to support Brexit was based on a knife-edge evaluation of where his own political advantage lay rather than any deep-seated convictions about the wellbeing of the UK. But the weaknesses of Johnson and the dangerousness of Trump are prices that Murdoch seems willing to pay in pursuit of malign personal power and influence at national and international level.

As Max Hastings pointed out, Vladimir Putin and his cronies just laughed at Johnson's recent efforts to deflect domestic attention from his own unsuitability for office by seeking to champion the people of Ukraine as their interlocutor with the Kremlin.

As I wrote here recently, the alliance between Xi's China and Putin's Russia, officially anointed in the run-up to the Beijing Winter Olympics, now threatens freedom and liberal democracy across the globe.

The canary in the coalmine of UK democracy is an independent BBC. That too is high on Murdoch's target list.

There is something truly Orwellian about his relentless buy-out and subversion of political decency and the inconvenience of objective truth.

Trumpism – A Danger to America and World Democracy

Why the pre-election rise of Trump is a global issue

27 March 2016

It is truly an irony that many sophisticated European liberals now look back at the presidencies of Ronald Reagan and George H. Bush Senior as periods when the Western world's fate lay in safe hands.

But the continuing degradation of rational politics in the US by the modern Republican Party is creating a nostalgia even for figures whose credentials to sense and reason were once derided by the self-styled intellectual elite and the fashionable 'commentariat' on this side of the Atlantic.

That Donald Trump could be a serious contender for the US presidency is deeply disturbing and is cause for profound anxiety.

That the GOP could find itself in the position of having Trump as its front-runner nominee is, frankly speaking, shocking.

But should we be shocked if the GOP willingly itself allowed itself to be hijacked by the Tea Party, by creationists, by media figures such as Glenn Beck and Rush Limbaugh, and by nitwits such as Sarah Palin?

The extraordinary polarisation of US politics whose early days were so well chronicled in the book *Right Nation*, and for which Fox News has been midwife, wet-nurse and nanny, has inexorably led to a decline in America's status as leader of the 'free world'.

A harsh and vindictive streak has become obvious in part of the American mainstream political discourse. Waterboarding, Abu Ghraib and Guantanamo are but symptoms of an extremist reaction to the difficulties America has encountered as the leading super-power in the post-Cold War world.

Rumsfeld and Cheney were responsible for the extreme damage caused to the moral authority of the US in the eyes of the world. I am glad that I took the opportunity when Minister for Justice to publicly condemn the Guantanamo regime as shocking, even if my remarks were greeted with less than enthusiasm in Iveagh House at the time.

If you doubt the implications of a Trump presidency, I advise you – implore you – to look at the entire 'speech' that Trump made to supporters at Fort Dodge in the run-up to the Iowa caucuses a few weeks ago. It is described as his 'best speech' ever on YouTube, where you can find it. The characteristics of self-infatuation, over-weening self-belief, intolerance, ignorance, vanity and predisposition to be violent are there to be seen in abundance.

That rambling, disconnected hour-long discourse displayed just how unfit Trump is to lead any democracy – least of all America. Just look at it – and be afraid.

It reminded me of an article in the Irish Jesuit quarterly *Studies* dating back to the spring of 1933, which I recently read online.

The author, Daniel Binchy, was the then recently retired Irish Free State 'minister' – or ambassador – to Berlin. The article's subject was none other than Adolf Hitler, who had just been appointed Chancellor in the dying days of the Weimar Republic.

Binchy had, by chance, seen Hitler ranting in the beer-halls of Munich in the early 1920s. He had later, as an Irish diplomat, watched his subsequent progress up the ladder of power. He identified many of the dangerous, psychotic tendencies in Hitler's personality – the hatred, the self-belief, the virulent anti-Semitism and, above all, his absolute determination to unleash war in Europe.

Binchy's article was hard-hitting and prophetic. It was, of course, unusual for a diplomat, on laying down his credentials, to launch a devastating critique of the new regime that was coming to power in the country to which he had been accredited. It must have been an embarrassment of sorts to his successor as Irish representative in Berlin.

But what Binchy said needed to be said. And if his opinion – and the opinions of those who thought like him – had been heeded, a great tragedy for the world might have been avoided or mitigated.

So also now it is vital that we do not simply greet the emergence of Trump in silent horror or disdain.

The Fort Dodge speech shows him to be a real menace. We would be foolish to look on his rantings as just some form of idiot buffoonery. That attitude allowed Hitler to take power.

Those of us who believe in democracy and believe in the potential of the US to be a force for good cannot sit silently by while American discourse is hijacked by such a menace.

There are even some who secretly hope that the GOP nominate Trump so that the Democrats can win with Clinton. There were people who held similar hopes that some success for Hitler would ensure his ultimate demise.

There is no guarantee at all that Hillary Clinton will sail home to the presidency in November. The plutocrats are lining up their PAC funding to destroy Clinton if they can. The Koch Brothers

PAC intends to spend $1 billion to secure a GOP win in November. Fox News is sharpening its fangs for Hillary.

They are just waiting to unleash mordant propaganda on topics ranging from classified emails to Benghazi to Monica Lewinsky. Just wait for it.

Ted Cruz is as problematic in many ways as Trump. The GOP – the party of Abraham Lincoln –has surrendered its soul and its legacy to the naked, vicious politics of anti-Obama dog-whistle racism, combined with intolerance, low rhetoric, and hostility to the migrants in a largely immigrant country.

If the GOP has allowed itself to become the political catspaw of a coalition of 'birthers', racists, homophobes, creationists calling themselves 'evangelists', plutocrats who regard state-funded healthcare as a threat to their savings, 'pacifists in the war on poverty', and nutters who want to waterboard and bomb their way to international respect, we should worry not just for America but for ourselves.

We have to call them out for what they have become.

The importance of calling out Trump for what he is

29 January 2017

Am I alone in detecting a whiff of raw evil in the Trump administration's utterances this week?

I spoke in the Seanad on Thursday about the evil plans of this man, the POTUS, to reintroduce torture, including waterboarding, for detainees suspected of having information useful to the US in its war on terrorism.

Lest we forget the 'facts' we saw in the pictures from Abu Ghraib and lest we start lapping up 'alternative facts', it is as well to remind ourselves of some of the torture techniques deployed by American interrogators. Apart from sensory deprivation techniques (and we have all seen pictures of hooded, ear-muffed, shackled men being wheeled around Guantanamo), the Bush administration encouraged its torturers to assault and inflict pain on shackled victims, to wrap towels around their necks and repeatedly hit their heads against solid walls, and to use drowning and waterboarding to break their will.

One disgusted Guantanamo serviceman wrote a book detailing what he saw there including sexual humiliation and degradation involving female US interrogators shackling a naked Muslim to a ring in the floor and then smearing him with what they claimed was menstrual blood. When I put this last scene to a conservative Republican, I was assured that it was probably fake blood.

Is all of this to start again? Are these practices all part of the shared values of 'freedom and human rights' underlying the 'special relationship' between the US and UK now being talked up by Theresa May? Or is Trump's appetite for a revival of these unspeakable wrongs not evidence of some evil psychopathy in what passes for his personality?

Is there not also something very redolent of the 1938 German bullying of the Czechoslovakian president, Emil Hácha, in this week's shocking attempt to bully the President of Mexico to come to Washington to have the cost of building Trump's wall imposed as some kind of economic reparation on the poor people of Mexico?

Why on earth should the Mexican people or state pay for Trump's wall? In moral terms, the idea is an outrage. Is it because those who live in comparative poverty must pay reparations for the fact that others have fled that poverty by becoming illegals working in the US? Or is it revenge for US job losses to Mexico by reason of NAFTA?

How would imposing a 20% import tax on Mexican goods to pay for the wall not result in the price being paid by US citizens – depending on price elasticity of demand on those goods?

The importance of calling out Trump for what he is

Is it because the Mexicans are collectively guilty as a people of damaging the US, in the same sense as when on Kristallnacht in 1938 the tiny 1% Jewish German population were forced by the Nazis to pay reparations for the assassination of a German diplomat in Paris by a young and desperate Jew, Herschel Grynszpan?

Only a shameless bully and psychopath would seek to revive the cruelties and international thuggish methods of the Third Reich as the means to make America great again.

I wrote here some months ago (and well before his election) about the dangers of not calling out Trump for what he is. I warned of the same complacency that allowed Hitler to ascend to power.

This week's warning by Trump's close adviser, Steve Bannon, to the US media to 'shut their mouths' and his description of them as 'the Opposition' could have come straight from the lips of Joseph Goebbels.

We have been told in recent weeks by 'wise' observers not to worry – that Trump's actions were what mattered, not his words. But the two are not that different.

Why has the EU not expressed solidarity with Mexico? Why is Canada and its young premier, Justin Trudeau, so silent about the blackmailing of its NAFTA partner by Trump?

Why are we all struck dumb as Trump's psychopathy is elevated to the status of US policy?

Why is our weakling government here in Dublin close-mouthed in the face of these events?

I think I know the answer – the 17 March presentation of shamrock at the White House would probably be cancelled if we opened our collective mouth and uttered even the most stifled squeak. One way or the other, POTUS will have no interest whatever in the future of Northern Ireland, by the way.

Such is our new world order.

Trump is a self-absorbed bully who wants the US to behave like a self-absorbed bully. He wants to re-create the US in his own image – 'great'. He wants to dismantle the EU and destroy the euro so that he can do 'Mexican deals' on the weaker individual ex-member states of the EU.

He wants to encourage the Israelis to complete their absorption of 'Judea and Samaria' as they call it – better known as the West Bank to us. He will move his embassy to Jerusalem in a short while.

He does not even seem to grasp that his inaugural speech's promise to exterminate Islamic terrorism cannot be delivered if he abandons any hope of statehood for the Palestinians. He may soon see ISIS driven out of Raqqa and Mosul; but he will only stoke up the jihadist terrorists' hatred and motivation if he permits Netanyahu to end the possibility of a two-state solution for Israel and Palestine.

If more terror follows in the wake of Trump's Middle East policy, it will be no surprise. It, alas, is how the weak and desperate typically wreak vengeance on the strong and unjust.

Nobody knows exactly why Putin moved might and main to assist Trump's election. But that strange alliance bodes ill for a new world order based on mutual respect, as the people of eastern Ukraine will appreciate.

In the 1930s the world entered a dark valley. Forgive me if I have a sense of foreboding that Trump is bringing us all into another dark valley. All the ingredients are stockpiled for a new world crisis – not least the personal characteristics of Trump himself.

Even the word 'carnage' seems to describe what is to come rather than what has already come to pass. His statement that the 'carnage stops now' seems so very unlikely.

Only Trump's successor can make America great again

27 August 2017

We are now eight months into the presidency of Donald Trump. The good news is that means that one sixth of his term is already over – assuming, that is, he is not re-elected in three years' time.

What is there to show for it? What will be there to show for it?

There is evidence that illegal immigration into the US has been curbed somewhat since Trump's election. But the anti-Muslim measures that he attempted to impose are probably irrelevant to the decline in such immigration, the main source of illegal migration being the Americas. Even then, his bombastic promises about deporting millions of migrants, starting on his first day in office, proved to be empty.

That campaign promise apart, Trump has achieved practically nothing so far.

His pledge to repeal and replace Obamacare has run into the sands of congressional opposition. His Mexican wall has petered out like a Mexican wave. His détente with the Kremlin has soured. His China policy has yo-yoed between cordiality and hostility. Kim Jong Un appears to have called his bluff; North Korea continues to build a lethal nuclear threat against the US. Syria has turned out to be far more intractable than Trump ever imagined.

US policy in the Gulf States, Iraq, Turkey and Kurdistan is all over the place. Iran is as problematic as ever from a US perspective.

In the Americas, his relationship with Mexico, Cuba, Venezuela is going backwards – unless he attempts and succeeds in deposing Maduro.

In Europe, Trump is despised, feared and despaired of – in equal measure.

Rex Tillerson is manfully standing in the credibility gap that surrounds Trump internationally.

The real issue now is whether Trump's US domestic voter coalition is going to stick with him or quietly desert him.

Money markets rallied greatly at the mere thought of a Trump-led economic revival. If market sentiment is important – and it is – share prices blossomed in a promising manner in the first semester of his presidency. Promised tax cuts for the wealthy were bound to have that effect. But will it last?

The real test of whether sustainable economic growth has any substance is the rate of investment in growth-producing industry, infrastructure and commerce. US employment growth to this point is more attributable to the backwash of Obama's policies than to anything Trump has done.

Now middle-class and working-class Americans, the core of middle America, need to see signs that America is becoming great again. Opening a few coalmines won't make the US great again.

Only a massive programme of infrastructural investment will bring hope to middle America.

And that is where Trump's difficulties come into sharp focus. Just how do you cut taxes, cut the deficit and increase capital spending at the same time? You can't – unless you slash current non-capital spending in areas like welfare, health, education, and defence. And such cuts won't make middle America feel great again.

Trump's chaotic reign at the White House and his bitter, confrontational relationship with majority leader Mitch McConnell bode ill for the implementation of a sustainable, radical budgetary policy that might be the foundation of economic 'greatness' for America.

In the unforgiving US political calendar, Trump's mid-term congressional elections are emerging into view. The question is whether the Democrats can get their act together sufficiently to recapture the House of Representatives or the Senate.

If there is a substantial Democrat recovery, both Republicans and Democrats will put their minds to ending Trump's presidency after one term. Strangely, the GOP might easily select another candidate at their next convention with the aim of holding on to the White House. The bigger problem for the Democrats is finding an electable candidate who is not in the mould of Hillary or Bernie – a candidate with charisma, vision, credibility, and optimism.

In that context, Trump's complete U-turn on Afghanistan last week raises even more credibility issues. He claimed that he is going to commit more troops to 'win' the war against the Taliban. He disavows any attempt to engage in 'nation-building' on behalf of the Afghans.

But what does 'winning' mean? As Trump puts it, winning means 'killing terrorists'. But is that really 'winning'? Is killing Muslims and occupying their lands 'winning'? Or is it stoking up fires of Salafist extremism across the globe?

The 'best' outcome that can be hoped for is that the US-supported Kabul regime survives long enough to force the Taliban to settle for an Afghanistan that becomes a mosaic of tribal fiefdoms run by regional warlords under the umbrella of a moderate coalition government in Kabul that is reasonably friendly to the US and that eschews any sympathy for Al-Qaeda and Isis.

We are not talking about creating a secular democracy, one in which oppressed Afghani women are guaranteed equality in all regions. Trump won't attempt to build up the Afghans' primitive infrastructure when he can't even tackle infrastructural deficits back home.

How many US and NATO soldiers' lives will be sacrificed in pursuit of such a limited and elusive goal?

This is a strategy that Trump promised middle America that he would definitely not follow. This is an Obama strategy that he derided. This is a military campaign that can't be 'won' in any intelligible way. The most that can be done with this strategy is to avoid humiliating military defeat and withdrawal under fire from Kabul in the next 18 months.

We in Ireland could perhaps afford to watch Trump's intended battle against Islamist extremism with a detached interest if it weren't for the atrocities in Barcelona and Turku last week. The jihadist terror group based in small-town Ripoll were immigrants. Their leader was an imam who used European civil rights law to avoid deportation to Morocco while at the same time he planned an atrocious slaughter of hundreds at Barcelona's Gaudí-designed Sagrada Familia cathedral – where any of us could have been the victims.

But the Manchester and London atrocities demonstrated that jihadi groups can be home-grown as well.

None of us is safe from these 'faith hate' Islamist extremists anywhere in Europe – even here in Ireland. I just hope that our security forces are active in pre-empting terror being unleashed on our innocent and vulnerable society.

In their perverted minds, Allah calls on mujaheddin 'martyrs' to kill infidel men, women and children in Europe as part of the Jihad against Western infidels and, in particular, allied drone strikes and cluster-bombs unleashed on men, women and children in Afghan, Yemeni, Syrian and Iraqi war-zone villages.

The big question is whether Trump is going to make the situation better or worse. Is he going to fan the flames of hatred or douse them?

It is hard to see any peace-making or de-escalation happening while Trump sits in the White House. He doesn't do subtlety or complexity. Nor does his core constituency.

Theirs is a confrontational, simplistic worldview. By irony, it is their sons who will come from Afghanistan in caskets draped with Old Glory – it won't be the sons of those making paper millions from Trump's boom in share prices on Wall Street.

I blame those in the GOP who brought us Trump's presidency. They could have beaten Hillary and won the election without

Trump. They flirted with the Tea Party, they subverted Obama because they couldn't stand having a black president, and they cheered Trump on in his bombastic buffoonery. They know so little of the world outside America that they cannot now see how diminished America has become in the eyes of the rest of the world.

Only Trump's successor can make America great again and that can only happen if the American people begin to appreciate the dimensions of the great mistake they made in empowering him to diminish America.

A Brexit-touting Trump is no friend to Ireland or the EU

9 June 2019

North America and Europe should see each other as friendly and supportive regional partner economies. Culturally the two regions have common roots and a conflict between them is unthinkable. The North Atlantic regional economic zone is and will remain the dominant economic force in world affairs.

That was not always so. Normandy in 1944 was the major start point of America's armed struggle to free Europe from tyranny and totalitarianism.

Within three years the faultline between freedom and tyranny in Europe was the Iron Curtain. America guaranteed the freedom of Western Europe while Stalin set about the totalitarian enslavement of Eastern Europe.

After the fall of the USSR and the end of the Cold War, the EU expanded rapidly to include the former Warsaw Pact countries not to rival or depose the US as the leader of the Western alliance but to consolidate the liberation and democratisation of its eastern member states. The EU enlargement of 2004 was a huge step towards the consolidation of peace and progress.

The Definite Article: TRUMPISM – A DANGER TO AMERICA AND WORLD DEMOCRACY

This is why the buffoon president, Donald Trump, is so dangerous and wrong-headed. For all his momentary solemnity at commemoration events during the week, he is a malign and poisonous ferment in world affairs.

There was little sense and much grotesquery in solemnly saluting the huge sacrifice of American GIs killed and wounded on the beaches and in the bocages of Normandy while at the same time actively encouraging the disintegration of the EU.

We should not forget that Trump has openly and consistently supported Brexit and those in other EU states who advocated withdrawal from the EU. He backed extremist politicians from a number of member states who want to Balkanise the EU states. He wanted to appoint an ambassador to the EU who vociferously opposed the existence of the union itself. He flirted with Putin.

He wants to reduce the states of Europe to economic satellites – to mirror the defunct Warsaw Pact with a new economic Washington Pact ruled by sanctions and tariffs imposed as executive fiats of the US presidency.

Let's be absolutely clear about it – Trump wants a hard Brexit. His offer of a tremendous trade deal to the gullible British is designed to encourage the hardest of hard Brexits. He couldn't give a fig about the consequences for Ireland – North or South. He is an impetuous and dangerous bully.

From his moronic statements in Shannon about the Irish border and 'wall', it is clear that he not only fails to read his brief but utterly misses the point about 30 years of US policy on Ireland.

Donald Trump is no friend of Ireland. If he were well disposed to Ireland, he would oppose a hard Brexit. His repugnant bromance with Farage and Johnson is a very serious danger for us.

As for the United Kingdom, do any members of the Conservative and Unionist party in the shires ever ask themselves exactly why it is that such large numbers in two of its four parts actually want to leave the UK? It's a good question that they can't bear to bother their little heads with.

Whether or not the secessionist vote in Scotland and Northern Ireland reaches 51% in the coming years, both parts of the ever-so United Kingdom clearly want to remain in the EU. So why is the UK once again becoming visibly an English state with vassal appendages?

Northern Ireland is, as a matter of international law, entitled to secede from the UK. Scotland's right to secede by a majority vote is conditional on acquiescence from Westminster.

The UK is not in good nick at all. England is riven by unstated class prejudice. It is a very unequal society in outlook and instincts. Its low unemployment rate masks a significant dis-empowerment of a working class dependent on low wages and poor employment law protections.

A decade of austerity has frayed the country's social infrastructural fabric to threadbare.

A Trumpian 'tremendous trade deal with America' simply won't make up for any of the damage done by a hard Brexit. A no-deal Brexit could produce a political and economic shock and the break-up of the UK.

The UK can, only with massive financial difficulty, build one aircraft carrier and then, after a further period, buy and install American planes on it. It can plan another. But the illusion that such investment will keep it a world power is ridiculous. The rest of Her Majesty's forces are dwindling in number and equipment.

Aspirations to deploy military force in the Near East, the Middle East or the Far East seem so unreal.

The last defence secretary's boast that the *Queen Elizabeth* might be sent to patrol the South China Seas is utterly absurd. What would happen if it hit a sea-mine off the Paracel Islands? War with China? About what?

Britain's steel-making business is in crisis. So is its car manufacturing capacity. The high street retail trade sector is imploding. A hard Brexit or a no-deal Brexit could do very serious damage to sterling. Add to that the massive costs entailed in meeting climate change targets and you have the elements of a real political and economic crisis. The possibility of a Corbyn-led government might provoke a financial exodus that could threaten London and sterling.

Britain, outside the EU, stands to become a second post-Imperial Netherlands. Even the Dutch Prime Minister has commented on Britain's slide economically and politically. The irony is that the leading contenders for the leadership of the Tory party and the keys of Downing Street are all spouting a pale imitation of Trump's political message, 'Make Britain Great Again'.

How real is the threat of a no-deal Brexit? You may think it unlikely by imagining that the British electorate and political establishment is incapable of such self-harm. But think back to the primaries and election that brought Donald Trump to power. Although some of us warned of the real danger that he might be elected, most believed that such an outcome simply couldn't happen.

To avoid a hard Brexit Britain must either negotiate a new deal with the EU or swallow the pill of accepting the existing deal with a new Tory leader or secure unanimous agreement among the EU member states to a further extension for the Article 50 process.

Which of these seems likely? That is the conundrum for Ireland.

Leo Varadkar faces very dangerous political waters. As a matter of law, there must be four by-elections held by 2 January to fill the seats of the newly elected TD MEPs. While three of the four seats are opposition seats (if you count Fianna Fáil as part of the opposition), and while he could probably stagger on having lost all four by-elections, most likely in November or December, his political fortunes would look very down at heel if he went to the electorate having lost a succession of by-elections.

The local and European elections, as I wrote here last week, are no guide to the outcome of a general election. But there is every reason to believe that the shine has gone off Leo in the eyes of the voters. Moreover, it is clear that Micheál Martin has been largely restored in the eyes of the electorate. It is difficult to see where Fine Gael will gain seats, bearing in mind that they will lose one seat in Dún Laoghaire on account of its being held by the former Ceann Comhairle, Seán Barrett.

An Irish general election in the early autumn looks increasingly likely – if only to avoid a difficult budget. With fail marks in his Leaving Certificates subjects in Housing, Health and Transport, Leo has a lot to ponder if term opens in September.

The fruits of populism are ripening, falling and rotting

29 June 2022

I suppose many people will have asked themselves whether there is not a contradiction of sorts in a society which appears to prohibit state legislatures from infringing the right of all citizens to keep and bear firearms on the one hand but upholds a right for the same state legislatures to prohibit all abortions, even for juvenile rape victims, on the other hand.

If all human life, from embryonic to centenarian, is sacred and requires protection, is it rational to allow hot-headed young men to buy, keep and carry multiple automatic weapons capable of inflicting slaughter of the innocents of whatever age?

And yet in a few short days the US Supreme Court has interpreted the US Constitution in exactly those ways. Reversing *Roe v Wade* has the effect of putting every state in the US in the same position as Ireland. It is for state legislators to decide on the circumstances, if any, in which any pregnant woman is legally permitted to terminate her pregnancy – as it is in Ireland.

Of course, Ireland and the US are coming to this issue from very different places – we had as a people by referendum enacted the Eighth Amendment to forestall any court decision such as *Roe v Wade* or any legislative decision to legalise any kind of abortion. The US, by contrast, had a Supreme Court decision enshrining as a constitutional right a woman's right to choose, so as to prevent conservative states from outlawing or radically restricting the same right to choose.

The US 2nd Amendment provides as follows: 'A well-regulated militia being necessary to the security of a free state, the right of the people to keep and bear arms shall not be infringed.'

In the *Heller* case in 1986, the late Justice Scalia delivered the majority opinion and in a very detailed historical analysis argued that the wording of the amendment did not imply that the citizen's right to keep and bear arms was in some way conditional on their potential use in a state militia. He viewed the right as part of the Bill of Rights in the US Constitution and that it derived from the right of individual self-defence rather than the idea of membership of an organised militia.

The recent mass shooting of schoolchildren in Uvalde, Texas is but a grotesque example of where America's gun culture has bought its citizens. There were 1.5 million gun deaths in the US in the period 1968 to 2017, which as the BBC pointed out recently is more than the entire death toll of American soldiers in battles and wars since the declaration of independence in 1776.

In 2020, there were 45,000 gun-deaths, a 43% increase since 2010. Of them nearly 25,000 were suicides while nearly 20,000 were classed as homicides. Of the 7.5 million new first-time gunowners

The fruits of populism are ripening, falling and rotting

in 2019 to 2021, half were women and 40% were black or Hispanic. What do they fear?

The American conservative right alliance which supports abortion bans but opposes assault rifle bans is growing in power. It opposes socialised medicine as a 'stepping stone' to communism or Nazism. It supports political action committees which spend vast sums of money raised from the wealthy to drive tax cuts and influence election outcomes.

As I wrote here some months ago, the Republicans are likely to win control of both Houses of Congress this autumn. Trump could easily emerge as their candidate for 2024 unless Florida's governor, Ron DeSantis, can head him off. The re-election of Biden or Kamala Harris seems very unlikely now. The Trump-packed Supreme Court may well target gay marriage in the coming months, if Justice Clarence Thomas is to be believed. His spouse was active in Trump's stolen election conspiracy.

The January 6th Committee has produced compelling evidence of the seditious plot by Trump and his cronies to quash the result of the 2020 election. But Teflon Trump supporters simply don't care. They are adept at targeting the people they don't like while shielding their own madmen from scrutiny or penalty.

Just wait for Trump to come up with a joint Trump–Putin 'solution' for Ukraine. Trump's silence on the Russian death goblin's savage war has been deafening.

Trump's erstwhile British acolyte, Boris Johnson, is using Ukraine to throw shapes on the international stage. But how long will his party allow him to sit figuratively at the wheel of a badly dented political Land Rover, a vehicular throwback to the glory days of Churchill and empire?

Economic out-workings of the Ukraine war have the potential to radicalise and polarise opinion in the Western democracies.

There is little room for complacency or optimism as long as Rupert Murdoch broadcasts Tucker Carlson's toxic views into the homes of middle America.

The fruits of populism are showing signs of ripening, falling and rotting.

QAnon well on its way to becoming America's new religion

27 July 2022

What is it about the Americans?

A recent picture of ecstatic young male Trump supporters, one clad in a 'Trump Won' T-shirt, posed a question for me: did he really believe that and on what evidence? Or is it a question of wishful thinking?

For a society that steadfastly refuses to 'establish' any religion, even though most of the founding generation were nominal Christians of one kind or another, the United States has embraced Christian fundamentalism and other beliefs to an extent far greater than any modern society.

But it goes further than that, There is an emotional blotting paper type of appetite to believe in things that would appear improbable to most modern Europeans.

The Church of Scientology is a case in point. Significant and well-placed figures seem willing to ignore the origins of Scientology in the far-fetched writings of a very dubious figure, science fiction writer L. Ron Hubbard, and to adhere to a sect that keeps most members in the dark as to its ultimate beliefs.

I cannot even attempt to explain their belief in thetans in the space allotted here, but they can be summarised as types of spiritual entities who have existed for billions of years and who willed the universe into existence – disembodied entities occasionally captured in human bodies.

The niceties of these beliefs are not revealed to people who become members of the church until they succeed in graduating through various challenging stages of development. The documentary *Going Clear* (available online) shines some light on Scientology and it is not a very pretty sight.

The church claims 8 to 15 million adherents worldwide but a US religious attitudes survey suggests this claim is a massive fabrication and that only 25,000 American are thought to be believers.

While European audiences may find the musical *Book of Mormon* an amusing piece of light-hearted comedy and while many of us are amazed by the zeal that sends earnest young Mormons to our doors seeking converts, there are, according to the Church of Jesus Christ of Latter-day Saints, more than 15 million believers worldwide – people who don't see the funny side of the musical at all.

The origins of that book – golden plates of text briefly given by the angel Moroni to one Joseph Smith in the early nineteenth century showing that Jesus was in America in biblical times and translated by him into the style and vernacular of the seventeenth-century King James Bible – might appear implausible to most modern Europeans. But Mormonism is a strong and growing church in the Americas.

QAnon is a new online phenomenon dating from 2017 which propagates theories including Trump's stolen election and another that America is controlled and manipulated by a cabal of liberal paedophiles which abducts and kills children as part of a satanic global conspiracy to dominate us.

They believe Donald Trump is secretly combating that evil cabal. While QAnon is not yet a church, it is well on the way to becoming a politico-religious sect in the way that Scientology morphed from science fiction into a self-styled church.

What do Americans make of QAnon beliefs?

While most Americans disbelieve and reject the beliefs of the QAnon conspiracy, recent surveys show that a fifth of Americans share some of its beliefs, including more than 60% of Republican voters who say they believe the last election was stolen. Some 14% of Americans told one recent survey that they regard themselves as QAnon supporters.

Trump has been careful not to alienate QAnon or disown its theories. He courts any form of fundamentalism and extremism he considers potentially useful to his forthcoming bid for re-election.

And that re-election is by no means improbable, notwithstanding the proceedings of the US Congress January 6th Committee. The Democrats are probably within months of losing control of both Houses to the Republicans. Trump is still the most dominant force in the Republican Party.

Can we in Europe feel morally superior and aloof in respect of all these American developments? After all, we rely on the US for our collective security, as the Ukraine war has once again emphasised.

Europe has been complacent and misguided in many ways, not least in its misreading of Putin. Those of us in Europe who are still happy to be called liberal feel helpless as the post-Cold War international order fractures and shows signs of crumbling.

Liberal democracy needs its own champions. At the time of writing, the UK is witnessing a nasty and vindictive, cynical political knife-fight among Tory factions – a struggle for control of what appears to be the bridge of a political *Titanic*. Europe too seems to be led by political nonentities.

Will anything save us from a remake of Make America Great Again? Is there any limit to American credulity?

Democracy has not hung on such a fraying thread since the 1930s

29 May 2024

In the year 2000, an episode of *The Simpsons* was broadcast entitled 'Bart to the Future', featuring Lisa Simpson becoming US president in 2016 and having to clean up the mess left by a Donald Trump presidency. What was the stuff of comedic cartoon shows in 2016 came to pass in 2000; Donald Trump was elected to the White House, defeating Hillary Clinton rather than Lisa Simpson. Comedy then descended into grotesque reality.

Trump now regularly rants during his comeback rallies about Joe Biden being America's worst ever president. Only the extraordinarily gullible and ignorant among American voters can have forgotten the reality of Trump's period in office. Can they really have forgotten the constant sacking of his appointees – only explainable either by idiocy in making those appointments or random caprice in terminating them – or both?

Can they have forgotten his utter failures in foreign policy, including his abandoned confrontation with North Korea's Kim Jong Un, which has left a legacy of intercontinental atomic ballistic missiles in construction to threaten the west coast of America? Can they forget the 'beautiful letters' from Kim to Trump which formed part of that foreign relations debacle?

Can they forget the deal Trump negotiated at Doha with the Taliban which left Biden with no choice but to evacuate and cut adrift the Afghans' somewhat democratic state?

Can they forget the appalling Trump misjudgements of Putin which clearly encouraged him to believe that the West would abandon Ukraine to Russian subjugation? Can they forget that Trump would betray the Ukrainians in the wink of an eye if doing so kept the US stock market's Ponzi scheme boom moving upwards? Can the people of Taiwan really trust him to preserve their democracy?

And yet, there is every reason to believe that voters in swing states may well deliver him the presidency against the wishes of a majority of all American voters.

I doubt whether a New York jury will unanimously convict him in the current proceedings. And even if they do convict, I doubt he will be serving a sentence by November, since he will exhaust every possible avenue of appeal, ending in his utterly compromised US Supreme Court. And even if he were jailed, his support base would probably try to vote him into the White House to get him out.

Trump tells gullible audiences that the world is laughing at the Biden presidency. And the audiences appear to believe that. I know of no democratic country in the world where it is suggested that a majority of its citizens favour a Trump presidency.

For the great majority of people in the world's democratic states, Trump is an appalling combination of unfitness and dangerousness. In Ireland, for instance, he seems to have the quiet support of 'sneaking regarders' based on their naive view that Trump is pro-life by personal conviction.

A recent documentary broadcast on BBC TV's Storyville series entitled *Praying for Armageddon* should be re-broadcast in Ireland and made compulsory viewing for all those here who are ambivalent on re-election for Trump. It revealed that Trump either is or pretends to be in deep-seated alliance with biblical Christian evangelists who believe that the present crisis in the Middle East is a portent of an end-of-the-world conflagration that will very soon happen at Megiddo in Israel – the last battle in which Jesus will return to vanquish the forces of evil as predicted in the Book of the Apocalypse.

If Trump is re-elected, power in the world will be shared personally by Trump, China's President Xi, and Russia's Vladimir Putin.

Trump and Putin are weaponising hardline religion for their own political ends; Xi is decommissioning or neutering all religions to preserve the Chinese communist party's dictatorship of the proletariat, as the Uyghurs, and other Muslims and Christians and other sects have found out to their extreme cost.

Democracy has never hung on such a fraying thread since the dark days of the 1930s when the tyrannies of Hitler, Stalin, Mussolini, and Imperial Japan loomed over the entire world – an era when Franklin Roosevelt struggled to make America a fairer society and stronger bastion of democracy against accusations of communism redolent of Trump's current rhetoric against Biden and Obama and against judicial reactionaries on the US Supreme Court.

Ireland belatedly found its collective tongue to speak out against the extremes of Islamism and Zionism in the utter barbarities of Gaza during the last nine months.

Standing up for, rather than speaking quietly about, the two-state solution to the Israel–Palestine conflict does not connote any antisemitism at all on the part of the Irish state. It does not reward Hamas barbarity. Along with Spain and Norway, our recognition of a Palestinian statehood is an essential exercise in speaking truth to power – so badly needed as the world looks into a valley of darkness not known for eighty years.

A Trump presidency will embolden Putin and Netanyahu

31 July 2024

So much depends on the outcome of the US presidential election in November.

It isn't just the Ukraine war, the war in Gaza, a possible war with Iran, a regional war in the Middle East, and war over Taiwan. The very future of the United States is now at stake as never before.

And bound up in that is the viability of the world's liberal democracies in the face of totalitarianism in one form or another.

As for Ukraine, the survival of a democracy is quite an achievement on the part of the Ukrainians and their Western supporters. The grotesque Putin invasion might well have snuffed it out – especially when the fact that the Kyiv government refused to believe that Putin was doing any more than sabre-rattling is remembered.

But now that the war has settled into a Flanders-style meatgrinder mode, the question arises as to whether or how the Ukrainians can repossess the heavily fortified occupied eastern territories seized by Russia since 2014, and whether they have the military resources to do so. Bearing in mind that conventional military wisdom is that an attacker needs at least three-to-one superiority and air superiority to dislodge defenders, the prospect of a successful counterattack on a large scale seems remote.

With or without a Trump presidency, it appears increasingly likely that some form of armistice, like that in the Korean War along a de facto line of truce, will eventually transpire.

Does anyone seriously argue that the Ukrainians, even greatly rearmed with planes, missiles, munitions, and intelligence resources, are likely to expel the Russians from all of the eastern provinces and from the Crimea which was added to Ukraine in 1954?

Unless Putin's regime collapses from the inside, it is more probable than not that such a stalemate will bed down as the outcome of Putin's folly and his war crimes. If this becomes inevitable, the only remaining issue is whether the West offers and delivers Ukraine a security guarantee and a path to EU membership. Anything less would endanger all of eastern Europe from the Baltic to the Black Sea. Finlandisation of Ukraine would be a disastrous first part of a domino chain of regional subjugation.

If Putin wants a new Cold War, so be it. His policy of covert, low-intensity subversion of Western Europe's democracies (which is to be seen in the attempted guerrilla-type attacks on the Paris Olympics) is serious but can be countered successfully.

As far as the Middle East is concerned, there is every sign that Israel has effectively destroyed most of the support it once had in the West, apart from the US. What has happened and is happening to the Palestinians at the hands of the Netanyahu government is simply unforgivable. The younger generation of Europeans and Americans will never forgive or forget what Israel has done.

After the horrific Hamas atrocity raid of 7 October 2023, I wrote here that the response of Netanyahu could be one that resounded though the ages if he refrained from doing what he now has done – unleashing a genocidal campaign of death and destruction on the innocent and helpless corralled in an enclave of hopelessness.

There is no forgiveness for what has happed to many tens of thousands of civilians, and hundreds of thousands of wounded, traumatised, bereaved, orphaned and childless human beings. Gaza is the scene of a crime against humanity. No legitimate purpose of Israel can remotely justify the scale and cruelty of what that state has released upon the innocent.

Extirpating Hamas is a forlorn aim – especially if an entire people are imbued with a hatred of the perpetrators who have condemned them to an existence of scrabbling for their relatives and their very way and means of life among the rubble of their world.

After a year, where are the hostages? Are many still alive? Can they survive the annihilation of their ruthless captors? Will they be yielded up as a prelude to the liquidation of every Hamas fighter or former activist? How does this savage bloodletting and genocide end up with a safe and secure Israel?

The UK is now distancing itself from Israel. So is public opinion right across the free world. At last, the Israeli settlements in the West Bank have been authoritatively declared illegal under international law. The perpetrators of the Hamas atrocity raid last October and the Israeli genocidal response will find themselves condemned as war criminals at the bar of international justice someday.

The war in Gaza must stop. It is not a war of self-defence by any rational measure. It is not an existential struggle for the survival of a democracy which is governed by Netanyahu. It is cruel beyond words. It is unspeakably disproportionate. It is futile and self-destructive for the honour and future of all Israelis.

Trump and American Republicans may flirt with Netanyahu's government, but they are courting a deeper and dreadful danger for America and the free world. That is what is in issue in November.

Referendums and Constitutional Issues

The Abbeylara referendum – a dangerous constitutional foray

23 October 2011

I will be voting No in the referendum this week on the proposal to give each House of the Oireachtas new constitutional powers of inquiry because I believe that the proposal is very dangerous, goes far further than is necessary and is very badly thought out. The phrase 'mad, bad and dangerous' truly applies to it.

The Government's proposals were finally published on 6 October 2011, and have received virtually no public scrutiny, and only a pathetically inadequate, toothless legislative consideration by the Dáil and Seanad.

The text of the proposed constitutional amendment amounts to an ill-judged overreaction to the decisions of the High Court and the Supreme Court in the Abbeylara case.

While I do support, and have always supported, the right of the Oireachtas to restore its rights to those which were generally believed to exist prior to the Abbeylara judgments, the terms of the proposed constitutional amendment go far, far further than is necessary.

We are, in effect, being asked to accept that two egregious wrongs make a right.

I have always believed that the High Court and the Supreme Court in the Abbeylara case failed to strike the proper balance between the rights of the individual and the rights of parliament under our Constitution and failed to give due weight to the constitutional separation of powers.

Because the courts in question (correctly in my view) found unlawful the process whereby a group of elected politicians were conducting their own mini-inquest/tribunal of inquiry into the shooting of an armed civilian at Abbeylara, they upheld the claim by the gardaí involved that the Oireachtas inquiry was an impermissible invasion of their constitutional rights.

I think that the High Court and the Supreme Court in the Abbeylara case arrived at the right decision in respect of the Abbeylara inquiry, but did so on the basis of a fundamentally flawed reasoning process which left the Oireachtas power of inquiry largely emasculated.

The courts' errors, at High Court and Supreme Court level, in dealing with the Abbeylara case have now created a constitutional mess in which the Oireachtas is asking the people to compound the original judicial error by granting to the Houses of the Oireachtas virtually unlimited powers to establish McCarthyite 'star chamber', highly politicised inquiries to investigate whatever and whomever future politicians of the day believe to be of 'general public importance' – a frighteningly wide category which potentially includes virtually everything.

This highly politicised power of inquiry would well be used to justify, say, the establishment of the Irish equivalent of a McCarthy-era congressional committee on Un-American activities. It also includes a vast range of public controversies.

This is a dangerous proposal in principle.

Since the elected politicians (principally the Government) are now attempting to bounce us into acceptance of this dangerously flawed proposal, it is incumbent that the media speak out loudly and clearly against the proposed amendment to the Constitution and demand that the Government abandons the proposal so that it can abide by its constitutional duty, which is to widely consult with the people and to carefully consider and debate how the constitutional balance can be properly restored post the Abbeylara judgments in a manner that respects the fundamental rights of ordinary citizens.

I should say here that, as Attorney General, I notified the Government of my intention to intervene in the Supreme Court appeal from the judgment of the High Court in the Abbeylara case. In the independent role of Attorney General, I sought to persuade the Supreme Court that the High Court decision had gone too far and that a fundamentally different approach to striking the balance between parliamentary and personal rights should be taken by the Supreme Court.

Although the submissions made by us on behalf of the State found some traction among a minority of the Supreme Court, it was unfortunate that a majority of the Court appears to have adopted the same erroneous analysis that characterised the original High Court decision.

We sought to persuade the Supreme Court that the Oireachtas and its Houses did not have an unlimited power of inquiry but, on the contrary, that the Constitution did allow for parliamentary inquiries by each House of the Oireachtas where that power was clearly and proportionately deployed in aid of the constitutional function of that House.

We submitted to the Supreme Court that Dáil Eireann was not merely a legislature. It was also envisaged by the Constitution to be a democratic organ of Executive accountability.

The Government is answerable to the Dáil for the manner in which the executive power of the State is exercised. The Seanad, by contrast, is a purely legislative body. The Government is not answerable to the Seanad in the same way that it is answerable to the Dáil.

We submitted to the Supreme Court that the general right of each House of the Oireachtas to establish a committee and to summon witnesses before it had to be exercised, in the case of the Dáil, primarily in respect of its legislative and accountability functions, and in the case of the Seanad in respect of its legislative function only.

The thrust of our submission to the Supreme Court was that the issue as to whether or not the good name of a citizen (elected or un-elected) could be damaged by the findings of a properly constituted parliamentary inquiry was not the central element of a test of constitutionality. We urged that the status of the person whose reputation was potentially concerned (i.e. were they or were they not a member of the Oireachtas) was not the appropriate determining factor in deciding whether a parliamentary inquiry was legitimate.

We sought to persuade the Supreme Court that the power of each House of the Oireachtas to establish an inquiry was derived solely from its own function and was not to be tested by reference to whether the inquiry had implications for the reputations of non-politicians.

Unfortunately, the middle way between the more obnoxious aspects of the Abbeylara inquiry and the rights of the Oireachtas that we argued for was not accepted by a majority in the Supreme Court. The common elements of the majority decisions were seen as radically curtailing the conventional parliamentary powers of inquiry as far as the Oireachtas was concerned.

The reaction of most democratic politicians to the Supreme Court's decision in the matter was to view it as a 'bull in a china shop' event that had damaged the delicate balance of the separation of powers.

This view, I regret to say, has now spawned the present grotesque overreaction which seeks to accord to each House of the Oireachtas not merely the limited functional power of inquiry that we argued to retain in the Supreme Court, but a power to inquire into 'any matter stated by the House or Houses concerned to be of general public importance' – a wide power that few imagined to exist pre-Abbeylara.

If the middle way proposed by us had been adopted by a majority in the Supreme Court, the Oireachtas would have retained what was generally supposed to be its conventional powers of establishing inquiries directly related to the constitutional functions of each House of the Oireachtas.

Unfortunately, the effect of the proposed amendment is to make *any* citizen answerable to either or both Houses of the Oireachtas in respect of *any* matter considered by either such House to be of 'general public importance'.

Arguably, a judicial calamity is now about to spawn a political calamity. An error in relation to the separation of powers made by the courts is being availed of to accord to the Houses of the Oireachtas very dangerous powers of a highly political kind to summon before each House or its committee ordinary citizens for judgment provided that the House in question considers the issue to be 'of general public importance'.

The proposed amendment also seeks to seriously reduce the power of the courts to protect the rights of ordinary citizens in such inquiries.

This is, frankly, a horrific outcome. And it is about time that those who know what is afoot speak out clearly and loudly against it.

Nor should we forget that we are amending our Constitution the only protection we have against a Government's abuse of power.

The terms of the Government's draft legislation, insofar as they are relied on as an assurance to the people that this power will not be abused, are largely irrelevant.

The difference between ordinary legislation (such as the draft Bill) and a constitutional amendment is that *any* future majority in the Dáil (assuming that we also proceed with the madcap scheme to get rid of the Seanad) will be able to amend the legislation so as to avail of the fullest scope of the power of inquiry on matters of 'general public importance'.

That this is potentially a form of political 'star chamber' should not be doubted.

The proposed amendment provides that the conduct of any person (whether or not a member of either House) might be investigated and that the House or Houses concerned may make findings in respect of the conduct of that person concerning the matter to which the inquiry relates.

This would allow any future Government of the day and its political supporters in the Dáil to establish, say, the Mahon Tribunal, the Moriarty Tribunal, or the Smithwick Tribunal, or the Beef Tribunal, as 'committees of inquiry' populated by politicians chosen by the self-same Government or its self-same supporters in the Dáil. It could be used by the Government to investigate the opposition (but not vice versa).

We could, for instance, have the question of where the truth lay in relation to Bertie Ahern's financial dealings decided by a committee of his enemies or, for that matter, his friends. The same applies to Michael Lowry. Politicians would be free to reject testimony of their opponents, effectively branding them as perjurers.

We could have political inquiries into press stories of public importance and into journalism. As long as the subject of a parliamentary inquiry was a matter of 'general public importance', *any*

The Abbeylara referendum – a dangerous constitutional foray

citizen, private or public, could be hauled before such a parliamentary inquiry for investigation leading to findings against him or her.

The Kenneth Starr process started with a public issue, suspected corporate fraud in Arkansas, and ended with Monica Lewinsky before a grand jury testifying about her clothing!

Even the implementing draft Bill published (which as the Chairman of the Referendum Commission, Bryan MacMahon, points out, may never be enacted and could be amended or repealed at a later stage) already envisages the appointment of a parliamentary investigator who can appoint authorised persons to interview any witness considered relevant and to require them to sign statements of proposed evidence.

A person authorised by the investigator may be given power to enter at any reasonable time any premises where it is believed there are documents or information in any form relevant to the inquiry and to secure for inspection such documents and to copy or remove documents or information and to direct any person on the premises to produce any document or any information.

The investigator will also be entitled to get a court warrant to have authorised persons search your home in the company of members of An Garda Síochána.

Is this the fantasy of Robespierre or the Christmas wish-list of the Stasi?

These proposals amount to a form of collective political insanity. They go far, far beyond anything that was necessary to restore the imbalance created by the Abbeylara judgments.

They set the stage for a new form of 'democratic' tyranny and for political witch-hunts along the line of Senator Joseph McCarthy's worst excesses in 1950s America.

I confess that I am absolutely shocked by what I find in the proposed constitutional amendment and in the proposed legislation (for what it is worth since it can be amended at any later stage).

This proposed amendment of the Constitution is utterly disproportionate, disgraceful and completely unjustifiable.

A different, moderate, well thought out, balanced amendment might well be justified.

This amendment is simply disastrous. It isn't merely a matter of throwing out the baby of our constitutional rights with the bath water of recent controversies. It is a permanent charter for political bullying and tyranny of the worst kind.

It proposes to accord to any future Government (no matter who is in it) dependent on the majority in the Dáil the right to haul before parliamentary committees ordinary citizens to have their behaviour examined on the pretext that the Dáil considers that the subject matter of the inquiry is a matter of 'general public importance'. This is sick.

Combined with their proposal to get rid of the Seanad on the ground of cost, this sets the scene for a malign future majority in the Dáil in the near future to be able to remove the President, remove judges, to haul ordinary citizens before them for behaviour to be condemned, to have the homes of citizens searched under court powers by investigators accompanied by gardaí, etc., etc., etc.

This madcap proposal has crept in under the radar without any proper democratic scrutiny.

If nobody in the present Government has had the courage to speak out against it when it was being cooked up in secret, how can we trust the Government in future not to abuse these powers?

All of this is truly shameful and the only thing standing between us and its terrible consequences is the voice of the people in the privacy of the ballot box this week.

Finally, lest it be said that I am motivated by the interests of 'fat-cat tribunal lawyers', I am not. I publicly spoke out repeatedly against the cost and length of tribunals. I established the successful alternative, the Commissions of Inquiry system. I initiated the reform process of excessive legal fees which is still undone five years later. I am not the mouthpiece of the judiciary or of the legal profession or of any greedy vested interest.

I think I can see this proposal for what it is – and isn't. Permit me to point out that the emperor is totally naked.

Vote No – while we still have a democracy.

Government power – abolition of the Seanad

6 June 2013

The Government today indicated its intention to wreck the Constitution by giving all power to the Dáil which it ruthlessly dominates by use of the whip system. Alone in the common law world, Ireland's democracy has already descended to a low ebb.

Any member of Dáil Éireann who votes against the wishes of the Government whips faces automatic expulsion from his or her party, sacking from any Dáil Committee, and de-selection as a Dáil candidate at the next election. A backbench TD is not allowed to speak unless his whip nominates him as a party speaker in any Dáil debate. Nor can he or she table a private members Bill or a motion without the approval of the party bosses. TDs are lobby-fodder for the whips. It was even recently reported that a small group of Fine Gael backbenchers were carpeted for setting up an informal group to promote and articulate party policy and threatened that they would face consequences unless they disbanded.

Legislation is routinely guillotined through the Dáil without debate by a Government with the largest majority in the history of the State.

Now they want to abolish the Seanad to suppress any voices in our parliament that are free to speak their minds. We will never again hear a Northern voice like that of Gordon Wilson or Seamus

Mallon in our parliament. We will never again hear a free and courageous voice like that of Mary Robinson, W.B. Yeats, Ken Whitaker, David Norris, Owen Sheehy Skeffington and many, many others in our national parliament.

Just remember that when Mary Robinson was fighting in the Seanad for the basic human right of contraception, Government whips were driving Dáil deputies through the lobbies to put into law a prohibition on condoms unless a medical doctor wrote out a prescription for a married couple that they were needed for bona fide family planning purposes.

The only way to become a future member of parliament will, if the abolitionists have their way, be to take a solemn pledge to obey the party whip or else to stand on local issues like Deputies Ming Flanagan, Michael Healy Rae and Mick Wallace. Is this the parliament we want? Is this a better parliament?

There will be no constitutional check or balance on the power of the whip-driven majority in the Dáil. Existing safeguards such as the right of the Seanad to petition the President to put a Bill to the people will be swept aside under Article 27.

The all-powerful Dáil, on a simple one-off vote any afternoon, will be able to surrender our EU tax veto, to surrender our constitutional rights and protections on a wide range of EU issues in areas like criminal law, and to abandon Ireland's right to insist on EU unanimity – measures which at the present require the consent of both Houses under Article 29. And there will be no comeback, no hope of reversing such measures, and absolutely no need to consult the people on such matters.

All of the window-dressing Dáil reform baubles cynically offered yesterday could be introduced at a stroke of the Dáil's pen tomorrow. And they could be undone the next day! They need no referendum. Why weren't they done two years ago?

If cost is the issue, then cut Senators' pay. Without any referendum, the Seanad Reform Bill now before both Houses would cut pay.

We could have a gender-balanced Seanad, with votes for Irish passport holders and Irish citizens in the Dáil tomorrow, without any referendum.

I am confident that the abolitionists' power grab will be rejected by the people. The great majority of the Labour Party opposes it and will campaign against it. A large section of Fine Gal opposes it quietly. Fianna Fáil and Sinn Féin oppose it. Civil society groups are forming to oppose it.

Real political reform is available and should be implemented. This proposal is a badly thought-out joke. The more ludicrous super-committee shadow Seanad idea was laughed out of the Bill when it was floated.

No constitutional amendment that was opposed by the main opposition parties has ever succeeded since 1937. This one is opposed by many in the Government's ranks and by broad swathes of civil society.

When our constitutional democracy is at stake, the people and not the Government whips will be the winners.

The politics of reform – reform the Seanad

An Address to the Daniel O'Connell Conference, Derrynane, Co Kerry

6 September 2013

When I was originally invited to address this conference on 'The Politics of Reform', I did not know that I would be speaking in the immediate run-up to a referendum on the future of our national parliament, the Oireachtas.

The Irish people are being called to the polls on 4 October to give their judgement on a proposal by the Government which will have far-reaching consequences for Irish democracy if approved.

The first question: consequences of abolition

I would ask every newspaper editor, every commentator, every political journalist, and every other citizen to look at the following passage, and to consider whether abolition of the Seanad amounts to 'reform', whether it improves and strengthens Irish democracy, and whether any substantial case at all has been made for it.

If the people vote to accept the Government's proposal, there are radical and irreversible consequences. A 'Yes' vote means that from 2016 onwards:

- There will be no system of parliamentary checks and balances in our Constitution at all.
- Those who control the Dáil will have absolute power in the Oireachtas.
- A majority in a single chamber, Dáil Éireann, will be able to decide under Article 15.10 which Bills will be debated, what procedures will apply to the debate on any Bill, what Bills will be guillotined, what Bills will be passed without debate and which and how many members will be heard in any debate.
- The courts will have absolutely no power to ensure time for debate or for legislation, or fair procedures, or speaking rights for minorities or independent members.
- There will be no body under the Constitution charged with the task of revising and amending Bills to make laws.
- There will be no chance of hearing voices in our parliament for people like W.B. Yeats, Mary Robinson, T.K. Whitaker, or for

famous Northern voices like Seamus Mallon, Gordon Wilson, Bríd Rodgers, or John Robb.
- The President, the judges and the Comptroller and Auditor General (our constitutional financial watch dog) will be removable by a single decision in a single chamber.
- A single decision on a single day in Dáil Éireann will enable EU laws, including treaty amendments, which will override our Constitution and decisions to abandon our EU right of veto in matters such as personal and corporate tax to come into effect without consulting the people, because the Seanad's important veto under Article 29 will be abolished.
- The possibility of having non-TD ministers, like James Dooge, as provided for in Article 28.7, will be totally abolished.
- The possibility of the President referring Bills to the people under Article 27 will be abolished.

Does anyone, anywhere, consider that the foregoing amounts to 'reform' in the commonly understood meaning of that term?

The second question: reasons offered for abolition

I now want to call on every newspaper editor, every commentator, every political journalist, and every citizen to carefully examine the case being made for abolition.

Two reasons only are advanced on Government posters: 'cost' and 'fewer politicians'.

Cost

The Government has falsely claimed that abolition would save the taxpayer €20 million per annum. We know that the real 'saving' is far, far less than that. The accounting officer of the Oireachtas testified that the direct 'saving' was €9.3 million gross. This amounts to an Exchequer benefit of about €6.5 million when the tax element is discounted – or less than €1.60 per person per year – the price of a container of milk.

- It is less than 1% of the annual budget of Dublin City Council
- It is far less than the €12.9 million annual payments that the Dáil gives from taxpayers' money to the political parties
- It is less than the total sum the Government spends annually on its non-elected political special advisors and the empty Farmleigh.

The costs 'saved' would not start for three years under the Government's proposed Constitutional amendment! If we cannot afford the Seanad now, it would be logical to scrap it now when we need the money, instead of in 2016 when we are told we will be past the crisis.

In the same three years in which there would be no Seanad savings, 2014 to 2016, the Dáil will have given the political parties €40 million and will have paid the political special advisors €10 million.

The referendum will have cost the taxpayer €14 million *this* year.

Cost, therefore, is not the issue. The cost argument is bogus. If the Government really wanted to reduce the cost of the Seanad, it would cut Senators' pay right now as is proposed in the Quinn–Zappone Bill.

Fewer politicians

The Government solemnly promised to reduce the number of TDs by 20. It has utterly broken that solemn promise, claiming that the terms of the Constitution prevent it from doing so.

Instead of keeping that promise by offering the people a constitutional amendment to deliver on their commitment, the Government slyly slithered away from it and proposed abolition of the Seanad in a referendum.

They hope the media and the people will not notice the U-turn in favour of the Dáil.

In truth, apart from throwing shapes and slogans, the 'fewer politicians' argument is really the bogus 'costs' argument put differently.

There is absolutely no reason to believe that backbench TDs, scared of losing their seats, are going to spend more of their time revising Dáil Bills as the Seanad presently does.

If fewer politicians means that Ireland's parliament does a worse and worse legislative job and never addresses EU legislation, we the citizens will be the losers, big time.

The third question: reform

I would ask every newspaper editor, every commentator, every political journalist, and every other citizen to look carefully at the Constitution itself and to see through the gross deception the Government is engaging in.

Many, many commentators have apparently swallowed the line that the Seanad cannot be reformed without yet another referendum. Nothing could be further from the truth. The Government is dishonestly trying to persuade the media and the people that the Seanad cannot be reformed and that the only choice is abolition.

There is nothing in the Constitution – *absolutely nothing* – which prevents this Government this month from giving by law every Irish citizen a vote for the elected members of the Seanad at the next election.

It was the Dáil, not the people, which enacted legislation giving politicians the only votes in Seanad panel elections. Every citizen could now by law be given a vote in the panel elections, if the Dáil will pass the Reform Bill which has already passed second stage and is currently awaiting committee stage in the Seanad.

Every citizen would then be in the same position as the university panel electors. And no citizen would have more than one vote.

Direct Seanad elections work well

And if you wonder how that would work out in practice, just look at the kind of person that one person, one vote, direct election to the Seanad has delivered.

The senators now directly elected are real, independent-minded additions to our parliament: Feargal Quinn (entrepreneur), Seán Barrett (economist), John Crown (oncologist), Ivana Bacik (law professor), David Norris (author and gay rights champion) and Rónán Mullen (conservative social commentator).

Each of them, in their own different ways, makes a hugely valuable contribution to our parliament, not only in the Seanad but also in joint Dáil–Seanad committees.

We need more of them: not 'fewer politicians'.

Without any constitutional change, all the panels could from now on be elected on the same basis by giving each citizen a right to register to vote on the panel of his or her choice – agriculture, labour, commercial, administrative, and cultural and education.

The Bill to do this is already going through our parliament. It is awaiting its committee hearing. It can be law by Christmas. That Bill is 'reform' in the real sense.

It is not a Bill for a 'Second Dáil'; it is a Bill to give to the Seanad the role the people gave to it in the Constitution, to give real participation to different, but valuable points of view in our parliamentary process.

The Bill also gives all Irish citizens who live in the North or emigrants who reside abroad a chance to register as Seanad voters in the same way as university graduates now can. That is not 'elitist' in any sense.

The Bill would also give the reformed, elected Seanad gender equality. Is that elitist?

Voting eyes wide shut

I want to make one last point. If the Government amendment is passed, there will be nothing left in the Constitution dealing with the way our laws are made.

Any new Dáil reform package will stand to be instantly reversed or bypassed by those who control the majority in the Dáil at any time in the future just as they think suits them. Article 15 makes that clear.

Reversible Dáil reform has no constitutional basis. This Government, with an enormous overall majority, promised two years ago to use the guillotine in the rarest of circumstances but has used it on 55% of Bills since then. No court can intervene.

If, at some future date, a citizen who supports abolition complains to the courts that a law was passed without debate or consideration, or if a TD who supports abolition complains that he or she was not allowed speak on the law, or even that the Dáil surrendered our EU tax veto without debate and without consulting the people, the judge might be inclined to answer:

I am sorry for your trouble. But that is exactly what you voted for 'eyes wide shut' back on 4 October 2013. You gave whoever controls the majority in the Dáil absolute power in these matters. You voted to dispense with parliamentary checks and balances. You made the Dáil party whip and the state-funded party machines supreme. You voted away the right of the Seanad to seek to have legislation referred to the people. You abolished the place where independent voices were always heard. You left the Constitution a tattered document with many articles deleted. You fell for the proposition that all that was done was 'reform'. And now you come here. There is nothing now that can be done for you in this place. Ask those whom you made your political masters for redress.

A demeaning wallop – the Seanad saved

28 December 2013

'Demeaning' was the term chosen this week by Minister Frances Fitzgerald to describe aspects of the Government's failed campaign to abolish the Seanad. We could add 'cynical', 'crass' and 'damaging' to that list.

While it is welcome that a Minister of the present Government would acknowledge that it had behaved in a demeaning way, her statement raises other important issues.

Was she simply hinting that the Government could have succeeded if it had been more subtle in its campaign? Was she herself still lamenting their failure to abolish Seanad?

After all, she herself participated in the abolition campaign – however half-heartedly and unconvincingly. But her face had shown her shock and displeasure way back when Enda Kenny first announced his 'personal initiative', as he called his stunt politics.

She was not the only Fine Gael Minister who secretly disagreed with the abolition proposal. Three other FG Cabinet colleagues have since admitted privately that they were also against abolition. A radio station poll during the campaign found even then that 46% of FG TDs also privately opposed the idea. The great majority of FG Senators were also opposed. All of which is hardly surprising, given that Enda crash-landed his 'personal initiative' on the party's decks.

As for Labour, a good 70% of their parliamentarians opposed abolition.

Is 'demeaning' not also very apt to describe the behaviour of all those parliamentarians who voted to support the Bill to amend the Constitution while privately believing it was wrong? What is it about the occupants of Leinster House that so many of them demean themselves in this way? Which comes first – loyalty to conscience, loyalty to the State's Constitution, loyalty to the whip, or loyalty to a leader?

Why did they lose their voices on the issue? I witnessed an FG parliamentarian openly admit to university students that s/he was opposed to abolition but could not be publicly seen to oppose the Bill. The students were taken aback in equal measure by the parliamentarian's candour and cowardice.

The truth is that they were afraid to stand up for their opinions. Afraid of the consequences for their careers. Afraid of the dud opinion polls which suggested that resistance to the 'personal initiative' was pointless. Nor were they alone in that fear. Many others were cowed by the prospect of openly opposing the Government. They included prominent public figures, NGOs, learned institutions, representative bodies and unions. Newspapers which had run opposing editorials trimmed their sails in the last week to advocate a Yes vote. Large swathes of civil society decided to keep schtum.

And now there is the issue of Seanad reform. Labour and Fine Gael Ministers recently meekly agreed in Cabinet to Enda Kenny's proposal to avoid Seanad reform by simply drafting a Bill and legislating to extend the university franchise, a measure of which 92% of the voters approved of decades ago in a referendum. Let's be very clear. That reform leaves 90% of the Seanad *un-reformed*. Only six seats out of sixty are affected.

How cynical can you get? Can you remember Government Ministers attacking the narrow base of the electorate for the Seanad's panel seats during the referendum campaign? They decried the fact that they themselves had seven votes while many citizens had none. Is that not to change now?

If Frances Fitzgerald found that her Government ran a 'demeaning' campaign for abolition, is she now satisfied to rubber-stamp a 'demeaning' pretence at reform?

What about Labour? Have they lost their compass completely?

There isn't going to be another referendum on Seanad reform. This Government is not going to sponsor two Seanad reform Bills in this term of office. If there is no real reform Bill passed now, the next Seanad will look more or less the same as this one.

Real reform starts now or is postponed for a decade. That is the choice we all face.

This issue will not go away. Those who championed Seanad reform are not going to lie down.

Without any referendum a Seanad Reform Bill could give a single vote to every citizen on the panel of his or her choice in the next Seanad election in two years' time. That could include citizens in the North and Irish passport holders abroad. The Bill could give us a gender-balanced Seanad – again without a referendum.

It is arrant nonsense to say that a reformed Seanad would become a rival Dáil or would make the business of government unworkable.

The Constitution was devised to ensure that the Dáil would enjoy supremacy. The limited powers given to the Seanad and President in relation to legislation mean that the Government does not have to control the Seanad's membership. The Dáil is and will remain the chamber which elects and removes the Government, and the chamber to which Ministers are responsible and accountable. The Dáil alone decides budgetary policy.

When you think about it, the very limitations on the powers of the Seanad were a clear acknowledgment that the Dáil and the Government could function properly *without* controlling the Seanad.

Enda Kenny thinks he can get away with leaving 90% of the Seanad seats in a rotten borough controlled by the political parties. He said he got a wallop for getting the referendum wrong.

He will get far more than a wallop if he rides roughshod over the vote of the people.

The people voted to keep a reformed Seanad in our constitution. Enda, Frances and Labour are asking for much more than a wallop if they shortchange us now.

REPEALING THE EIGHTH

Making a vote to repeal into a vote to endorse the twelve-week on-demand regime could be an unforced political error

25 February 2018

As someone who believes strongly that the Eighth Amendment should now be repealed and that the issues of abortion should be one to be dealt with by laws enacted by the Oireachtas as it considers right and just, I hesitate to become involved in any heated or bitter debate or campaigning because I know well how intense the emotional feelings are on either side of the argument.

But I thought it appropriate to devote some space here to aspects of the controversy that may be swamped in the to-and-fro of predictable debate.

The Definite Article: REFERENDUMS AND CONSTITUTIONAL ISSUES

From a lawyer's point of view, I think we should be very clear as to what can and cannot be achieved by law – whether it is constitutional law, statute law or judge-made common law.

The Constitution is our supreme law. It cannot deal with very complex issues without extensive interpretation. Ultimately, the Constitution means what the Supreme Court says it means – subject to the capacity of the people to amend it.

The Eighth Amendment seemed so harmless and simple to a majority of the electorate when it was passed. It was proposed by those who claimed that we could not rely on the judiciary in the 1980s to uphold as constitutional the criminal law which prohibited abortion. It was put to the people in a referendum by political parties which feared the electoral consequences of being seen to be in any way soft on abortion.

And yet the Eighth Amendment gave rise within ten years to the X Case, in which the Supreme Court, by a majority, ruled that the Eighth Amendment justified granting travel injunctions but permitted abortion in Ireland on the basis of a risk of suicide. That decision, in turn, gave rise to a remedial amendment of Article 40.3.3 to prohibit travel injunctions and to permit information on abortion outside the State to be made available here in limited circumstances. An amendment to exclude suicide as a basis for abortion in the State was, however, rejected by the people twice in twelve years.

Hard cases such as Savita Halappanavar's and cases concerning fatal foetal abnormality kept coming to the surface. The last government's Protection of Life in Pregnancy Act caused great political difficulty and achieved very little change in practical terms, save to provide in statute law for termination of a pregnancy in the case of established suicide risk – a result on which the Supreme Court had already decided in the X Case twenty years previously.

The major new contextual development has been the increasing availability of pharmaceutical abortifacients – from the 'morning-after pill' to pills capable of terminating a pregnancy up to twelve weeks.

The issue that faces us now is simple and stark: Do we want to make or keep it a criminal offence punishable in law for a young woman to use such an abortion pill six weeks into a crisis pregnancy?

If so, do we want to jail such an offender or her friend who supplied her with such a pill? And, again, do we want simply to shame such a girl if discovered and convicted by a fine or a suspended sentence? Do we want such a girl to go without any medical treatment arising from such a termination for fear of prosecution? Do we want to attempt to prevent such pills from being brought into the country? Who is going to prevent that and how? Do we want to strike a doctor off the Medical Register for telling a girl abut such a pill or advising her to take it?

These questions must be answered truthfully and honestly by all of us. We may like or dislike, approve or condemn, abortion as a matter of principle or moral conviction. But we must address these questions fair and square.

And if we do not want, and are not prepared, to criminally sanction the use of such pills or to take any of the foregoing steps to punish and sanction those involved in their use, are we simply being asked to turn a blind eye to the emergence of a de facto twilight abortion regime in the State that is too embarrassing to prevent? Are we to allow the Eighth Amendment to remain but somehow to wither into desuetude and irrelevance?

Such a scenario, coupled with a constitutional right to travel and a constitutional right to information about these pills (but only on the basis they are taken outside the State), and a ban on terminations which are sought to end fatal foetal abnormalities and continued monitoring for foetal heartbeat as in Savita's case, and a ban on any termination to preserve the mother's health (as distinct from her life), seems increasingly indefensible and unsustainable.

These issues are the issues that confronted the Citizens' Assembly and the All Party Oireachtas Committee. These issues fully explain their considered reports.

Having said all that, I have to say one thing more.

Most people have not given the issues the sustained consideration that the Citizens' Assembly or the Oireachtas Committee have. Most people have not been confronted with these issues, the evidence, and the consequences.

It would be a mistake for politicians who favour repeal to presume that the thinking of the Assembly or the Committee is obvious or easily discoverable.

I think that those who would vote to repeal the Eighth Amendment may not all accept that the twelve-week on-demand legalisation is the only and inevitable consequence of repeal. Some may, like Simon Coveney, wish to approach the issue in two stages – first repeal the ban on legislation; second let the Oireachtas formulate the laws dealing with the matter.

Making a vote to repeal into a vote to endorse the twelve-week on-demand regime could be an unforced political error that tips the scales against repeal in a narrow contest. The two-stage approach may be the wiser approach.

There is a danger that the experience of the marriage equality referendum justifies linking proposed legislation to the constitutional referendum. This referendum is, with respect, quite a deal more complex than the marriage equality referendum; compassion is a two-way street on the subject of abortion.

Loss of the referendum would be politically catastrophic for the Government and for the Taoiseach and, I think, for the country. Today's *Sunday Business Post* Red C poll should remind those in government that nothing is to be presumed or taken for granted.

I am not suggesting timidity; I am just counselling against presumption. I am suggesting that the pro-repeal vote is probably more complex and less unanimous in supporting the Government's proposed legislation than some in Merrion Street and Kildare Street might think.

I suggest the immediate imperative is to get repeal over the line on the basis of maximising the repeal vote. The Oireachtas is there to legislate on this complex issue if, and only if, the people give it that role.

Let's not rush our fences and come a cropper to a No vote swollen by political presumption.

The Eighth Amendment repealed: the circumstances that brought us to this moment

27 May 2018

The outcome of Friday's referendum marks, I hope, the beginning of the end of a particularly fraught period in Irish politics and law.

If the Eighth Amendment had never been made in 1983, the complexity of all the issues surrounding the circumstances in which a pregnancy may be ended would most likely have been reflected in a series of enactments by the Oireachtas to adapt our laws to modern realities and attitudes.

But elevating those complexities to be governed by a simplistic constitutional formula was a profound error, albeit an error made in good faith by many people.

People these days often have only a dim and fading appreciation of the circumstances that brought us to this moment. And it as well now to call them to mind.

Ireland in the 1980s was a very different place. The State had in 1935 criminalised contraception and family planning until the Supreme Court in 1973 held that the law in question violated the rights of a married woman, Mrs McGee, to matrimonial privacy.

An attempt in 1971 by Senator Mary Robinson to repeal the 1935 legislation was not even granted a first reading in parliament; the Catholic hierarchy condemned her Bill as a 'curse upon the country'.

Even then, our legislators (who the pro-life movement have recently spent months telling us are not to be trusted) reacted very ponderously to the McGee decision.

The then Taoiseach, Liam Cosgrave, voted against his own Government's remedial Bill in 1974. It failed. Charlie Haughey, in 1979, pushed through legislation with some difficulty, restricting all forms of artificial contraception (including condoms) to married persons who had obtained a doctor's prescription for bona fide family planning purposes.

Conservative Catholic bodies campaigned to prevent any legalisation of contraception. Those bodies then coalesced and expanded into a pro-life movement which had decided to prevent any further judicial reform in the area by having a pro-life article inserted into the Constitution.

By that means, they hoped, neither the legislature nor the courts could relax in any way the total ban on abortion without a referendum.

Because of the highly competitive political balance between Garret FitzGerald's Fine Gael and Charlie Haughey's Fianna Fáil, the major parties were very vulnerable to the pro-life movement's disapproval on the grounds of being 'soft on abortion'.

As part of Garret's modernisation of Fine Gael, one of its vice-presidencies came to be occupied by a young medical student who was a member of Young Fine Gael. In a media interview, she expressed the view that there were some limited circumstances in which she thought abortion was justified.

This brought in the roof on her. Her views were immediately disowned and she was 'encouraged' to resign as a party vice-president. But the damage had been done.

The pro-life movement now had a pretext to label FG as 'soft on abortion'. To staunch the bleeding political wound, Garret engaged with the idea of a pro-life amendment. Naturally Fianna Fáil followed suit and drafted the Eighth Amendment Bill. Fine Gael and Labour won the election.

Despite the clearest warnings from the newly appointed attorney general, Peter Sutherland, the Eighth Amendment was put to the people and passed in 1983.

Now SPUC (the Society for the Protection of Unborn Children) commenced a campaign to prevent bodies like students' unions and the Dublin Well Woman Centre from giving any information about the fact that abortion was available in England to women and girls in Ireland.

SPUC obtained injunctions from the High and Supreme Courts threatening any person or body from disseminating information or counselling any woman about her option to go to England for an abortion. The sanction they held over their defendants was imprisonment for contempt of court.

Nearly all of the older leading figures in the No side in Friday's referendum were active supporters of the SPUC drive against information and counselling in the 1980s.

Then came the 1992 X Case, which convulsed the country.

The High Court, at the insistence of the Attorney General, handed down an injunction to a 14-year-old rape victim and her parents requiring her to return to Ireland and prohibiting her from having an abortion in England.

Most people were rightly shocked. They had been assured by the pro-life movement back in 1983 that such an order would never be made.

On appeal to the Supreme Court, a majority held that the injunction should be lifted. But the court did not find that travel injunctions were wrong; on the contrary, the Supreme Court only held that the uncontested evidence that the pregnancy, if continued, constituted a real and substantial suicide risk for the schoolgirl made it lawful to terminate the pregnancy – whether in England or, horror of horrors, in Ireland.

The pro-life movement was outraged. They immediately demanded that suicide be excluded as a ground for termination in Ireland, saying the people had never voted for that. Their supporters spread the rumour widely that the whole case had been contrived.

The liberal majority too had had enough. They demanded that the Constitution be amended to stop any more travel injunctions and to stop SPUC injunctions on providing information in Ireland concerning the availability of abortion in England.

Albert Reynolds responded to the public disquiet with three separate proposals for constitutional change – the Twelfth, Thirteenth and Fourteenth Amendment Bills. The people rejected the Twelfth Amendment Bill disallowing suicide as a ground. They approved the Thirteenth Amendment Bill prohibiting travel injunctions for pregnant girls and women. And they approved the Fourteenth Amendment Bill allowing for the provision of abortion information, subject to legislation.

This outcome meant that the legislature should make provision for suicide as a ground for abortion in Ireland. But the 'never to be trusted' legislators (including myself) never did so; it took the death of Savita Halappanavar for the highly restrictive 2013 Protection of Life In Pregnancy Act to be passed. Bertie Ahern had in the meantime committed to revisiting the suicide issue, but his proposals were rejected in 2002 by a combination of liberal voters and hard-line pro-life voters.

Friday's vote shows that Ireland has changed.

The people, or a majority of them, have moved on from the Ireland of the 1980s in which the Catholic social conservatives still live – and would wish to have us all still live.

A large amount of this arises from the institutional and theological obsessions of the Catholic Church with sexuality, purity, celibacy, and subordination of women.

From the 1930s encyclical *Casti Connubii*, which equated family planning with the 'sin of Onan' and proclaimed the husband to be the naturally ordained head of the family, to *Humane Vitae* in 1968, the Catholic Church has been on a self-destructive theological journey over a cliff. Ironically, John Paul II was one of the principal advocates of *Humanae Vitae*.

The clerical hardliners have left many, many people who aspire to be Christian behind them.

The cost to the institutional Church and its standing has been enormous. Its influence on Irish society has collapsed. The signs were on it with the marriage equality referendum result. While social attitudes vary geographically and by age cohort, modern Ireland has moved on.

In terms of politics, things are changing too. While the pro-life campaigners insisted politicians are not to be trusted, they must now realise that the contrary is the case.

The people, their elected politicians, and their duly appointed judges are to be trusted. Women are to be trusted.

Maybe some people should now ask themselves whether their own atavistic attitudes and dogmas are to be trusted.

The Eighth Amendment was meant to be the ultimate bastion of moral conservatism. But its wording was so extreme as to carry with it the seed of its own destruction.

Referendums are the occasion for a simple binary choice. By making their beliefs and values subject to a simple binary judgement, the well-meaning and the zealots have repeated their mistake of 1983.

Things are not always black and white. Relativism may be a dirty word in some theological circles, but it is the coinage of politics and the antidote to absolutism.

Now I and the other legislators must use our skills to enact workable and compassionate laws. We have been entrusted with that task by the Irish people. We will not rush into laws that are ahead of the centre of political gravity.

But we have no reason to be afraid of doing what we feel to be right and just according to our own judgements now; we should reclaim that right and that duty from the long shadow of harmful absolutism in which it languished for thirty years.

THE FAMILY AND CARE REFERENDUMS

I'm voting No–No as reckless amendments will only cause uncertainty

3 March 2024

Last week Minister Roderic O'Gorman had an extensive and searching interview with Hugh O'Connell in these pages in which he blandly asserted that critics of his referendums were wrong. As I read the piece, it became increasingly clear that it's the referendums that are 'wrong' – not their critics.

We are being asked by two separate ballot papers to decide on amendments to one single article in our Constitution.

One of the proposed amendments asks us to decide that the family as provided for in Article 41 of the Constitution need not be based on marriage but can be based on 'durable relationships' in future.

It's good to remind ourselves of what the Constitution says in Article 41.1 about the family. This definition would not change on 8 March.

The constitutional family is stated to be 'the natural primary and fundamental unit group of Society', and 'a moral institution, possessing inalienable and imprescriptible rights, antecedent and superior to all positive law', having 'its constitution and authority', and as 'the necessary basis of social order' and 'indispensable to the welfare of the Nation and the State'.

The Supreme Court held in the recent O'Meara decision that citizens are and must be entirely free to choose *not* to marry if they want to avoid the burdens and obligations or if they do want any State involvement in their private lives, and that marriage is a 'legal status freely chosen by the parties with knowledge that it involves a corpus of rights and obligations, burdens and benefits'.

Everyone knows whether or not they are married. Nobody knows who is or who is not in a 'durable relationship' unless a court decides in a disputed case that it is 'durable'. Nobody knows how and when a 'durable relationship' between two adults ends in the eyes of the law.

Asked by Hugh O'Connell whether a married person who separates from his or her spouse would be free, without getting a divorce, to become part of a second constitutional family based on a different 'durable relationship', Minister O'Gorman couldn't answer 'yes' or 'no' but said that it would depend on the 'magnitude of that relationship'. With respect, that is nonsense.

But it is legal and logical nonsense that lies at the very heart of the referendum proposals. He proposes that such undefined non-marital 'durable relationships' will create constitutionally recognised families that are 'moral institutions' with 'inalienable rights', each with their own 'constitution and authority', and will be regarded as 'the necessary basis of social order' and be regarded the courts as 'indispensable' to the State's welfare. Is he serious?

He ignores the inconvenient fact that the Constitution requires, and will continue to require, that applicants for divorce obtain a court order that must be refused unless proper provision has been made for spouses and dependents. None of those safeguards will apply to persons exiting non-marital 'durable relationships'. They will end in the case of two childless adults informally and without court orders. The non-marital 'family' involved will simply evaporate.

But if, as the minister now proposes, a single mother is recognised as a constitutional family with her child, and she later cohabits with a man and has a second child, could their 'durable relationship' make them a second constitutionally recognised family? If he later moves out and into a second 'durable relationship' with a different woman, will that give rise to a second or third constitutionally recognised family?

Where will that leave the first single mother? Will she be in a different constitutionally recognised family with two children?

Will the man be simultaneously a part of two constitutionally recognised families?

Is any of the foregoing seriously described as being the 'the necessary basis of social order' or 'indispensable to the welfare of the Nation and the State'? And yet, Minister Thomas Byrne told RTÉ's *Upfront* viewers last week that these domestic situations occur all the time.

Minister O'Gorman blithely assured Hugh O'Connell that the Government had the Attorney General's assurance that the amendments would not impact tax law, family law, social welfare law, succession law, pensions law, and immigration and pensions law. I find that hard to credit, having been Attorney General myself.

The Attorney General recently unsuccessfully defended existing social welfare provisions in the recent O'Meara case, which invoked Article 40 equality rights and Article 42A children's rights to force the Government to afford Mr O'Meara a widower's social welfare payment, despite the fact that he was unmarried.

Take this example. Two neighbouring households, each with parents and four children, have existed for 20 years. The father in each case owns the house, and in one case the unmarried father dies. His partner does not inherit his estate and the house tax-free as would happen next door. The unmarried household is much poorer than the married household and the tax bill is devastating for them, possibly requiring sale of their home.

If the unmarried woman, like Mr O'Meara, sues the State claiming that she is part of a constitutional family based on a 'durable relationship' recognised as such because of its 20 years' existence, and claims the family is being 'arbitrarily' discriminated against solely because it was not based on marriage, would the Attorney General be any more successful than he was in the O'Meara case, relying on the special status of marriage?

When we alter our Constitution, we as citizens need to understand the effects. When the Eighth Amendment was proposed in 1981, my late and very close friend Adrian Hardiman, then a barrister and later a great Supreme Court judge, warned on *Questions and Answers* that it would bring travel injunctions on women travelling to England for abortions. His warning was dismissed by the amendment's proponents.

In 1992, the Supreme Court was invited to uphold just such a travel injunction in the case of a juvenile rape victim by counsel for the then Attorney General. We needed two referendums just to reverse that decision. And we eventually repealed the entire Eighth Amendment with a third referendum.

Putting words into the Constitution that nobody clearly explains or understands is collective madness and reckless. Reversing unwanted judicial interpretations needs a referendum, not just a statute.

The 39th Amendment would introduce gross social uncertainty; the 40th Amendment removes all recognition of mothers and women from the Constitution and offers no new enforceable rights to carers or people, including people with disabilities, who need care. All of the major issues are dealt with in the *Lawyers for No* paper available online at www.michaelmcdowell.ie.

I advise rejection. No and No.

Irish people victims of referendum campaign of concealment by Government

22 May 2024

There are profound ethical, accountability and constitutional issues in light of the belated discovery of documents demonstrating that the Irish people were victims of a campaign of sustained concealment by their own government in the course of the referendums on the family and care.

It isn't a matter of those who opposed the referendums engaging in some kind of 'I told you so' lap of honour at this point. There should be personal and political ministerial accountability on these matters.

In retrospect it is blindingly obvious that the proposed family amendment was always going to have profound implications for family law, succession law, taxation law, immigration law, welfare law and pensions law.

In all those areas, constitutional equality provisions, and family and children's constitutional rights were going to oblige the courts either to re-interpret or to invalidate many existing laws referring to the exclusive rights, entitlements, and obligations of members of families based on marriage so as not to unfairly prejudice the rights of similar persons in non-marital, 'durable' relationships.

And those who pointed out those implications were systematically contradicted and accused of scaremongering by Government ministers and others in the media – an offensive and groundless implication of political manipulation or recklessness on the part of those opposed to the amendments.

Of course, politicians and lawyers have the right to differ in the course of public as well as private debate. But the matter becomes much more serious if the people's Government actively misrepresents or minimises knock-on implications of a decision that is reserved by our constitution for determination by the people in a single binary process.

By dishonestly claiming that the durable relationship family amendment could have no consequences for statute law in those areas and at the same time dishonestly claiming that the care amendment (which had been carefully neutered in its wording to prevent significant entitlements) could have beneficial knock-on constitutional implications, the Government and their supporters now appear to be the cynical manipulators of public opinion.

It is wrong that ministers should now hide behind what they claim was the advice of the Attorney General, to justify their misrepresentation of the implications of their proposals and seek by that means to defend the indefensible.

I have absolutely no problem with the general rule and convention that the Government is entitled to obtain and to keep confidential the advice of the Attorney General of the Government in all 'matters of law and legal opinion' under Article 30 of the Constitution. No holder of that office would differ with that. It follows that the Government must be extremely careful and circumspect in ever departing from that convention.

But we are all equally bound to uphold the Constitution, and ministers cannot simply engage in bland assertions about the meaning of proposed amendments, invoking the confidential advice of the Attorney General to prevent proper scrutiny of their own proposed amendments.

If it was proper to inform the public that the Attorney General had advised that there were simply no knock-on implications in the areas of family law, succession law, taxation law, immigration law, welfare law and pensions law in extending the constitutional family to 'other durable relationships', one would have expected that there was in the hands of ministers a separate, detailed analysis of each of those fields made by the Attorney General personally to that effect.

Such analysis would have had to deal with and refute each and every adverse implication or risk we now know was identified by agencies of state involved in the interdepartmental process which had oversight of the referendum proposals.

I cannot believe that such categorical advice was, or could have been, given to the Government, especially in the light of the O'Meara decision of the Supreme Court.

Nor can I believe that the newly established Electoral Commission could or would ever have offered any such advice to the people – even if it had the time and resources to analyse those matters in the rushed time frame it was afforded.

The Attorney General's internal advice was redacted from the recently published records of the interdepartmental process leading to the referendum proposals. Even those redacted records were wrongly withheld from the public until after they had voted.

The bottom line is this: if the Government claims in a referendum on constitutional amendment that *their* proposal (not that of any Attorney General) will or will not have knock-on implications for the people, their laws or the state, and seeks to convince citizens to make constitutional change on the basis of Attorney General's advice, the people as sovereign in our state must have a constitutional right to examine, accept or reject that advice. The Attorney General is the legal advisor of the Government – not of the people or even the Oireachtas.

Referendums are not mere political games. What we now belatedly know happened seems disgraceful and should have political consequence.

Citizens' Assembly is a phony piece of window dressing

7 August 2016

The Citizens' Assembly which the Government has decided to convene is, in my view, a somewhat ridiculous idea. That is why I spoke and voted against it in the Seanad.

The media have, in general, left the public largely in the dark about its purpose and its composition. Anyone that I have spoken to believes that it has been only convened to consider the whole question of the Eighth Amendment (which inserted a constitutional right to life for the unborn into Bunreacht na hÉireann).

But that is not true. The same Citizens' Assembly, surprisingly, has also been charged to consider and report on a number of other completely disparate and puzzlingly chosen topics, namely:

- Global warming
- How we should plan for the growing number of elderly people in society
- How we handle referendums
- Whether we should amend the Constitution to provide for fixed-term parliaments.

Does any of this surprise you or strike you as strange? Why should public money be spent on getting 99 people chosen at random from the electoral register by a polling company to consider these wholly unconnected topics?

The Assembly will be chaired by a member of the Supreme Court, Ms Justice Mary Laffoy, who is by any standard a very capable and independent-minded person. Its secretariat will commission expert advisers and reports, hear submissions from interested lobby groups, and deliberate on all these issues with a view to reporting its views to the Oireachtas, our national parliament.

The first point that needs to be made is that these issues are ones which under the Constitution are the business of the Oireachtas and its two chambers, composed in all of 218 members. These are issues of policy to be considered by legislators in any democracy. So why do the constitutional deliberative assemblies now need to convene a randomly selected group of 99 citizens to do their thinking and deliberation for them?

This is not a case of seeking a report from a group of experts on difficult and complex issues which are beyond the competence of legislators unguided.

On the contrary, the 99 randomly chosen citizens are being assembled precisely because they are not expert. If they are to hear experts and receive submissions from interested parties, why cannot the parliamentarians simply receive the same input directly?

What does the interposition of 99 randomly chosen citizens add to the process of receiving the evidence and considering it?

To take one issue, the Eights Amendment, any change to the Constitution will have to be considered by the Dáil and Seanad.

Why should the members of those Houses not hear at first hand the experts in question and deal with the interest groups for themselves directly? In what sense does the collective opinion (or more likely the set of diverse opinions) among 99 randomly chosen citizens on the issue refine the issues or winnow out the irrelevant? In what sense are they considered to be wiser or better informed than parliamentarians?

Citizens' Assembly is a phony piece of window dressing

Is the Citizens' Assembly anything other than an elaborate political focus group? Is the Government using it as a risk-free exercise in market research?

Or will we be told that because the Citizens' Assembly has heard expert evidence or the evidence of interest groups there is no need for the Oireachtas to examine the issues in the same degree of detail?

I am afraid that the dreadful truth is that the Fine Gael dominated Government simply wants 'political cover' on the issue of the Eighth Amendment.

The Assembly provides 'cover' for doing nothing in the meantime while we 'await' its reports. If the majority of the Assembly recommends repeal or further amendment of the Eighth Amendment, that too will provide further 'cover' for scared politicians. If the result is inconclusive, yet more 'cover' for doing nothing. Like the Lion in *The Wizard of Oz*, our political class is heading off down the Yellow Brick Road in pursuit of courage.

Why are we even thinking of having a constitutional change in relation to fixed-term parliaments? Who came up with this idea?

We have had long-lasting parliaments and governments for twenty years. And before that we had a change of government from the FF/Labour coalition to John Bruton's Rainbow coalition without an election in 1994.

The present constitutional arrangements work well as regards stable government. The minority government situation that we have now arises purely from political cynicism and certainly does not need to be sealed in place with a fixed-term parliament amendment to the Constitution.

If a coalition government falls apart, and the members of the Dáil are not minded to replace the coalition with a different coalition as they did in 1994, the people are entitled to decide on the issue. We already have a constitutional role for the President to refuse a dissolution to a Taoiseach who has lost the support of the Dáil. What more do we need?

What good would be served in denying a Taoiseach the right to seek a new mandate from the people?

And for heaven's sake, what new insight are 99 randomly chosen citizens going to give us on global warming? Or on the issue of ageing?

Is the other extremely vague Assembly issue of 'how we run referendums' a smokescreen for reintroducing a right for politicians to use taxpayers' money to persuade us to vote the way they want us to? Or is it to change our right to be consulted by referendum on EU issues?

Having seen the somewhat similar Constitutional Convention (a mix of politicians and randomly chosen citizens) established by the last government at first hand, I strongly believe that the agenda and thinking of such bodies is largely driven by the secretariat's agenda – especially in choosing expert advisers and witnesses.

Regretfully, I consider the Citizens' Assembly to be a phony piece of window dressing, of political procrastination and bullet dodging, and a cynical waste of time and money.

Maybe its theme song should be 'Ninety-Nine Lead Balloons'.

Fixed-term parliaments, child voting, and proxy voting subvert the Constitution

23 October 2019

Watching the procedural trench warfare at Westminster over the last weeks, you cannot fail to be struck by the consequences of not having a written constitution in the United Kingdom.

To take a simple example, their hugely problematic Fixed Term Parliament Act simply could not have been enacted in Ireland.

Fixed-term parliaments, child voting, and proxy voting subvert the Constitution

Why not? The Constitution provides that the President must dissolve Dáil Éireann when advised to do so by the Taoiseach – except in the case of a Taoiseach who has lost the support of a majority in the Dáil, when a dissolution may be refused in the President's absolute discretion.

Our Constitution only provides an outer limit to the life of a Dáil – seven years or such lesser term as may be fixed by law. And the present law fixes a five-year term.

Likewise, a Taoiseach can only be appointed if Dáil Éireann has nominated him or her for appointment by the President. In the UK, the Queen chooses the Prime Minister by an unwritten convention, inviting a person from the largest party to form a government. Thus Boris Johnson was never actually chosen by a majority in the House of Commons.

The Dáil approves individual members of our government proposed for office by the Taoiseach. Not so in Westminster.

The infamous power to prorogue parliament vested in the Crown does not exist in Ireland. Each House of the Oireachtas decides on the length of its sessions and adjournments. Suspending sittings for political advantage against the wishes of parliamentarians (as recently invalidated by the UK Supreme Court) is not possible under our Constitution.

More topical is the question of 'absentee voting' in the Houses of the Oireachtas.

Article 15.11 of our Constitution is very clear. Every question in either House must be decided by a majority of those of its members who are both present and voting.

So proxy voting is unconstitutional. Any attempt knowingly to vote on behalf of an absent member is therefore nothing less than an attempt to subvert the Constitution.

On every division, tellers are appointed. Where the vote is electronic, those tellers try to ensure that votes are only cast by members who are present. On walk-through votes, the tellers stand in the Tá or Níl lobbies and mark off those members as they pass through to vote.

Electronic voting does speed things up. But it also depends on trust. The tellers cannot oversee every hand on every button. That trust would be shattered if tellers cannot depend on the electronic record.

Likewise, standing orders of each House allow tellers to demand a walk-through vote as of right rather than accept the electronic voting result. Sometimes this right is used to ensure that a person locked out for a speeded-up electronic vote has a second chance to attend and vote.

Voting electronically for an absentee TD is a very serious matter. And it must be treated as very serious unless it can be shown to result from a bona fide mistake.

Bona fide mistakes can and do occur on every side of each of the Houses. It is quite easy to make a voting mistake. As a teller, I have seen members vote the 'wrong way' simply by pushing the wrong button or by confusing whether a resolution phrased in the negative is what they had actually wished to support.

In cases of bona fide error, tellers readily amend and initial in manuscript the corrected electronic printout before the result is reported to the Chair for announcement.

The matter could be easily addressed by requiring TDs to remain in their designated seats for the one-minute electronic voting period and storing photographic images of the deputies while seated with the result for comparison.

Micheál Martin was right to act decisively in relation to the Dooley–Collins matter. They have a case to answer. He was equally right to accept Lisa Chambers' explanation of a bona fide error.

We should reject any suggestion of amending our Constitution to allow distance or proxy voting in parliament. Public dissatisfaction with low attendance in the Dáil would be compounded if

Fixed-term parliaments, child voting, and proxy voting subvert the Constitution

members were allowed to vote electronically from their constituencies or from ministerial offices or other places in Leinster House.

In 2018, the Citizens' Assembly voted narrowly to amend our Constitution to introduce fixed-term parliaments. This was a classic case of a 'solution in search of a problem'.

What is wrong with having flexibility in the lifetime of a parliament? What is wrong with giving the Taoiseach the right to request a dissolution of the Dáil and allowing the people to re-elect it? Why change that when the President has discretion to refuse a dissolution to a Taoiseach who has lost majority support and where there is a prospect that the Dáil will nominate another Taoiseach?

Look at Westminster, if you have doubts.

The Citizens' Assembly also recommended lowering the age of eligibility to become President to 21. That notion was overwhelmingly rejected by the people – and rightly so.

I seriously question their other recommendation to lower the voting age to 16.

If 16-year-olds can't legally drive, buy drink, buy Lotto tickets, be bound in contract, or be named in juvenile courts, and are classified as child refugee applicants, it is very difficult to justify according them votes in referendums and elections. Nobody is suggesting lowering the general age of majority to 16.

Our Constitution is a solid foundation for our democracy. It is not immutable; neither is it a test bench for faddish reform. Just as it prohibits absentee voting in the Dáil, it also avoids the constitutional chaos we are witnessing in Westminster.

There is real work to be done on real issues that affect our democracy. The Taoiseach should now deliver on his government's clear, but shamefully abandoned, commitment to reform the system of electing the Seanad. And there is no excuse for not having the long-delayed independent Electoral Commission – except perhaps that the relevant department is also responsible for housing policy.

Judicial Appointments Commission Bill is unconstitutional

15 March 2023

The Government hopes before Easter to pass legislation that amounts, in my view, to a gross subversion of the architecture of Bunreacht na hÉireann and a massive breach of the constitutional separation of powers between legislature, executive and judiciary that has existed in Ireland for 100 years. That legislation is the Judicial Appointments Commission Bill 2022.

If enacted, it will become unlawful for the Government to appoint at least five and possibly seven current ordinary members of the Supreme Court to the position of Chief Justice whenever next that position becomes vacant. How can that be?

The proposed commission, a group of eight people, four of them serving judges and four lay members, will submit a shortlist of three names from which alone the Government may choose one for the President to appoint Chief Justice. There will be no casting vote on the names to be included in the shortlist. The Commission will include the Attorney General but he or she will have no vote.

Since the Supreme Court now consists of a Chief Justice and eight ordinary members (there is one vacancy) and two ex officio members (the Presidents of the Court of Appeal and the High Court), by definition, submitting a shortlist of three names will render a majority – at least five, and conceivably seven – of members of the Supreme Court legally incapable of becoming Chief Justice.

For the first time in a century, the Government will be legally prevented from choosing freely among the serving members of the Supreme Court whom to appoint as Chief Justice.

The Constitution provides that the Government advises the President on whom to appoint Chief Justice. It has always been the case heretofore that the Constitution was understood as vesting the discretion to make such an appointment in the executive and not in the legislature.

But the Oireachtas is now being asked to pass a law taking that constitutional discretion away from the Government and giving it by law to a group of four judges and four laypersons – giving an effective veto to the four judges on appointing from among a majority of the members of the Supreme Court.

The Bill also accords to the same judicial bloc of four an effective veto on any appointment of any new judges or on the promotion of any judge to any higher court or to the presidency of any court.

Simply by excluding any person from a shortlist of three, the four judicial members of the Commission will hold a self-selecting veto over the entire future composition of the judiciary.

No major common law country with a written constitution – Australia, New Zealand, Canada, or even the United States – permits such a system. The executive or government is the body given sole discretion in selecting judges. The only exception is South Africa, where the constitution explicitly provides for a shortlist system.

Among the three EU member states with common law elements to their constitution – Malta, Cyprus and Ireland – the choice of judges is generally vested in the executive.

It is, of course, lawful for the Oireachtas to prescribe by law minimum eligibility requirements to be appointed a judge. Those cannot be discretionary. But when it comes to a very different matter – discretion as to who among eligible candidates is to be appointed – the Irish Constitution has vested that discretion in the Government.

It is solely a function of the democratically elected government to evaluate the suitability of candidates for judicial office by reference to their philosophical outlooks – conservative or liberal or radical. No commission – not even of judges – can or should be given that function. The fig leaf of a shortlist leaves discretion largely with those drawing up the list who can exclude at will.

Our system has served Ireland well for a century. We have a really good, independent, competent and impartial judiciary. This Bill is the classic 'solution in search of a problem'; it is no solution of a non-problem to accord a veto over all judicial appointments to a four-member blocking group of judges pursuing their own discretionary views about the entire future judiciary.

If this curtailment of the Government's constitutional role can be enacted, why not go one step further and reduce the shortlist to one? Or give the power of shortlisting to a Dáil judiciary committee?

Despite the Bill's long title, which cites inapplicable EU civil law opinions on the matter, I believe that this Bill is manifestly unconstitutional and *ultra vires* the legislature.

The huge constitutional issue involved cannot be decided on the secret advice of an Attorney General. A very, very different view was taken by Attorneys General in 1994 and later.

The Bill ought to be referred to the Supreme Court under Article 26 before it becomes law. A later invalidation could be very damaging.

100 years ago the fuse was lit – now we owe it to ourselves to deliver a true democracy

3 April 2016

There is absolutely no constitutional reason why the majority of the Seanad should continue to be elected by a tiny electorate, consisting of less than one in every four thousand of the citizens – namely TDs, county and borough councillors and outgoing senators – or, for that matter, why this tiny electorate should continue to have five votes each.

There is no impediment in the Constitution to opening the five vocational panel elections to ordinary citizens. A simple Act of the Oireachtas could provide for that.

100 years ago the fuse was lit – now we owe it to ourselves to deliver a true democracy

The Quinn/Zappone Bill by Feargal Quinn and Katherine Zappone proposed that every citizen should be permitted to register as a voter for one of the vocational panels of interest to that citizen. The seats in each such panel could, in this way, be filled by senators elected by ordinary citizens who had an interest in, say, education, agriculture or cultural matters.

A recent report by a cross-party group chaired by Maurice Manning suggested a compromise between the Quinn/Zappone proposals and the present system, in which the citizen voters would elect the majority on each vocational panel and elected politicians would elect a minority.

It was hugely disappointing that Enda Kenny, following the defeat of his abolition referendum, accepted the need for reform, established the Manning group to find an all-party consensus on the nature of that reform, but promptly did nothing to implement its findings.

Was it cynicism or just carelessness for a Taoiseach to engage in planning Seanad reform and then to walk away from the process?

And now that we are again being told that reform of the Oireachtas is a priority for the new Dáil, why should we trust Mr Kenny to lead that reform when he had the 'reform ball' at his feet in front of an open goal and failed to kick it in?

If the Seanad had been abolished, the architecture and text of Bunreacht na hÉireann would have been left a tottering wreck. All checks and balances would have been swept away. The Dáil would have been left all-powerful on paper, but in reality under the thumb of the all-powerful government whip.

Since the politicians opted by default to keep their multiple votes on the vocational panels, it is all the more vital that the university panel seats be kept out of the control of the party whips. They are the last bastion of independence in the Seanad.

That is why, when Mr Quinn invited me to stand for the Seanad to continue the campaign for reform in his place, I was persuaded that I should do so.

I believe strongly that the Seanad should be a house for independent, experienced minds to participate in the legislative process and to strengthen our parliamentary processes against the inevitable localism and clientelism of the party system based on a Dáil elected by multi-seat PR.

The Oireachtas is failing abysmally to play its part in the post-Lisbon EU legislative process. The Seanad can help fulfil that role.

Nor is there any reason why the expressed wish of the people that the university Seanad seats should include other universities and third-level institutions such as DCU and UL should not be implemented some 37 years after the Constitution was amended to that effect in 1979.

We need reform badly. It cannot be delayed further. The Dáil and the Seanad have been under-functioning as parliamentary institutions. The discussions on reform have concluded; the choices must now be made.

It was for these reasons that I, along with Mr Quinn, Ms Zappone, Joe O'Toole and Noel Whelan, in 2013 established Democracy Matters, a non-party civic society group committed to keeping and reforming the Seanad. We cannot walk away from that agenda now.

In 2016, 100 years after the fuse was lit to transform Ireland from a decaying province of empire into a sovereign, independent republic, we owe it to ourselves to ensure that the institutions of that republic function in a manner that serves the people rather than the interests of a small, self-serving political elite.

It is on that basis that I am seeking a mandate to ensure the Seanad is reformed and plays a part in building the true republic to which we all, as citizens, owe a duty of loyalty.